Sociology, Work and Industry

THIRD EDITION

■ Tony J. Watson

First edition published 1980
Second edition published 1987 by Routledge &
Kegan Paul Ltd

Reprinted 1988, 1991, 1993 and 1995
by Routledge
11 New Fetter Lane
London EC4P 4EE

Third edition published 1995

© 1980, 1987, 1995 Tony J. Watson

Text design: Barker/Hilsdon
Typeset in Janson and Futura by
Solidus (Bristol) Limited
Printed and bound in Great Britain by
TJ Press Ltd, Padstow, Cornwall

British Library Cataloguing in Publication Data

A catalogue record for this book is available
from the British Library

*Library of Congress Cataloguing in Publication
Data*

A catalogue record for this book has been
requested

ISBN 0-415-13373-4 (hbk)
ISBN 0-415-13374-2 (pbk)

Soc
Wo

THIRD

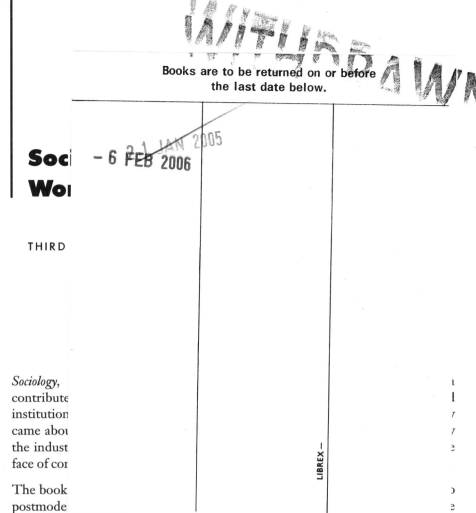

Sociology,   l
contribute   l
institution   7
came abou   7
the indust   ɔ
face of con

The book   ɔ
postmode   ɔ
discipline of sociology is introduced from basic principles in the early chapters
of the book. All the main areas are also developed: occupations; organizations;
work experience; industrial relations; industrial society and theory. The author
ends with a thoroughly revised chapter covering the important questions of how
work experience and global patterns of relationships are changing now and may
change in the future.

This third edition of *Sociology, Work and Industry* is an expanded and thoroughly
updated version of what has been one of the most successful and popular texts
in its field since 1980. Presented in a new and easily approachable format, the
new edition will be accessible to an even wider audience.

Tony Watson is Professor of Organizational and Managerial Behaviour in the
Nottingham Business School of The Nottingham Trent University.

LONDON AND NEW YORK

Contents

3 The industrialised society 81

4 Work: meaning, opportunity and experience 111

5 The structuring of work: occupations and the social division of labour   169

6 The structuring of work: organisations 233

7 Conflict, challenge and control in work 281

8 The restructuring of work and employment

331

Figures

Introduction

THE AIM OF *Sociology, Work and Industry* is to present an integrated account of how the discipline of sociology can contribute to our wider understanding of the variety of work practices and institutions which exist in modern societies. The fact that the nature, terminology and basic rationale of the discipline of sociology is introduced from basic principles in the early chapters of the book means that a reader new to sociology can derive the full benefit from reading the contributions which sociologists offer to help make sense of what is happening in the sphere of work. The sociology of work and industry can play an important role in informing the understandings and choices which human beings will make about their roles in the changing world of work and employment.

The book has been written both to explain the 'classical' traditions of industrial sociology and to give an overview of new developments in the broader 'sociology of work and industry'. It travels the full journey from the founding ideas of the discipline to postmodernist departures. Full account is taken of issues which have the traditional industrial enterprise as their focus, but the text goes beyond this. It considers the impact upon work experience and organisation of societal trends in the areas of gender and class relations, unemployment, global economic change, technological innovation and the restructuring of work organisations and employment insititutions in the latter part of the twentieth century. Sociology partly came about in the first place to make sense of the original upheavals of industrialisation. Its potential is no less in the face of contemporary upheavals.

Whilst preparing this third edition of *Sociology, Work and Industry* I have experienced a range of the pains and delights which we all associate with the work we do. Among the mass of material I had to read was a great deal of impressive research and theorising. At times wading through this was a delight and at other times it was a torment. Some of the greatest torment came, however, when I had to leave out or treat with daring brevity ideas which could have have taken up pages of the text. The book is a guide to a massive field. It attempts to cover all the basics of the subject and to help the reader new to it learn its distinctive language and style of analysis. It also tries to give an overview of what is being 'found out' about the working world by the research endeavours of sociologists.

This new edition of the book was written as I was emerging from a long period of intensive research in an industrial setting. That experience, together with the other personal values and interests which influence all authors, has helped shape the work. I hope that those who engage with the book which has emerged from this shaping will learn as much from reading it as I did in writing it.

■   ■   ■

Sociology and
social analysis

Introduction

Work is an activity in which everybody in the world is involved. People may work in their own small field, growing food to keep themselves alive. They may work in an office or a factory and, after a day working in the office or the factory for an employer, may return to do their housework or to work in their garden. Even those who do not themselves perform any of these labours are nevertheless involved with work: as owners of land on which other people work, as investors in industrial enterprises or as employers of servants. To understand the way of life of people living in any society we therefore have to pay close attention to work activities and to the institutions associated with those activities. If our main interest is the industrialised type of society and the way such societies are changing, then our main – but by no means exclusive – focus will be on activities associated with work organisations within which people are employed. Sociology provides us with a range of insights, concepts, ideas, theories and research findings which help us understand these activities in the context of the broader social and cultural arrangements in which they occur.

What is sociology?

> ### Sociology
> The academic study of the relationships which develop between human beings as they organise themselves and are organised by others in societies.

Sociology is primarily a form of study and analysis rather than a collection of formulae or principles telling us how we should organise our social life and our social institutions. Nevertheless, it should be seen as more than just another 'subject' in which we can take classes and sit examinations. Its ultimate rationale is one of helping people reach a better understanding of the human predicament, with specific reference to the social arrangements which they make. It contains the promise of helping people cope with the world, whether coping is seen as involving attempts to change, preserve or simply adjust to particular institutions or ways of living. Sociology, like many other scientific and artistic pursuits, can be seen as an activity which can help *inform the choices which people make about their lives*.

There is nothing new about social thought, of course. Thinkers have reflected on and made generalisations about social life since ancient times. However, two factors distinguish sociology within broader social thought and, at the same time, make it a distinctively modern enterprise:

1 It involves a particularly systematic or 'scientific' attempt to analyse social relationships.
2 It tends to deal with problems which have developed in an especially acute form in modern times.

These problems are associated with all those changes which have occurred in societies which have experienced the process of industrialisation:

- The disruption of traditional communities.
- The stress placed on the individual and the smaller family unit.
- The development of factories, large bureaucracies and large-scale urban living, and so on.

Accompanying this, if not underlying it all, have been substantial changes in the ways that work is organised and experienced. And this means that the sociology of work and industry is necessarily at the centre of the sociological enterprise.

We might say that the defining characteristic of the sociological perspective is that it ultimately relates whatever it studies back to the way society as a whole is organised. The essential insight which sociology provides is that no social action, at however mundane a level, takes place in a social vacuum. It is always linked, in some way, back to the wider culture, social structure and processes of the society in which it takes place. And these structures, processes, norms and values, with all their related inequalities, ideologies and power distributions, are the source of both constraints and opportunities which people meet in conducting their lives. The better and more widely these cultures, structures and processes are understood and the better the connections between specific actions or arrangements and these basic patterns are appreciated, then the greater is the opportunity for human control over work, industry and every other kind of social institution.

The rise of sociology paralleled the rise of industry and of modern capitalism and it can be seen as having the potential for an ongoing and critical examination of the institutions associated with industrialised societies. But such examination and appraisal of our social arrangements has a relevance for more than just the professional academics and their specialist students. The sociology of work and industry, for example, has the potential to help the worker, the manager, the engineer, the trade unionist, the provider and the user of goods and services make better-informed judgments about the world of work and perhaps contribute more effectively towards ensuring that human beings control economic institutions and do not experience them, as many seem to nowadays, as controlling us. To do this, we need some conception of the alternatives which might exist.

Sociology and conceptions of alternatives

Sociology as a discipline is still very dependent on the insights, concepts and theories of the leading intellectual figures who inspired its growth in the nineteenth century. The reason for this is that people like Emile Durkheim, Max Weber and Karl Marx – to name the big three 'key thinkers' – can give us special insights into our twentieth-century world. These individuals lived in the same type of society in which we find ourselves today but they, unlike us, lived in a period when the essential features of this societal type, together with its fundamental problems, were more visible and could be observed more acutely. Industrial capitalist institutions and practices were, in nineteenth- and early twentieth-century Europe, sufficiently well developed for their basic features to be observable whilst they were, as yet, insufficiently established for the assumptions and values underlying them to have become as near to being taken for granted as they are today. For example, whereas we see it as normal for a person 'being in work' to be employed for a wage or salary, these earlier observers were closer to an historical period in which this was unusual or aberrant. This helped them recognise the social invention of 'wage labour' for what it is: just one of many possible ways in which work relationships might be organised.

The founders of sociology can be seen as striving to make sense of the dislocations of their age. Their attempts to make sense of their situation are invaluable to us because, in an historical location more marginal than our own, they were better able to look at the industrial capitalist world in the light of *conceptions of alternatives*. This is their humanistic significance. They were perhaps more aware of alternatives on a societal level than we are because they were better placed historically to contrast the modern with the traditional, the urban with the rural and so on. This, combined with the great interest of their age in primitive and ancient social orders, helped to inspire their analyses with the most basic sociological insight of all: that there is more than one way and one way only for men and women to organise their lives. To put this another way, we might say that the way society is, is not necessarily the way society has to be. In the realm of work this means that the way we currently organise production and distribution does not possess some immutable inevitability. It is only one of a range of possibilities.

In the later part of the twentieth century, it could be argued that we are in greater need than for a long time of an ability to conceive of alternative social and economic arrangements. More and more parts of the world are becoming industrialised and links between different areas and cultures are becoming closer and more immediate with fast-developing information technologies. Alongside this, many of those societies whose economies were based on socialist rather than capitalist principles have moved towards market-based systems. All this could mean that we are seeing a world becoming more and more part of one big industrial capitalist system. There is little evidence, however, that the diverse interests and aspirations of people across the range of cultural backgrounds and the range of levels of economic development in the world will readily be met by the emerging world pattern. Imagination and creativity will play a vital part in devising ways of matching economic and work activity to the provision of human welfare. Sociology emerged in the first place as a way to apply such imagination to a world in which industrial and capitalist institutions were making their first appearances.

Sociology and industrial capitalist society

Sociology is an academic discipline which emerged in the nineteenth century as both a reaction to and a reflection of certain social and cultural shifts which had been occurring for some hundreds of years in Europe. For some centuries prior to the emergence of sociology, the glue which held together the fabric of European society, giving it stability and a widespread *taken-for-grantedness*, had been weakening:

- The Reformation saw a questioning of the authority of a centralised Catholic Church and with the emergence of Protestantism and dissent came a growing stress on the individual rather than the corporate, and the rational rather than the traditional.
- The Enlightenment brought under rational and critical scrutiny institutions of religion, inequality, kinship, property and monarchy.
- The Industrial Revolution and the French Revolution ensured that these institutions were further shaken and indeed often overturned.

A bourgeois revolution had occurred in England in 1688 limiting the power of the monarchy and in France the monarchy had been toppled. Notions of democracy were current but the problem of finding appropriate institutions for democratic politics was increased by the complications introduced by the Industrial Revolution. Capitalism had been growing in strength for centuries but by the early nineteenth century had become combined with an industrial spirit and associated techniques which carried revolutionary structural implications. Arising partly within and partly from outside the established bourgeois class was the new industrial middle class and even more threatening to stability was the appearance of a new social phenomenon – an industrial working class.

Some sense had to be made of these massive processes of change, indicated in outline form in Figure 1.1. How could people come to terms with processes of urbanisation, industrialisation, a growing division of labour, secularisation, bureaucratisation, democratisation, national state centralisation and the rest? Sociology has been seen by a number of commentators as an intellectual coming to terms with these processes and as an attempt to understand their impact.

It has been argued that there was a total breakdown of society at this time, a breakdown which called for a total reconstruction of the social

Traditional world's emphasis on	Modern world's emphasis on
Community and kinship	The individual and their immediate family
Rural and village life	Urban life
Work on land or in small manufacture	Factory and large-scale bureaucratic work organisation
Landed interests	Business and industrial interests
Monarchy	Democracy
Tradition	Reason
Religion	Science
Church mediated social thought	Science-based social thought, including SOCIOLOGY

FIGURE 1.1 Transitions from traditional to modern worlds following the Reformation, the Enlightenment and the French and Industrial Revolutions

order. Piecemeal reconstruction was seen as inappropriate when the 'entire fabric of institutions was falling apart' which meant that there was a need for a 'body of knowledge about society as a totality of institutions' (Fletcher 1971). It was this need which the founders of sociology were to attempt to meet. The key concepts or 'unit ideas' of sociology, according to Nisbet (1970), were developed as part of an attempt to achieve a 'theoretical reconsolidation' of the various elements on which social order had once rested – kinship, land, social class, religion, local community and monarchy – but which had now been 'dislocated by revolution' and 'scrambled by industrialisation and the forces of democracy'.

Sociologists, in this view, developed concepts like society and community to provide a consolidating or overarching perspective which was needed to counter the divisive, contradictory and individualistic tendencies of life in this period of emerging modernism. The founders of sociology were preoccupied with the analysis of industrialism and were engaged in creating a 'powerful vision or "image" of a society in the making' (Kumar 1978) and, says Giddens (1971), the overwhelming interest of Marx, Durkheim and Weber was in the 'delineation of the characteristic structure of modern capitalism as contrasted with prior forms of society'. Contemporary sociology has inherited this role and has 'as its main focus the institutions of "advanced" or "industrialised" societies, and of the conditions of transformation of those institutions' (Giddens 1982).

Sociology was – and continues to be – both a reaction to and a part of the social and cultural changes in which it was involved. And this often meant that it was ambivalent towards the institutions with which it concerned itself. This is especially the case with regard to industrial institutions. Marx, for instance, whilst the arch critic of many of the

Worries	18th/19th centuries	late 20th century
The condition of labour	Industrialisation sees working people degraded as they are torn from their traditional guild, village and family settings	Industrial change sees increasing numbers discarded from employment with redundant skills and little prospect of work
The transformation of property	Abstract shares, stocks and the depersonalised medium of cash encourage a calculative morality; relationships increasingly mediated by cash payments and calculations of pecuniary gain	The quality of attachment of employees to work based on low-trust cash relations inhibits both satisfying work relationships and high quality performance/ initiative-taking
The industrial city	Rootlessness and alienation in the urban sprawl replace the natural rhythms of the countryside	'Inner city' problems of crime, poverty and racial tension threaten social integration
Technology and the factory system	Regimentation, the intense division of labour and the machine-pacing degrade both the work and the worker	'New' technologies displace people from employment and lead to the deskilling of others

FIGURE 1.2 Social concerns 'evoking a sociological response' in early and later industrial societies

manifestations of industrialism, clearly welcomed the potential in it for improving human well-being. Saint-Simon in France and Herbert Spencer in Britain positively celebrated industrialism as part of human progress. But others reacted against it. Nisbet (1970) shows strong similarities between early sociologists and other social thinkers of the time who were appalled by the excesses of the industrial revolution. He sees an important stimulus to the growth of sociology in reactions to industrialism, suggesting that a sociological response was evoked most significantly by five aspects of the industrial revolution. These are shown in Figure 1.2 and alongside them are some corresponding worries which are expressed about work and social conditions in contemporary industrial societies.

It is important to remember, as was argued earlier, that we still live in the type of society and economy over which the nineteenth- and early twentieth-century theorists were agonizing. We have come to take for granted a great deal of what they puzzled about. And this is why we need to take their concepts, insights, theories and their critical edge as our starting point for contemporary analysis. As Figure 1.2 suggests, we have a set of conditions in late twentieth-century industrial capitalism which can 'evoke a sociological response' which very much parallels those identified by Nisbet.

All of these areas of concern call for an ability to analyse them systematically and rationally and in a way which does not look at any of them in isolation. Just like the founders of sociology, whose ideas will be examined in the next chapter, we have to confront fundamental questions about the nature of industrial capitalism and the place of work, employment, technology and organisation within it. These are questions of social arrangements, social processes and culture – the subject matter of sociology. But before we can apply sociology to these problems and issues we must clarify the nature of the discipline and how one thinks sociologically and engages in sociological investigation.

Thinking sociologically

Sociology is concerned with how people relate to each other. It examines how human beings organise both themselves and each other. In looking at how people behave and think it looks for patterns or 'structures' in social life. These patterns are seen both as the outcome of the activities of individuals and as something which, in turn, influences, encourages and constrains the individual. Let's take such a pattern which we might observe if we were to go into a secondary school classroom and ask which children were interested in careers in engineering and which were interested in nursing careers. We are unlikely to be surprised if we find that most of the would-be engineering workers are boys and most of the aspiring nurses are girls. Let's assume that this is the case in the school we happen to have entered. How do we explain this pattern?

One approach is to look at this pattern as an outcome of a series of individual choices. There are clearly choices being made. Nobody is forcing the children to name one or other of these areas of employment. Each human individual is an *agent*, with wants, aspirations and a sense of identity which they bring to any decision to speak or act. But an alternative approach would be to look at the pattern as an outcome of the way 'society' channels male and female children into certain spheres of activity. There are clearly pressures on each child from the world around them: from examples provided in literature and entertainment media to examples seen in the work activities of the men and women they see around them as they grow up.

These two types of explanation can easily come to be seen as alternatives. To use terms which have been around as long as there has been social thought, we can speak of explanations which emphasise free will and explanations which stress determinism. However, sociologists see a need to go beyond this. What is needed, to develop an explanation of the patterns observed in the school, is an analysis which considers the way these individual children have come to shape their career interests and 'choose' their aspirations *in the light of* their previous experiences in life and what they have learned from cultural and parental influences to be the appropriate and possible types of work for them to enter. There is an interweaving of individual and social factors, of free choice and of constraint. We might simplify this, as Figure 1.3 does, by saying that individuals make society and society makes individuals.

The dualism between a focus on the individual and a focus on the 'social' does not fully parallel the free will and determinism dualism, however, because it is possible to talk of an individual's actions being determined by factors such as genetic ones which are intrinsic to them as individuals. Equally, it is possible to see social structures as providing

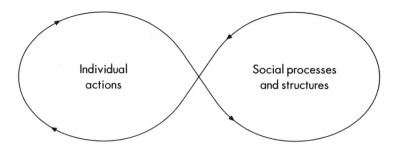

FIGURE 1.3 Individuals make society and society makes individuals

opportunities for individuals to realise their individual interests ('climb-ing the ladder' of the class structure, say) as well as seeing people constrained by such a structure (being excluded from an activity because of one's class or race, for example). In dealing with these matters, sociologists commonly refer to a dualism between *agency* and *structure* and one of the most significant attempts to overcome this has been in Giddens' (1984) call for us to focus on what he calls *structuration* processes in social life. Human beings are both makers of social patterns and are made by them. These patterns both constrain us and enable us to achieve our purposes. But these patterns or 'structures' are not objectively existing entities outside of human patterns of interaction, even though it may at times feel as if they have this kind of forceful presence. Structuration is an ever-unfolding process.

Structuration

The ongoing process whereby individual initiatives are interwoven into the patterns of human interaction which sometimes constrain and sometimes enable those initiatives.

Sociology is not simply the study of the social, of societies, of social structures. Neither, of course, is it a study of individuals' activities, aggregated in some way to give us a view of societies as little more than the sum of their parts. It is, rather, a study of the interrelationships between the individual and the social whose greatest potential lies in examining the processes whereby human initiatives and choices shape and are shaped by patterns of human interaction and power. The concept of structuration may not fully capture every aspect of this, as Layder points out whilst nevertheless noting that its greatest strength lies in its attempt 'to incorporate the full force of the human ability to make a difference in the social world while recognising the limitations imposed by the social context' (1994).

Sociology, like every other discipline, makes use of a distinctive range of concepts. Structure, process, culture, norm, value and institution are concepts widely used, for example. Figure 1.4 briefly explains these

Structure	Regularities or patterns in social behaviour, observed as 'frozen in time'
Process	Regularities or patterns in social behaviour, observed in movement
Norm	Part of the underlying pattern of social life — the standards to which people are expected to conform or the rules of conduct whose infringement may result in sanctions intended to encourage conformity
Values	Notions of what is good and bad, right and wrong, within a society or a part of a society
Institution	A regularly occurring and therefore normal pattern of actions and relationships
Culture	The system of meanings which is shared by members of a human grouping and which defines what is good and bad, right and wrong, and what are the appropriate ways for members of that grouping to think and behave

FIGURE 1.4 Some key sociological concepts

concepts. To illustrate the use of the key concepts explained in Figure 1.4 in a way which also illustrates the general style of sociological thinking, we can look at the case of change in a steel industry. Applying the *sociological imagination* involves switching an initial focus on the private problems of, say, a steelworker faced with redundancy to various contextual *public issues* (Mills 1970). These issues range from the state of the international market in steel and managerial, governmental and trade union policies, to patterns of technological change and the different nature of involvement in that industry of technical and managerial staff on the one hand and manual workers on the other. Sociology, then, shifts the level of focus from that of the close-up to that of the 'big picture', but sociology is not simply to do with producing the broad picture; it necessarily goes beyond this to look for underlying regularities or patterns, *structures* and *processes*. Sociologists in this case of steel redundancies will want to know about the occupational structure of the industry and the industrial relations processes which go on; they will look at the managerial structures and the ongoing processes of technological change. All this will be set in its historical context and the general structure of society, its industrial base and its capitalist or its socialist nature. In analysing these structures and processes the sociologist would try to show how they potentially both constrain people as well as enable people to further their personal wishes, noting how they both result from the initiatives of individuals and can be seen to restrain individual initiatives.

We can illustrate the interplay of tendencies towards initiative and tendencies towards constraint by considering the implications of the threatened steelworkers considering a possible initiative. Let us assume that they get together and decide that they would like to share out the remaining work – each becoming a part-time worker. The union structure might be used to pursue this aim and existing bargaining arrangements used to argue the case with management. These negotiations might succeed but, before they did, the constraining aspects of social structure would soon become apparent to those involved. For example, the *norm* in that society or town of each household having a male as the main breadwinner might need to change. Changing these norms would involve changing *values* with regard to the place of work in people's lives. Thus the *institutions* of work and family would be affected as, potentially, would be the *culture* of the society as a whole.

All this may appear to stress the constraining rather than the enabling aspects of social structures and, indeed, sociology often leans this way – afflicting the mind with a pessimism about possible change in social life. Nevertheless, what a full sociological analysis would do would be to examine how these structures developed historically – this analysis in itself reminding us of the existence of social and cultural relativity and suggesting that varieties of social organisation are possible. The maintenance of the status quo, this suggests, is not inevitable. Here we are back to our conceptions of alternatives and to the existence of human choice – choices which sociology may be used to inform.

Sociology, economics and psychology

The foregoing arguments and examples are intended to show the distinctiveness of sociological analysis, particularly in contrast with everyday thinking. But it is clear that many of the issues raised are ones where we might expect a contribution from other social sciences. Indeed, it is sometimes argued that the study of the social aspects of work organisation or business should not be performed by a variety of different disciplines but by a general 'behavioural science'. The very rationale behind the present work suggests a rejection of this position. In the first place, the term 'behavioural science' is to be rejected. This is not so much because of its being coined by social scientists nervous of business clients and worried that research fund donors might confuse social science and socialism but, rather, because of its inaccuracy. Sociology, for example, is not just about social behaviour but about socially meaningful behaviour or, in Weber's terms, social action. Sociology operates by considering meanings, ideas and the interpretations of human beings as much if not more than by studying their behaviour as such. The actual behaviour of a coalminer preparing for his end of shift shower could well be technically identical to that of a strip-tease dancer in mid-shift. To fail to take into account the different meanings, the social significance and the motives behind these acts would make sociological nonsense. The rejection of misleading titles is not terribly important, however. It is perhaps inappropriate to attempt to conceive of a general 'social scientific' approach for studying any given area. Human life has too many dimensions for any one discipline to develop models, concepts and theories which do sufficient justice to this complexity whilst remaining simple enough to be manageable. What we need is a minimal division of theoretical labour with people operating within each specialism whilst taking into account the work of those in other specialisms (economists advising on incomes policy, for instance, taking into account psychological and sociological factors). Out of the multiplicity of the disciplines involved in the study of social life we can pick three which are distinguishable primarily by their particular conceptual and analytical styles: psychology, economics and sociology. These are distinguished from other disciplines in the way shown in Figure 1.5.

If we were to seek a general social scientific explanation of, say, the case of a particular married woman who is unable to get a job, we might seek the following dimensions:

- A psychological dimension – perhaps her personality and intense nervousness lead to her failing interviews.
- An economic dimension – maybe wages paid to women in this area would be insufficient to allow her to pay bus fares or a child minder.
- A sociological dimension – her husband possibly comes from a culture where working wives are frowned upon.

Disciplines distinguished by their methods, concepts, styles of analysis	Disciplines distinguished by the aspect of human activity which they study
Psychology	Organisation studies
	Business and management studies
Economics	
	Industrial relations
	Social and public administration
Sociology	
	Political science

FIGURE 1.5 The relationship between the three primary social sciences and other disciplines which study the social

It is conceivable that a single social scientist could give an adequate explanation here, but once we move up to the complexities of explaining, say, a case of substantial industrial strife, this would be unmanageable. The greatest challenge to a general explanation would face the person left trying to weave together the contributions from the three disciplines. Any argument that the sociologist is potentially the best fitted for this task in cases of social complexity is inevitably and perhaps justifiably open to charges of sociological imperialism. Nevertheless, it could be argued that the whole point of sociology is to relate the individual to the social and that this means taking into account the contributory individual and economic dimensions of the social.

The sociologist trying to explain a particular strike could usefully listen to a psychological analysis of such matters as the personalities of the individuals leading each side and would be dependent on the economist for an expert appraisal of labour market conditions, relative wage rates and local living costs. All of this has to be thrown into the much bigger picture which is the realm of the sociologist:

- The patterns and conflicts of interest (employer–employee, craft–semiskilled, male–female).
- The solidarity or otherwise of local communities.
- The expectations of work and incomes currently prevailing in the culture both nationally and locally, and so on.

Let me stress here that in no way is this to argue for the superiority of sociology in status terms. The very level of generality at which it operates, compared to economics and psychology, is as much the source of its weaknesses as its strength. Its concerns are so diffuse that it often reaches a level of abstraction where its analyses become almost meaningless to those outside the sociological community. The psychologist's talk of people's needs, attitudes or personalities or the economist's talk of numbers of unemployed, rates of inflation or economic growth will, understandably, be more readily listened to than the sociologist's talk of cultural factors, the changing social structure, or work ideologies. The former ideas are not necessarily more simple, somehow they are more easily grasped – their relative specificity if not their simplicity makes them manageable.

The suggestion that the level of abstraction involved in applying a sociological perspective makes it difficult to manage implies that people in the 'practical' rather than the academic worlds might be likely to prefer psychological or economic approaches to sociological ones, and, indeed, might think more happily in such terms. Particularly important is the fact that economic and psychological variables are often more manipulable than those of sociology or, at least, they are often seen to be so. Economic variables are characteristically measurable and economic policy and much business activity is devoted to manipulating them. Psychological variables are correspondingly manageable. If a management difficulty can be put down to some individual's personality problem you can either sack the individual or send them for therapy. If managers' or employees' attitudes need to be changed you can attempt persuasion or 'improve communication'. Paradoxically, psychological thinking also has the opposite virtue. Psychological factors which are not manipulable – for example basic human needs or 'instincts' – cannot be changed and therefore simply have to be lived with. Sociology does not have a comforting potential in the same way. On the one hand, its variables of social structure, culture and patterns of expectation sound too complex to be thought of as manipulable whilst, on the other hand, the discipline's underlying assumption of social and cultural relativity suggests that, although these may be difficult to change, we cannot expect to take comfort in their inevitability and thus ignore them.

Where social scientific thinking has penetrated the practical world of work – and this, not surprisingly, has been largely on the management side – it has been in the *psychologistic* form rather than the sociological. The word 'psychologistic' is deliberately used here rather than 'psychological' because the form which this thinking generally takes tends to lack the rigour associated with academic psychology and because it tends to be 'psychologically reductionist' – that is, it excludes considerations of wider social, political or economic factors.

Psychologism

A tendency to explain social behaviour solely in terms of psychological characteristics of individuals.

This is illustrated in a study of personnel specialists, people who are shown to be the most highly qualified group within management in social science disciplines and yet who, in replies to a range of questions asked about problems of both a workplace and a wider social nature tended to be very markedly individualistic if not crudely psychologistic in style and content (Watson 1977). Structural insights at either the organisational or the wider social-structural levels were little in evidence. This can be explained to a large extent by the fact that people in management are paid to solve short-term problems, to be pragmatic, to get the job done – in short, to be practical. To analyse structures, let alone change them in other than a piecemeal way, is generally out of the question. Even where social scientists are actually employed as such in industry they are likely to find those with whom they work highly reluctant to operate in the structural terms characteristic of the sociological perspective (Klein 1976).

The problem with the prevalence of psychologistic thinking in the industrial world is not that it deprives the sociologist of work or influence but that it often leads to woefully inadequate, not to say simplistic, diagnoses of problems and, following from this, a reduced chance for people to control work institutions. Explaining strikes in terms of communication breakdown or people's greed, 'poor motivation' in terms of basic human needs, payment systems or organisational structures in terms of 'human nature' is simply misleading. More adequate theories of work activity will inform better managerial, employee, social and political decision-making. A supervisor's decision on how to reorganise a shop-floor layout; a union decision on whether to negotiate for increased cash or reduced hours; or a social policy decision on national leisure provision – each has a sociological dimension. A simple and straightforward statement of how sociology can be applied to these issues is not possible. That is part of the problem of the discipline and is why the present work is a book and not a pamphlet!

Perhaps most usefully at this stage we can point out again that sociology looks at how people organise themselves and each other. Whilst recognising that individuals have different personalities, needs and attitudes, we must recognise too that work organisations and the associated institutions in the wider society have a reality over and above these factors. People in industry have tended to see the relevance of social science to their problems in terms of how it can help 'change attitudes', 'improve communications' or 'involve people better'. Without looking at the structure of the work organisation, the administrative system, technology, management and trade union structure and the relationships between these and other such factors inside and outside work, little can be achieved. The way much industrial, social or behaviourial science is written and applied gives the impression that it is all based on the ludicrous proposition that you rewrite a play by changing the actors rather than by rewriting the roles. Perhaps you can – but only marginally.

Sociology, science and the need for theory

It has been implicit in what has gone before that sociology is in some sense a scientific discipline and that the developing of sociological explanations involves rigorous investigation of phenomena. We must now consider how it goes about investigation in the course of analysing the kinds of structures, patterns and processes discussed above and in what ways it tries to formulate generalisations about the social world.

First, we must examine the notions of science and the scientific. Earlier, science was put in the context of the ways in which modes of thinking tended to move away from an emphasis on religion and tradition in the course of changes in western societies. To talk of science today inevitably brings us up against the image of the typical scientist as a cool, objective and precise white-coated laboratory investigator doggedly discovering laws of the universe (the inspired but absent-minded and half-mad scientist figure being archetypal but atypical), and this first image must be rejected, at least in part, if sociology is going to claim any scientific validity for itself. This can be achieved to some extent by pointing out just how far physical scientists have moved towards the social scientist in their new preference for talk about 'probability' rather than prediction and to their willingness even to admit that their own involvement may affect their investigations. But a more fruitful approach to deciding the distinctiveness of the scientific approach in general is to view it as merely one way of making sense of the world – a way that can be differentiated from others. It can, for instance, be contrasted with a religious approach or a literary one. Thus, to make sense of the use of industrial robots we could perhaps consider what part they play in God's (or the gods') purpose or, alternatively, we could write a poem to express our emotional reactions and describe our experience of robots. But the third possibility is a scientific one. Here we would formulate concepts or working definitions of what a robot and its constitutive elements are, collect data on robots, make comparisons of specific aspects of robots, and draw up classifications of robots, noting the circumstances of their introduction and the apparent effect of their appearance on the scene. Out of this we might propose tentative explanations (or hypotheses) which can be tested as a generalisation through collected evidence. In a similar way we could attempt to understand or account for phenomena such as growth in small businesses theologically, through novels or in a scientific manner.

A scientific approach to industrial events and activities can be differentiated from literary, emotional, religious or philosophical approaches, but is the approach any different in reality from the attempts made to explain this strife by workers, journalists, managers and politicians? Do not these people develop concepts, put forward explanations and even act on the basis of the theories which they develop? To this one can only respond by accepting that there is a very positive continuity between scientific thinking and everyday practical reasoning. The householder works out a theory of why the local refuse collectors are working to rule just as the baby in its pram works out for itself some notion of gravity. The differences between common sense and science, then, are not differences of essence but differences of degree – in three main respects.

Science and practical reasoning

Science is

- more formal, systematic and precise;
- more rigorous in testing propositions;
- more committed to building up a body of knowledge and theory.

The scientific approach has the following characteristics:

- It is more formal, systematic and precise in its observing, classifying, conceptualising and interpreting.
- It is more rigorous in the extent to which it submits its procedures,

testing, etc. to critical examination (seeking to falsify rather than prove its tentative explanations for example).

- Where everyday or common-sense analysis is merely interested in the short-term pragmatic practicalities of everyday life, formal science is committed to building up a body of knowledge and a series of generalisations which go beyond immediate and practical needs. This body of knowledge is, therefore, available to be drawn upon when there is a practical issue to which it may be relevant.

Science is about generalisations, we might say. An important product of science is obviously knowledge but its more characteristic product is that part of knowledge which we call theory or theories, and here we have a problem with regard to the industrial scene.

Theories

Ideas about how phenomena relate to each other and, especially, about how particular events or actions tend to lead to others. Theorising is about generalising and is at the heart of all scientific endeavour.

There is a strong tendency, at least in the British industrial world, to associate anything academic with the irrelevant and to regard theories as useless. Whilst accepting that many academics are indeed 'out of touch' and that many theories are built on sand, we must necessarily recognise the nonsense of this position. What 'practical' people often forget is that their actions are as much based on theories, in the sense of generalised propositions about phenomena, as are those of the scientifically aware. Moreover, a reluctance to examine consciously the theories on which one's practices are based can lead to real difficulties. This can be illustrated with the example of a trainee manager whose first managerial assignment was to take charge of a department of skilled men and women. In this job he applied what amounted to a 'common-sense' theory of employee motivation. This suggested that people will more or less do what their manager requires of them as long as that manager takes a close personal interest in them 'as people'. This seemed to work. But when, as his next assignment, this young college-educated man was put in charge of a yard-gang of tough unskilled male workers, he found his management style scorned and derided by his staff. Instead of abandoning or revising his 'theory of motivation' to take into account such concepts as group culture, varying work expectations or orientations, he simply argued that the men were 'unmanageable' and he sought a move. His theory was not totally 'wrong'. But it was poor as a set of understandings which could inform practical choices. It was simplistic in that it did not include the recognition that different types of employees in different circumstances react differently to managerial personnel and hence respond to different managerial styles. More conscious attention to theories of work behaviour and context would have enabled the individual to cope better with these circumstances and, even more important, to be better able to deal with whatever other assignment he might be given in the future.

The above example illustrates a general problem with sociological theories or generalisations. This is that because sociology deals with the exceedingly complex world of human activity and relationships its general propositions can rarely take the simple form 'a causes b'. Much more typical would be something on the lines 'to understand the relationship between a and b in any given situation, we must look at the influence of c, d, e, f, g, etc.'. Thus the sociologist trying to generalise about, say, employee behaviour will examine such factors as technology, local community, union structure and general management style. However, to examine events sociologically one does not start afresh in each situation; the body of knowledge and theory already existing within the discipline guides this analysis, so leading to a more informed conclusion and potential practical action.

The extreme complexity of social life and the consequent difficulty of making usable generalisations is often taken to deny the sociologists' claim that they are scientific in approach. It is because of this complexity, the fact that every individual is different and every human act unique, that it is seen as impossible for the scientific observer systematically to observe or experiment. Furthermore, since sociologists are human beings like those they study, they are inevitably 'involved' and are therefore incapable of being objective. To make sense of the complex human world they are forced to indulge in moral argument, to make use of imagination and insight and to succumb to the influence of personal experience. They are thus no different, this argument would continue, from the literary observer or the journalist. Nevertheless, as long as we do not use the scientific label as some kind of fetish but regard it as providing a set of guiding principles (as opposed to concrete rules), then sociology can and should be seen as a scientific discipline.

There is some debate among social scientists about what is the appropriate conception of science for the kind of work they do. A powerful, and once dominant, tradition was that of *positivism*.

Positivist conceptions of social science
- see social science as equivalent to the physical sciences and therefore able to use similar procedures;
- see the social world as an objective reality external to those who study it;
- seek explanations in the forms of general theories or 'covering laws' which can be used to make predictions.

Alternative conceptions, in the *interpretive* as opposed to the positivist tradition, are less concerned to follow the traditional or natural sciences and they place great emphasis on the fact that the researcher is part of the world that they are researching, as opposed to a neutral investigator looking at it from a distance. Patterns in social life are sought, as in the positivist approach, but these are seen as rooted in the meanings which people attach to their circumstances rather than in objectively existing structures. Instead of aspiring to theories in the form of universal propositions, the interpretive researcher attempts to develop *understandings*. These still take a theoretical form – in that they make use of concepts and in the sense that there is a concern with making generalisations. These generalisations are about the social processes which occur in social life (the general way in which people develop a concept of self-identity, for example) as opposed to universal laws which can lead to specific predictions (people unemployed for more than one year will develop a stress illness, for example).

Interpretive conceptions of social science
- see social science as requiring different procedures from physical sciences;
- see the social world as a reality accessible only through the meanings developed by social actors;
- seek understandings of social processes and the patterns within them rather than explanations of social behaviour.

Contributors to the debate about the virtues of these two basic approaches vary in the way they define them. It can be argued that the differences between the two approaches have been overstated and there are attempts by some writers on methodological matters to find ways of compromising between the two emphases. An important way in which this is being attempted is suggested by such writers as Hammersley (1992) and Silverman (1993), who have worked predominantly within the interpretive tradition but are now insisting on looking to the broader scientific tradition, often associated with the allegedly alternative positivistic emphasis, to call for rigour and stringency in the way ideas are developed and tested. Although the social sciences may differ in some important ways from the physical sciences (especially in the fact that the difference between sociologists and the people they study is of quite a different order from that between, say, chemists and the contents of their test tubes), their activities have enough in common for them both to be classed as sciences. There are key characteristics of science which should guide all scientists.

Sociology is a science.

Sociology as science
It makes generalisations as systematically as possible in the light of available evidence.

What makes sociology a science is not a sterile value-neutrality or a concern with amassing facts uncontaminated by subjectivity. Neither is it a pursuit of final laws. Sociology does use insight, imagination and even inspiration; it is motivated by moral concern and even by political commitment, and it is characterised by internal debate and rivalries of both method and interpretation, but, in the end, it falls in the category of the sciences rather than the arts. Sociology is a scientific pursuit because it goes about detecting regularities and because it makes its generalisations on as systematic a basis as possible given its subject matter. This involves the testing of propositions and the basing of statements on evidence – this being collected, explained and interpreted in such a way that others can scrutinise that evidence and make their own judgments on the generalisations which are offered.

Coping with complexity: the role of concepts, models and types

One of the greatest problems in the development of a science of sociology has been its inevitable entanglement in a horrible methodological paradox. This arises because sociology, to be able to proceed, has to simplify the vast complexities of social life whilst, in going about this and stating its assumptions, developing sets of concepts and working out models, it seems to be trying to complicate matters. Sociologists are often accused of making matters too complicated when, in fact, they are drastically simplifying them. The paradox is resolved when we realise that sociologists recognise the extent of the complexity in their analyses to a greater extent, typically, than does the everyday practical man and woman. This is illustrated, in a slightly tongue-in-cheek way, in Figure 1.6.

What Figure 1.6 implies is that sociology is totally incapable of ever giving a full account or any final explanation of the social world. And, indeed, there is no objectively existing ultimate social reality. But what, it might be asked, is being suggested here other than that sociology is merely an upgraded form of common-sense understanding? A reply to this would be that this 'upgrading' is such that the sociologically informed will be better able to understand the complexities of what is the case and, just as important, will comprehend better the possible outcomes – the intended and unintended consequences – of actions which might be

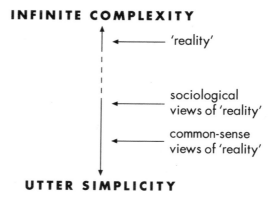

FIGURE 1.6   Sociological and common-sense perceptions of the complexity of social reality

taken. The point of all social science investigation is to give a more effective rather than a true understanding.

We can now turn to some of the ways in which the sociologist simplifies the vast buzzing confusion of the social world in order to render it amenable to analysis. The basic method is the development of a model or general theoretical scheme which picks out certain aspects of reality whose interconnections are felt to be important. Metaphor is often used to make the abstract more manageable: system, structure, stratification, for example. The last is a good example. To study the inequalities which exist between human beings, sociologists often picture society as if it were a geological diagram and this helps give a sense of structure or pattern. People are located in 'strata'. Models like this are made up from concepts.

Models

Analytical schemes which simplify reality by selecting certain phenomena and suggesting particular relationships between them.

In the present example of stratification we often find the groups into which people fall conceptualised as 'classes' – upper, middle and working classes perhaps. The characterising of class as, say, dependent on the ownership or non-ownership of capital is not a 'definition' but a concept. A concept is a working definition, if you like.

Concepts

The building blocks of models and theories — working definitions of factors playing a part in a scientific analysis.

The nature of concepts as *working* definitions rather than once-and-for-all definitions is stressed because we are not saying that class exists in an objective sense when we talk of it in sociology. We are, rather, suggesting that it provides a useful tool for analysing human inequality. This does not mean that 'class' is a mere linguistic plaything of the intellectual. Ultimately, sociological concepts have to relate to what people experience in their lives. Although people may believe that 'class is dead', they may well meet with certain experiences which are best understood by being related to what the sociologist calls 'class'. Were those people to look at some sociological analysis in this area, they might well come to understand their own situation better. To put this important point another way, the sociologist is not really concerned to look at any person and say that he is working class or that she is middle class. The concern is, rather, to decide in which class it is analytically most useful to place him or her. This is in order to understand what is happening to these persons and what they are doing in that society.

Connected with the development of both concepts and models in sociology, and fundamental to the process of simplification, is the use of types or to use Weber's term, *ideal types*. Sociology universally constructs these. As the discipline is interested in generalising, it looks at the typical rather than the specific in directing its analysis. Thus if we wished to find out whether the employees of a factory were generally more interested in money rewards or job satisfaction we might envisage an ideal typical instrumentally oriented worker (a totally money-oriented person) and then their opposite – an ideal typical expressively oriented worker (one only concerned with intrinsic satisfactions). Clearly, neither would exist in reality, but these extreme types can be held in mind whilst we construct our questionnaire, which will provide data to enable us to find what

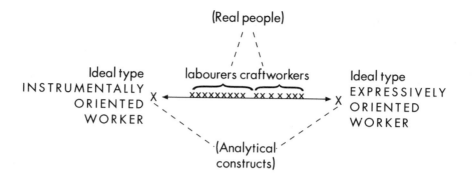

FIGURE 1.7 Application of IDEAL TYPE constructs in the study of orientations to work in one industrial workshop

patterns exist in that factory. We might find a pattern in one workshop like that in Figure 1.7.

It is very important to stress that all of these analytical devices – concepts, models, ideal types and theoretical schemes – are merely tools or means and are not ends in themselves. They are to be judged by their usefulness and not by any criterion of correctness. This is not to suggest any one is as good as any other and, throughout this book, various approaches to different phenomena will be examined in order to reveal their value.

Sociological techniques of investigation

Having considered what are properly termed *methodological* questions about sociology (questions about the logic of its concern with studying the social world scientifically), we can now consider some of the research *methods* or techniques of investigation used. There is a range of these available and the particular ones chosen will depend on various factors such as the following:

- The theoretical assumptions the researcher holds about social life. If a researcher sees the class structure as a principal factor behind the phenomena being studied, for example, he or she would tend to choose a different method from that which they would adopt if personality factors were seen as a key factor.

- A leaning towards either positivist or the interpretive conceptions of science discussed earlier. Interpretive researchers, with their characteristic interest in human meanings, are more likely to use a method which enables them to get close to the people in the setting they are studying whereas the positivist is more likely to be content with large-scale survey material.
- The type of research access which is available. The sociologist wishing to use direct observation techniques to study boardroom behaviour, for instance, will be lucky indeed to gain such access.

To give an account of the available techniques we can sketch out an imaginary research project in which practically the whole range of techniques is used. We will assume that the research team will engage in the various methodological debates, which have been introduced here, when making sense of the material they have collected.

Let us envisage a research team who take on the task of giving a sociological account of the running down of a manufacturing concern in a town where it was a significant employer. The owners of the company, all of whom are intending to retire shortly, have given open access to the sociologists. One member of the team is a former worker in the factory and their *personal experience* has been used to direct their colleagues towards various organisational and industrial relations issues and they will also contribute certain qualitative material to the final research reports. This person is being temporarily employed in the personnel department of the firm to help with the tasks of carrying out early retirements, redeployments and redundancies. Valuable data on both managerial and employee experiences will be collected by this *participant observation*. A second researcher is engaged in combing through company records and local historical documents to build up a picture of the firm's past and the background to the present situation in the company and in the surrounding community. The quantitatively-inclined team member is running through various *statistics* varying from figures supplied by the marketing department to ones on labour turnover and on disputes provided by the personnel department. A survey designed to reveal the expected impact of the firm's decline on surrounding small businesses and other parts of the community will use *postal questionnaires* and *structured interviews* with key people in the community. Both structured and more informal *unstructured interviews* will be used to collect data from samples of company employees at each level in the organisation.

Here we have, then, a fairly large and no doubt expensive sociological research project which is deploying a battery of techniques of investigation. But to what end, we might ask, and in what way will this material be brought together and interpreted? It might be the case that the style of this research team is to pursue what Glaser and Strauss (1967) call 'grounded theory' which means that they will hope to see concepts and hypotheses emerging from this mass of data, which can be applied and tested within the project. But let's assume that this is not the case in this particular piece of research. The leader of the team, as it happens, was born in the town where the research is occurring and she is concerned about the problems of industrial decline in this part of the world. An early paper written for a sociological conference suggests that the academic rationale for the research is an investigation of the impact of unemployment resulting from technological change and patterns of investment on a community with a record of industrial decline. Theoretically, the concern is how expectations in the community affect the orientations of employees and others towards job loss in such a community context. However, the foundation which is funding the research views its expenditure as an investment which will yield useful information to give guidance to other companies and to government agencies in similar cases in the future. The company board members who agreed to give access, on the other hand, welcomed the project as a possible way in which the 'human problems' of the rundown might be reduced by the involvement of sociologists – people with special knowledge of the human aspects of work.

It is hoped that this fictional example of a research project reveals something of the processes by which sociological material is generated. What we see is a complex web of personal values, private and public concern, theoretical interests and research skills. Despite the range of motives and interests behind the project, a set of research reports will eventually appear and will be scrutinised by other sociologists and by lay commentators, reviewed in the literature and discussed at conferences and seminars. And at the end of this process of evaluation there should be an increased understanding of a range of issues among the academics and the practically-involved alike. But what this material will not do, as we shall see shortly, is tell government, employers, trade unions or whoever what they should do in such situations.

Objectivity and value relevance

In the research example discussed above we saw how a variety of motives and values underlay the work which was done. It would not be surprising if, in a corresponding way, the findings of this project were taken up to argue for a range of different political ends and commercial interests after their publication. It is exceedingly important to stress this point. Social scientific investigations simply cannot in themselves produce political, commercial or individual programmes for action. Yet they may well be used as if this were the case. A study indicating the overwhelming pecuniary attachment of workers to their jobs, for example, could be taken to 'prove' that the best action to take in that industry is to forget the possibility of improving job satisfaction and simply to organise for wage maximisation. This is highly illegitimate, not to say dishonest. The type of decision about work design to be made here must ultimately be based on values – on social and political preferences. To expect to arrive at such decisions as a result of scientific investigations such as industrial surveys or perhaps 'cost-benefit analyses', is to ignore the fact that the social world contains a diversity of value positions and many conflicting material interests. Science can be no substitute for political activity and is incapable of settling moral questions. Sociology, like any other science, has to be kept in its place. It is an invaluable tool. But it is only a tool. It is a means of improving understanding, informing decisions and indicating the implications of proposed alternatives.

To argue in this way that sociological investigation should be subservient in the realm of practical activity to democratic processes in the formal political sense or in the industrial and collective bargaining sense is not enough. We have to remember that the idea of science can be a powerful legitimating symbol. The political activists inspired by Marx are likely to claim scientific validity for their actions just as are the employers who attempt to persuade their employees of the 'clear economic need' for the redundancies which have been 'recommended by highly objective consultants'. This tendency means that there are considerable ethical problems for the sociological investigator in the industrial sphere and one way in which this can be handled is to argue that the sociologist should be value-free or ethically-neutral.

The term 'value-free' has been used with various different emphases since it was taken up from the arguments of Max Weber developed early in the history of the social sciences. Weber's true position was probably very like the one argued above about the necessary subservience of science to politics but, partly because he probably overstated his case in the course of reacting to the politically biased work of some German academics of his day, his notion has been taken up by some sociologists to distance themselves from the moral implications of their work. This involves suggesting that sociologists' work is uncontaminated by values and moral issues and that their contribution to social life is merely a technical one. In contradiction to this, it is nowadays increasingly accepted in the world of academic sociology that sociological work is value-oriented from the start. From the choice of research topic, the assumptions made about social life, the concepts applied to the problem, the investigative techniques used, the source of funding and the place of publication, value judgments and choices are ever present. The sociologist, then, cannot be value-free. This does not mean that objectivity is out of the question, however.

The arguments about value freedom and the possibilities for objectivity are about the relationship between analysis and evaluation in sociology. Whereas it is indeed impossible for sociologists' work to be value-free it is nevertheless incumbent upon them to pursue a certain objectivity. This does not mean that they should totally separate their analysis and evaluations. This would be impossible. What they can be expected to do is to go as far as possible towards revealing the grounds on which their interpretation is based. That is, they might reveal where their evidence came from, how it was collected, upon what assumptions these procedures were based and, as far as possible, reveal the ways in which the investigators themselves were implicated in the ways their work was done. As long as sociologists work in this way, their readers or students will be able to make their own evaluations of the generalisations made. To justify the type of acceptability indicated by the scientific label, sociology must not deny its audience the opportunity to draw its own conclusions.

The position taken here is clearly value-based in itself, and it is prescriptive. It sets criteria of judgment which students and readers are encouraged to apply in evaluating sociological material. It also demands much of sociologists themselves in researching and writing. It is very easy to do this in the comfortable role of the writer of generalisations about sociology. In practice, life is not so simple. Both the sociologist wanting to do empirical research and the sociologist wanting to teach or write material for a 'practical' audience face problems. And many of these come down to the question of access.

Industrial sociology and the problem of access

Sociology, in the form bequeathed by the sociological tradition described earlier, always tends to raise 'big questions' and go to the root of the nature and tendencies of the democratic, industrial and capitalist world which saw its birth. In this sense it can be seen as radical – probing deep down and raising potentially unsettling questions. Its equipment of concepts, which includes class, alienation, anomie, industrialism, power, capitalism and conflict may well unsettle a seminar of industrial managers and, more importantly perhaps, strongly discourage the owners or managers of any work organisation from giving access for sociological research on their territory. Not only can we expect resistance to any apparently radical analysis on the grounds that it is 'political' (the organisation of work being seen as somehow non-political) but we can also expect the retort that it is pointless going into basic issues or those relating to the structure of society since nothing can be done about these anyway. This might seem to be a good justification for keeping macro-sociological interests out of micro-scale investigations. But this is to deny the very rationale of sociology, which is to locate

- the specific within the general;
- the local within the structural;
- the individual within the societal.

This whole book is, of course, dedicated to the proposition that these large-scale matters are highly relevant to people wishing to understand the goings-on within the smallest and least significant workplace. But where this is not recognised by those controlling access to researchers, as it rarely seems to be, then investigators have to look hard at how they are to present themselves to these gatekeepers.

Largely as a result of these considerable problems of access, twentieth-century industrial sociology has frequently stayed at a parochial level of analysis, often using value-laden concepts such as 'worker resistance to change' and 'organisational goals' in an unreflecting way and as if these were purely scientific concepts whose assumptions did not happily resonate with those of their patrons. The double problem of access – access to do research and access to an audience – has strongly influenced the development of industrial sociology and given much of it a heavily managerial bias. But, ironically, managerial bias in industrial sociology may be helping managers themselves very little in the long run. Telling people what they want to hear or happily leaving their prejudices untouched is hardly the way to improve their understanding. This point is simply illustrated by the need frequently recognised in industrial relations training courses to point out that industrial conflict cannot successfully be understood or 'managed' if procedures are based on the naive assumption that there are not really 'two sides' in employment relationships and that the plant or office is a unitary and family-like entity.

Many industrial sociologists have been wary of becoming what Baritz (1960), in a classic criticism of much early industrial sociology, called 'servants of power' and are frequently reluctant to work directly for organisational interests. This means that some have entered industry covertly whilst others have studied it from a distance or through interviewing participants outside of their work (Beynon 1988). However, a different strategy has been followed by other researchers. This is the 'action research' approach which involves collaboration in solving problems of a client organisation in such a way that problem-solving and knowledge acquisition gain from one another so that advantage accrues to the action researcher, the client and the scientific community alike (Bryman 1989).

The sociology of work and industry: role and purpose

It is possible to recognise three possible roles which can be played by the sociology of work and industry.

> **Three possible roles for the sociology of work and industry**
> - as a servant of power;
> - as a private and marginal activity of academics;
> - as a resource helping inform human choices.

1   *A 'servant of power' role* along the lines already mentioned. Here, those trained as industrial sociologists would primarily be employed as specialist human manipulators by large organisations in the way Baritz (1960) saw beginning to happen in pre-war USA where such people were

> doing what they were told to do and doing it well – and therefore endangering those other personal, group, class and institutional interests which were opposed to the further domination by the modern corporation of the mood and direction of American life.

Sociological knowledge and insight will inevitably have a relevance to practical problem-solving in large organisations and can be shown to help solve problems in certain relatively bounded situations (Klein and Eason 1991). One would be naive and wrong to deny the right of any group to make use of knowledge in this way. What can be objected to, however, is the exclusive development of industrial sociology as a manipulative instrument for the pursuit of sectional interests (Watson 1994c).

2   *A marginalised and disengaged role* which can arise from too strong a reaction to the above possibility. It is a role which is in danger of becoming the most likely one, if care is not taken by the academic creators and communicators of sociology. This is the danger of the subject becoming marginalised with sociologists and their students coming to know the world only through their texts and where texts, monographs and research reports become substitutes for experience. There is a real danger of the sociology of work becoming encapsulated in its own private world of

scholarly production, polemic and career rivalry, thereby reducing its potential for informing social action outside the academy. There is a tendency for many sociologists to become either too obsessed with their naive political utopianism or too caught up in dense conceptual mystification – and quite frequently to be trapped in both of these – to be seen as worthy of attention by other than their own acolytes.

3   A role for the sociology of work and industry as *a resource* which helps those living in an industrial capitalist society to understand better the possibilities and choices which exist with regard to how work is organised and experienced in those societies. Its role should be to inform choice. Here, the subject is not the sole preserve of the expert – be they 'marginalised' or 'servants of power' – but is something to be disseminated through both formal and informal educational institutions and communication media. It becomes something in whose development the individual is first involved as a student, and which is subsequently drawn upon and further engaged with in their later life and career as employees, managers, voting citizens, trade unionists, self-employers or consumers. It is a resource vital to a democratic society. As Eldridge, Cressey and MacInnes say, in considering the role that industrial sociology might play in coming to terms with the various economic and social crises, 'To show what possibilities may exist for political choices in an active democracy is to exercise the sociological imagination' (1991).

In the past, social thinkers were a tiny minority addressing a slightly larger minority of the population. The modern age is one of vastly increased literacy and access to schooling and communication media. This means that critical reflection on the values and institutions of society need no longer be the preserve of the privileged social philosopher or the dilettante intellectual of a leisured class. An ability to be analytical about social, economic and political issues can be developed in every citizen – this furthering the ideal of democratic control of society and its institutions. As Burns (1962) suggested, at a time when industrial sociology scarcely had a foothold in Britain, we can see it as the sociologist's business 'to conduct a critical debate ... with the public about its equipment of social institutions'. Institutions of work and industrial organisation are central to the very nature of society. And they nowadays require perhaps closer and more rational scrutiny and rethinking than ever before.

■   ■   ■

Chapter 2

The sociological analysis of work and industry

Introduction

Work and how it is organised and experienced is central to the traditional concerns of sociology – a discipline which developed to provide a critical understanding of the industrial capitalist society. In spite of this, there has never emerged an integrated industrial sociology or sociology of work. This, in part, reflects the fact that the sociological discipline itself contains a variety of different theoretical traditions. But it also reflects the fact that sociologists interested in work have tended to specialise and to concentrate on such separate areas as work organisations, occupations, employment relations, or work behaviour and attitudes. Figure 2.1 gives examples of the concerns of these various areas of the sociology of work and industry and indicates that each of these represents one facet or another of industrial capitalist societies.

A degree of diversity is welcome in any discipline which deals with important social issues about which members of society have a variety of views and preferences. A degree of division of labour or specialisation within a discipline also has the advantage of achieving a sharper focus on particular areas of activity or concern. But this can be taken too far and can lead to confusion and frustration on the part of those who come to sociology with a desire to see what the sociological perspective can offer to their understanding of contemporary problems of work and how it is organised. It can be off-putting if the person involved in industrial problems discovers, for example, that they are located in a work organisation which has one sociology, that they belong to an occupation which has another distinct sociology, and that they are involved in employment or industrial relations issues which have their own separate literature. And it can be even more discouraging when they discover that different studies or analyses within these compartments tend to vary quite considerably in the set of concepts which they use and the extent to which they stress, say, co-operation in social life or, alternatively, conflicts of interest.

To come to terms with this problem, the student interested in the sociological analysis of work and industry needs to appreciate just how the

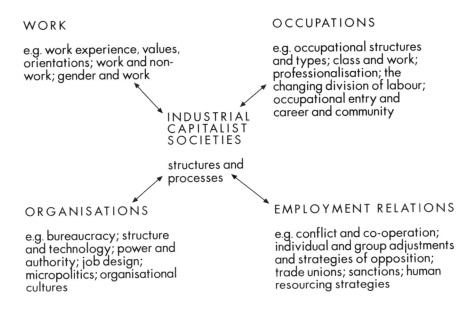

FIGURE 2.1 The components of the sociology of work and industry

discipline is fragmented into both theoretical traditions and substantive areas of study. To help with this it is convenient to recognise that the sociology of work and industry (a) tends to cover the five areas of study shown in Figure 2.1; and (b) tends to approach these through six different theoretical traditions or strands of thought. These are shown in Figure 2.2. It is not a matter of there being a specific theoretical approach for each of the areas of study, however. Different contributors within each of the areas will tend to favour one theoretical tradition rather than another.

The strategy which is chosen here for overcoming the problems of diversity of focus and approach in the sociology of work and industry is to concentrate first on establishing the main characteristics and interests of the six theoretical strands. As each of these has important insights to offer, it is well worth looking at each of them in their own terms. Once this has been done, it becomes possible for more general theoretical schemes to be developed which draw on insights from the various existing traditions. It will therefore be argued, towards the end of the chapter, that any particular investigation within the broad area of the sociology of work and industry can follow a theoretical strategy of *pragmatic pluralism*

Theoretical strand	Applications and developments
Managerial-psychologistic	Scientific management
	Democratic humanism
Durkheim-systems	Human relations
	Systems thinking in organisational analysis
Interactionist	Occupations and professions in society
	Organisations as negotiated orders
	Ethnomethodology
Weberian-social action	Social action perspective on organisations
	Bureaucratic principles of work organisation
	Orientations to work
Marxian	Individual experiences and capitalist labour processes
	Structural contradictions in society and economy
Postmodern	Discourse and human subjectivity
	Postmodern organisations

FIGURE 2.2   Six theoretical strands in the sociology of work and industry

in which elements are taken from the various existing traditions to create a theoretical framework which is most appropriate for that particular investigation.

The six strands of thought should not be seen as constituting watertight 'schools' of thought. My 'map', which is designed to help the reader through the jungle of different perspectives, is simply one possible scheme for organising ideas by bringing together contributions which appear to have something in common. The arrows crossing some of the 'boxes' in Figure 2.2 indicate developments which have been influenced by more than one of the theoretical strands. In the case of three of the strands we see approaches which have been especially influenced by a particular founding figure of sociology, Durkheim, Weber and Marx. The first strand, however, contains what are usually seen as quite separate and indeed contrasting schools of thought. These strange bedfellows are brought together here to represent a style of thinking about people and work which the five other strands can be seen as reacting to and reaching substantially beyond.

The managerial-psychologistic strand

Strictly speaking, neither of the two approaches brought together here should be seen as part of a sociology of work and industry. Yet they are vitally important to an understanding of the strictly sociological way of thinking because they provide an ever-present general style of thinking with which sociologists of work have to come to terms and advance beyond.

Scientific management and democratic humanism are the ghosts at the banquet, in effect. It is much easier to appreciate the sociological guests at the feast if we have a good view of these strictly non-sociological approaches which tend to haunt most occasions when sociologists of work come together. Although the two are diametrically opposed in underlying sentiment and assumptions about human nature, they both represent a style of thinking about work which is highly individualistic and which is concerned to prescribe to managers how they should relate to their employees and should organise workers' jobs. Both approaches are, in the sense discussed in the previous chapter, psychologistic. They See page 17 both concentrate on questions of 'human nature' and, as a consequence of this, tend not to recognise the cultural dimension of social life and the range of possibilities of work organisation and orientation implied by this. The concern of each of the approaches is to harness scientific method to discover and make legitimate what are, in effect, techniques of manipulation rather than disinterested concerns with understanding.

Scientific management

The leading advocate and systematiser of what he named scientific management (and others frequently call 'Taylorism') was F. W. Taylor (1856–1915), a US engineer and consultant. Taylor's importance as the leader of the movement which has given the world work-study, piece-rate schemes, and time-and-motion study has to be set in historical context. The increasingly rationalised division of tasks and the mechanisation of work reached a point at the beginning of the twentieth century where the need to co-ordinate human work efforts not surprisingly invited the attentions of men interested in applying scientific and engineering criteria to the human sphere as they had to the mechanical. Taylorism sees the worker basically as an economic animal, a self-seeking non-social individual who prefers managers to do their job-related thinking for them. Given this, the management simply has to work out the most efficient way of organising work and then tie the monetary rewards of the work to the level of output achieved by the individual. This would produce results which would benefit employer and employee alike, removing the likelihood of conflict and the need for trade unions.

Scientific management involves the following approaches:

- The scientific analysis by management of all the tasks which need to be done in order to make the workshop as efficient as possible.
- The design of jobs by managers to achieve the maximum technical division of labour through advanced job fragmentation.
- The separation of the planning of work from its execution.
- The reduction of skill requirements and job-learning times to a minimum.
- The minimising of materials-handling by operators and the separation of indirect or preparatory tasks from direct or productive tasks.
- The use of such devices as time-study and monitoring systems to co-ordinate these fragmented elements and the work of the de-skilled workers.
- The use of incentive payment systems both to stabilise and to intensify worker effort.
- The conduct of manager–worker relationships at 'arm's-length' – following a 'minimum interaction model' (Davis 1966; Littler 1982).

Taylor's successors within scientific management soon modified his refusal to accept a place for organised labour in the workplace but the approach has always retained its individualistic emphasis. Books on management thought and much management teaching imply that scientific management, on being shown to fall short psychologically, was consigned to the history of management as part of its 'classical' past. This is far from the case, however, concerning the practicalities of job design in the modern world. Systematic research carried out by Davis, Canter and Hoffman in the 1950s and followed up in the 1970s by Taylor (Davis and Taylor 1979) on a representative sample of US companies showed that job design practices in manufacturing continued to be dominated by a concern to minimise the unit production time in order to minimise the cost of production. Job design criteria included skill specialisation, minimal skill requirements, minimum training times, maximum repetition and the general limiting of both the number of tasks in a job and the variation within those tasks and jobs. Subsequent to this, as we shall see later, evidence continues to be presented to support Braverman's (1974) claim that scientific management and its associated deskilling is becoming more dominant and is covering increasing sectors of the working world in the latter part of the twentieth century. Braverman stressed the association between Taylorism and the logic of capitalist accumulation in explaining this but we might also see the continuing influence of scientific management as a reflection of the extent to which psychologistic assumptions hold sway among practical managers.

The psychologistic assumptions of scientific management are best illustrated by reference to Taylor's concept of 'soldiering' as described in *The Principles of Scientific Management* (1911). Soldiering in Taylor's sense is 'the natural instinct and tendency of men to take it easy'. When this is combined with people's economic interests and the failure of managers to design, allocate and reward work on a scientific basis, it leads employees to get together and rationally conspire to hold production down. They do this to maximise their reward without tempting the incompetent management to come back and tighten the rate (which only needs tightening because it was originally guessed at and not fixed scientifically). This is 'systematic soldiering' and is an inefficient evil. It is not, however, seen as an inevitable phenomenon which results from the natural sociability of human beings, as others have seen it. If the management relate directly to each individual and satisfy their personal self-interest then they will get full co-operation. A proper understanding of human nature, it is implied, would demonstrate that this is the case. The ultimate explanation of work behaviour, then, is a psychologistic one. It can be so labelled because scientific management is reductionist in its precluding of wider social considerations and because it is not an explanation which has stood up to more academically rigorous psychological study – on human factor industrial psychology, for instance (Rose 1988b).

Democratic humanism

The prescriptions offered to managements by democratic humanist writers and researchers are very much in conflict with those of scientific management. It is suggested that organisational efficiency can be achieved through 'participative' approaches, which may take the following forms:

- Subordinates becoming involved in setting their own objectives.
- The 'enriching' of jobs by reducing the extent of their supervision and monitoring.
- The development of more open and authentic colleague relationships.

These represent the sort of ideas which have become popular with more 'enlightened' managers since the writings, manuals and training films of a group of American psychologists and management consultants encouraging such an approach began to have an influence in the 1960s. It is the opposite of scientific management but in some ways it is a mirror image of it. It bases its approach to human work behaviour on a theory of human nature and one of the popular early writers of this school made quite clear the equivalence of the two opposing propositions by labelling them Theory X and Theory Y.

McGregor (1960) characterised the scientific management approach adopted by unenlightened managers as based on Theory X. This sees human beings as naturally disliking work and therefore avoiding it if they can. People prefer to avoid responsibility and like to be given direction. They have limited ambitions and see security as a priority. The manager therefore controls and coerces people towards the meeting of organisational objectives. The effect of this is to encourage the very behaviour which managers wish to avoid; the employees' passive acceptance of the situation may be encouraged, leading to a lack of initiative and creativity on their parts, or their resentment may be fuelled and hence their aggression and lack of co-operation. But Theory Y, which McGregor advocated and which social science research was said to support, states that people are not like this but would generally prefer to exercise self-control and self-discipline at work. He believed this would occur if employees were allowed to contribute creatively to organisational problems in a way which enabled them to meet their need for self-actualization.

The notion of a *self-actualization need* within all human beings is taken from the work of the US humanistic psychologist Maslow (1954) whose starting point was the belief that scientific investigation of human behaviour should be oriented towards releasing in people the various potentials which they possess. The basic scheme which has been taken from Maslow and used by numerous 'enlightened' management writers and teachers is the 'hierarchy of needs' model. This suggests that there are five sets of genetic or instinctive needs which people possess and that as one satisfies most of the needs at one level one moves up to seek satisfaction of the needs at the next level.

- At the first level are *physiological needs* such as for food, drink, sex and sensory satisfaction.
- At the second level are *safety needs* which motivate people to avoid danger.
- At the third level are what Maslow calls *love needs*. These include needs to belong and to affiliate with others in both a giving and a receiving sense.
- At the fourth level are *esteem needs* which cover prestige, status and appreciation from external sources as well as internal feelings of confidence, achievement, strength, adequacy and independence.
- At the fifth level is the need for *self-actualization*, which is the desire to realise one's ultimate potential.

> ## Self actualization
> 'to become more and more what one is, to become everything that one is capable of becoming' (Maslow 1943).

Maslow's model is frequently used as a stick with which to beat traditional managerial approaches, these being seen as failing to obtain employee co-operation because they do not provide the intrinsically and naturally sought rewards which employees 'need' once they have satisfied their basic low-level requirements. An influential example of such thinking is Herzberg's 'Motivation-Hygiene' or *two-factor theory of work motivation* (1966) which was originally based on a study of engineers and accountants who were asked to describe events in their working lives which made them feel good or made them feel bad. Herzberg suggested that the factors which made them feel good when they were present were different from those which made them feel bad when they were absent.

Herzberg went on to differentiate between the following factors:

- Contextual or 'hygiene' factors like salary, status, security, working conditions, supervision and company policy which can lead to dissatisfaction if 'wrong', but which do not lead to satisfaction if 'right'.
- Content or 'motivation' factors such as achievement, advancement, recognition, growth, responsibility and 'the work itself'. These have to be present, in addition to the contextual or 'hygiene' factors, before satisfactions can be produced and people motivated to perform well.

These 'motivators' clearly relate to Maslow's 'higher level needs' whilst the hygiene factors only satisfy the 'lower level' ones. Managers are therefore encouraged to see that getting 'right' such matters as wages, supervision and working conditions would produce little by way of positive motivation. Instead, the 'motivators' have to be built into the way jobs are designed. Jobs should be enlarged and managerial controls over how they are performed reduced. Workers themselves would set targets, plan the work and, as far as possible, choose the working methods to be used. This represents a complete reversal of the job design principles advocated by scientific management, as we shall see when we look at job design issues in Chapter 6.

Discussion

At first it might appear that those interested in scientifically investigating work behaviour have a fairly simple task: to test these two propositions about work and human needs to find the validity of either scientific management's 'Theory X' or the democratic humanists' 'Theory Y'. Alas, says the sociologist, this cannot be done. Such an attempt would involve reductionism and psychologism in its belief that understanding work behaviour is a matter of reaching a correct understanding of human nature – a set of principles about people which would apply to all human beings in all circumstances. In so far as there is such a thing as human nature it is much more complex than this and leads people to act very differently in different circumstances. To a much greater extent than other animals, humans are what they make of themselves. They do have some minimal instincts and some inbuilt physiologically based needs. But, beyond these, they very much mould themselves and each other to need the following:

- A little simple food *or* a lot of rich food.
- The assurance of safety *or* the stimulation of danger.
- Self-aggrandizement *or* self-abasement.

Our socially or culturally defined nature is far more important than any universal 'human' or species nature; we have socially-mediated wants rather than built-in needs.

In evaluating scientific management and democratic humanism we can easily get into a paradoxical muddle. In effect, both are right and both are wrong. To make sense of this statement, we must add the magic words *depending on the circumstances*. And by circumstances is meant the structural and cultural factors which were shown in the previous chapter to be central to a sociological approach to analysis. Thus, if we have on the one hand, (a) a culture which lays primary value on money and an industry structured on the basis of mechanisation and minute task-specialisation, it is possible that people will deliberately choose to do such work and will happily accept close supervision and a degree of boredom in return for cash; and on the other hand, (b) a wider culture which places central value on 'doing your own thing' and sees work as a key to identity, then we might expect the scientific managers to lose out to the self-actualizers as guides to appropriate managerial policy.

See page 118
The difficulty we face in industrial sociology in practice, however, is that we find a mixture of these circumstances in modern societies. Consequently we need a more sophisticated sociological approach to studying work behaviour and attitudes. This we will examine later but, for the moment, we must stress that the choice which is made to adopt either cash-reward oriented work organisations or self-actualizing ones is not a scientific choice. It is to a large extent a value or a political choice. The role of sociological analysis is to inform that choice with a consideration of what is possible in which circumstances.

The Durkheim-systems strand

In contrast to the psychologism of the first strand of thinking, we see a turning away in the second strand from an emphasis on human individuals and the 'needs' which they are said to share. Instead we see an emphasis on the social system of which individuals are a part. The social system may be that of the society as a whole or, alternatively, it may be that of the work organisation or even a sub-unit of the organisation. The key, and essentially sociological, idea is concentrating on the patterns of relationships which exist between people rather than on the people as such. This emphasis was at the heart of the work of one of the most important founders of sociology, Emile Durkheim, and it provides the theoretical underpinning of the first recognisable 'school' of industrial sociology, that of human relations. More recently it has inspired systems approaches both to industrial relations thinking and to the sociology of organisations.

Emile Durkheim

Emile Durkheim (1858–1917) is often described as the sociologist *par excellence*. In this we see his importance and perhaps the principal problem with his work. His position as the first sociologist to hold a university professorship meant that there was considerable pressure on him to establish the distinctiveness of the new discipline. This fact probably explains in part his overemphasis both on science (which, in contrast to the position taken here, can give moral guidance) and on the 'reality' of an autonomous and externally-existing 'society'. Ideas which stress the primacy of community over the individual have a strong ideological and conservative potential, but to picture Durkheim as an intentionally conservative thinker in this way is quite wrong. He was concerned neither to return to the past nor to justify the status quo. Yet he was reacting strongly against certain aspects of the prevailing individualism of his age. On a methodological level he was opposed to psychological reduction-ism, showing that even a highly individual act like suicide has to be understood in terms of the extent of the individual's integration into a community or group rather than by simple reference to the individual's mental state. To study social life one had to isolate and examine 'social currents' and 'social facts'. These are to be seen as *things* and as existing external to individuals, exerting constraint over them. Values, customs, norms, obligations and suchlike are to be considered in this way.

Perhaps most influential in taking Durkheim towards an over-emphasis on the structural side of the agency–structure relationship was his See page 10 morally inspired reaction to the disintegrating effects of the egoism and self-interest which he saw developing in the European societies of his time. He saw the organic solidarity so necessary for a healthy society being threatened by *laissez-faire* economics and a utilitarian philosophy which encouraged an egoism strongly contrasting with the healthy individualism which could exist in an industrialised society. A 'healthy' individualism could exist as long as that society provided regulation, directing principles or norms. Without this we have the pathology of *anomie*.

Anomie

A form of social breakdown in which the norms which would otherwise prevail in a given situation cease to operate.

The particular form of anomie which worried Durkheim was one in which the 'organic integration' of society would be threatened by unrestricted individual aspirations and hence a lack of any kind of social discipline, principle or guiding norms.

Human relations

Durkheim's analysis of anomie and his concern about social solidarity and integration was a strong influence on the work of Elton Mayo (1880–1949) who has come to be seen as the leading spokesman of the human relations 'school' of industrial sociology. Whereas Durkheim's sympathies were not with the ruling or managerial interests of capitalist society, Mayo's were. In place of Durkheim's seeking of social integration through moral communities based on occupations, Mayo put the industrial workgroup and the employing enterprise, with the industrial managers having responsibility for seeing that group affiliations and social sentiments were fostered in a creative way. Like Taylor, Mayo was anxious to develop an effective and scientifically informed managerial élite. If managements could ensure that employees' social needs were met at work by giving them the satisfaction of working together, by making them feel important in the organisation and by showing an interest in their personal problems, then both social breakdown and industrial conflict could be headed off. Managerial skills and good communications were the antidotes to the potential pathologies of an urban industrial civilisation.

The context of the contribution of the human relations group was the problem of controlling the increasingly large-scale enterprises of the post-war period and the problem of legitimating this control in a time of growing trade union challenge. The faith of the scientific management experts in a solution which involved the achieving of optimum working conditions, the 'right' method and an appropriate incentive scheme proved to be blind. Practical experience and psychological research alike were indicating the need to pay attention to other variables in work behaviour. Here we see the importance of the Hawthorne experiments.

The Hawthorne investigations had been started in Chicago by engineers of the Western Electric Company's Hawthorne plant. They had investigated the effects of workshop illumination on output and had found that as their investigations proceeded output improved in the groups investigated, regardless of what was done to the lighting. In 1927 the Department of Industrial Research of Harvard University, a group to which Mayo had been recruited, was called in. Their enquiry started in the Relay Assembly Test Room where over a five-year period a wide range of changes were made in the working conditions of a specially segregated group of six women whose job was to assemble telephone relays. Changes involving incentive schemes, rest pauses, hours of work and refreshments were made but it was found that whatever changes were made – including return to original conditions – output rose. The explanation which was later to emerge has been labelled 'the Hawthorne effect'. It was inferred that the close interest shown in the workers by the investigators, the effective pattern of communication which developed and the emerging high social cohesion within the group brought together the needs of the group for rewarding interaction and co-operation with the output needs of the management. This type of explanation was also encouraged by the other stages of the investigations. The employee interviewing programme was seen as showing that many of the problems of management–worker relationships could be put down to the failure to recognise the emotions and the 'sentiments' of the employees and the study in the Bank Wiring Observation Room was taken to show the part played by informal social group needs in worker restriction of output. The Hawthorne studies were most fully reported by Roethlisberger and Dickson (1939) and their reports and interpretations can be compared with those of Mayo (1933) and Whitehead (1938).

We have already noted the relationship between Durkheim's ideas and those of Mayo but perhaps a more important influence on all of these interpreters was the classical sociologist Pareto (1848–1923). A key figure in the Harvard sociological circles of this time was the biologist and translator of Pareto, L. J. Henderson. He introduced the ideas of this Italian former engineer to those Harvard thinkers who, at the time, were highly receptive to ideas which might counter those of the liberals or Marxists (Gouldner 1971). The effects of Pareto (via Henderson) on this first specialised school of industrial sociology were twofold:

1   The suggestion that workers' behaviour can be attributed to their 'sentiments' rather than to their reason. Apparently rational behaviour, like Taylor's 'systematic soldiering', could be better understood as deriving from irrational fears, status anxieties and the instinctive need of the individual to be loyal to his or her immediate social

group. The problems did not arise from economic and rationally perceived conflicts of interest and were therefore not open to solution through 'scientific' management.

2   An emphasis on the notion of *system*, this conveniently according with the holistic tendencies of Durkheim. Here we have the organic analogy with its stress on integration and the necessary interdependence of the parts and the whole. Only by the integration of the individual into the (management-led) plant community could systemic integration be maintained and the potential pathologies of the industrial society avoided.

Human relations industrial sociology has been widely criticised for its managerial bias, its failure to recognise the rationality of employee behaviour and its denial of underlying economic conflicts of interest (see Landsberger 1958). The investigations which were carried out have also been examined and found wanting (Carey 1967). Some of the writers in the tradition are more vulnerable to criticism than others, but what cannot be denied is the enormous influence these researchers, and especially Mayo, had on subsequent social scientific investigation of industrial behaviour (J. Smith 1987). Although the Hawthorne works in Chicago have now been replaced by shopping malls, researchers on work organisations are turning back to the classic studies carried out there as they debate a range of theoretical and methodological issues which were initially raised by this work (Schwartzman 1993). Gillespie (1991) argues that we can most usefully regard the accounts and discussions of the Hawthorne experiments as 'manufactured knowledge' in which Mayo and his fellow human relations writers drew on their social scientific investigations to construct a 'message' – one which played down the possibility of an active role for workers, especially a collective role, and which stressed the role of managers as experts in control.

Systems thinking in industrial sociology

Durkheim's message to sociologists was that they should look beyond the individuals who compose society to the level of the underlying patterns of social activity. The institutions, which are part of this pattern, are to be studied not only to locate their 'genesis' but to understand their 'functioning' – that is, the contribution of the parts of the society to the continuation and survival of the whole.

Systems thinking

Social entities such as societies or organisations can be viewed as if they were self-regulating bodies exchanging energy and matter with their environment in order to survive.

The idea of looking at society itself or at industrial organisations as social systems (and, later, as socio-technical systems) is rooted in the old organic analogy which views society as a living organism constantly seeking stability within its environment, and has come down into contemporary sociology through the work of Durkheim, Pareto and various anthropologists working in the Durkheimian tradition. Perhaps the most influential single sociologist of the twentieth century, Talcott Parsons (1902–79), is much taken up with biological analogies and was a member of Henderson's Harvard 'Pareto Circle' along with Elton Mayo. His influence has been enormous, establishing an intellectual ambience in which a considerable proportion of existing contributions to industrial and organisational sociology have been fashioned. Added to this has been the growing popularity of cybernetics in the industrial world and a growing interest within management thought in the so-called 'general systems theory' of von Bertalanffy.

The greatest impact of systems thinking in the sociology of work and industry has undoubtedly been on the study of work organisations. Between the mid-1950s and about 1970 the view of the formal organisation as an open system functioning within its 'environment' virtually became an orthodoxy shared by various different schools of organisation theory. These include the socio-technical systems approach and the very influential contingency approaches which we will look at in detail later (Chapter 6). The systems approach, essentially, amounts to the replacement of the classical managerial metaphor which sees the organisation as a rationally conceived machine constructed to meet efficiently the goals of its designers with the metaphor of the organisation as a living organism constantly adapting in order to survive in a potentially threatening environment. Systems views are still widely followed in the study of organisations even if their use is sometimes more implicit than explicit (Brown 1992). They have two significant strengths:

- First, they properly recognise that organisations are much more than the official structures set up by their initiators. They are, rather, patterns of relationships which constantly have to adapt to enable the organisation to continue.
- Second, they stress the importance of close interrelationships between the different parts, or 'subsystems', of the organisation. The tendency for changes in one part of a system to have implications for other parts of it is strongly emphasised.

See page 287

The influence of systems thinking in industrial relations has been less long-lasting, at least among those taking a more sociological view of industrial conflict. The British Oxford School of industrial relations writers whose most significant impact came with their influence on the Donovan Commission, uses a systems approach (Schienstock 1981). However, such an approach is made more explicit in the US tradition which is based on the model offered by Dunlop (1958). This locates all industrial disputes and their management within an 'industrial relations system', composed of the following:

- Groups of actors (managerial, worker and outside, especially governmental, agencies).
- A context.
- An ideology which binds the system together.
- A body of rules which govern the behaviour of the various actors.

Central to this, and central to the kinds of objections which have been made by sociologists to the approach, is the notion of the ideology which holds the system together. This, according to Dunlop, is the set of ideas and beliefs 'commonly held by the actors' involved. To sociologists of the generations active after the mid-1960s who were turning away from orthodox systems-oriented sociologies of the Durkheimian and 'structural-functionalist' type and moving more towards the power and conflict-oriented insights of Weber and Marx, this was heavily to overstress the degree of consensus which exists in modern societies about work and its rewards. It was felt that the sociologist should set issues of industrial conflict much more in the context of the basic power and material inequalities of society as a whole and give attention to the role of domination, exploitation and class conflict in work relationships.

Discussion

The greatest weakness of all of the components of this Durkheim-systems strand of thinking, as seen by later sociologists, has been the tendency to overemphasise integration and consensus both within societies and within work organisations at the expense of attention to underlying conflicts and fundamental differences of interest. Differences of interest are recognised but interest groups tend to be conceived within a 'pluralist' political model which sees the parties in conflict as being more or less evenly matched in power terms. As we shall see in later chapters, contemporary approaches to understanding industrial capitalist societies, work organisations and industrial conflict, attempt to give a more balanced view through attending to basic power structures and patterns of inequality as well as to matters of co-operation and shared norms.

Systems models are not only seen as one-sided in their overemphasis on integration and consensus. They are often seen as too readily viewing the organisation, or the society of which it is a part, from the point of view of managerial or other dominant interest groups. Often implicit in analyses of social relationships as 'systems' is the priority given to considering ways of maintaining that system. Conflicts and differences over anything more than minor matters of adjustment thus become seen as pathologies – or sicknesses of the organism which have to be cured if the organism is not to die. This tendency is not inevitable, however, since highly oppositional, and especially revolutionary, analyses are fond of talking about 'the system', usually implying a wish for the system to 'die'. Such radical types of systems thinking are, of course, no less one-sided than their managerial counterparts.

Systems thinking is valuable in its stress on structures and patterns in social life. It is therefore a useful corrective to over-individualistic approaches to explanation or to what was labelled 'psychologism' in Chapter 1. However, it does face the danger of over-reacting to individualistic perspectives. It is always in danger of leaving out of the analysis the people involved. Structures come to replace human beings as the focus of attention so that the approaches which make up this present strand of thinking do not really meet the criteria established for a successful sociology in Chapter 1. In making individuals secondary or derivative of the social system in which they are located, systems approaches tend to pay insufficient attention to the degree of interplay between individual initiative and social constraint in human societies. And systems views tend to fall especially short when taking into account the extent to which the social world is the creation of interacting individuals and groups assigning *meanings* and making interpretations of their situations. To consider an approach which gives prime emphasis to meanings and to interaction rather than to systems and structures existing outside the individual, we now turn to a quite different strand of the sociology of work and industry.

The interactionist strand

The interactionist strand has its roots firmly in the sociology department of Chicago University in the USA. Theoretically, the interactionist perspective, with its focus on the individual, the small group and on meanings, is almost a polar opposite of the Durkheim-systems strand described above. Yet in the contributions of interactionist sociologists to the study of work, we find important continuities with the work of Durkheim. This continuity can be seen in a common interest taken in occupations as central social institutions and also in a recognition of the importance of the division of labour in society. But to appreciate fully the interactionist approaches to work, it is necessary to give an account of the theoretical approach of the wider school of sociology of which these sociologists of work are a part – the school of symbolic interactionism.

The Chicago school and symbolic interactionism

The particular brand of sociological theory known as symbolic inter-actionism has developed alongside the more empirical study of work which has taken place within the same Chicago circles. Those sociol-ogists who have performed the studies which we will look at in later chapters have drawn on and contributed to this theoretical perspective to varying degrees and, to make their generally shared theoretical orientations clear, the main characteristics of symbolic interactionism need to be briefly described. The origins of the approach lie in the work of Cooley (1864–1929) and Mead (1863–1931) and its basic position is that the individual and society are inseparable units; their relationship is a mutually interdependent one, not a one-sided deterministic one. Human beings construct their realities in a process of interaction with other human beings. Individuals derive their very identity from their interaction with others.

Symbolic interactionism

Studies social interaction through a focus on the ways in which people develop their concept of *self* through processes of communication in which symbols such as words, gestures and dress allow people to understand the expectations of others.

According to the symbolic interactionists, all interaction and communication is dependent on the use of symbols such as words, gestures, clothes, skin colour and so on. The infant acquires an identity – a consciousness of *self* – through the socialisation or social learning process. This process involves the internalisation of symbols, which are organised round the concept of self to make social life meaningful. Awareness of self is acquired through 'taking on the role of the other'. It is through taking on the role of the other, particularly what are called 'significant others', that we learn about the expectations which others have of us. This helps us in deciding what role we will play in any given situation. Similarly, by taking the role of the other, we learn what to expect of that other. To orient us as we make our way through life we look to a variety of what are termed reference groups and as we move through a series of situations which bestow identity on us we are said to follow a career. Not surprisingly this concept of career is, as we shall see, a key contribution of this theoretical perspective to the sociology of work.

The man who established the investigative tradition of the interactionist strand was Park (1864–1944), a former journalist who encouraged researchers to make detailed ethnographic observations of both normal and deviant Chicago life in the participant observation tradition previously confined to anthropological studies of tribal life. In this and in his Durkheimian interest in what he called the 'moral order' (an ordering of expectations and moral imperatives which tend to routinise interaction) he influenced Everett Hughes who, in turn, has influenced an impressive proportion of those sociologists currently contributing to the sociology of work. Where Durkheim tended to look to occupations as offering possible solutions to the problem of social order, Hughes tends to take the study of occupations as his starting point; his way into learning about society.

Hughes' approach is to focus on the social drama of work – the interaction which takes place at work – taking note of the problems or tensions which are created by the work itself and by its social situation. The concern then turns to how the individual copes with or adapts to those problems, and especially, relates them to the problem of maintaining their identity. Here, perhaps, is the great fascination of this approach, a fascination which will become apparent later in this book when we look at how members of different occupations cope with the particular problems of their work. Hughes encouraged his students to focus on the offbeat, the 'dirty' or the deviant types of occupation (in the notorious Chicago 'nuts and sluts' tradition). This was not only because these occupations are interesting in their own right but because their study can highlight factors of general relevance to work experience which we might not notice in more conventional kinds of work where we too easily take them for granted. Thus, for example, when later we consider the way See page 229 prostitutes heavily stress the extent to which they control their clients in order to maintain self-respect, we are prompted to consider just how this may also be done in the more normal service occupations which we come across – the retail worker, the garage mechanic or the nurse. Light is thus thrown on the significance of the common tendency of car mechanics to insist that any theory put forward by the motorist about what is wrong with their car cannot be correct. Expertise must be protected to defend the mechanic's sense of self-respect *vis-à-vis* the client just as the female prostitute must protect her sense of emotional non-involvement to defend her notion of 'self' and personal autonomy *vis-à-vis* the male punter.

The influence of the Chicago school on the sociology of organisations has tended not to be in the area of industrial organisation but the work of Strauss and colleagues (1963) which shows how 'order' in a hospital can be understood as the outcome of a continual process of negotiation and adjustments between groups has implications for all work organisations.

> ### Negotiated order
>
> A view of social or organisational patterning as the *outcome* of interactions between people and their mutually developed meanings.

And the study by Goffman (1968) of 'total institutions' such as prisons, monasteries and mental hospitals in which inmates' lives and identities are almost totally dominated by organisational rules provides generally relevant insights about organisational life, especially with regard to how those in the least powerful positions in organisations nevertheless 'make out' and defend their identities in spite of the determination of the 'system' to reduce them to a cipher.

Ethnomethodology

Ethnomethodology takes interactionist insights nearer to their logical conclusion. It combines the thinking of the Chicago school with ideas from the European tradition of phenomenological philosophy and insights from Weber's methodological thinking.

> ### Ethnomethodology
>
> is concerned with the way ordinary members of society in their everyday lives make the world meaningful by achieving a sense of 'taken-for-grantedness'.

Ethnomethodology denies any objective reality to social phenomena; it suggests that there are no such things as societies, social structures or organisations. Instead, there are conceptions of this type within the heads of ordinary members of society which are *made use of* by these 'members' in carrying out their every day purposes. Thus, as Bittner (1974) suggests for example, we should see the idea of 'the organisation' as a common-sense construct of ordinary people rather than as a scientific concept, and we should concentrate on how people exploit the concept to make sense of what it is they are about. We do not follow organisational rules and procedures but carry out a range of personal projects which we then 'make sensible' by claiming to be acting in accordance with the organisation's requirements.

See page 308 Ethnomethodological thinking has been applied by a number of researchers to organisational settings. It was applied by Silverman and Jones (1976) to show how interviewers in a job selection process 'made sensible' the decisions they reached by utilising 'typifications' like 'acceptable behaviour' or 'abrasive behaviour'. It has also had an impact in the occupational sphere in the study of the work of scientists and the ways in which scientific knowledge emerges from the processes whereby scientists work together to produce 'accounts' of the physical world (Woolgar 1988). Neither the science produced by scientists nor the decisions arrived at by the job selectors are to be seen as outcomes of a rational analysis of an objective 'reality' but reflect the mundane sense-making work which all humans beings do all the time.

Perhaps ethnomethodology's importance is far greater than is implied by the very limited number of people in the sociology of work and industry who wholeheartedly adopted it. The impact of the ethno-methodologists' powerful critique of conventional sociology which was mounted in the early to mid-1970s was to make sociologists much more sensitive than perhaps they had been to the dangers of turning conceptual abstractions like 'society', 'class' or 'organisation' into concretely existing 'things' which have a life of their own outside people's minds.

Discussion

The interactionist strand of the sociology of work and industry clearly pays great attention to individuals and their role in social life and it pays very necessary heed to the human interpretative process which the more structural or systems-oriented approaches tend to neglect. The approach is clearly not psychologistic but we do have to ask whether, in turning from attention to social wholes, it is doing sufficient justice to the influence on human interaction of those ongoing historical processes and 'structures' of power and material interest which provide the context for individuals and their social role. To see how an interest in social meanings and individual motives can be combined with a more power-conscious and historically aware perspective we must return to the European tradition and to the work of Max Weber.

The Weber-social action strand

This strand is seen by many as taking us much closer to a sociological approach which takes into account both the meaningful activity of the individual and the larger-scale questions of historical change and economic and political conflicts. Despite the early interest shown by interactionists in the societal 'moral order' and the general division of labour, their interests have subsequently proved to be largely confined to the group or occupational levels. They have not successfully related meanings at the micro level to historical and cultural patterns at the macro level. A concern with such a relationship is basic to the work of Weber.

Max Weber

The work and ideas of Max Weber (1864–1920) have been much misunderstood and misrepresented. This is partly because of the incompleteness of his written works, his awkward style of writing, his own ambiguity on various issues, his tendency to separate his political writing from his sociological work and, especially, because his work was brought back into contemporary sociology largely via US sociologists who wished to use the name of this massively impressive European figure to legitimate their own positions or interests. Thus we find Weber misinterpreted at times as one who totally opposed Marx's position on the nature and rise of capitalism; as one who denied the importance of class divisions in society by arguing that a plurality of interest groups counterbalanced each other; as one who 'advocated' bureaucracy as 'efficient'; as an armchair thinker without interest in carrying out empirical investigations; and as one who encouraged the sociologist to be a neutral and uncommitted individual. There is some element of truth in each of these interpretations but each of them tends to be quite the opposite of what was his essential position.

Weber's advocacy of value freedom and his attempts to fill out (rather than totally contradict) the one-sidedness of Marxian thinking have to be understood in the light of his social and historical context. In trying to separate scientific analysis from political interpretation and advocacy he was reacting to contemporary academics whom he saw as abusing their academic status and, as was suggested in Chapter 1, he was interested in relegating sociological study to a role which was secondary to moral thinking and political activity. His reaction to the Marxist thinking of his time was not to try to demolish it but to take from it what was most useful in understanding modern capitalism whilst balancing its emphasis on material factors with fuller consideration of the role in history of ideas, individual agents and culture. It is true that in his more political writings he showed a clear preference for capitalism over its socialist alternative but his enthusiasm for capitalist social organisation was not much greater than that for socialism. Both of them involved the threat to individual freedom which he saw in bureaucracy. Such was the pessimism which runs through Weber's world view.

See page 14
Weber defined sociology as the study of social action (discussed above). The discipline would examine the ways in which people, through the attribution and inference of subjective meanings, would be influenced by each other and thereby oriented in their actions. Weber avoided ever talking of structures or systems and he related these social meanings to the wider society through the concept of a 'legitimate order'. This is a patterning in social life which individual actors *believe* to exist and to which they may conform. To understand how the order becomes valid to actors it has to be seen within the human meaning creating processes which, in turn, have to be related to the conflicts and power struggles which take place in a world where there are a variety of material interests. The interplay between ideas and interests is basic to Weber's sociology:

- As a first stage of investigation the sociologist attempts to gain an interpretative understanding (*verstehen*) of actors' behaviour.
- As a second stage of investigation the sociologist moves to a causal explanation. Since the actors who are being studied think in causal terms about what they are doing and because they base their actions

on certain rationally based assumptions of regularities in the world, some causal explanation of their behaviour should be possible.

Weber's sociology is underpinned by a set of philosophical assumptions about the world which include a view of reality as infinitely diverse and leading to the existence of fundamental conflicts of value, interest and perspective. Social life is thus characterised by perpetual conflict, struggle and the exercise of power. Humans are seen as rational beings pursuing ends, but there is no direct relationship between their efforts and the resulting social order. There is a *paradox of consequences* in social life.

Paradox of consequences

Human actions often have unintended consequences which may be quite different from or even in direct opposition to what was intended. This is because their fulfilment typically depends on the actions of others who will have their own interests, interpretations and priorities.

This tendency is profoundly important for the discipline of sociology generally and is especially well dealt with in the Weberian perspective. To illustrate this paradoxical aspect of social initiative as well as the other aspects of Weber's approach described above, we can make reference to some of his most famous substantive work.

In Weber's study *The Protestant Ethic and the Spirit of Capitalism*, which we will look at in detail below, we see how the ideas developed by See page 101 individuals like Luther and Calvin, who were primarily concerned with religious and spiritual ends, had the unintended consequence of helping to foster a 'spirit of capitalism' and an increasingly rationalistic world view, one of the consequences of which was the eventual undermining of religious belief. The ideas which encouraged asceticism contributed to a later materialism in western culture which would have horrified those who first set out these ideas. But Weber, in this kind of analysis, is not suggesting that ideas autonomously wing their way through history, changing their forms as they go. It is their coming together with the material interests of historical actors which give ideas force. Weber talks of an 'elective affinity' between ideas and interests: people tend to choose, develop or adopt ideas which fit with their material interests – these interests in turn being influenced by available ideas. Weber is by no means replacing Marx's stress on material interests as a force in history with an equally one-sided stress on ideas. Instead, he is showing that the cultural or subjective aspects of social life have to be seen as equal partners in any analytical scheme.

Weber sees a process of *rationalisation* underlying western history.

Rationalisation

A trend in social change whereby traditional or magical criteria of action are replaced by technical, calculative or scientific criteria.

With rationalisation, social life is 'demystified' or disenchanted, rational pursuit of profit motivates work behaviour and efforts are increasingly co-ordinated through bureaucratic means. This means that people more and more use calculative devices and techniques as means towards the achieving of ends (these are *formally rational* means) – the division of labour, sets of rules, accounting methods, money, technology, and so on. However, because of the ever-present tendency for unintended consequences to occur, these often turn out not to lead to the goals for which they were intended (thus making them *materially irrational*). In fact, the means may subvert the very ends for which they were designed. This may be difficult to understand and it is perhaps not surprising therefore that many writers on organisations have taken Weber to mean that bureaucracy is 'efficient', thus implying that he was unaware of its tendencies to develop 'dysfunctions' – tendencies towards inefficiencies (Albrow 1970). Weber was in fact pointing merely to the *potential superiority* of bureaucracy as an administrative instrument (its formal rationality) whilst being fully aware that it could manifest features which rendered it materially irrational, even going so far as to threaten individual freedom in a society with an attachment to such a goal or value. But this misunderstanding of Weber (perhaps partly deriving from a failure to realise that his ideal-type construct of bureaucracy was an intentionally one-sided representation) has been such that it has led to the development of a whole area of industrial or organisational sociology, and therefore part of the present strand. This is the work in the tradition of Merton's analysis of the so-called dysfunctions of bureaucracy, something we will look at later. See page 248–9

Weber's perspective allows us to take into account the individual social actor whilst seeing ideas and actions in the context of the vast political and dynamic patterns of history. The great sweep of Weber's interests (note that he applied his historical and comparative approach to both western and non-western societies) does not mean, however, that he was uninterested in detailed empirical investigation. He was, in fact, closely involved in what might have become one of the classical studies of industrial sociology – factory studies which predated the Hawthorne studies by twenty years or more. For a variety of reasons, these uncompleted studies have only recently been brought to the attention of those interested in the sociology of work and industry. Weber was interested in investigating a range of issues which are very close to those which have become central to industrial sociology in practice only some fifty or sixty years later (Eldridge 1971b). Weber's 'Methodological Introduction' to the proposed study shows an intention to study the effects of large-scale industry on the 'individual personality, the career and the extra-occupational style of living of the workers', thus taking into account the 'ethical, social and cultural background, the tradition and the circumstances of the worker'. All this is set in the context of economic, technical and capital-investment patterns in a way which is still very relevant to industrial sociology today.

Work orientations approach

The Weberian strand of specialised industrial sociology could well have started early in the century had Weber's research investigations not been abandoned. But various British sociologists have recently applied a generally Weberian perspective to industrial questions and performed studies very much in the spirit of Weber's own projected work. Most outstanding here has been the 'Affluent Worker' studies of Goldthorpe, Lockwood *et al.* (1968) which have given sociology the important concept of 'orientation to work', a notion with great potential for investigating connections between actions in the workplace and the external community and cultural life of employees. Much of the recent work which uses the Weberian 'social action frame of reference' has developed in reaction to that which emphasises the systemic aspects of social life and which puts special emphasis on the importance of technology in organisations. In Chapters 4 and 7 care will be taken to ensure that the enormously valuable 'orientation to work' concept does not become over individualistic or too subjective in emphasis by relating it to the logic of capitalist work organisation in the tradition of Weber (and indeed Marx) through the use of the idea of Baldamus (1961), one of the first contemporary sociologists to bring an essentially Weberian perspective to bear in industrial sociology.

Discussion

The recent renewal of interest in Weber's relevance to the sociology of work and industry is part of a process whereby investigations are increasingly moving away from the managerially oriented tradition which has prevailed for half a century towards a concern with some of the basic 'dilemmas of modernity' (Ray and Reed 1994). This accords with a more truly sociological concern with seeing work behaviour and patterns in the wider political, social and cultural context. A similar concern leads others to retain a commitment to the analytical potential of Marx's thinking. For some sociologists who want a critical and historical perspective on work Weber does not fit the bill. His anxious desire to separate sociological analysis and political evaluation is partly responsible here; his arguments were seen to be used too often to justify what more critical thinkers saw as the indifference of much mainstream sociology to the persisting inequalities of the modern world and the constant tendency for the ever-present underlying conflicts to manifest themselves. In addition to this we have the range of misrepresentations of Weber which prevailed and these, together with Weber's self-identification as a bourgeois and his own political nationalism and antipathy towards socialist reorganisation, have led to an understandable reluctance to look behind the complexities and ambiguities of Weber's writing to find a perspective which, in analytical terms, extends rather than rejects the strengths of Marxian thinking. The extreme subtlety, ambiguity and complexity of Weber's analysis, we have to recognise, does reduce the analytical value of his perspective in some ways. The full potential thrust of a Weberian perspective in sociology is perhaps only possible when combined with some of the more immediately coherent insights which are offered by the Marxian model.

The Marxian strand

Since its first appearance on the intellectual and political scene, Marxist and Marxian thought has influenced the development of sociology (Marxist to mean after Marxism and Marxian to mean after Marx). Marx and Engels created one of the most influential theories of social life ever made available to those trying to make some systematic sense of the modern industrialising world. Its influence in contemporary sociology can be understood as part of a reaction to an earlier tendency of much academic sociology to be consensus-oriented, to be non-critical at best and justifying the status quo at worst and also to its tendency to restrict its attention to the 'social' at the expense of the economic and political. Much of the older sociology was also seen to be too static and tending to ignore history.

Marx and Engels

Underlying the ideas of Karl Marx (1818–83) and Friedrich Engels (1820–95) is an assumption about the nature of human beings. This is the assumption that human beings achieve the fullness of their humanity through their labour. It is through labour – an essentially social process – that the human world is created. This is the basis of Marx's 'materialism'. However, the conditions under which the labour is performed make a crucial difference to the extent to which the human being is fulfilled. Under capitalism the workers are forced into an unequal relationship with the owner of capital, to whom they sell their labour power. The relationship is unequal, since the owner of capital always has sufficient means of subsistence whether production goes ahead or not, whilst wage workers are dependent on work being available to them. Furthermore, the employer requires workers to do more work than the workers themselves would need to do to meet their own needs; that is, the capitalist extracts the surplus value and in this way exploits the workers. Work within a capitalist context does not allow the workers the creative fulfilment which labour could potentially give them. Since the workers do not use tools and materials which are their own and since they neither own nor control the products of their labour any more than they have control over the methods which they apply in their work, they cannot achieve their potential self-realisation. They are thus *alienated*. Although this condition clearly has subjective implications, fundamentally it is an objective condition. A contented worker is no less alienated in this sense than a frustrated one.

Marx sets the above ideas in a historical model of the way in which one form of society develops to a point where it is superseded by another (for example, feudalism is transcended by capitalism which, in turn, is transcended by socialism). These ideas are also set in a structural model of capitalist society – or, more accurately, a capitalist mode of production. This is represented in Figure 2.3.

According to Marx, it is the nature of the economic base which characterises a society. The way in which production is organised and the social relations accompanying that organisation are the more decisive factors – ideas, culture, law and politics being secondary. This again illustrates the materialist basis of Marx's work and perhaps indicates how the rather crude accusations of 'economic determinism' have come to be made against him. His approach is often described as 'dialectical materialism' and the dialectical element of the analysis can be illustrated here by pointing to the tendency of the base to contain within it conflicts

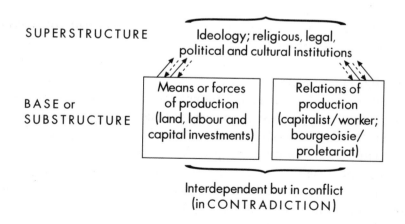

FIGURE 2.3   The capitalist mode of production

and contradictions which represent the seeds of its own destruction (or, rather, supersession). The dialectic operates in history by the growth of one element out of another in such a way that the new comes into conflict with the old, leading to its overthrow. Thus the bourgeoisie, we might say, created the proletariat but, in so doing, created the condition for its own overthrow.

Marx sees the capitalist mode of production as inherently unstable and ultimately doomed. This is because the social relations of bourgeoisie and proletariat are relations of fundamental conflict since their relationship is a one-sided and exploitative one. All of those who sell their labour power are, objectively, members of the proletariat. They are all 'exploited'. The proletariat is thus a 'class in itself', but it will not act as a class – so releasing itself from exploitation – until it overcomes its 'false consciousness' and becomes aware of its common interest. Class action is therefore dependent on the growth of class-consciousness. The proletariat will become a 'class for itself' and act out its historical destiny through creating socialism. To recognise the full force of the notion of *contradiction* in Marx we have to note that the efforts of the bourgeoisie themselves, to a considerable extent, hasten their own demise. For example, the bringing together of larger and larger numbers of employees into ever-larger work units will create the very conditions in which workers, through being thrown together, can become aware of shared economic and political interests. Thus class-consciousness increases and the challenge is invited.

Marxian industrial sociology

Marx's key concepts of class, exploitation, labour process and alienation have played a growing part in the sociology of work and industry since the 1960s, sometimes being used as analytical instruments and sometimes in a more directly Marxist way when their discussion is tied to an interest in actually affecting consciousness. There has been an especially strong Marxist attention to various aspects of conflict at work (Beynon 1984; Nichols and Beynon 1977) and Hyman has exerted considerable influence through his persuasive attempts to establish a Marxist political economy of industrial relations (1989).

The greatest impact of the ideas of Marx on modern industrial sociology has undoubtedly been through the use of his concept of 'the labour process' to develop a perspective which combines interests in employee behaviour, employment relations and questions of work design and organisation. The considerable 'labour process' literature which has grown up since the publication of Harry Braverman's seminal *Labor and Monopoly Capital* in 1974 focuses on the process within capitalism whereby managements design and control work tasks in order to extract surplus value from the efforts of employees in order to facilitate capital accumulation on behalf of those who employ them. A great deal of time and effort has been given to deciding the extent to which this process inevitably leads to a general degradation or 'deskilling' of work tasks and this debate will be given full and detailed attention later.

See page 260

Discussion

The ideas of Marx and Engels constitute more than simply a sociological theory. Marxism provides a particular method of analysis – one which does not divide polity, economy and society and one which attempts to unite theory and practice. Despite the fact that Marx wanted to bring together theory and practice, sociologists can nevertheless derive a great deal of analytical value from Marx and Marxian thought, without necessarily accepting Marxist evaluations or programmes for action. In doing this, however, sociologists are clearly differentiating their enterprise from that of the Marxist and, given the central concern of Marx and Engels with human labour and their interest in relating individual experience to large-scale matters of history, economy and societal power structure, it would be surprising if there were not important insights to be gained with regard to the sociology of work.

The chief problem with Marxist analysis from the point of view of those who do not share Marxist political values is that it is primarily concerned with problems of class, exploitation and large-scale historical changes out of which is expected to emerge a socialist order in which there will be work satisfaction, peace and plenty. The concepts which are deployed to analyse specific situations thus tend to be selected to highlight issues relevant to these problems and play down issues which are not felt to be of strategic political relevance. However, many of the issues which are underemphasised within the Marxist frame of reference or 'problematic' are areas of considerable importance when it comes to examining actual work or employment problems at a particular point in history – even if in the 'final instance' they may not be regarded as crucial to those hoping for the millennium. There are people who will look to the sociology of work and industry for insights relevant to their concerns with such matters as organisational redesign, the improvement of workplace relations and the attempt to reduce ethnic or gender discrimination within the existing basic social and economic system. Marxist and Marxian thought has useful insights to offer on questions such as these. Such insights are perhaps more likely to be taken up if they are offered alongside insights and concepts from other theoretical and value traditions within the sociology of work and industry.

The postmodern strand

A postmodern perspective has only recently been explicitly taken up by sociologists studying work and industrial issues. It has its roots in the French intellectual tradition of *post-structuralism*, an approach which puts the consideration of human language and how it is used at the centre of the study of all aspects of human existence. It develops the key insight in the linguistics of Saussure about the 'arbitrariness of the sign' – the recognition that there is no necessary connection between a word (or other sign) and what it stands for. The word 'book', for example, does not connect with the item which you at this moment have in front of you apart from the social convention that such a sound, to an English speaker, is conventionally taken to stand for such objects. In post-structural or postmodern thinking, reality itself comes to be treated as if it were a text; as a set of arbitrary signs which are not tied into a pre-existing reality. This implies that there is no basic truth outside language and that there is no reality separate from the way we write and talk about the world. There are no universal human values and we cannot rely on overarching systems of thought, like science or religion, to give us a basic understanding of the world and to provide guidance on how to act within it.

> **Postmodernism**
>
> A way of looking at the world which rejects attempts to build systematic explanations of history and human activity and which, instead, concentrates on the ways in which human beings 'invent' their worlds, especially through language and cultural innovation.

Postmodernism as a way of approaching the world contrasts with a *modernist approach*. Modernism emphasises the following:

- *Reason*: science, systematic investigation and codified generalisations about 'how things work' are applied to the world.
- *Control* is achieved through this application of reason and science.
- *Progress* becomes apparent in history as a result of this enhanced control and the human condition improves as time goes by.
- *Expertise* becomes important in achieving human progress with key roles going to scientists, technocrats, administrators and avantgarde artists (who take human fulfilment and reflection on to evergreater heights through their artistic innovations).
- *Grand narratives like those of Marxism or Freudianism* emerge to offer blueprints for making the world a better and more easily controlled place.

Postmodernism reacts against all of this. It encourages what Lyotard (1986) calls a stance of 'incredulity towards metanarratives' and encourages us to look at the world in terms of the way we 'make it up' through talk, speech and other communicative behaviour. A central concept is that of discourse – a notion which is increasingly playing a role in the study of work and work activity.

Discourse and human subjectivity

> **Discourse**
>
> A set of concepts, statements, terms and expressions which constitute a way of talking or writing about a particular aspect of life, thus framing the way people understand and act with respect to that area of existence.

Postmodern perspectives are said to 'decentre the subject'. They question the notion of an autonomous thinking and feeling human subject who acts upon the world from a position of a confident belief in an essential and unique personality or 'self'. Postmodernists stress the way human beings' notion of who and what they are is shaped by the discourses which surround them. Foucault (1980) observes historically how various discourses have exerted power over people by creating the categories into which they are fitted: 'the homosexual', 'the criminal', the 'mentally ill'. Such notions help people define what they are and create notions of how such people should be treated by others. This is clearly relevant to people as workers and employees ('a loyal employee', 'a skilled worker') and we shall see in Chapter 4 some of the ways in which researchers have looked at the role of discourse in shaping human subjectivities in work contexts. In Chapter 6 we shall see how discourses play similar roles when they are developed by those managing work organisations as part of an attempt to shape behaviour 'through culture'.

Postmodernity, societies and organisations

So far, postmodernism has been presented as a way of looking at the world. It is a way of thinking or a style of analysis. Sometimes, however, it is used to characterise what might better be labelled *postmodernity*:

> ## Postmodernity
>
> A state into which the world is moving which departs from the key organising principles of modernity.

Postmodernity sees a reshaping of activities across the globe with trends towards both globalisation and more localised activity. A greater plurality of interest groups appears, 'image' and consumption play a key role in people's consciousness with pleasure replacing the old emphasis on work as a virtue in its own right. Work organisations become much more decentralised and people's experience within them changes. These broad changes will be considered, alongside older claims about 'post-industrialism' in Chapter 5 and the alleged changes in the nature and shape of work organisations will be a key concern of the final chapter.

Discussion

Postmodernism as a way of looking at the world and associated claims that the world is moving into a new epoch of postmodernity have been received with varying degrees of acquiescence and disdain by industrial and organisational sociologists. Thompson (1993), for example, sees both trends as amounting to a 'fatal distraction' and a retreat by sections of the intelligentsia from engagement with important issues in the world. He describes postmodernism as a reactionary trend. Although there are progressive dimensions to postmodernist thinking – the decentring of the sovereign subject, the exploration of multiple identities and the challenge to traditional hierarchies of knowledge – the interest in 'multiple realities' and the making of multiple interpretations of the world leaves a situation where, in effect, the world become 'all things to all people'. If we let this become the case, it would allow us no opportunity to take action to change that world.

An alternative position is to play up the virtue of those aspects of the turn to postmodern analysis which Thompson is willing to label pro-gressive. The most significant idea in the postmodernist style of analysis is the notion that, as Hassard and Parker (1993) put it, 'the world is constituted by our shared language and . . . we can only "know the world" through the particular forms of discourse our language creates'. This has great appeal to many social scientists who have, as Gergen (1992) suggests, a yearning for an alternative to modernist and romanticist beliefs that there are 'essentials of the universe' which can be discovered through observation and reason and which are then *reflected in* or represented by language. Within modernism, language is in some way secondary to that which it 'describes'. Gergen points to ways in philosophy and the social sciences, ranging from the type of ethnomethodological thinking we met earlier to ideas such as those of Foucault which reject this position. These can be seen as part of a 'postmodern transformation' reversing 'the modernist view of language as picturing the essentials of reality'. Language now loses its 'servant' or 'picturing' role. It is part of a process whereby people, through joint action, make sense of the world. We might say that we cease to speak of language as something which *describes action* and see language as *action in itself*.

We might label this broad approach *soft postmodernism* (Watson 1995c). It retains a concern with reason and analysis but recognises, along with Weber, the limits of formal rationality. It recognises the centrality and power of language, without suggesting that there is nothing in the world beyond the words we use to talk about it. It comes to terms with the plurality of interests and perspectives in the world but does not descend into a moral relativism where any one idea or activity is said to be as good or right as any other. Postmodernism considered in this 'softer' way can indeed be seen as a perspective developed *within* modernism rather than as something which supersedes it. Baumann (1992) points out that we might see it as *modernism coming to terms with itself* by recognising what it had tried to deny: its own discovery that 'human order is vulnerable, contingent and devoid of reliable foundations'.

Sociology emerged as a characteristically modernist activity with the project of applying reasoned analysis to the changes which were coming about with industrialisation and helping people make a better world within the new possibilities which were emerging. This aspect of the 'enlightenment project', so powerfully defended by Habermas (1987), need not be totally abandoned, as a hard postmodernist position would suggest. But social science is inevitably going to play a much more modest role in helping social change and achieving human control over circumstances than was once hoped. The sociology of work and industry can helpfully be characterised in 'soft postmodernist' terms as a bundle of *discursive resources* which people can use in various ways to create their own interpretations and understandings of the world with which they have to deal. It is a world full of ambiguities, paradoxes and contradictions which will never finally be 'sorted out', classified or pinned down in terms of sociological laws. The various perspectives or strands of thought in the sociology of work and industry covered in this chapter each have something to offer. How might they be used?

Drawing the strands together: a pragmatic pluralist strategy in the sociology of work and industry

There are ideas and insights in all these six strands of thought within the sociology of work and industry to which one can turn when analysing work-related issues in the contemporary world. To suggest this, however, is not to call for a straightforwardly eclectic approach to industrial sociology in which almost 'anything goes' and in which we take 'a little bit of this' and 'a little bit of that' until we feel that every angle is covered. What is needed whenever a specific aspect of work or industry is investigated is a conceptual framework or analytical scheme which draws on the range of relevant ideas from the different traditions whilst maintaining a coherence and an internal consistency.

Such an approach is given the label *pragmatic pluralism* (Watson 1995b) and it is advocated that each researcher when developing an analysis of a particular aspect of social life draws on concepts and ideas from any theoretical perspective as long at is helpful in achieving that analysis. This approach is

- *pluralist* in that it brings together ideas from a variety of theoretical or disciplinary sources;
- *pragmatic* in that it uses those ideas to enable the research to inform the choices of those who receive that research.

To stand as a coherent conceptual foundation for their research, however, the framework which investigators develop must maintain an internal consistency and a methodological integrity. A theoretical scheme which uses a concept of human personality as a fixed set of human character-istics which one takes through life, for example, would lose such integrity and consistency if it also used, say, a concept of self-identity which is seen as changing as the individual's circumstances change.

Important as these matters are, it is argued that the basic criterion for judging theoretical schemes is one of the *truth* of the research which emerges when it is applied to an area of social life. And the concept of 'truth' drawn upon here is one derived from pragmatist philosophy. A piece of research can be seen as 'true' to the extent that a person entering the social setting dealt with in the research would be more competent to act socially in that setting if informed by that research than if they were informed by a piece of research that was less true. A research project focusing on the management of a particular industrial plant in order to generalise more broadly about the nature of managerial work (Watson 1994a), was shaped by precisely this notion of the pursuit of truth, which

> means that any social actor entering that plant – be they a manager, an industrial spy, a customer, a trade union representative or a management researcher – would be better placed when trying to 'learn the ropes' than someone who was informed by a 'less true' research account. They would have greater 'power to act' in relation to that environment than someone less 'truthfully informed'. [Truthful research] in this sense would indeed be helpful to managers. But this does not make the producer of the analysis automatically a servant of those managers, it would be relevant to the actions of *any actor* entering that managerial environment, whether they were allies, enemies or simply observers of the managers operating there. To take a parallel outside the manage-ment research context, a 'true' account of human physiology in this sense could equally assist the life-saving surgeon or the life-taking assassin.

> (Watson 1995b)

The concepts, theories, models and perspectives presented in this chapter are, in effect, an enormous bank of resources which can be drawn upon when one wishes to analyse any aspect of the sociology of work and industry. In advocating a pragmatic pluralist strategy for those wishing to carry out such analyses a link back to some of the key issues of Chapter 1 has been made. The arguments put forward here clearly relate to the first chapter's view of sociology as playing a role in *informing human choice*. The pragmatist conception of truth also suggests a particular position on the value problems of sociologists of work and industry raised in that chapter; suggesting criteria of evaluation which judge research in terms of potential relevance to all readers of it, and not just to particular interest groups.

It was suggested in the previous chapter that the defining characteristic of the sociological perspective is that it ultimately relates whatever it studies back to the way society as a whole is organised. It was also argued that the underlying rationale of the discipline of sociology was and still is one of attempting to understand the nature and implications of living in industrial capitalist societies. In accord with both of these claims we now move on to consider the nature and dynamics of the industrialised society – the type of society which provides the context of both our work and our non-work experiences and institutions.

■　■　■

The industrialised society

Introduction

To enable human beings to cope with the potentially chaotic world around them they need to develop some idea of an ordered reality. Life has to have some pattern or order to be manageable. People therefore develop sets of images and assumptions about the 'way things are'. This means that when people look at their own society they will do so with a degree of *taken-for-grantedness*. To give themselves a sense of certainty and security people tend to view their own particular social order as 'natural', if not 'inevitable'. Life is the way it is because that is the way it has to be. Yet, at the same time, people know better than this. They frequently come across conceptions of alternatives.

Sociology as a form of reflection on the social world depends on the assumption that there are potentially alternative ways of life and that the 'way things are' is not necessarily the way they have to be. It follows from this that if we are to use sociology as a means towards making more informed choices about our social arrangements, we must suspend those often practical and necessary everyday assumptions which we hold about our social world. One intention of this chapter is to argue that the particular type of society in which we find ourselves is by no means the inevitable outcome of some autonomous historical process. Both the structural arrangements on which our social order is based and the ideas and assumptions which we hold with regard to those arrangements are the outcome of human efforts – outcomes which are both intended and unintended and which can be comprehended only if set in their context of human conflicts and competition.

This chapter will examine the background and basic features of the advanced industrial capitalist society. Without an appreciation of these basic features, it is argued, one cannot fully appreciate the nature and problems of the specifics of work organisation and will therefore be less able to recognise the scope for potential choice. But at the same time as stressing the need for structural analysis, we have to remember that it has been emphasised in previous chapters that a successful sociology is one which does full justice to the interplay of individual and structural factors in human life. The present chapter emphasises the structural element but is very much setting the scene into which the individual actor will walk in the next chapter and into which further structuring processes of occupation, organisation and employment relations will be introduced later. The chapter is based on a particularly sociological view of history.

A view of history

History is made by human initiatives and group efforts, rather than by the popularly suggested forces of evolution, technical progress or physical determinism.

Determinism and choice in social change

Living in the twentieth century in a society where social and techno-logical innovations are introduced daily into one area of our lives after another, it is not surprising that people should feel that they are caught up in some inevitable process. Much change is undoubtedly beneficial but even where individuals feel themselves harmed by such changes they may be reluctant to be seen as standing Canute-like in an inevitably advancing tide. At various stages of modern history, particular groups have resisted the tides approaching them:

- Machine-breakers of early industrialisation, concerned to protect their jobs.
- Objectors to the advance of the first motor cars, wishing to preserve peace and safety.
- Contemporary protestors against environmental damage to the earth.

They might equally well be met with the advice not to 'stand in the way of progress', especially where technology is involved. Every form of work involves technology – universally in the sense of using some kind of technique and particularly in the sense of utilising mechanical devices – and there can be few modern occupations which have been untouched by technological change. These changes are again frequently seen as part of a historical trend which we cannot resist – as part of human evolution. 'Automation is bound to come', people say.

Assumptions like these of the inevitability of changes in a general though not totally unspecific direction tend to permeate everyday thinking. The likelihood of technological progress, industrial advance and economic growth, even when clearly presenting problems of management, is fundamental to lay assumptions about the modern world. Both their inevitability and their desirability are frequently taken for granted, and a necessary requirement for the democratic control of industrial, technical and economic change is that this *taken-for-grantedness* be questioned. First we must examine how social scientific thinking has frequently matched lay tendencies in the ways in which it has approached the question of industrialisation and continuing social change.

Evolution, progress and industrial society

One of the most popular analogies borrowed from biology and applied to industrial societies and economies is *growth*. To see social change in terms of this metaphor is to imply a number of things. Growth of an entity implies change that is 'intrinsic to the entity, . . . change that is held to be as much a part of the entity's nature as any purely structural element' (Nisbet 1979). It implies the following:

- Directionality
- Cumulative change
- Irreversibility
- A sequence of stages
- An underlying purpose

The metaphor of growth does not in itself imply that societies develop over generations in a direction which can be interpreted as leading to the improvement of the human condition. Yet such a notion emerged and rapidly gained ground when the novel idea of *progress* caught on in the eighteenth-century world of the European enlightenment. This, of course, was the seedbed period for both the coming social sciences and large-scale industrialisation (see Chapter 1) and it is not surprising that the social sciences, from the start, took to their heart some idea of societies growing and improving *with inevitability* through history until they achieved some eventual state of industrialised peace and plenty.

Two of the very early sociologists, Saint-Simon (1760–1825), who coined the term 'industrial society', and his one-time disciple Comte (1798–1857), who invented the word 'sociology', suggested theories of change in which societies are seen as passing through stages. In both cases the final – and favoured – form is the industrial and scientifically-based social order. The ideas of the Saint-Simonians influenced later thinkers as different as Durkheim and Marx. Durkheim attempted his understanding of the industrial world by examining its evolution from less complex societies whilst, in England, Herbert Spencer (1820–1903) combined the biological metaphors of organicism, growth and evolutionism to show how 'militant society' develops into the more moral industrial society in which individual freedom can flourish.

'Growth' and 'progress' views of industrialisation imply that it is

- natural;
- inevitable;
- universally beneficent.

Evolutionary views of industrialisation suggest that it is a 'natural' process. Such a suggestion gives industrialism a certain legitimacy deriving from an implied inevitability and a potential, if not always realised, benevolence. Marx, of course, stressed the capitalist nature of the industrialising society and aimed his criticism at the characteristics of capitalism rather than at industrialism itself. But Marx's analysis, despite a central recognition given to the part played by human agency and conflict (partly following Saint-Simon here) does see societies passing through various stages. The socialist society will emerge as inevitably out of the capitalist as the capitalist did out of the feudal. Whilst it is unfair to accuse Marx of simple economic or technical determinism, there is an element of historical determinism here which brings much of Marxism into the category of 'historicist' thinking which we shall shortly submit to critical review.

A logic of industrialism?

The concept of *industrial society* lies at the centre of the twentieth-century version of evolutionary social thought. Associated with the concept is the idea that industrial growth creates certain problems for any society and that there is only a limited range of alternative ways in which any society can respond to those problems. Any society which is industrialising is thus bound to conform more or less to a certain pattern as it follows the imperatives and indeed the logic of industrialism. The sociological characteristics of any society are likely to be pulled into a certain shape by the basic forces of the developing economy and its associated technology. In many ways this is reminiscent of the Marxian model of development and it is ironic that the revival of the notion of 'industrial society' by the French sociologist Aron in the mid-1950s (see Aron 1967) was intended to help attack Marxism by showing that both capitalist and socialist societies had certain cultural and structural features in common. This was by virtue of their being industrially advanced and in spite of their different patterns of ownership and control. Yet the concept was taken over by various US writers, who were as much if not more opposed to the Marxist doctrine, in such a way that theories of industrialisation were developed which seem 'to rival that of the Marxists in both their evolutionary cast and often too in their emphasis on the determining force of technological and economic organisation' (Goldthorpe 1971).

One of the most influential analyses in this vein is that of Kerr *et al.* in *Industrialism and Industrial Man* (1973, first edition published 1960). They see a compelling logic underlying industrialism which means that whatever choices are exercised by human beings they cannot avoid, in the long run, having the technology of industrialism without a set of concomitant structural and cultural features.

The convergence thesis

Societies which industrialise become increasingly alike in their social, political and cultural characteristics as well as their work organisations.

Industrial technology, it is argued, requires a highly skilled and pro-fessional labour force which is controlled by a range of norms and rules. For this labour force to exist and to be motivated there must be a certain kind of open educational system accompanied by social mobility and relative social equality in society at large. This society will inevitably be a large-scale one with the consequent requirement for close government involvement but with consensus being achieved through the develop-ment of values of progress, science, mobility, materialism, a work ethic and, especially, pluralism. No one group dominates the world of 'pluralistic industrialism'. Various groups compete but do so within an accepted web of rules with the government holding the ring. Following from this is the suggestion that in many basic respects all societies which are industrialised must, because of the very logic of industrialism, become similar. This notorious 'convergence thesis' will be returned to when we consider the occupational structures of industrial societies (Chapter 5).

Social change and the end of history

As we saw in the last chapter, a central theme of modernist thinking has been a tendency for grand narratives to appear and large-scale schemes of thought to provide guiding principles about how social life might be organised. Socialism and Nazism are two of these which have played significant roles in the twentieth century. Such schemes provided a view of history as moving in particular directions and when they have appeared to fail or go into decline arguments have appeared suggesting that history was coming to an end. This occurred in the period after the Second World War with thinkers of both the left and right interpreting the failure of both Fascism and socialism in western Europe to shape the post-war world as a matter of *posthistoire* (Niethammer 1993). The big stories were fizzling out. A later 'end of history' thesis has been offered by Fukuyama (1992) to make sense of the collapse of the authoritarian states in central and eastern and in Latin America in the late twentieth century. Fukuyama speaks of 'the endpoint of mankind's ideological evolution and the universalisation of Western liberal democracy as the final form of human government'. He sees two driving forces behind this development:

See page 74

- Economic forces whereby there has emerged 'a single market for German cars, Malaysian semiconductors, Argentine beef, Japanese fax machines, Canadian Wheat and US airplanes'.
- Political forces whereby the 'liberal project' has enabled human instincts which push people to seek supremacy over others ('mega-lothymia') to be managed so allowing a greater influence for that part of human nature which seeks dignity and equality with others ('isothymia').

Fukuyama's thesis is not put forward without qualification but in spite of his recognition that there are still parts of the world which are firmly anti-liberal and anti-democratic, his is an optimistic view of world trends. The fruits of industrialisation and its associated social institutions have enabled the 'better side' of the human species to triumph over the darker side. He nevertheless recognises a tendency which corresponds See page 65 with Weber's notion of the paradox of consequences. Human beings (in the form of the 'last man' of the book's title) may come to be bored with the peace and plenty which comes into their grasp and wilfully act to destroy it.

These various theories of change and development are not mere neutral formulations which exist in an academic vacuum. If we are persuaded that there is only one 'correct' pattern of growth for industrial or industrialising societies, then political decision-makers can more easily be allowed to correct deviations from the proper path by treating them as pathological. To understand the nature of our particular industrialised society we must examine how it came about as well as characterising its essential features – these two being closely interrelated. To enable ourselves to do this effectively, we must first exorcise the evolutionary ghost with its associated technical determinist spirit which effectively haunts much of our everyday thinking about society as well as much influential social science thought.

Historicism and bad faith

Most of the theories which we have examined can be characterised as more or less historicist in the sense established by the philosopher Karl Popper in *The Poverty of Historicism* (1957). Popper's intention was to show the invalidity of approaches which examined the way in which history had unfolded in the past in order to predict the form which societies would take in the future. He was not saying that specific sociological propositions could not be made on the basis of historical data but that large-scale patterns of change in societies are logically unpredictable. Any substantial change in society is the outcome of so many different causal factors and human acts that any particular conjunction of events is to an extent adventitious. Had not certain people made particular choices at a specific time, for instance, and had not this economic development coincided with that political change in British history, then the industrial revolution might not have occurred or might have taken a quite different form. Further, if future stages of social change are capable of prediction on the basis of knowledge of past stages, why should not people act on that knowledge to contradict their own prediction? It is feasible, for example, that some advantaged and politically powerful social group might read Kerr et al.'s (1973) thesis of an increasing degree of equality and, as a consequence, act differently from the way they otherwise would have, choosing alternative means of meeting the problems created by industrial organisation.

These logical or methodological problems of historicism and evolutionary thinking are closely connected with the tendency for social thought to utilise biological metaphors. However, metaphors can be misleading if given anything but temporary validity. To talk of societies 'growing' is to draw a parallel with the way, say, a tree grows, but the pattern of growth of a tree is genetically coded. Every tree of a given species will end up taking a form more or less identical to that of every other tree of that species. The roots cannot make any choice of the tree's future shape any more than can the leaves, the branches or the bark. Similarly, no branch is likely to engage in disagreement or enter into conflict with another branch about its share of the available moisture or sunshine. Societies are not trees and, whereas they may indeed increase in size and they may become increasingly complex over time as might such an organism, they are not structured by a genetic code. Social orders are built, we might say, to adopt a more appropriate metaphor, and in the building of the structure some people are likely to direct and some are likely to be directed, some will live in the best rooms and some in the worst. The design, for all that it is constrained by environmental and physiological factors, is likely to be the subject of choices and disputes over alternative conceptions, and disagreements, conflict and compromise will constantly threaten. Theories of social change must shift away from an emphasis on inevitability and irreversibility towards an emphasis on 'human agency, the contingency of events and openness of the future' (Sztompka 1994).

Human understanding of the nature of life and social change is inevitably restricted by the metaphorical apparatus we use. Humans must simplify the world to cope with it and we might almost say that it is as 'natural' to turn to the biological notion of evolution to simplify the vast complexities of history as it is to turn to the system of organic analogy to simplify the equally complex nature of 'society'. But ideas are not neutral! It was argued in the previous chapter that human ideas tend to develop in a close relationship with the pursuit of material interests. And we should note that the organic analogy of society has great potential for use by powerful groups to help justify the status quo (the status quo being made to appear 'natural' and inevitable).

The evolutionary approach to social change is equally amenable to ideological use and political manipulation. It could be used to justify the building of nuclear power stations, the extension of a motorway network or the automation of a manufacturing plant, for example. It is the way history is going, it can be claimed. This is to act in bad faith – whether or not the proposal is generally beneficial or not. It is to speak immorally:

- In its denial of politics.
- In its suspension of values.
- In its attempt to avoid contest, debate and informed choice.

The ideologically suspect nature of most of the historicist theories of 'industrial society' or the end of history is further suggested once we observe that the bulk of theorists tend to take as the future which they claim to predict the particular society in which they themselves live or, at most, some modification of their own society which they – evaluatively – favour. Is it coincidence that the generally US theorists of convergence see other societies moving towards the US pattern – albeit an often liberalised version of the present USA? We can each decide for ourselves whether this tendency is the result of ideology, an ethnocentric lack of imagination, or simple defeatism; as Baechler (1975) says, 'To declare the necessity of one outcome is only to avow one's inability to explore other possibilities.'

Technology, science and social change

Technology is frequently spoken of in terms of the physical devices or 'hardware' that people use when carrying out tasks. Sociologically it is seen as involving much more than this.

Technology
The tools, machines and control devices used to carry out tasks and the principles, techniques and reasoning which accompany them.

Technology in this sense is often brought into the determinist views of history and social change that were considered earlier in this chapter. There is a popular tendency to invest technical inventions and their associated technique with causal power. Hill (1988) has described this as part of the 'tragedy of technology', something which is experienced as a 'remorseless working of things'. Individual human action appears to be

> so completely enframed within the technical properties of systems that there seems to be no way that the individual can stand outside and kick the system into new life or wrestle it into a trajectory that departs from the apparently intrinsic system expansion that has characterised industrial history.

The view of technology as having causal power is often encouraged in the educational process. Many of us in our early history lessons at school are encouraged, for instance, to see the scientific inventions which were made in the period of the industrial revolution as key causal factors in the occurrence of that revolution. Technical changes in both of these cases might indeed constitute *necessary conditions* for the social changes with which they are associated but it is mistaken to regard them as *sufficient conditions* for change. When considering the economic advances which occurred in Europe in the eighteenth and nineteenth centuries, we have to ask why the level of technical sophistication achieved by the

Chinese in ancient times did not lead to industrialisation. The answer must be in terms of human initiative. The Chinese did not *choose* to apply their knowledge to economic ends.

It is pointed out by Hobsbawm (1969) that the early industrial revolution was technically rather primitive. He suggests that what was novel was not technical innovation but 'the readiness of practical men to put their minds to using the science and technology which had long been available and within reach'. The motor of change was not the machinery itself or new scientific knowledge but the motivation of these practical individuals. The novelty was 'not in the flowering of individual inventive genius, but in the practical situation which turned men's thoughts to soluble problems'. Hill (1988) claims that science did not play a role as a leading edge in industrial progress until after the Second World War when existing markets for capitalist expansion were saturated. The early inventors were, in fact, 'more motivated by curiosity than "practical intent"'.

Technology is only a means, it is a piece of machinery or equipment with an associated technique which is used for carrying out certain tasks. Yet developments in technology may have massive implications for individuals and for society at large. Those implications arise only when particular people choose to adopt them and apply them to achieve human ends. Technology is not a force in its own right. To talk of the 'iron hand of technology' as do Kerr *et al.* (1973) is to avoid the important and necessary question of who is applying technology and to what ends.

Although technology is in itself only a means, a mere device, it is difficult to see its role as a neutral one in human affairs. *Actor-network theory* stresses this and goes as far as abolishing the distinction between human and inanimate actors; people, machines, techniques and operational principles can be analysed as equivalent actors in a network of activities (Latour 1987). Latour (1993) says that the distinction between the natural and the social world can be regarded as a myth of modernism and Grint (1991) illustrates the power of this perspective with reference to the actor-network which existed in Berlin for nearly forty years and which included the East German Communist Party, the armed forces and a proliferation of bureaucratic controls. This was 'regarded by many as impermeable and its power appeared complete'. The significance of the meanings attached to situations by human actors is, however, revealed by the fact that when 'a large proportion of the population's interpretation of the power of that network altered so did the "reality"'. This example illustrates the interplay which occurs between 'hard' technological artifacts and their social or organisational context. This interplay is equally important when we examine technology within work organisations. Technology and organisation can perhaps best be seen as 'fluid and interlocking *processes*' in which 'technology and organisation evolve and overlap together rather than separately or in opposition to each other' (Scarborough and Corbett 1992). Work organisations are often designed as if they were 'big machines' in themselves. They are conceived within what Hill (1988) calls the *technology text*, 'the design principles of human organisation':

- Efficiency.
- Instrumentally powerful, controlling information flows.
- Standardisation – to make this 'system' work.

Hill observes that these principles apply particularly within commercial enterprise, but also increasingly shape government activity and provision of services.

Technology may be a means towards certain ends, then, but the meeting of ends implies the fulfilling of human material interests, and all human material interests do not coincide. One man's airfield takes another man's land and one woman's capital requires another woman's labour. Thus the importance of technology in human life can be appreciated only once it is set in the context of social, economic and political relationships. Machinery itself can do neither good nor harm to human beings – it is what human beings do to themselves and to each other with machinery that is crucial. Any argument about the logic of industrialism, the inevitability of technological change or the automatic unfolding of 'progress' has to be treated with suspicion. All these notions have ideological power. They frequently justify the self-interested actions of some people which are as likely to threaten the interests of others as they are, indeed, to further them.

The nature of industrial capitalist society

Having rejected evolutionary type approaches to the process of industrialisation and noted the dangers of technical determinism does not mean that we cannot examine the specific development of western capitalist industrial societies in a sociological way. This will shortly be attempted and the analysis will stress the importance of human agency in social change and emphasise the part played by power relationships in the emergence and ongoing development of the particular social form with which we are concerned. First, however, we must clarify this particular characterisation.

Three characterisations of 'advanced' societies
*   As industrial societies.
*   As capitalist societies.
*   As industrial capitalist societies.

Here it is most useful to characterise the majority of economically 'advanced' societies as *industrial capitalist*. This is in recognition that it was a conjunction of capitalist forms of activity and industrial methods of production which led to many of the most significant social changes which have occurred in recent world history. What occurs in the so-called developing countries of the world as well as in those states which retain a commitment to 'socialist' principles and a 'command economy' can be appreciated only if put in the context of what has occurred and is happening in the industrial capitalist sphere. Socialism itself, the most significant of alternatives to capitalism, arose in very large part as a critique of industrial capitalist developments.

In a study of the sociology of work and industry it might well be expected that the focus would be on 'industrial society'. However, to choose this focus would be to neglect the extent to which industrialised societies are the way they are as a result of the growth of capitalism. It is reasonable to argue that industrialism, in anything like the sense in which we know it either in the West or the East, would never have come about but for capitalism. In addition to this, there are strong objections to the concept of 'industrial society' which derive from the way this term has tended to be used since its first appearance. The term is a far from neutral one: it supports the image of an industrial Leviathan, a Prometheus unbound, marching through history (Badham 1984). The idea of an industrial society is very much associated with an evolutionary perspective and with a basic assumption that the industrial nature of production in any society is the prime determining feature of social structure and culture. It may well be that technology does have certain imperatives with regard to social organisation but it would be a mistake to prejudge the existence of these at this stage as a result of the way in which we choose to conceptualise the social form with which we are concerned. We have to decide on the basis of analysis which features of our society are essentially concomitants of industrial technology and which relate more to the capitalistic aspects of social activity. Where we wish to allude to the basic industrial features of certain societies, we can adopt the usage 'industrialised society'. This has less implication of determinism, is less of a reification and can apply to any society in which large-scale or complex technology plays a leading part.

When we turn to the concept of 'capitalism' we encounter a series of problems. Not least of these is the pejorative loading which the word carries. This is largely a result of the fact that it has been the critics of capitalism who have used the term, whilst its defenders have preferred such expressions as 'free enterprise'. However, there is no reason why the concept cannot be used analytically. Both the leading theorists of capitalism, Marx and Weber, recognised that capitalist activity has occurred in various forms and settings historically, but both of them became centrally concerned, as we are here, with the relatively modern phenomenon in which capitalistic activity becomes a predominant factor underlying the way in which whole societies are organised (cf. Bottomore 1985). Marx's characterisation of the capitalist mode of production was described in the previous chapter and central to it is his emphasis on the way in which the property-owning *bourgeois* class buy the labour power of a propertyless proletariat to meet their own ends. Weber fills out this picture. Whilst placing less central emphasis on the importance of property interests he nevertheless recognises their importance but he stresses the way in which, under modern capitalism, *formally free labour* is organised on a rational basis: the work of free citizens is administered on a routinised and calculative basis not known in any other kind of economic system.

From the work of these two leading thinkers, Marx and Weber – one the arch antagonist and the other a partial defender of capitalism – we can elicit several key features which are basic to modern capitalist societies.

Principles of capitalism

- Ownership and control of wealth (and therefore the means of production) are in private hands.
- A free market operates.
- The pursuit of profit motivates economic activity.
- The capacity to work of those without capital is 'sold' to those who own capital – or to their agents.

Within a capitalist society are the following features:

- A basic inequality in the distribution of resources with certain social groups controlling the means whereby wealth is produced.
- Most other social groups merely possess a capacity to work under the direction of others, this being their only means of earning a living.
- These groups are subject to the systematic and calculatively rational pursuit of return on capital by those who own or control that capital and buy people's capacity for work.

The predominance of these features could not have occurred, however, without their conjunction with industrialisation. Thus we get the following working conceptualisation of the form of society with which we are concerned.

> ## Industrial capitalism
> Large-scale or complex machinery and associated technique is widely applied to the pursuit of economic efficiency on a basis whereby the capacity for work of the members of some groups is sold to others who control and organise it in such a way that the latter groups maintain relative advantage with regard to those resources which are scarce and generally valued.

Baechler (1975), after his detailed examination of the analysis of capitalism by both Marx and Weber, comes to the conclusion that the specific and defining feature that belongs only to the capitalist system is 'the privileged position accorded the search for economic efficiency'. We must note that 'efficiency' can be understood only in terms of specific goals and that the privileged significance given to the pursuit of economic ends over other values such as religious, military or political ones, is privilege given to the fulfilling of goals which may not be shared equally by all members of society. For example, it is quite common to see employees – at various occupational levels – becoming unemployed as a result of their employers' honest and conscientious pursuit of efficiency. Reducing manning levels or deskilling work is clearly in the interests of efficiency, but it is not necessarily 'efficiency' from the point of view of those experiencing job or skill loss. Whether such actions are to be judged efficient or otherwise at the level of whatever goals are widely shared within a society is a judgment which, ultimately, can be informed by, but not made by, social scientists.

Interests and ideas in the rise of industrial capitalism

From feudalism to capitalism

It has been a traditional and indeed valuable method used by sociologists to accentuate the characteristic features of industrial capitalist societies to compare these with some model of a feudal society. The most famous attempt to do this is perhaps that of Ferdinand Tönnies (1855–1936) who

Community *Gemeinschaft*	Association (society) *Gesellschaft*
Small-scale, intimate, stable Rural Religious and traditional	Large-scale, individualised, rapidly changing Urban Scientific and rational

FIGURE 3.1 Tönnies' notion of a transition from community to association

contrasts the modern form of association or society (*Gesellschaft*) with the older, traditional, small-scale community (*Gemeinschaft*) (Figure 3.1).

See page 7 To fill out this simple image of transition (which corresponds to Figure 1.1) we will now look back to the pre-industrial and pre-capitalist world, remembering that we are not dealing here with irrelevant and purely academic matters but are considering a world which has left us images of life which still underlie many of our contemporary ideas about how human lives could be lived.

People undoubtedly worked very hard to exist in the medieval period but this work was performed on a basis which fundamentally differs from that which we take as normal today. One's work was seen more as an inevitable burden than as a way of developing oneself. It was not a duty to work hard nor was hard work a way of improving oneself. Hard work was done because survival demanded it. Further, there was little separation of home and workplace and a quite alien notion would have been that of working for somebody else. This does not mean that the rich did not exploit the poor but that even the poorest and most exploited serfs tended to have their own land to work – even if they were forced to supplement the income derived from this with some wage labour. However exploitative relationships were between social groups, the hierarchical relationship existing between people was nevertheless based on a certain recognised mutual dependence and some sense of reciprocity. There was a commitment from both sides of the master–servant relationship of a diffuseness quite lacking in the modern employment relationship (Fox 1985). The essential feature of work was that it was performed to meet clearly and generally recognised needs and its rhythms, or lack of them, were given by natural and immediate human needs themselves, like the need for food, shelter and clothing, or by the rhythms of nature itself in the shape of the changing seasons, the needs of animals to be milked or crops to be harvested.

The most advantaged groups of this period not only had the greatest share of wealth, which was predominantly in the form of land and the comforts which accrued from that land, but also were served by a Church which provided ideologies helping to stabilise order. Christianity itself contained much which might encourage challenge to the feudal order and such challenges indeed did arise in combination with Christian 'heresies' and millenarian hopes on a number of occasions. However, the Roman Catholic Church and its doctrines, which put its priests as intermediaries between individuals and their destinies, was able to counteract challenges with organic models of society like that developed by Aquinas in which each person plays his natural part in the wider scheme of things.

In an organic model of society

each person serves or contributes to this scheme for the sake of the whole community. Those who rule are merely doing so for the benefit of the community.

Given a largely illiterate society with the insecurities resulting from dependence on agricultural production, dangers of war and disease, it is easy to see how the Church, with its near monopoly on literacy, could maintain a stabilising affinity between ruling interests and the realm of ideas.

All processes of social change centrally involve conflicts and competition between social groups. Throughout history, groups form around common interests and the formation and activities of groups are closely involved with processes whereby ideas are developed and expressed. Advantages with regard to scarce and valued resources are sought and, once they have achieved these, the advantaged groups attempt to regularise and make legitimate their advantage in the face of challenges from rival groups. Applying this basic theory of social change, we should expect to see groups arising within feudalism to challenge the above feudal order and the advantages of the feudal lords. Peasant groups did indeed provide such challenges at different times but this was not the challenge which prevailed. Instead, the challenge came from the one part of feudal society which was not fully incorporated into the feudal order. This was the urban trading element which contained a class whose interests did not fit with a stable, landed and rural order. It is among the growing bourgeoisie of later feudal society that we find an economically motivated group with interests which potentially challenged the status quo. This was a group lacking social legitimacy and which needed to find appropriate ideas to give force to its motives and thus power to its pursuits of economic ends, as well as to give itself legitimacy in its own eyes and those of others.

Before turning to Weber's analysis of the role of Protestant ideas in this process and to historical evidence about the later social groups whose initiatives developed capitalism into industrial capitalism, it is important to note the extent to which we are simplifying a highly complex set of processes. We are warned against such dangers when, in his review and critique of the various existing accounts of the transition from feudalism to capitalism, Holton (1985) shows how the three main types of approach to this (economic or 'Smithian', Marxist and Weberian) have considerable limitations. In each case the account is said to leave out certain elements which cannot be fitted into the basic perspective. Holton believes that there is a degree of evolutionary thinking in all of these classical approaches and that what is needed is a post-evolutionary or 'conjunctural' approach in which we do not seek a 'prime mover' in the transition to capitalism. Although he recognises the general importance of centralised political authority and of the Graeco-Roman, Christian and Germanic cultural legacies, he argues that we should examine, in the case of each specific society, how a particular combination of factors came together at a particular time. Holton's preference for historical specificity is perhaps closer to Weber's own position than he admits, however. Such a view is supported by various recent writers on the 'rise of capitalism' (Baechler, Hall and Mann 1988) who emphasise specific features of north-western European medieval society which made capitalist initiatives a possibility:

- Political pluralism – given the lack of a dominant single power.
- Stability – resulting from the common ideology of the Church.
- Good communications between areas.
- A system of marriage and family based on couples – encouraging

economically active households.
- An emphasis on individualism going far back into English history.

The following account of the interplay between interests and ideas in the rise of capitalism attempts to compromise between an emphasis on this kind of historically specific factor and a consideration of underlying sociological trends. It is an analysis which both uses Weber's insights and recognises Holton's warning about disguised evolutionism.

Protestantism and the spirit of capitalism

Weber's study *The Protestant Ethic and the Spirit of Capitalism* (1965) has aroused fierce controversy. Weber is often seen as suggesting that Protestantism caused capitalism whereas, in fact, he was merely investigating one aspect of the chain of events which led to the specific phenomenon of modern capitalism. If one looks at his *General Economic History* (1927) and *Economy and Society* (1968), especially his chapter on 'the city', it is clear that he sees the influence of Protestantism as just one factor to be put alongside the type of change in city life alluded to above, the growing separation of home and workplace and many other technical and commercial factors. Weber was concerned to counter the one-sided materialism and the determinism of Marxian accounts of the rise of capitalism and he chose to examine the part played by ideas in social change. This was by no means an alternative to concern with material interests but an attempt to demonstrate the necessity of examining how the congruence of certain interests and particular ideas produces forces leading to change. His analysis brings into historical analysis the variable of human agency, countering any tendency towards determinism with an emphasis on human motivation. Weber stressed that it is interests and not ideas which govern men's conduct (Bendix 1965). Nevertheless he sees world views created by ideas frequently acting 'like switchmen indicating the lines along which action has been propelled by the dynamics of interest'. In his version of Goethe's concept of *elective affinity* Weber suggests that people adopt ideas to fit in with their interests.

The spirit of capitalism, aided by the Protestant ethic, brought a new force and a legitimation to the proto-capitalists of the cities. It encouraged hard work not just in order to meet basic needs or to produce short-term capital gain but as a virtue or duty in its own right. A religious doctrine which suggests that one is serving God by following one's mundane tasks in a self-disciplined and efficient way and which combines this with a demand for an ascetic or frugal form of existence has obvious potential for fostering such a spirit and indeed encouraging the accumulation of capital. One makes money by hard work and application but confidence of membership of the elect is risked if one slacks in one's efforts or if the fruits of one's labours are indulged in. The fruits of labour are not now hedonistic ones but confidence of salvation. Under Catholicism a 'calling' from God involved transcendence of the mundane but the novel Calvinist notion of seeing one's mundane work itself as a 'vocation' overturned this. The almost revolutionary change in religious thought brought about by the Reformation was its removal of the Church and its priests as intermediaries between the individual and God. In a sense, every one was to be their own priest and the demand was now less that one should be guided in one's actions by the Church hierarchy than that one should look to one's own conscience in deciding how one should act.

There had been earlier tendencies in Christianity which looked to motives of the heart in this way but such ideas were able to take root only once there were social groups well placed to sustain opposition to prevailing values and 'in a society where custom and tradition counted for so much, this insistence that a well-considered strong conviction overrode everything else had a great liberating force' (Hill 1974). Protestantism does not cause capitalism but gives force and legitimacy to the pursuit of economic interests by already emerging social groups. As Hill puts it, 'the protestant revolt melted down the iron ideological framework which held society in its ancient mould. Where capitalism already existed, it had henceforth freer scope.' Weber's whole point is to show how the ethical posture of inner-worldly asceticism engenders within certain groups 'already involved in the practice of business . . . a certain occupational ethic' (Poggi 1983). This is 'the spirit of capitalism'.

At this stage it is worthwhile to pause and consider just why looking back so many centuries to changes in theological thinking should be relevant to a study concerned with work and industry today. Attention to these matters is justified by the need to locate the roots of norms and values which underlie the culture of industrial capitalist society. Protestantism played a significant part in liberating people from the forces of tradition – forces which ensured that by and large one played one's allotted role in a drama scripted elsewhere. This laid a massive stress on the individual, on a striving for individual achievement, on human competitiveness. Campbell (1987) has argued that the particular form of 'sentimental' (as opposed to Calvinist) Protestantism prevalent among the English middle class contained within it the seeds of modern consumerism. A 'cult of sensibility' developing within these beliefs led to a concern with good taste and a following of fashion which, in turn, led to a strong demand for luxury goods. And alongside these particular shifts was the unleashing of what Weber sees as a leading process which runs through all subsequent social change in western Europe: the process of *rationalisation*. This process involves a replacement of the criterion of tradition (we do this because it is the way it has always been done) with a criterion of rationality (we must work out the most efficient means of achieving this end).

See page 66

Rationality and change

The criterion of rationality involves submitting actions to constant calculative scrutiny and produces a continuous drive towards change.

The essence of rationality is *calculation*, and, historically, this process led to the undermining of the primacy of religious or magical thought (including, ironically, those forms which gave impetus to this process) and is a force pushing forward the growth of science and technology with an accompanying expansion of the technical division of labour and the bureaucratic organisation of work.

It is interesting to note that many of the changes made in contemporary work organisations, especially changes which lead to the replacement of human skills or even basic human involvement at all by technology and advanced techniques of control, are frequently described by those implementing such changes in terms of 'rationalisation'. The disturbance to human lives caused by these programmes can be seen as part of the long-running tendency of Weber's process of rationalisation and its accompanying individualism, materialism and acquisitiveness given such impetus by the Protestant Reformation, to threaten social solidarity. The modern 'work ethic' – a secularised form of the old

Protestant ethic – has long been seen as posing a threat to social cohesion or solidarity (Rubenstein 1978). This is a tendency which, as we shall see shortly, creates basic tensions within the contemporary industrial capitalist society.

Social groups and the rise of industrialism

We have to be careful when examining the importance of changing ideas not to underestimate that their force only becomes manifest when they interact with changing material and political conditions. If we turn our attention towards England, where the industrial revolution was later to occur, we see a rising bourgeoisie challenging the old order in such a way that by 1688, their political action and parliamentary triumph had brought about a bourgeois revolution. The wealth of this rising class was made possible in part by other aspects of the decay of feudalism. Massive rural changes were displacing increasing numbers from the land (as many as half a million by the mid-seventeenth century) and from traditional crafts. People were thus made available as wage labour for employment or as domestic manufacturers to be exploited by merchants. These commercial groups were not unopposed in their ascendancy, of course, and it was the very opposition of established groups to their interests which helped mould them into, effectively, a coalition of interest. England had a relatively permeable class structure by general European standards and this encouraged aspirations towards advancement (Israel 1966). The Crown, however, pursued a policy of suppressing middlemen and the 'proto-industrialists' in ways which increased the revolutionary challenge to the established order. Various proto-industrial cliques were driven into a united front, their consolidation being 'promoted by this clear perception of a common foe, the Establishment' and they were helped in their new solidarity by Puritanism which was, as Israel puts it, 'the only available ideology that could effectively legitimise opposition to church and state simultaneously'. Here again we see the dialectical interplay of interests and ideas.

Opposition to the rising groups had also helped foster the scientific spirit. The effective forbidding of non-conformists to Oxford and Cambridge universities after 1660 encouraged the application of minds away from traditional academic pursuits towards pursuits of a more rationalising spirit. But to see the resulting scientific developments *leading to* the industrial revolution would be mistaken, as was suggested earlier. Nevertheless, the conditions were set for yet new groups of men to emerge and apply the rationalising spirit with a vengeance to employment and to manufacture. Studies of the early industrial entrepreneurs suggest that a large proportion of them were from relatively low origins and, like their merchant predecessors, they too, Bendix argues, found the opposition of ruling groups 'an important stimulus to the formation of this social class' (1963). Yet whilst Foster (1974) shows the importance of money made in the previous century of capital accumulation in the establishing of new manufacturing concerns in Oldham, Crouzet (1985) produces evidence to suggest that very few pioneer industrialists came from either the upper or the working classes. Most rose from the lowest strata of the middle class and servicing the larger new firms were numerous small firms led by members of a 'reserve army of capitalists' who probably had even humbler origins.

What clearly did occur in the latter part of the eighteenth century in Britain was the beginning of a great leap forward of the capitalist spirit, a revolutionary advance facilitated by the new processes of industrialisation. In what is probably best seen as an alliance between the established capitalist groups and some of the new thrusting industrial men who managed to establish themselves with these groups, a massive initiative was taken with fundamental structural and cultural implications.

The specifically novel development of the industrial revolution was the bringing together of the now available *wage labour* in special premises to work under the supervision of the employers (or their agents), using the employers' tools and machinery and their raw materials. The impression is frequently given, following the lead of Adam Smith's *Wealth of Nations* (1776), that the splitting down of work tasks among the employees in these factories simply follows some 'logic of efficiency'. In contrast to this, it can be argued that this division of labour was not the result of a search for a 'technologically superior organisation of work but for an organisation which guaranteed to the entrepreneur an essential role in the production process' (Marglin 1980). There is thus no determining force making the appearance of the factory inevitable. There is, rather, a choice on the part of certain people to provide themselves with a niche in society – one which involved the control and co-ordination of the labour of others in the pursuit of capital accumulation and their own material advantage. It was no technological imperative that brought people into factories and set underway new methods of work organisation.

The increasing bureaucratisation and growing scale of work organisations which later occurred is central to the concerns of Chapter 6 but what we will do at this stage is to look at the ways in which the new forms of work organisation, the accompanying societal changes and the emerging legitimations of both, contain within them inconsistencies, conflicts and contradictions which gave industrial capitalism a basic instability requiring it to be continually adapted.

Contradictions, adaptations and change

The preceding analysis has strongly opposed the popular tendency to view history or social change as an autonomous force which pulls human beings along with it. Instead, the importance of human agency and the pursuit of material interests have been stressed in our outline of the rise of industrial capitalism. Nevertheless, any sociological analysis is bound to show that social structures are by no means the simple result of conscious human design. What Weber calls the paradox of consequences is constantly operating; the pursuit of any human goal can set in motion tendencies which may not only create unforeseen and incidental effects but completely undermine the original human purpose. A large part of that which we call social structure is the result of these *unintended consequences* of purposive human action. The most basic example that we can give of this tendency is social class. We can see modern class systems as an outcome of the historical actions of industrial capitalist entrepreneurs, but these individuals never intended to create a class of human beings with all the potential which such a creation might have for the growth of opposition to industrial interests. They did want a pool of landless wage-labourers, of course, but this is not the same as a potentially self-organising social class.

See page 65

Tendencies of elements within social structures to undermine those structures can be conceptualised sociologically as *structural contradictions*.

> **Contradictions**
>
> arise within a social structure when certain principles on which the structure is based clash with each other in a way which undermines that structure.

Whereas Marxian usage of the term contradiction emphasises the ways in which contradictions lead to the collapse of particular 'modes of production', the usage here is more open – it accepts that constant adaptation is as likely a possibility as collapse or revolutionary supersession. If the early industrial employers created a class which might well have brought them down they equally readily adopted policies which would cope with such a challenge, giving us, for example, the dynamic behind shifting employment policies over the years.

See page 71

Weber's thesis of an increasing rationalisation of life in the West might be interpreted as suggesting that what this notion implies – an increasing tendency to calculate the most appropriate means to achieve a given goal – would mean that contradictory tendencies in the resulting social organisation would be less than those found in less 'rational' times. However, precisely the opposite is the case. The increasing concentration on *means* (rules, techniques, money, machines, accounts, etc.) which the rationalisation trend involves can mean that the original human goal or purpose for which the means was chosen becomes lost or subverted. Formal rationality (applying technically appropriate means) paradoxically does not necessarily lead to material rationality (advancing the originally inspiring goal). For example, it is formally rational for a society to use money as a means towards the efficient exchange of goods which people want and need. As long as the medium of money enables people to gain the fulfilment and satisfactions which led them to adopt the device in the first place, its use is also materially rational. Should money-making become an end in itself, with the consequences that the originally motivating desire for comfort, pleasure or whatever is not fulfilled, then the use of money is materially irrational. Its use is still formally rational, however.

The rise of industrial capitalist societies has occurred in such a way that these societies contain a range of structural contradictions. This means that they are in constant need of adaptation (to avoid collapse or chaos). The various contradictions which arise can be related to two principal trends which underlie the processes whereby industrial capitalist societies have developed:

1   *Rationalisation*: the increased application of formally rational criteria of action. This has led to an ever-present instability as chosen means tend to subvert the ends for which they were designed.
2   The increased *cultural emphasis on individuals* and their needs, wants and fulfilment, as opposed to the social collectivity or community. This raises problems for social cohesion and is another potential source of instability.

Examples and implications of specific contradictions will be examined throughout the present work. Figure 3.2 sets out examples of contradictory tendencies which can arise in industrial capitalist societies. Several of these relate to analyses provided by the founding figures of sociology:

* Marx on the tendencies for oppositional forces to arise as a result of the efforts of the very interests to which opposition arises.
* Weber on the contradictory tendencies of bureaucracy.
* Durkheim on the two-sided potential of individualism.

The notions of structural contradiction or a paradox of consequences may not be simple to grasp but an appreciation of them is vital to the insight which sociology offers. In arguing that industrial capitalism has created unintended consequences and fundamental instabilities, it is not being suggested that such a society necessarily creates an 'unnatural' way of life for human beings. The instabilities arise as a result of clashes between the principles underlying social arrangements; between a culture emphasising individuality and a production system stressing a loss of individuality, for example. Such clashes or tensions, in one form or another, arise in all social orders and they are not reducible to any simple notion of 'human nature'. The critical issues are sociological, not psychological.

Many of the problems inherent in industrial capitalist societies which have been raised briefly here will appear throughout the following chapters in areas as diverse as problems of class, race and gender

The workplace	In bringing people together in single premises employers not only act to further their own ends but also create conditions in which opposition to those interests may arise.
Mobility and freedom	To achieve the degree of mobility of labour needed in a market economy, people have to be formally freed from feudal, geographical or kinship ties. Such 'freedoms' tend to influence demands for political freedoms and interest in democratic participation, which again enables labour to challenge employing interests.
Control and initiative in work	Employers need a workforce willing to be controlled and co-ordinated yet, at the same time, the complexity of industrial techniques requires employees to use a certain degree of initiative, thereby encouraging possible demands for independence from control.
Bureaucratic work organisation	Bureaucracy, whilst having great potential for efficiency in task performance, at the same time contains tendencies towards rigidity, formalism and the like, which can make it inefficient.
The technical division of labour	The splitting down of jobs into small components can lead to efficiency. At the same time it can, in its tendency to bore, tire or contribute to the alienation of the operator, encourage inefficiency.
Individualism	Reducing traditional social attachments and putting the emphasis on individualism, calculation, self-interest, achievement and competition may improve economic performance but also risk its benefits through a tendency towards anomie and a possible 'breakdown of community'.

FIGURE 3.2 Examples of contradictory tendencies within industrial capitalism

inequality, work alienation, bureaucratic inefficiencies, industrial conflict and the changing meanings of work in society. For the present, however, we turn our attention to the human individual within the industrial capitalist society and to his or her experiences both in work and outside it.

■ ■ ■

Chapter 4

Work: meaning, opportunity and experience

Introduction

All living creatures expend some kind of effort in the process of acting upon and taking from their environment whatever they need for survival. Human beings are not different from any other animal in this general respect. They are, however, different in three important ways:

- Humans, as a species, have devised an infinitely greater variety of ways of dealing with their material situation.
- Humans are unique in the extent to which they have divided up and allocated particular tasks to individuals and groups within the general task of subsisting.
- Human beings differ from animals in the way they bring value-based conceptions of alternatives to the problem of maintaining life.

The human capacity to make choices on the basis of values means that both the methods of work which human beings adopt as well as the social organisation which accompanies them cannot be explained by reference to any clearly definable set of instincts. Human agency, choice, values and interpretations are essential factors to be appreciated in any examination of work forms and experiences.

Work is basic to the ways in which human beings deal with the problems arising from the scarcity of resources available in the environment. The scarcity of resources in the world influences the patterns of conflict and competition which arise between social groups. It follows from this that the social organisation of work will reflect the basic power relationships of any particular society. But patterns of social relationships do not relate to power structures alone. They are also closely connected to patterns of meaning. Thus the ways in which people think and feel about work will closely relate to their wider political and religious doctrines and to their general cultural orientations.

Work, meaning and culture

> **Work**
>
> The carrying out of tasks which enable people to *make a living* within the environment in which they find themselves.

This definition is not as simple or straightforward as it at first appears. The notion of 'making a living' implies much more than just producing enough material goods to ensure physical survival. People do not simply extract a living from the environment. In many ways work effectively transforms environments and, in the process, creates for many a level of living far in excess of basic subsistence. Not only this but the work which people do becomes closely bound up with their conception of self. In 'making a living' we are dealing simultaneously with the material and the cultural aspects of our existence.

A society, or a part of a society has its distinctive culture.

> **Culture**
>
> The system of meanings which are shared by members of a human grouping and which define what is good and bad, right and wrong and what are the appropriate ways for members of that grouping to think and behave.

As Williams (1981) argues, a culture is a 'signifying system' and through it a social order 'is communicated, reproduced, experienced and explored'. People, as this implies, do not simply follow the culture into which they are born, but both take from it and give to it in the process of dealing with the problems of human existence. And these problems of human existence are shared by all social groups. As Bell (1977) stresses, there are recurrent existential problems which are common to all human groups:

- The meaning of death.
- The nature of obligation.
- The character of love.

All cultures offer those who live within them ways of coming to terms with these basic problems but, of course, different cultures vary in the particular way the problems are approached. And since the problems of how 'properly' to go about working and 'making a living' face all human groups, we would expect every society, through its culture, to have its distinctive way of making sense of the question of work and a distinctive set of values and priorities giving guidance on how its members should proceed with it.

It is important to recognise that the meaning which work has for people in any particular setting and at any particular time is influenced by a wide range of factors (Joyce 1987). We can nevertheless note some broad patterns of difference which have existed historically:

- The ancient Greeks regarded the most desirable and the only 'good' life as one of leisure. Work, in the sense of supplying the basic necessities of life, was a degrading activity which was to be allocated to the lowest groups within the social order and, especially, to slaves. Slavery was the social device which enabled the Greeks to maintain their view of work as something to be avoided by a full human being: what human beings 'shared with all other forms of animal life was not considered to be human' (Arendt 1959).

- The Romans tended to follow the Greek view; the Hebrews viewed work as unpleasant drudgery which could nevertheless play a role of expiating sin and recovering a degree of spiritual dignity (Tilgher 1930).

- Early Christianity also modified the relatively extreme Greek view and recognised that work might make one healthy and divert one from sinful thoughts and habits. Leading thinkers of the Catholic Church, such as Aquinas, were influenced by the Greek view but a doctrine did emerge which gave a role for work in the Christian scheme whereby it was seen as a penance arising from the fall and original sin. It also contributed to the virtue of obedience but was by no means seen as noble, rewarding or satisfying; 'its very endlessness and tedium were spiritually valuable in that it contributed to Christian resignation' (Anthony 1977).

- The Reformation and the emergence of Protestant Christianity saw work coming to be treated positively within western cultures. With Luther we see the suggestion that work can itself be a way of serving

God. The historical implications of this Protestant work ethic were fully discussed in the previous chapter and the future of it will be considered in the final chapter. What we must note here is that it established the all-important idea that one's work was a 'calling' of equivalent value to that of a religious vocation which had previously involved a turning of one's back on the mundane and a movement 'upwards' towards virtue and other-worldliness.

See pages 101, 365

• With the growth of modern industrial capitalism we see the work ethic spreading further and wider.

The modern work ethic

makes work the essential prerequisite of personal and social advancement, of prestige, of virtue and of self-fulfilment.

Where not to work and membership of a 'leisured class' had once been an indicator of prestige and a 'good life' it is now associated with failure and even disgrace. Although this may not be formally underpinned by religious faith it has a religious tone to it. The ideas of a duty to work and to be dutiful in work are essentially moral and go deeper than our rational attachment to how we make a living. As Max Weber put it, 'the idea of duty in one's calling prowls about in our lives like the ghost of dead religious beliefs' (1965).

Associated with the notion that people can achieve self-fulfilment or self-actualization in their work and their careers is its opposite: work alienation. This notion, which is derived from Karl Marx's analysis of capitalist society and his view that the essence of human existence is found in people's capacity to labour and transform the material world, has been very influential in sociology. It has been widely used by those wishing to understand the dehumanising potential of industrial or capitalist organisation of work.

The basic notion underlying the concept of alienation is one of 'separation' (Schacht 1970) and, in Marx's usage, various forms of 'separation' within human experience under capitalism are indicated. The fragmenting of experience which Marx discusses is the result of the capitalist organisation of work activity and not, as it is sometimes wrongly

See page 70 taken to be, an outcome of the use of any particular kind of machinery or work method.

Marx sees the worker under capitalism

- Alienated from other people.
- Alienated from the product.
- Alienated from one's own labour.
- Alienated from one's self.

Individuals are seen by Marx as alienated in various ways in capitalist society:

- They become alienated or estranged from other people as relationships become merely calculative, self-interested and untrusting.
- They become alienated from the product of their efforts since what is produced is expropriated from them and was not, anyway, conceived by the workers themselves to meet their own ends or needs.
- They are alienated or separated from their own labour in that they do not derive the satisfactions or the delight that is possible in labour since that labour is forced upon them as a means of meeting other needs and because they put themselves under the control of other people in the work situation.
- In all this, the work of individuals becomes an alien thing which oppresses them. Yet, potentially, it could be a source of human fulfilment, and here we come to the essential element of the Marxian notion of alienation – people can be alienated from themselves.

Marx's conception of human nature assumes that people realise their essential nature, as a species, through productive work which is carried out for their own purposes and not under the control and exploitation of others. What this implies – and many users of the concept of alienation forget this – is that alienation is basically an objective state. Alienation is not necessarily reflected in felt job dissatisfaction or in frustration. A person may be very happy sitting at a desk in someone else's factory five days per week, sorting pieces of paper which mean little to them in return for a wage. Yet, in the Marxian conception of alienation, this person is alienated; they are not fulfilling themselves in the way they might be were they working under different conditions. People are alienated when they are not being what they possibly could be, and for people to become what they could be – to fulfil themselves or achieve 'self-actualization' – they must create a society which, although taking a basically different form from capitalism, is still one in which work, as a source of fulfilment in its own right, is central.

Because work is still seen as central to human self-fulfilment, the apparently radical Marxist critique of capitalist work forms can, ironically, be criticised as functioning as a conservative work ideology: 'the essential paradox of alienation is that it emerges with any meaning only as a result of an overemphasis on a work ethic and work-based values' (Anthony 1977). People can be seen as alienated from their work only when they have been subjected to an ideology of work which requires them to be devoted to it. Anthony sees alienation as a 'managerial conception' functioning within an ideology of work which, like all ideologies of work, is essentially a defence of subordination. He argues that a stress on the importance of work which goes beyond the necessary part which it must play in meeting other needs is required only when some groups require the labour of others to meet economic ends other than those of the people in whose mind the required work has to be justified. Thus Marxist stress on the problem of alienation is precisely equivalent to the stress on self-actualization in the work of the 'enlightened' management theorists discussed earlier. Both ideas, or rather how See page 46 they are used, serve to close off human options. They imply that, whatever we do in the future, our work must be central to our lives, psychologically as well as materially.

Whatever the possibilities for the future may be, we have to recognise that work currently takes up a large proportion of many people's lives and that the satisfactions and deprivations which it – or the lack of it – involves are not equally shared across the social structure. We must now explore the various ways in which these experiences and meanings are patterned in modern societies. And our starting point will be at the level of the individual and how individuals vary in the way they approach and experience work.

Work orientations and worker behaviour

The key concept to be used here is that of work orientation.

> **Orientation to work**
>
> The meaning attached by individuals to their work which predisposes them both to think and act in particular ways with regard to that work.

The notion of orientation to work is used to investigate the various ways in which different individuals and groups approach their work and it takes as its starting point a fundamental distinction which was implicit in much of the thinking discussed above: a distinction between work meanings in which work offers intrinsic satisfactions to people and meanings which recognise only extrinsic satisfactions. From this dichotomy we can set up two extreme ideal types of work meaning and suggest a continuum along which people's actual positions can be located as suggested in Figure 4.1.

Unfortunately, this essentially binary way of looking at what work means to people has encouraged an 'either/or' type of debate. Much discussion of work attitudes and work motivation has centred upon the question of whether people generally are intrinsically or extrinsically oriented towards their work. It is therefore frequently debated whether, on the one hand, people generally go to work 'just for the money' or 'basically for company' or, on the other hand, they primarily want 'job satisfaction' or self-fulfilment. But this is simplistic and industrial sociologists have developed the concept of work orientation to go beyond this and to show how people's approach to their work typically includes mixtures of these basic inclinations whilst nevertheless containing specific leanings in one or other of these general directions. And the concept has been employed to help explain the factors, both individual and structural, which influence people's attitudes and behaviour with regard to their work.

In the social sciences, much of the thinking about attitudes and behaviour at work has derived from a concern with manual workers. Two reasons can be suggested to explain this:

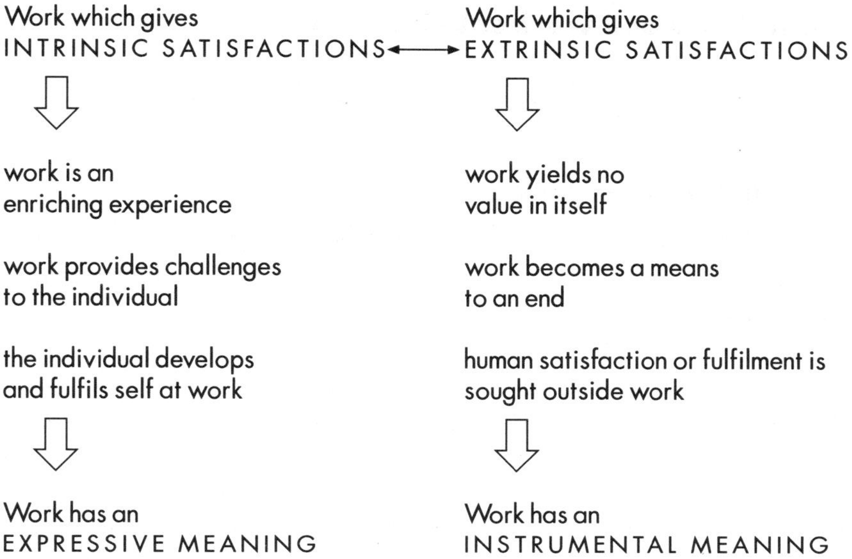

Work which gives
INTRINSIC SATISFACTIONS ⟷ EXTRINSIC SATISFACTIONS

Work which gives

⬇   ⬇

work is an
enriching experience

work yields no
value in itself

work provides challenges
to the individual

work becomes a means
to an end

the individual develops
and fulfils self at work

human satisfaction or fulfilment is
sought outside work

⬇   ⬇

Work has an
EXPRESSIVE MEANING

Work has an
INSTRUMENTAL MEANING

FIGURE 4.1 Meanings of work: a continuum

- Such groups have been more accessible to investigation.
- Manual workers have been regarded as a particularly problematic group.

This second factor applies in an immediately managerial sense in that managements are always interested in ideas which might give them insight into the motivations and activities of those whose efforts they have to direct. A corresponding concern also exists at the socio-political level. The 'working class', its loyalties, aspirations and accommodations has been a focus of concern ever since its creation. Sociologists have been at the forefront of those showing this concern. In looking at the development of theoretical perspectives on the relationship between work and the individual, therefore, we inevitably find ourselves examining the changing ways in which sociologists have attempted to explain shopfloor attitudes and behaviour. My intention now is to look at the progress which has been made in this field and then attempt to build on what has been achieved in such a way that we can use one theoretical apparatus to look at work as it is experienced at various levels and in various spheres.

Traditional thinking about industrial behaviour tended to focus on the assumed 'needs' of workers, concentrating sometimes on the econ-

See page 44

omic needs of the employees, as with the scientific managers, and sometimes on their so-called social needs, as with the human relations

See page 52

tradition. A significant breakthrough in distinctively sociological analysis was made, however, once closer attention was given to the influence of technology in the workplace. The technological implications approach discussed later in this chapter stressed the influence that technology can have on the way people act and think at work.

Although the orientations to work perspective gives a less central role to technology as an influence on work attitudes and behaviour than the technological implications approach, the importance of its insights should not be underestimated. It is vital, however, not to assume some relatively direct causal link between the technology being applied and the attitudes and behaviour of those applying it. In practice, we often find that there are differences in attitudes and behaviour between organisations which have similar technologies and that even within a given organisation changes may occur which are the result of adjustments other than to the technology itself. This can be illustrated by looking at two studies of the car industry. Turner *et al.* (1967) in their investigation of industrial relations in the car industry pointed out that the differences in strike records of different car manufacturers could not be put down to variations in technology and Guest's (1962) US case study demonstrates the possibilities of changes in conflict and general interpersonal behaviour which can be achieved by changes in managerial policy and staff.

The research study which first introduced the notion of 'orientation to work' also looked at workers in the car industry. As part of their wider study of social class in Britain in the 1960s, Goldthorpe, Lockwood *et al.* (1968) examined the attitudes and behaviour of assembly line workers in the Vauxhall plant in Luton. These workers did not appear to be deriving either intrinsic or social satisfactions from their work experience. Yet they did not express dissatisfaction with the jobs which they were doing. The possible paradox here was removed by the authors' explanation that these workers had knowingly chosen work with these deprivations, regarding such work as a means to a relatively good standard of living which could be achieved with the income made on the assembly line. The workers were said to have an *instrumental orientation* to work. The sources of this orientation were in the class, community and family backgrounds of the employees and not in the workplace itself. The technological implications approach was strongly questioned by the finding that workers in other technological situations investigated (a chemical plant and a batch-production engineering plant) had similar work orientations with consequently corresponding patterns of behaviour and attitude. Technology thus appears to be less important a variable than had previously been suggested. The motives, interests and outside-work background of the worker had to be taken into account if not given central emphasis. These authors accepted that technology does have an influence but argued that this influence has to be put into the context of what it is people are looking for in their work.

The work orientation perspective

takes the employee's own definition of the situation as an 'initial basis for the explanation of their social behaviour and relationships' (Goldthorpe, Lockwood *et al.* 1968).

This approach has the great strength of encouraging us to recognise the variety of meaning that work can have for employees.

Whilst accepting that all work in industrial societies has an instrumental basis, Goldthorpe, Lockwood *et al.* suggest that a typology of work orientations can nevertheless be offered. These are indicated in Figure 4.2. We see here the following orientations:

- An instrumental orientation associated with the study's affluent manual workers.
- A bureaucratic orientation reflecting patterns found among white-collar employees.
- A solidaristic orientation inferred from the authors' understanding of more 'traditional' working-class employment situations like coalmining and shipbuilding.

In the same way that the technological implications approach represented a move towards an approach which was more sociological than those approaches which had emphasised universal human needs, so this move towards an analysis in the social-action tradition can be

ORIENTATION TO WORK	PRIMARY MEANING OF WORK	INVOLVEMENT IN EMPLOYING ORGANISATION	EGO-INVOLVEMENT	WORK AND NON-WORK RELATIONSHIP
INSTRUMENTAL	Means to an end. A way of earning income	Calculative	Weak. Work not a central life interest or source of self-realisation	Spheres sharply dichotomised. Work relationships not carried over into non-work activities
BUREAUCRATIC	Service to an organisation in return for career progress	'Moral' elements: some sense of obligation	Individual's position and prospects are sources of social identity	Not sharply dichotomised. Work identity and organisational status carried over
SOLIDARISTIC	Economic but with this limited by group loyalties to either mates or firm	'Moral' when identification is with firm. 'Alienative' when this is more with workmates than with employer	Strong social relationships at work are rewarding	Intimately related. High participation in work-linked formal or informal associations
PROFESSIONAL		No details given		

FIGURE 4.2   Four possible orientations to work

Source: Based on Goldthorpe, Lockwood *et al.* (1968): 38–41

seen as progressing towards an even more fully sociological understanding. It recognises the importance to any appreciation of what goes
on within work of both the individuals and their social context. This
had not been totally ignored previously. Such an approach became
central to industrial sociology, however, only with the appearance of
Goldthorpe, Lockwood *et al.*'s Affluent Worker study, despite the fact
that Weber himself foreshadowed such developments early in the
century. The analysis provided by Goldthorpe, Lockwood *et al.* has been
shown by researchers who have revisited the Luton setting to have

exaggerated the amount of choice being exercised by the 'instrumental workers'. Devine (1992a) and Grieco (1987) have pointed to pressures of avoiding unemployment and looking for better housing which were as relevant as a desire to maximise earnings. The study can also be criticised for going too far in stressing the factors which influence workers' initial choice of job and for failing to recognise that the individual's work orientation, once in that job, is constantly liable to change as a result of both factors operating within and factors located outside the workplace. Subsequent work in this area has suggested that attention to 'prior orientation' to work has to be balanced by a greater recognition of the structural conditions in which these orientations then operate and a recognition that orientations or definitions of the situation are not necessarily fixed but are dynamic.

Changing orientations and the individual worker

By showing that the workers whom Goldthorpe and Lockwood studied in Luton acted at work and thought about their work in a particular way which was most strongly influenced by their deliberate choice to move into the car industry for extrinsic rather than intrinsic rewards, the authors tended to underplay the potential degree of influence which factors within work itself might have on work attitudes and behaviour generally. To apply the notion of orientation to work to a wider range of work situations we have to take into account several arguments which have been made by researchers subsequent to the publication of the Luton study.

Beynon and Blackburn (1972), as a consequence of their detailed study of a factory involved in the manufacture of luxury foods, argue that although employees tend, as far as possible, to select employment in keeping with their priorities in what they want from work they nevertheless make important accommodations and adjustments once in work, as their experience is influenced by such workplace factors as work processes, pay levels and power structures. Orientations are also shown to be influenced by biographical factors in the worker's life outside the factory. The authors argue that the rejection of the adequacy of explanations based on technological determinacy and systems needs should not lead us to adopt one which replaces an analysis of the work situation with one based on prior orientations. They felt that the Luton study came 'dangerously near to being stuck the other side of the factory gates'. Wedderburn and Crompton (1972) who studied three chemical plants, make a similar point. These authors found that the workers whom they studied generally displayed the instrumental orientations to work described in the Luton study. However, they found that within specific work settings different workers displayed different attitudes and behaviour which 'emerged in response to the specific constraints imposed by the technology and the control setting'. As Bechhofer (1973) puts it, we should not ignore the influence of factors such as technology on work orientations but might most usefully regard these as non-social *conditions* of action rather than actual *sources* of action.

In a significant critique of their work, Daniel accused Goldthorpe, Lockwood *et al.* of failing to recognise the complexities of what it is workers look for in their jobs. He argues that the researchers paid too much attention to the job choice situation and thus failed to recognise that, once in work, employees display varying priorities, attitudes and interests – depending on the context in which we look at them. Daniel (1973) suggests that different attitudes will prevail, for instance, in what he calls the bargaining context from those which are indicated in the work context:

- In the *bargaining context* priority is given to the material rewards accruing from the job. The negative aspects of the job are stressed (these justifying appropriate compensation) and the management is seen as being the 'opposite side'.
- In the *work context*, where the work content itself is the focus of interest, we find that there is more concern with the quality of work experience and with the social rewards of contact and communication with others, and we find that the relationship with management is 'more characterised by a sense of common interests'.

The importance of Daniel's contribution here is considerable. It suggests that every employee is likely to have different priorities at different times and in different contexts. Definitions of the situation vary with the aspect of the situation which is of primary concern at any particular time. The employee acting to improve his or her pay packet or salary is not likely to show much interest in job satisfaction at that point in time. However, once the individual returns to the machine or desk, the intrinsic satisfactions to be gained in that specific context may come to the fore. The study of ICI's attempt to introduce 'participation' among a semi-skilled workforce in a nylon-spinning plant illustrates this tendency. The improved quality of working experience was recognised and appreciated by the workforce yet, as the authors comment, 'this does not extend to any radical change when it comes to pay and effort-bargain. On this there are still two sides facing each other over a table in collective bargaining' (Cotgrove *et al.* 1971).

What is becoming clear is that to understand work behaviour we must recognise the importance of dynamic orientations and that, instead of relating work attitudes and behaviour in a direct way to either fixed psychological needs or technological constraints, we must recognise that individuals see things differently and act accordingly in different situations and at different times. This may seem fairly obvious but, as with so many generalisations which emerge from sociological study, this insight is not always present in our everyday thinking. We can illustrate this by looking at the common practice in industry of labelling individuals in specific ways, as 'an ambitious career woman' or as 'a poor team member', say. Let us consider several examples of the ways in which the appropriateness of such labels might change as an individual's orientation changes. These are all examples from personal experience in the engineering industry.

- An apprentice was widely regarded by supervisors as a 'poor worker' and as something of a trouble-maker. The apprentice's girlfriend became pregnant, they got married and he not only settled to his training but applied himself to his work in a way which he hoped would help him achieve eventual promotion.

- A long established foreman was regarded by managers as the epitome of the 'loyal company man'. But, like many other 'loyal company men' among his colleagues, he became increasingly angry at the erosion of supervisory authority in a period of rapid organisational and technical change. He encouraged his colleagues to unionise and present a militant opposition to the management, the ferocity of which had previously been unimaginable.

- A graduate trainee was assessed as 'having little interest in the firm'. He then found himself in a training placement which he saw as giving him access to the type of advancement he had previously felt unlikely to occur.

- A shop steward who was perceived by managers and workers alike as especially 'militant' and anti-management effectively defeated a set of managerial proposals to which his shop was strongly opposed. After this he became, in the eyes of the management and his colleagues, one of the most 'reasonable' and co-operative of all the stewards.

These characterisations or labels are important since they influence the way such individuals are treated by other people. The tendency is to assume that these characterisations are fixed qualities of the individuals involved. But these four cases show how changed circumstances can be associated with changed orientations which, in turn, lead to changed perceptions on the part of others and hence to changed behaviour and relationships.

Self-identity and subjectivity at work

The illustrations of people whose work orientations changed with certain work circumstances raise the question of the extent to which the human individual is an entity with some internal consistency over time. Each individual may, through their life, modify their attitudes and behaviour but it does not do justice to the integrity of individuals to view them as mere chameleon-like beings changing with each backcloth on which they are to be viewed. To help us here, we can turn to the ideas of the See page 59 interactionist strand of industrial sociology and make use of the concept of *self* as it is used in that tradition. It is valuable to see each human being in terms of their *self-identity*, something which each of us develops in the light of our interactions with other human beings.

Self-identity

The conception which each individual develops of who and what they are.

As we move through different situations and circumstances and interact with different 'others' so we adjust ourselves to achieve a sense of selfhood. The life of the individual can be seen as a process. It has a certain pattern, whether this is one viewed by the observer or by the actors themselves. This process is referred to in the interactionist tradition as *career* – a vital concept in linking the subjective aspects of life with its objective circumstances.

Career

A sequence of social positions filled by a person throughout their life.

Looking at individuals' work life objectively, for instance, we see them moving through various structural 'statuses' which may be viewed as making up *occupational careers* (each occupation involves various typical stages through which a member may pass) or *organisational careers* (each organisation has a series of positions through which individuals may move in typical sequences). But individuals also have their own view of the process which their life is following, what Hughes (1937) refers to as the 'moving perspective in which the person sees his life as a whole and interprets the meaning of his various attributes, actions, and the things which happen to him'. This is the individual's *subjective career*.

Subjective career

The perceived pattern which emerges as individuals make sense of the way they move through social positions in the course of their life.

The concept of subjective career is a necessary one if we accept the proposition that 'people seek to achieve overall stability in the outward life and coherence in their inner world' (Collin 1986), a proposition which is central to the interactionist strand of the sociology of work. This further implies that if we wish to understand the work experience of individuals we have to look at their whole life career. We have to trace through their upbringing and education to appreciate what might happen to them in their later work career. Their work experience is likely to be fundamentally influenced by the wants and expectations of work which they derive from their upbringing as well as by the skills and abilities with which their physique, intellect and social milieu has endowed them.

In explaining the postmodern strand of thinking in Chapter 2, it was noted that various theorists have pointed to the role of discourse in shaping people's subjectivities. Discourses, as we saw, are sets of concepts, statements, terms and expressions which provide a framework within which people come to understand and act towards whatever area of life any given discourse covers. If, say, a discourse is current within a work organisation which uses the expression and concept of a 'conscientious worker' then there will be a tendency for people to locate themselves and others within such ways of speaking. And in doing so, their behaviour is influenced. There has been a tendency in the sociology of work to combine this type of insight with insights from other traditions to analyse processes whereby individuals' identities are shaped at the same time as consent and control are achieved at the organisational or occupational level. Knights and Willmott (1989), for example, combine Marxian labour process concepts with Foucauldian insights to argue that subjectivity can be understood as 'a product of disciplinary mechanisms, techniques of surveillance and power-knowledge strategies'.

The concept of career is used by Grey (1994) to link a series of 'discursive and non-discursive practices' associated with accounting careers. The idea of a career 'provides a meaning and a rationale for the otherwise disillusioning grind of accountancy training'. Regulation of behaviour is thus achieved in the form of a self-discipline which follows from trainees' acceptance of a 'discourse of career'. Sturdy (1992) combines this kind of insight with interactionist notions of the individual striving to achieve a sense of self to throw light on the way the employers of the clerical workers he studied achieved the 'consent' of the workers to carry out managerial requirements. And Collinson (1992) focuses on the subjective experience of shopfloor employment and the role of gender and class elements in employees' subjectivities and how these are linked to patterns of both conformity and resistance in the workplace. He shows, for example, how 'manual workers' socially skilled and culturally embedded practices of resistance, compliance and consent' were 'heavily "saturated" with specific masculine subjectivities'.

Anxiety, emotion and sexuality at work

One outcome of the growing interest in human subjectivity within the sociology of work and work organisations is the attention beginning to be paid to the anxieties, fears and emotions which are part of the human condition. The human being, in order to survive psychologically, has to overcome 'the precariousness of identity implicit in the unpredictability of social relations' (Knights and Willmott 1985). The world is potentially an utterly ambiguous place and, without the set of meanings which is supplied by human culture, people would be unable to cope. Without a sense of order or *nomos* (which comes from culture) the individual would become 'submerged in a world of disorder, senselessness and madness' (Berger 1973). The anxiety or *existential angst*, which people can handle only with the help of culture is more than a matter of specific fears. It has to be understood 'in relation to the overall security system the individual develops' as part of their self-identity (Giddens 1991). However, the human is not a simple creature of its culture in the same way that other animals are largely creatures of their instincts. Cultures are constantly being made by people and each individual has their own interaction – their own pattern of giving to and taking from – the cultures within which they live. This means that a sense of order and self-identity is constantly in the process of being won from the social environment in which we find ourselves. Angst is an ever-present condition which we, each and every one, have to handle. The work context is one of the key arenas in which we experience and learn to handle, more or less effectively, the angst which is inherent to the human condition.

See page 113

A study of managers in US corporations (Jackall 1988) seeks to demonstrate that managerial work of this kind is especially anxiety-making with managers constantly attempting to hide their daily fears, panics and anxieties behind a mask of self-control and amiability. Jackall shows his managers terrified by the unpredictability and capriciousness of their employment and work experience, a terror which they mask with a demeanour of enthusiasm. A different emphasis is to be found in a British study of managerial experience (Watson 1994a). Here anxiety is seen much more as the normal human condition but it is argued that the nature of managerial work and, especially, its expectation that managers have to exert control over others (directly or indirectly) as well as over their own lives can exacerbate this basic human condition. The fact that managers have to face a 'double control problem' in this way leads them to seek comfort in managerial 'fads, fashions and flavour of the month' (Watson 1994d) as well as encouraging them to engage in ill-tempered behaviour, threats of violence, interpersonal rudeness as well as more benign joking behaviour. Most of the classic texts on management, Taylor's and Mayo's most notably (see Chapter 2), portray managers as rational non-sentimental beings. This has been to deny the very humanity of those holding command roles in modern bureaucracies.

The image of the bureaucratic office-holder as one who puts sentiment to one side and operates rationally is central to Weber's analysis of bureaucratic functioning. Albrow (1994) argues, however, that Weber's interest in irrationality and affectivity was 'submerged by twentieth-century rationalistic models of organisation'. Following the example of what he calls the 'other Weber', Albrow puts the case for paying much more attention to the place of emotions in organisations 'but as byproducts, interferences or even repressed potentialities and resources, but as integral and essential modalities of organisational performance'. Fineman (1994) argues similarly and points out how being in organisations 'quintessentially' involves us in worry, envy, being comfortable with something, resentment, hurt, sadness, boredom, excitement, happiness, anger and so on. He notes that even the 'dull indifference which pervades some people's work experience' is usually spoken of as 'a feeling'.

Issues of emotionality at work do not arise only because people are people and are therefore continually at the mercy of their feelings. Certain types of work formally require people to engage in what Hochschild (1985) calls *emotional labour*.

Emotional labour

A type of work activity in which the worker is required to display particular emotions in the course of providing a service.

Hochschild shows how the emotional labour required of airline flight attendants who were required continually to wear the 'mask' of a smile when in the presence of passengers took its toll of these workers – whether they were those who complied zealously with the requirement or were those who handled it self-consciously as a form of 'acting'. There was always the danger of feelings of anger or irritation breaking through the façade of pleasure and happiness. Emotional labour is normally associated with routinised 'lower level' service work but, as Fineman (1993b) points out, skills of emotion-management are also important in the work of doctors, nurses, counsellors or social workers. Serious consequences can follow if the mask slips and there is a failure to 'look serious, understanding, controlled, cool, empathetic' with their patients or clients. Not only this but expulsion from a professional body could follow if 'inappropriate' emotions are expressed. Sexual emotions or behaviours are the most obvious issue here.

There are sexual dimensions to almost every aspect of organisational life, as Hearn and Parkin (1987) show, even if they become clearly manifest only when formal complaints are made about sexual harassment or where events occur such as the hospital 'works do' observed by these authors where open sexual acts occurred with couples making 'blatant use of the premises, both cubby holes and semi-public "back regions"'. Burrell (1984, 1992) points out how managements in organisations ranging from monasteries, prisons and ships at sea to factories and commercial organisations attempt to repress sexual relations and expel them from the organisation into the 'home'. Yet managements may also collude in a degree of expression of sexuality as part of the delivery of what is not formally seen as a kind of sexual service. This is effectively shown in Filby's (1992) research in off-course betting shops where there is an 'elision... of emotional labour and sexuality' similar to that described by Hochschild. Filby shows how a 'minority undercurrent' of the conversations which occur between staff and between staff and customers involves 'sexy chat' – speech acts 'which themselves are experienced as pleasurable as well as sometimes discomforting and hurtful'. Sexuality is also 'embodied in gaze, deportment and clothing, and sometimes more obviously in expressive physical encounters'. In the light of certain unspoken assumptions which exist about 'what men and women are and what male punters want' there is an extent, says Filby, to which 'these moments are related to the milieux of service delivery as implicitly constructed by management, a milieux which is envisaged as an aid to business'. Put more simply, the management is more than happy for customers to receive a little light sexual amusement. And it might or it might not suit the employees who are expected to provide it.

Having examined these facets of work experience, work meaning and identity we now turn to the processes which in part precede them. In the following section we discuss the factors which influence the individual's life career up to the point at which they enter work.

Entering work

Choice and opportunity structures

A successful sociology is one which does full justice to the interplay between individual characteristics and initiatives on the one hand and structural factors and contingencies on the other. In the large existing literature on the processes leading to people's entry to work there has been a tendency for authors to stress either the individual's *choice* of occupation or the *determining* influence of external factors. Much of the literature on the so-called process of occupational choice is psychologically based and examines the way in which the individual develops and passes through a series of stages during which the self-concept grows as abilities, aptitudes and interests develop. Two very influential theories of this type are those of Ginzberg *et al.* (1951) and Super (1957), the latter giving relatively more attention to the situational factors which condition the eventual occupation which is chosen. Musgrave (1967) attempts to be more sociological by concentrating on the series of roles through which the individual passes at home, in education and early work experience. These roles provide the settings in which the individual is socialised and learns to select the work role in which he or she will eventually settle. However, the problem which arises with this approach is that the structural limitations on choice are underplayed.

In reaction to approaches which exaggerated the degree of free 'choice' which people have about the work they enter, Roberts (1975) stressed that, for many individuals, entry to work is a matter of fitting oneself into whatever jobs are available given the qualifications which one's class and educational background has enabled one to attain. Roberts argues that it is careers which tend to determine ambition rather than the other way round. Careers can be regarded as developing into patterns dictated by the *opportunity structures* to which individuals are exposed, first in education and subsequently in employment, whilst individuals' ambitions, in turn, can be treated as reflecting the influence of the structures through which they pass.

In an attempt to do equal justice to the extent to which there are both individual choice factors and structural circumstances working interactively, Layder, Ashton and Sung (1991) make use of the notion of *structuration* (Giddens 1984) as a model which recognises that 'structure and action are inextricably interwoven and should be given equal analytical weighting'. Their research on the transition from school to work shows that structural variables (ones over which they had no control) such as the social class of their parents, their sex and the local opportunity structure (measured by their place of residence and the level of unemployment at the time they entered the labour market) played a more significant role for people entering the middle and lower level jobs in the youth labour market than they did for those entering the higher levels. In the upper segments of the job market it was found that 'the factors which individuals perceive as being a product of their own efforts and achievements are indeed the most significant factors in determining the level at which they enter the labour market'. Individuals here had a greater ability to control their circumstances through strategic activities of job search and behaviour informed by values and attitudes. Research by Banks *et al.* (1992) reveals a similar picture and their findings trace the subtle interplay which occurs between young people's self-identities and the structural circumstances in which they grow up.

See page 11

Such research indicates that if we wish to produce a model which identifies the various factors which influence how individuals approach work, we must consider both objective and subjective factors. Objectively, the individual has certain resources such as cash, skills, knowledge or physique. Subjectively, the individual has certain motives, interests and expectations such as to make a living, achieve power or gain job satisfaction. Both of these sets of factors are, in turn, strongly influenced by structural factors. These are, on the one side, the structural settings of the individual's family, class, ethnic and educational background and, on the other side, the occupational structure and the prevailing job market. All these factors are interlinked as indicated in Figure 4.3, with the structure of opportunities acting as an influence alongside the various non-work influences on the individual's approach to work.

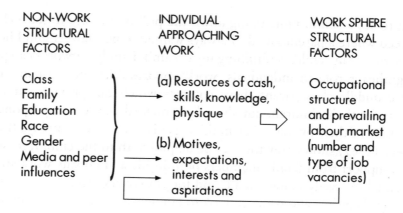

FIGURE 4.3 Factors influencing the individual's approach to work

Class, family and educational influences

The life career of the individual is influenced to a very considerable extent by the class–family–education cluster of structural factors. The occupational structure of society which people enter when they begin to work (whether their role be in paid or unpaid work) is structured and segregated on a basis of class, status, gender and ethnic factors (Ashton *et al.* 1990). This is something we shall consider in the next chapter, which concentrates on the occupational structure, the division of labour and labour markets. But people do not enter that structure with equal opportunities. Both the resources they take with them and the aspirations which they hold will be influenced by their class, family and educational background together with the way this affects their perception of themselves as members of a particular gender or an ethnic group or as male or female.

Parental occupational and class background is likely to make a significant difference to the individual's life chances both through the material advantages which can be given (buying education or providing books and other learning aids in the home, for example) and through the encouragement or discouragement which is provided. There may be direct pressure on the child's job preferences, with the parents either encouraging or discouraging them from entering work like their own ('I would like my daughter to follow me and go into medicine', 'I do not want to see a son of mine going down the pit') or a desire to see a child succeed where a parent failed ('I always wanted to be a lawyer and I hope to see one of my children fulfilling my dream'). Family networks can play a significant role in individuals' work opportunities, not just in cases where middle-class parents have contacts which can provide entry to careers for their children, but also where manual workers may 'sponsor' members of their own families in the organisation which employs them. Grieco (1987) shows how this can be helpful both to the employee, who gains support from family members both inside and outside work and is sustained in steady employment, and for employers, whose recruitment costs are kept low and who can look to employees' relatives to help train them and teach them to 'fit in'. Whipp (1992) in a study which shows the significant role played by family networks in the British pottery industry notes that potters frequently 'employed' their own relatives in subcontracting relationships. And in the contemporary Asian small businesses studied by Ram (1993) the employing of family members is shown to have a practical rationale in which family labour is cheaper and easier to supervise (cf. Ward 1987), and an ideological rationale in which there was a concern to develop a 'family culture' for the organisation, one intended to promote trust and to align the goals of managers and employees (though what came about in practice was a form of 'negotiated paternalism', arising as family members resisted impositions).

More generally, socialisation in the home and in society at large, especially through the images seen in the communication media, not only provides information about and evaluations of different occupations, it suggests what kind of work might be appropriate for members of each gender. The evidence for the enormous extent to which boys and girls are socialised differently, from a very early age indeed, is considerable and this is strongly tied to ideas about work roles. Child socialisation strongly colours work career aspirations with influences ranging from those of the games played in infancy through the cultural models provided by fiction and advertising to the personal observations made of existing patterns of occupational segregation. For example, little girls tend to be given nurses' uniforms rather than doctors' garb to play with, they see more male than female doctors in televised fiction and they are actually likely to meet mainly female nurses and male doctors as they grow up. Existing patterns are thus reinforced.

Formal schooling operates alongside the general cultural and family socialisation processes with, for example, school curricula and practices influencing pupils' ideas of what kind of work is appropriate for each gender. Devine (1992b), for example, shows how the 'gendered' nature of subject choices within the education system 'accounts for the small number of women who embark on technical degree courses in pursuit of high-level careers in industry'. But the educational system plays a crucial role in linking all the non-work influences on the individual's work aspirations, expectations and capacities. If one looks at British evidence ranging from the recommendations of the Taunton Commission of 1868, through to the various reports on education of Hadow, Spens and Norwood, and the way the Education Act of 1944 was implemented (on the tripartite basis of grammar, technical and secondary modern schools) one can see the extent to which both the organisation of institutions and the thinking of educators have concentrated on the 'process of sorting and grading' people rather than on developing and reinterpreting culture (Williams 1965).

Educational structures have been stratified in ways which match the class and occupational grades which they feed, and to a large degree, reproduce. But, according to certain theorists and researchers, the relationship between educational and work patterns does not stop at this external level of structure. Bowles and Gintis (1976), with their 'correspondence principle', point to the ways in which the internal structuring of educational institutions facilitates 'a smooth integration of youth into the labour force'. The stress here is not on the extent to which teachers, lecturers and administrators consciously and specifically prepare pupils and students for occupational roles but on the way that the structuring of relations within education closely mirrors those of work organisations. Pupils are seen as lacking control over their curriculum in a way which prepares them for the lack of control they will experience at work. As a whole, it is claimed, the relationships of authority and control 'replicate the hierarchical division of labour which dominates the workplace'. Even the ways in which certain school pupils resist authority at school is seen by Willis (1977) as a form of preparation for the way those particular individuals will need to live with their subservient roles once they enter paid employment. The research on youth career entry carried out by Banks *et al.* (1992) is taken by the researchers to 'confirm the centrality of educational career in the reproduction of social inequality'.

A variety of informal factors also comes into play during the educational process. It is quite possible, for instance, that liking or disliking a certain teacher may influence which subjects a 14 year old opts for and this may lead to the opening-up or the closing-off of spheres of work at a later stage. A rejection of scientific subjects in mid-adolescence, for example, switches the individual out of one educational channel or career area. This kind of process, together with the type of school which the child is attending, the stream or 'sets' to which they are allocated and the perceptions which the teachers develop of the child, all influence the way the child comes to perceive themselves and their future interests. And alongside this are the 'role models' seen in both their personal life and the communication media as well as their general career knowledge and the information they receive from formal career counselling or vocational guidance.

Individual capacities and values

Although, sociologically, we tend to stress structural factors when we examine the factors which influence the life career of the individual approaching work, it is important not to ignore such factors as the preferences and the mental and physical capacities of the individual. Various work careers, especially in the manual categories, require particular physical characteristics and many of those occupations to which children may be attracted by the cultural communication media also require specific individual characteristics, such as the skills of the footballer, the physical beauty and presence of the model and the talent of the entertainer.

The values which the individual holds will also play a part in whatever occupational choice is open to them in their particular milieu. Blackburn and Mann (1979), for example, show how individuals have preferences for outdoor work or for work which provides an opportunity to 'care'. Students in higher education tend to have a relatively wide scope for choice and certain values have been noted by researchers as affecting choices of types of career by students. Rosenberg (1957), for example, showed that students indicating 'people-oriented' values were more strongly oriented towards careers in medicine, social work or personnel management. Students who valued pay and status to a greater degree looked towards business, whilst those putting values of self-expression foremost were more inclined towards careers in journalism, art or architecture.

There is a danger with studies of this kind that it might be inferred that personal 'values' are determinants of choice. It is equally likely that the values which one would indicate by completing the social scientist's questionnaire would be those which one felt to be congruent with the career towards which the structure of opportunities and the influences of family, education and the rest were pushing or pulling one. Again, we have to be aware of the interplay between individual and structural factors. This is stressed by Banks *et al.* (1992) who also show the interplay between two aspects of individual identity:

1   A self-concept involving such matters as 'self-efficacy, self-esteem and self-confidence, as opposed to depression, poor motivation and estrangement'.
2   Social identity which includes 'various attitudes, values, beliefs and commitments in relation to society and social institutions'.

Personal values are very much influenced by the culture of a society and by the groups within it. If, for example, the non-work culture stresses values which do not coincide with those central to certain areas within the work sphere there may be considerable problems of recruitment to that sphere. An example of this would be the alleged reluctance of the 'most able' youngsters to enter industrial careers in Britain. At the individual level, however, an opportunity to fulfil one's personal values may be a significant 'reward' which one may seek in one's work. It can become part of the implicit contract which the individual makes with their employer, a concept to which we now turn.

The employment relationship and the implicit contract

As individuals move nearer to the point where they are to enter work so we can see a 'prior orientation' to work beginning to crystallise as values, wants and preferences are matched against the jobs which are available and for which they are qualified. Typically, the individual will enter an employing organisation, although the decision to set up one's own business or enter a partnership will involve very similar considerations.

Central to the orientation to work which will influence subsequent attitudes and behaviour will be the way the individual perceives the *implicit contract* which is made between the employee and the employer.

The implicit contract

The tacit agreement between an employer and the employee about what the employee will 'put in' to the job and the rewards and benefits for which this will be exchanged.

The implicit employment contract is the largely tacit agreement made between the two parties with regard to what will be given by each and what each will take from the relationship. The employee's priorities, the resources which they take to the labour market and their personal circumstances all influence what kind of bargain they can make. This model is similar to Schein's (1978) notion of a *psychological contract*. This is formed as a result of 'various kinds of symbolic and actual events' which define what the employee will

> give in the way of effort and contribution in exchange for challenging or rewarding work, acceptable working conditions, organisational rewards in the form of pay and benefits, and an organisational future in the form of a promise of promotion or other forms of career advancement.

Schein says that this contract is 'psychological' in that the 'actual terms remain implicit; they are not written down anywhere'. However, 'the mutual expectations formed between the employee and the employer function like a contract in that if either party fails to meet the expectations, serious consequences will follow – demotivation, turnover, lack of advancement, or termination'. In Figure 4.4 we see the principal elements which make up the implicit contract which, it is claimed, is at the core of every employment relationship.

Within the individual's personal priorities – conditioned as these are by personal resources brought to the labour market and by the knowledge and the reality of the jobs available – a certain degree of calculation will be involved in the taking of any job. The individual will balance the likely

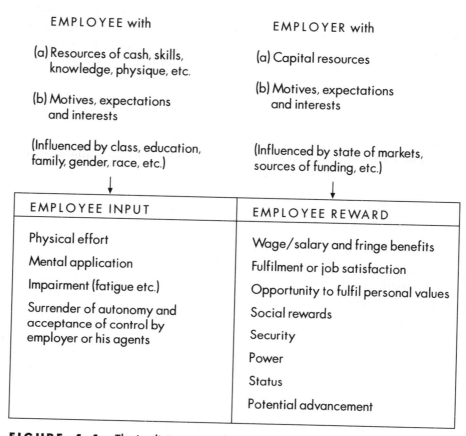

FIGURE 4.4   The implicit contract between employer and employee

personal costs in the shape of the amount of physical and mental effort to be expended, together with the likely deprivations of fatigue and the loss of freedom involved in accepting the instructions of others, against the available rewards. For certain employees cash may be a priority, for others there may be more concern with the career advancement possible in the future, yet another person may be more interested in intrinsic job satisfaction, the status of a given job, the chance to control other people or simply the opportunity to fulfil personal values afforded by a job which, say, involves 'helping people'.

Whatever the individual's priority, the various factors indicated in Figure 4.4 will have to be balanced against each other. The schoolteacher giving up the satisfaction to be gained in the classroom to earn a higher level of income selling goods, for example, will make particular calculations as will the individual entering a theological college to train for a calling which is likely to involve little by way of future material advantage. In each case the calculations made prior to the decision to enter into a particular type of implicit contract will orient the subsequent attitudes and behaviour of the individual once engaged in a work career within that organisation.

The implicit contract is never fixed, nor is it ever fully stable and two particular factors tend to threaten its stability – the push towards increased efficiency on the part of the employer and the tendency towards collective action and challenge on the part of the employee, as we shall see in Chapter 7. What is important to us at present is the way in which different implicit contracts are made in different types of work and, especially, at different levels within work settings. Individuals located in different positions in the hierarchical pattern of experience and condition in society are likely to make different types of implicit contract with an employer:

- Those in the higher positions in the class structure, typically in managerial or professional positions, tend to have a relatively *diffuse implicit contract* which means, as Fox (1974) shows, that they will be required to use discretion in their work and experience a high trust relationship with their superiors. The high trust which is put in this type of staff and the relatively high level of rewards (in the form of cash, status, opportunity for intrinsic satisfaction and career advancement offered) are reciprocated on the part of the employees with a willingness to comply with organisational requirements on their own initiative. The type of control to which they are submitted is characterised by Friedman (1977) as *responsible autonomy*. Organisational norms are, in the psychologist's terms, 'internalised' and individuals, in other words, control themselves (as well as their subordinates) on behalf of their superordinates.

- Those in lower class positions, typically in less skilled manual or routine clerical and service work, are more likely to experience a *restricted type of implicit contract*. The generally lower level of rewards is associated with what Fox (1974) describes as institutionalised low-trust relationships with superiors. Work tasks are much more closely

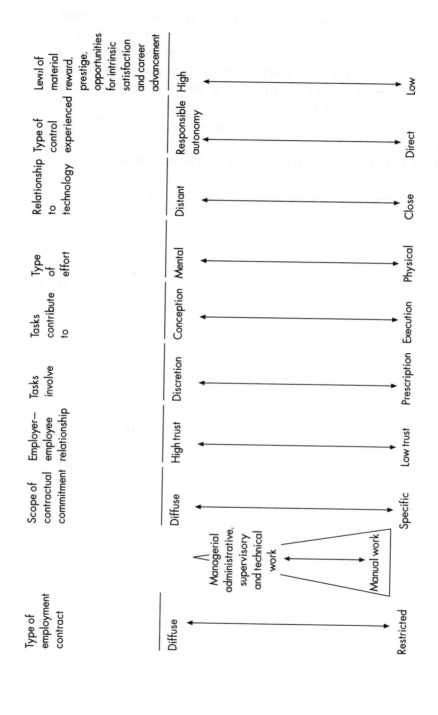

FIGURE 4.5 Two ideal types of relationship between individual and employing organisation (seen as two ends of various continua related to the hierarchical structure of organisation)

prescribed and these are executed (their conception occurring elsewhere) on the basis of a contractual commitment which is specific rather than diffuse. This specificity is represented by there typically being an hourly or weekly wage as opposed to an annual salary, by the much tighter specification of what is required of them and, especially, by the lack of an inducement in the form of potential career promotion. The control mechanism is traditionally that referred to by Friedman (1977) as *direct control* which removes worker responsibility and submits them to close supervision.

The broad pattern here is represented in Figure 4.5. It shows general structural tendencies within which individuals each have their own unique experience of work and satisfaction.

Work and satisfaction

The implicit contract approach emphasises the rational and generally instrumental aspects of the choices people make about work. People tend to know the limitations to which they are likely to have to adjust as they weigh up the possible satisfactions and the likely deprivations offered by the particular jobs available to them. Given this tendency, it is not surprising that surveys which involve asking people about work satisfaction frequently report a large proportion of people registering satisfaction. However, satisfaction is not a totally individualistic notion. In any given society there will be certain basic notions of what is desirable and we can expect people with different degrees of access to the means of these satisfactions at work to recognise this. Some indication of the distribution of these satisfactions can be derived if only in a very general way, by looking at the variations in response to questions about 'satisfaction' between people working in different settings.

In a review of a number of work satisfaction studies, Blauner (1960) found that professionals and businessmen claimed relatively high levels of satisfaction, that clerical workers claimed higher levels than manual workers, whilst skilled manual workers appeared more satisfied than unskilled workers or assembly-line operators. We may well observe that these accounts fall into a pattern closely relating to the social class hierarchy – itself a patterning of the way those resources most valued in society at large are distributed. But this does not invalidate our seeking factors in the work itself which appear to relate to these differences. Blauner offers four principal areas:

- The importance of the relative prestige of the occupation.
- The degree of independence and control over the conditions of work – covering freedom from hierarchical control, freedom to move about, opportunity to vary the pace of work and allocate one's time.
- The extent to which social satisfactions to be gained from working within an integrated group are noted.
- The degree to which people who work together share non-work activities (in something approaching an occupational community).

In a later review of work satisfaction surveys, Parker (1983) notes some additional factors such as opportunities to achieve the following:

- 'Create something'.
- 'Use skill'.
- 'Work wholeheartedly'.
- Work together with people who 'know their job'.

Dissatisfactions are likely to involve formulations which simply oppose these but Parker also usefully locates the following specific factors:

- Doing repetitive work.
- Making only a small part of something.
- Doing useless tasks.
- Feeling a sense of insecurity.
- Being too closely supervised.

All the factors emerging in these studies relate to those characterised earlier as intrinsic satisfactions, that is, those relating to factors inherent in the work itself rather than the extrinsic rewards which may be obtained. However, if we look at the type of implicit contract which people at various levels in the class structure of society are able to make with employers, we may note that those likely to gain the highest intrinsic satisfactions of the type listed above are also often those most able to gain higher material or other extrinsic rewards. Let us therefore examine the patterning of work rewards and satisfactions by work level. Having done this, we will then return to examine the patterning which may be connected with technology – a factor which indeed often relates to work level.

Different researchers have used different methods to elicit information about the nature of people's involvement in their work and hence the rewards and satisfactions which are sought or expected. Morse and Weiss (1955), for example, asked respondents whether they would continue to work if they had sufficient money to live comfortably. People in middle-class occupations pointed to the loss which would result with regard to the interest which they found in their jobs and the sense of accomplishment to which they were used. The type of loss mentioned by those in working-class jobs, however, was typically more in terms of the lack of activity with which to keep themselves occupied. Another classic study in this area is that of Friedmann and Havighurst (1954). Here the lower status workers were those most likely to stress the importance of money as the principal reward. The relationship between the nature of rewards and satisfactions and job level is also suggested by studies which have followed Dubin's method of attempting to elicit whether the individual's *central life interest* lies inside or outside the work sphere. Dubin (1956) himself, in his original study based on a large sample of industrial workers, found that three out of four individuals in this manual work had central life interests *outside* their work. Yet Orzack (1959) found that four out of five of the professional nurses whom he studied, using a procedure similar to Dubin's, indicated a central life interest *within* their work. More recent international studies using the central life interest notion, among others, suggest that there are occupational similarities in work meanings across different countries, this implying that national cultural factors might be less influential than structural matters such as the market situation of the occupational activity (MOW International Research Team 1987).

It is important to bear in mind that most of the 'data' on which these generalisations are based derive from the accounts given to researchers. The evidence is such, however, that at the very least, we can take it that those in higher level work expect more by way of intrinsic satisfactions than do those in more routine manual work. Using Daniel's (1973) distinction between satisfaction *in* work and satisfaction *with* work, we might say that routine manual workers both find and seek satisfaction *in work* less than do those in managerial, professional or highly skilled work. But this does not mean that they are not *satisfied with* their job. The 'affluent' car workers studied by Goldthorpe, Lockwood *et al.* appeared to be *satisfied with* jobs in which they achieved little or no intrinsic job satisfaction. They did not seek or expect such satisfactions. As Mann (1973) points out in his study of workers moving with a relocated factory, the fact that the instrumentally-involved worker sets little store by intrinsic work activities is, paradoxically, all the more reason for their staying firmly attached to their job. One stays in a job in order to increase its stability and predictability, thereby lowering one's 'emotional investment' in work.

Lowering emotional involvement in work is not so easily achieved for the worker in the professional or managerial sphere. The prior orientation to work is likely to be quite different and the absence of intrinsic satisfactions may lead to a greater degree of dissatisfaction and felt deprivation than is likely among working-class employees operating in settings at first sight far more potentially depriving. A picture consistent with this point was painted of the work orientations of British managers in a study by Scase and Goffee (1989). The people they called the 'reluctant managers' were people who were 'less than fully committed to their jobs and who have great reservations about giving priority to their work, their careers and, indeed, their employing organisations'. They were warier than they had been in the past about becoming completely 'psychologically immersed in their occupations'. They were reluctant to strive for career success if this could be gained only at the 'expense of personal and family relationships'.

Similar pressures on the work of managers were observed in a study by Dopson and Stewart (1990) but they found different orientations towards these from those observed by Scase and Goffee on the part of the managers they interviewed. In large part because they felt that they had greater control and responsibility in the 'flatter' managerial hierarchies than they had experienced in the older taller ones, they felt that their jobs had become more challenging and they 'enjoyed the additional responsibilities and variety of their work'. A third study of managerial work in Britain (Watson 1994a) suggests that either of these patterns of orientation are possible in different circumstances within the broad changes occurring in work organisations. The managers closely studied in one industrial organisation were shown to display a strong ambivalence towards their work. It was common within the firm for managers to say they felt rewarded by the opportunities presented in their immediate jobs to achieve tasks, to be 'in control' and to have the respect of the people with whom they worked. But they were increasingly 'becoming concerned about whether their energies were being directed towards the sort of overall business success' that would give them the security and involvement that they had once experienced.

The subjective experience of work, in practice, is influenced both by the prior orientation which individuals bring to that work and the changing work and organisational circumstances in which they find themselves. And the perceptions and priorities shaping the implicit contract entered into with an employer vary considerably up and down the occupational hierarchy.

Technology and work experience

When we look at the part which technology plays in the patterning of work experiences, we find that most of the existing discussions confine their attention to manual work. We may wonder why this should be, given that work of all types has its own technology in one way or another. Medical general practitioners have their medical bag, prescription pad and motor car for visiting patients and concert pianists have their pianos and musical scores. Why, then, has the relationship between working-class manual work experience and technology been the centre of attention? The answer lies partly in the general point made earlier about the tendency to treat the working class as a 'problematic' group but it specifically relates to that element of the input which the employees make in their implicit contract with the employer – the surrender of autonomy and acceptance of control by the employer or their agents.

Technology, for the majority of employees, is central to their work experience and is often something which, down to its finest detail, is chosen, is designed and its mode of use dictated by persons other than those applying it. In addition, these persons are frequently those with higher status, higher level of material rewards and, especially important, greater apparent autonomy in their own work experience than those directly applying the technology. Given cultural norms which encourage the valuing of personal autonomy, individuality and self-expression, we can see why technology is potentially such a source of resentment, conflict and opposition and hence concern among those studying manual work in industry. We are looking at a point where one of the primary structural or cultural contradictions described in the previous chapter (where the culture values autonomy whilst the economy demands submission to control by many) comes to bear on the individual's work experience.

Industrial sociology in the 1960s paid considerable attention to investigating the ways in which workers applying different types of technology were likely both to think and to act differently. Such an approach has been labelled *technological implications*.

Technological implications thinking

The technology being used determines, or at least closely constrains, the way in which tasks are organised which, in turn, significantly influences the attitudes and behaviour of workers.

Following this approach, investigators like Woodward (1965), Blauner (1964) and Sayles (1958) argued that workers' social relationships with each other, the quality of their work experience and their propensity to engage in conflict with management would be heavily dependent on technology. To make this clearer, let us compare a situation where the technology is craft-based, like printing, with the very different technology of the car assembly line.

- *Printers* will be closely bound up with their workmates through the craft group which they will have joined as youths and, because of the nature of the tasks which they carry out, they will be relatively free to interact with their colleagues.
- *Car workers'* social experiences will be quite different. The lack of skill required by the work will mean that there is not the craft tradition and resulting cohesiveness. The fact that the workers are paced by the machines, rather than the other way round, will mean that they are less free to interact with others even if they wished to.

These differences affect the social satisfactions which can be derived from the two types of work and will have implications for the type of industrial conflict engaged in, if not the amount of such activity generally. The nature of the tasks themselves – potentially interesting and fulfilling in the craft case and typically boring and frustrating in the assembly-line case – will strongly influence the feelings, thoughts and hence preparedness to act in certain ways of the two groups. Other technological situations will each have their own particular determining influence. More advanced technologies, like automated process production for example, could be expected to bring about attitudes and behaviour more in line with those of the traditional craft worker and away from those of the alienated and resentful mass-production operative.

Individuals will tend to be aware of, and take into account, the general nature of the technology they are likely to use when they shape their prior orientation to work. Once in work, their subsequent attitudes and behaviour may be conditioned by more specific factors such as the extent to which the technology enables them to mix with others, the freedom it allows them to use discretion, and so on. Wedderburn and Crompton (1972) in the study cited earlier, found that, although they were studying 'a group of workers with primarily instrumental attitudes to work', there were nevertheless distinct differences of attitude and behaviour between different parts of the plants examined, and technology was taken to be the key variable in this. The degree of interest expressed in the job, the attitude to supervision and the level of grievance activity were all found to be more 'favourable', for instance, in the continuous flow plant than in the batch production plant (even though pay levels were higher in the latter area). These authors stress the importance of two factors which relate to technology:

- The structuring of the job itself.
- The way in which the relationship between the supervisors and the operators was shaped.

It is thus not the technology itself which operates on the individual. It is the opportunity which the technology allows for personal discretion and the part it plays in the power relationships between the managers and the managed.

Blauner's influential study, *Alienation and Freedom* (1964), attempted to bring together several of the factors thought to influence work satisfactions and to relate those to work experience in different technological settings. He used the concept of alienation to bring together those factors influencing satisfaction. He termed these four 'dimensions of alienation':

- *Powerlessness*, or lack of opportunity for control.
- *Meaninglessness*, or lack of opportunity to feel a sense of purpose by linking one's job with the total production process.
- *Isolation*, or an inability to relate closely to others at work.
- *Self-estrangement*, or a lack of opportunity to achieve self-involvement or personal fulfilment at work.

Blauner used a variety of research materials to measure alienation in four types of industry: printing, textiles, car assembly and chemicals. There were four distinct types of technology here: craft, machine-tending, assembly line and process technology and Blauner found that alienation was relatively low in the craft printing industry and the process chemical industry, higher in the machine-tending textile setting and highest on the

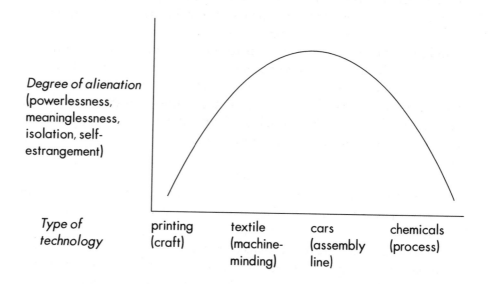

FIGURE 4.6 Blauner's 'inverted U curve' relating alienation and technology
Source: Based on Blauner (1964)

car assembly line. We thus get the famous 'inverted U-curve' shown in Figure 4.6.

Critics of Blauner's thesis such as Eldridge (1971a) have suggested that it trivialises Marx's notion of alienation by conceptualising it in subjective terms; its inferences from attitude survey data can be questioned, and the representativeness of the areas surveyed can be doubted. Although the study has important points to make about the relationship between certain technical settings and sources of work satisfaction, its greatest inadequacy lies in its failure to locate technology within its *political* context. Blauner suggests that as technology becomes more automated in the future so will the opportunity for people to experience control, purpose, meaning and self-realisation at work increase. What this does not recognise is that technology is a means to the ends of those who employ labour rather than those who are employed. The 'deskilling' of work is as great a possibility arising from the employer's introduction of new technologies to increase their control over work effort as is the evolution of a workforce of autonomous skilled, integrated and satisfied control room workers and maintenance engineers. Automation is merely one way of increasing control over work process on the part of the owner or manager and its combination with other methods of achieving control such as partial automation combined with deskilling is just as feasible.

Justifications for the type of reservations expressed here can be found in a study conducted in the British chemical industry more than a decade after Blauner. Nichols and Beynon (1977) found that in six out of the seven plants of a leading British chemical company which they visited, control room operatives – the archetypal non-alienated worker of automated industry – were a minority: 'for every man who watched dials another maintained the plants, another was a lorry driver and another two humped bags or shovelled muck'. This study has, however, been criticised for selecting evidence which fitted the ideological preconceptions of the researchers and, especially, for completely ignoring the category of workers in the plant who were classified as skilled – the maintenance workers (Harris 1987).

Care has to be taken not to make generalisations about the effect of technological change on work experience on the basis of quite real differences of experience within specific and limited work settings and without recognising that any given technology is typically a mediating factor between those who control work and those whose efforts are controlled. Since the managers of work are typically under constant pressure to maintain and increase this control we can expect their efforts to introduce technical change to be a constant influence on the 'dynamic orientations' of the employee, that is, on their ongoing definition of their situation and their preparedness to act in certain ways.

Technology, then, is a principal factor in people's work experience and their orientations to work. As was stressed in the previous chapter, technology involves a great deal more than simply the tools and machines which people use at work. What Hill (1988) called the 'technology text' pervades every aspect of work and its organisation. It is often difficult to separate the technological from the organisational. As Scarborough and Corbett (1992) observe, it is increasingly difficult because of 'the fluidity and interpenetration of technological and organisational forms' to 'know the dancer from the dance'. Hence we will return to the relationship between technological factors and work experience again and again, whether it is in the process of considering claims about the progressive deskilling of work in Chapter 6 or when looking at the implications of the increased use of information technology in Chapter 8.

Work and non-work

The relationship between the work and non-work aspects of our lives is complex and two-way. At the highest level of generality the two spheres interrelate to form a particular type of society; the industrial capitalist type examined in Chapter 3 being that with which we are concerned. This society is ever-changing, with changes at work influencing those in society at large and vice versa. As was argued in the earlier chapter, much of the impetus to social change comes from structural contradictions, many of which derive from aspects of work organisation, control and experience. The structures of work and the technology used are located in the power structures and cultural understandings of the wider society with social class, family, education and other social structural factors having a significant influence on individuals' prior orientation to work as well as on their socially conditioned predisposition to act and think in a certain way once in work. We may, however, examine a variety of further ways in which one's work and non-work experiences are interrelated.

Mobility, class and imagery

Following entry to work, one's occupation, through the income earned and the other social class correlates of the position, is a principal determinant of one's own life chances and those of one's dependants. The career structure of either the occupation or the employing organisation will offer or deny opportunity for social mobility and hence improvement in their life chances. Different approaches to mobility can be noted, however. For example, W. Watson (1964) located a particular type of aspiring middle-class employee, the *spiralist*, who moves upwards in career by moving from organisation to organisation and locality to locality. This type of person, one who occupies what Gouldner (1957) has called a *cosmopolitan* latent role, can be contrasted with what he calls a *local*, someone more inclined to seek whatever advancement is desired within the local setting.

These various categories of people, with their contrasting orientations to work and career, are recognisable in a study of the British class structure by Roberts *et al.* (1977) who clearly distinguished the spiralist middle-class workers as a group with both distinct political, social and job attitudes within the middle class as a whole. Differences of experience between people with careers in large corporations and middle-class workers in smaller firms were later pointed to by Savage *et al.* (1992) as shaping different political views. The latter are said to be adopting a more individualistic, consumerist and conservation position than the former, who retain a more corporatist or collectivist politics.

Studies like this support what research has indicated over the years: that the social class images which people have are related to the work they do. The findings support what Goldthorpe, Lockwood *et al.* (1968) found in the mid-1960s: that achievement of relatively high levels of income by some manual workers does not lead to their assimilation into the middle class in either behaviour and attitude (thus invalidating the so-called 'embourgeoisement thesis'). Devine's (1992b) return to these informants decades later found that their image of themselves was one of 'ordinary working people' who contrasted themselves with the 'idle rich'. They were cynical about party politics and although they retained a basic loyalty to the Labour party and regarded trade union membership as a necessary protection from managerial initiatives and a means of improving earnings, they were sceptical about trade unions' real commitments and effectiveness and many had been deterred from supporting the Labour Party in the 1980s as a result of the pattern of labour movement activity in the late 1970s.

This research gives important insights into particular patterns of social imagery and political stance and Mackenzie (1975) provides an overview of the range of factors in people's work situations which are likely to influence class imagery, arguing that this in turn influences such factors as their child-rearing attitudes, political viewpoints and ways of using leisure time. He examines the following factors as conducive to either middle-class imagery or working-class imagery:

- The size of the workplace.
- The organisation of the workgroup.
- The workgroup's relation to supervisors and management.
- The degree to which the worker has control over the work process.
- The extent to which the job facilitates or prevents communication between workers.
- The rigidity of the distinction between staff and workers.
- Security of tenure.
- The progressiveness of earnings.
- Job discipline.

The recognition that people's work situation influences their wider world view has led various authors to speculate that moves towards greater automation in the workplace would help create a 'new working class'. Blauner (1964) expected the typically non-alienated workers of the automated plant to become quite different in outlook and behaviour from the traditional working class, manifesting less loyalty to the trade union, more to the employer and generally a more characteristically middle-class orientation. In his version of the new working class ushered in with advanced technology, the French writer Mallet (1975) foresees an opposite tendency with workers making use of a new sense of power and a greater knowledge of the firm to act through their unions in efforts to challenge the employer and gain greater control. However, this type of argument, in both versions, tends to infer too much direct influence of work experience on outside orientations, underestimating structural and cultural factors in the wider society. This has been shown in Gallie's (1978) study of four oil refineries, two in France and two in Britain. His results question both the above theses, suggesting that advanced technology itself appears to have no significant effect on class attitudes and aspirations, or on attitudes to the employer and to trade unions. The study suggests that more significance has to be attached to the structure and culture of the society outside the plant, this being indicated by the distinctly more conflictual and class-conscious orientations of the French workers compared with the British (see also Gallie 1984).

Personality, home and family

An important theme in writing about modern work organisations has been the alleged tendency for their managements to create a type of person whose first loyalty in life is to the corporation. These 'organisation men', graphically described by Whyte (1961), show a willingness to fit in and co-operate with others at work; they are unwilling to challenge or disturb the order of which they are a part and their superficial suburban home life reflects the lack of initiative and their docility at work. This thesis gained wide currency and is found in similar forms in various other US works such as Wright Mills's *White Collar* (1953). However, Kohn's (1971) investigation of the personality types associated with bureaucratic employment found little support for this popular stereotype, arguing that there was no evidence that bureaucracies produced placid conformists. It was argued in fact, that the reverse tended to apply, the secure base provided by the bureaucrats' employment enabling them to consolidate their own values and 'develop a life style reflecting his personal preferences'. Nevertheless, it is clearly recognised that careers which involve long absences of the individual from the family setting and frequent geographical moves do create tensions in home life (Pahl and Pahl 1972, Tunstall 1962), this being exacerbated where both spouses work. But this is again an area where individual orientations to work are important. Rapoport and Rapoport (1976) in their study of dual-career families show that the stresses involved in this form of family life are reorganised and accepted as a 'cost' involved when such a way of life is chosen, and Sofer (1970) reports that where the managers in his sample were able to achieve a separation between their working and non-working lives, there was less mental conflict engendered by aspects of the husband's work career.

The family is the most significant setting for most people's life-cycle and here we would expect there to be a significant type of pressure on the individual's orientation to work. The arrival and different stages of children's growing up may, for instance, exert significant pressures on parents' interests in such items in their implicit contract as income level and degree of security. Child-rearing practices themselves have been related by researchers to the employment of the parent. Kohn (1969), for instance, noted the commitment to different value-systems by manual workers and non-manual workers, these affecting the extent to which they stressed conformity or self-direction in the child socialisation patterns. He argued that the restrictive nature of working-class employment reinforced the relative lack of education of the parents in its influence on the higher level of conformity encouraged in their children. Similar findings have been reported by Miller and Swanson (1958) and Aberle and Naegele (1961) and, as Mackenzie (1975) points out, this has an important influence on the class imagery of the children themselves. And this, in turn, will have significant implications for the future work life of these children as well as for their non-work attitudes and behaviour.

Gender and family

Gender differences are a principal patterning factor in all societies and in most of the activities which occur within them. In the next chapter we shall examine the extent to which the occupational structure or societal division of labour is patterned on gender lines and how patterns of discrimination occur in association with this. We shall also look specifically at the occupation of 'housework'. At this stage we are concentrating on the impact of family life on the work meanings of men and women.

In discussing these matters we have to be careful to avoid the sexually discriminatory assumptions which have influenced the sociology of work in the past and, particularly, take care to avoid the trap noted by Feldberg and Glenn (1982) whereby male participation in the labour force has been considered within a 'job model' and female participation within a 'gender model':

- Men's work is considered in a *job model* – in terms of working conditions, opportunities and problems, with non-work aspects seen as influenced by work activities (as in the discussion of 'bureaucrats' above, for example).

- Women's relationship to employment is looked at the other way round, within a *gender model* – 'as a derivative of personal characteristics and relationships to family situations'.

As these authors say, what is needed is an integrated approach which takes into account the interaction between job and gender factors and the ways in which 'the work people do can be located within the context of their whole lives'. Such an approach is followed in a study of a post-war generation of British managers by Roper (1994) who takes as his starting point the concept of the 'organisation man', introduced in the previous section. This notion, says Roper, conjures up the image of a classless, genderless, disembodied administrator who – in contrast to the owner-manager of old – 'can exercise complete neutrality in decision-making'. Such people are anything but genderless in reality and Roper shows how the organisation man's 'extreme devotion to company and career was, after all, facilitated by the servicing work of secretaries and wives'. And this servicing work included emotional support given by wives and secretaries to help men maintain the appropriate masculine image of a character 'driven by intellect' rather than by emotion.

It is widely argued that the distinction between male and female roles in both the working and the non-working sphere of life was much less stark in pre-industrial and pre-capitalist Europe before the modern separation of home life and working life. In the feudal period the home and work spheres were generally one, with both men and women contributing to furtherance of the family's economic interests, whether these were simply a matter of economic survival in the case of the peasantry or the maintenance of superiority and honour among the nobility. But this unity of home and work and of production and consumption was eroded as the economic basis of social life changed. The steady conversion of the peasantry into wage labour meant that female tasks of bearing and suckling children could less easily be combined with the productive work which was increasingly being performed in a setting away from the home. Where women could obtain work, their vulnerability to exploitation was much greater than that of men who were, in effect, 'biologically freer'.

These general trends took place at different rates in different industries and in different areas (Tilly and Scott 1978). In certain contexts, women employees were preferred to men and in some areas there was a pattern of employing family units (Joyce 1980). Nevertheless, the trend was towards women becoming increasingly dependent on men and, at times, when the wages of male manual workers became too low to support wives and children, these became a charge on the community. In middle-class circles, the women were not left at home as domestic drudges as were working-class women but as 'useless' domestic decorations or bearers of male property-inheritors. In the more recent stages of industrial capitalist development where middle-class homes largely lost their ability to employ servants and where working-class wages made it more possible for males to support non-employed wives and children, it more or less became the cultural norm for women to play the domestic role whilst men 'went out to work' and earned the basic family income.

Cultural support and legitimation of this pattern developed historically with the growth of certain 'patriarchal ideologies' identified, for example, by Hamilton (1978). She notes the effect of Protestant thinking in giving 'unprecedented ideological importance' to the home and the family and in establishing the ideal for women of the faithful and supportive 'proper wife'. By the nineteenth century this had evolved into a powerful 'domestic ideology' which enabled working wives and mothers to be presented as unnatural and immoral (Hall 1979). The cultural basis of the sexual division of labour was thus obscured and 'the split between men and women came to be seen as naturally ordained. Nature decreed all women were first and foremost wives and mothers'. Making a material 'fit' with this cultural trend, was the trend towards the two-child family in the late nineteenth and early twentieth centuries and the association with this of a family model in which a male breadwinner's wage was sufficient to support a family who were looked after at home by a full-time wife and mother (Lewis 1984).

When engaging in this kind of analysis it is vital to separate that which is mythical or 'culturally normal' from that which actually occurs. It is important not to use myths or people's beliefs as simplistic explanations of the way people behave. Purcell (1978) is critical of those who suggest that women have 'internalised' the 'myth of the division of labour by sex' or the 'myth of motherhood'. Women do not fully accept the idea that their employment should be valued less than their domestic role because they wholeheartedly embrace the values associated with this.

They comply with these values because they perceive no realistic alternative. Their approach to employment and the apparent acceptance of their dual workload reflects 'their enforced experience and the range of alternatives available rather than a legitimation of a deferential mode of interaction between the sexes and uncritical acceptance of the myths and the division of labour by sex and motherhood'. According to Purcell, the facts of labour market life and the cultural precedence given to mother-wife roles reinforce one another.

Women's attitudes to work and family do not simply follow labour market opportunities according to Dex (1988) who provides historical evidence to show that between the 1940s and 1965, attitudes 'changed independently of women's employment experience ... that is, attitudes appeared to change before women's employment experience had grown'. More recently, Dex argues, the structures of employment in Britain have been 'changing to accommodate to women's availability and attitudes towards work'. It is not a matter of women simply reacting to changes in demand; 'the fact that women are prepared to accept primary responsibility for child care, and then structure their employment participation around the availability of their husband to fill in the child care gaps, has its roots, in part, in attitudes'.

It might have been expected that there would be a shift towards men and women sharing domestic tasks as a result of the increased level of employment among married women and mothers and the simplification of household tasks brought about by 'labour-saving' devices. Such a belief was strongly encouraged by a study by Young and Willmott (1975) who saw the 'symmetrical family' as the pattern for the future. Subsequent research in the 1970s was consistently less optimistic about a trend towards equality in the distribution of family work tasks. A US study of 750 urban households showed, for example, that where men did contribute to domestic or child-care tasks, they tended to play their part at a time of the day when the pressure has lessened and the tasks to be done are the more pleasant ones – tasks like reading a bed-time story to the children (Berk and Berk 1979).

Later studies like those of Gershuny (1992) indicate a shift to a situation where the total amount of housework done by men and women is shared almost equally and Wheelock (1990), on the basis of a study in which the women were employed and the men were unemployed, suggests that the shifting pattern of paid work roles among men and women is seeing a trend towards a more egalitarian approach to domestic work. However, Morris's (1988) study of the families of unemployed steelworkers suggests less of a role for the employment situation of men and women in influencing domestic activities. Morris (1988) reports her 'general impression ... that within working class culture there are strong feelings against male involvement in tasks commonly regarded to be essentially female'. Inevitably, the differing pictures emerging here are in part the outcome of different research designs. This is recognised by Warde and Hetherington (1993) who attempted in their investigation to produce evidence which could, as effectively as possible, be compared to material from the 1960s. This suggests that, with some qualification, 'gender stereotyping of specific work tasks and unequal contributions between men and women *cannot* have changed much in the last twenty years'.

Such patterns appear to apply across social class boundaries. Edgell (1980) shows that the majority of the middle-class families which he studied had a pattern of role segregation in which the wife 'typically performed a distinct range of domestic and child-rearing tasks considerably more often than the husband, and generally deferred to the husband's authority in the "more important" areas of decision-making'. The chief influence on the pattern of role allocation was not the work or the family career cycles but the husband's orientation to paid work and the wife's orientation to domestic work. Again, the importance of the meaning which individuals attach to their work roles – whether employment roles or domestic roles – is demonstrated. And this continues to apply, it would appear, when families are able to afford to employ domestic labour. The late 1980s in Britain saw a dramatic expansion in the use of waged domestic labour by high income dual-career households according to Gregson and Lowe (1994a), whose research indicates that the employment of cleaners and nannies does not create a more egalitarian pattern of role allocation between men and women. What are emerging here are 'new domestic divisions of labour which involve just women' (Gregson and Lowe 1994b).

Significant findings on gender roles have also emerged from research on those involved with small businesses. Scase and Goffee (1982) showed that wives of men who had established and were running such businesses tended to be economically, socially and psychologically subordinated to the needs of their husbands and that, without the largely unrecognised contributions of wives, many small businesses 'would not even get off the ground'. Not only do the wives contribute unpaid time and effort to the business, but they are left to cope single-handedly with domestic work, often with limited financial resources, as their husband devotes himself to the fledgling business. When women entrepreneurs are studied, however, they do not appear to get anything like this degree of support from their spouses. Goffee and Scase (1985) say that their interviews with such women suggest that husbands rarely contribute to the running of either homes or businesses. They are nevertheless forced to be dependent on men for financial and technical assistance. This is a pattern which is socially reinforced by such experiences as those, which Vokins (1993) reports, of successful women entrepreneurs approaching banks for assistance; '"Where is your husband?" was a frequent question, as were the condescending and sexist comments like "Well, do your best dear".' Businesswomen are liable to be reminded in such ways of their subordination in the sexual division of labour, as are the women married to men in occupations varying from the church or medicine to farming, military service or fishing where wives are often incorporated into their husbands' careers (Finch 1983).

When women are in paid employment, their work orientation is still heavily influenced by the implications of their feminine gender and all that this implies for their life career. A leading study of over five-and-a-half thousand women of working age in Britain indicated that girls tend to base their educational, training and job decisions on the assumption that they will be wives and mothers (Martin and Roberts 1984). Whereas boys expect to be the primary wage-earner and to have employment as their main lifetime occupation, girls look forward to a working life 'interrupted by childbirth and childrearing, usually characterised by partial employment so as to enable them to do the domestic work involved in looking after a husband, children and a home'. Indeed, even where they worked full time, only a minority of the women in the study said that they shared housework equally with their husbands.

Studies show that economic factors are highly significant within the work orientations of women workers. But, as the implicit contract model introduced earlier would suggest, there is range of other 'rewards' pertinent to people's orientations. Sharpe (1984), for example, suggests that it was the 'social characteristics' of working which gave most meaning to the jobs of the wives and mothers she interviewed and that this was especially the case after a period of not working. Pollert (1981) talks of the 'ray of light' provided in the factory she studied by the company of others for women with children who were experiencing the double burden of home and work. Cavendish (1982) adds to this the point that her participant observation study of factory life gave her a feeling of being 'more rooted in social life', enabling her to becoming more outgoing and socially relaxed than she had previously been. On the basis of her sharing this life, 'it seemed only sensible to get married and benefit from the economies of scale of two wage packets'. To consider role reversal would have been 'economic suicide'.

In discussing the considerable importance of women's non-work roles and obligations for their employment experience, we must not forget that work attitudes and orientations are also significantly influenced by factors in the workplace itself. McNally (1979) claims that this is often done and she stresses the importance of such factors as the nature of the work tasks, the prospects for promotion and the policies of employers with regard to recruitment and conditions of work. But she attempts to show that women do not passively accommodate the constraints which they meet through her study of temporary office workers who, she says, 'exemplify par excellence women's capacity actively to negotiate the limiting structures which confront them'. Resilience and creativity in the face of constraints is also shown by Brannen and Moss's (1988) account of the considerable lengths to which women go on returning to work after having babies to make arrangements for childcare in the face of hostile attitudes to working mothers, inadequate leave arrangement and a poor supply of childcare facilities. Finch and Mason (1993) similarly comment on the determined initiatives taken by working women who have to look after older relatives whilst staying in employment.

In spite of this evidence of the power of human agency in the face of cultural constraint, it is important, sociologically, to recognise the power of the constraints faced by women in employment. Kanter (1982) takes as one of the most significant factors influencing women's attitudes and behaviour at work the opportunity structure in which they find themselves at work. She argues that the widely observed tendency of women to be less committed, involved and aspiring than men in their work careers has less to do with their socialisation and upbringing than with the structure of opportunities which they face. She argues that what is normally seen as a sex difference – the greater tendency for women at work to limit their aspirations, seek satisfactions outside work, dream of escape and create sociable peer groups in which interpersonal relationships take precedence – is really a 'structural' one. The point is made by observing that men tend to show the same characteristics when they are disadvantageously located in the opportunity structure.

Leisure

In stressing the significance of the institution of the family for both class and gender patterns we should not forget that it is also the setting for a great deal of people's leisure activity. In this way it has a double implication for the work and industrial sphere:

- It provides a demand for goods and services such as the family car and the family holiday.
- It provides a context in which people can go beyond their workplace and domestic task obligations and engage in activities which they enjoy.

There are many other sites for leisure.

Leisure

Those activities which people pursue for pleasure and which are not a necessary part of their business, employment or domestic management obligations.

And there are numerous different types of leisure activity, these not only varying with personal taste but also with different types of employment. The hours left free for leisure by different kinds of work and the money available to spend on leisure are factors which clearly relate work and leisure forms. However, other factors are also relevant and, to help indicate a pattern in these, Parker (1982) has suggested that we can see three types of relationship between work and leisure: extension, opposition and neutrality.

- Leisure is likely to be experienced as an *extension* of work where a relatively high degree of autonomy and intrinsic satisfaction is experienced in work. The academic's work and leisure reading may well shade one into the other and engineers may well apply their expertise to hobbies and read professional literature in their non-work time (Gerstl and Hutton 1966). Parker's research indicates that social workers tend not to see a sharp distinction between their working and non-working lives, and Evans and Bartolemé (1980) argue that for the majority of managers in their study the relationship between work and non-work was one of 'spillover', generally with the work experience influencing individuals' private lives much more than the other way round.

- Leisure is likely to have a neutral relationship to work where there is less autonomy and potential self-fulfilment. People in jobs such as those involving routine clerical work reflect their lack of involvement and passivity at work in their leisure pastimes.

- Leisure operates in *opposition* to work where the worker who is liable to be frustrated and unfulfilled at work concentrates on the fulfilling and comfortable pastimes of home and family (this privatised lifestyle fitting with the instrumental orientation to work considered earlier) or they may pursue the more gregarious and even riotous type of leisure associated with the coalminer or deep sea fisherman (Tunstall 1962).

Some writers have pointed to the opportunities which some workers may find to compensate for work experience in the exercise of skill and the obtaining of social satisfaction in activities like pigeon racing (Mott 1973). But the general likelihood of this type of compensatory effect has been strongly argued against by people such as Meissner (1971), who diagnoses what he calls 'the long arm of the job' and argues that the suppressing of the capacity for initiative in the work setting will tend to reduce the capacity for engaging in leisure activities which involve discretion, planning and co-ordination. But for many in the future, and especially the unemployed, leisure will increasingly be more significant than work as a site in which personal fulfilment and satisfaction can be sought (Seabrooke 1988; Rojek 1989).

Unemployment

The experience of being unemployed in a society in which there is a work ethic which puts considerable value on being 'in a job' and where a reasonable level of income can come for most people only from employment is likely to be both psychologically and materially distressing. Fineman (1987) writes of 'an experiential gap that can exasperate the jobless' in the face of 'the sheer force of the effect of no longer being creditworthy in a society that builds so many of its transactions, in one way or another, on cash'. Our concern here is with these subjective aspects of unemployment and we shall return in the last chapter to issues of the future of employment and of the changes which may be occurring with regard to the work ethic.

In her study of the experience of unemployment, Jahoda (1982) concentrates on what people tend to lose, in addition to a source of income, when they become unemployed. A person's job provides the following functions:

- It imposes a time structure on the day.
- It enlarges the scope of social relations beyond the often emotionally charged ones of family and neighbours.
- It gives one a feeling of purpose and achievement through task involvement in a group setting.
- It assigns social status and clarifies personal identity.
- It requires one to engage in regular activity.

These socio-psychological functions of employment are not easily replaced when unemployment is experienced. However, a variety of other factors also influence how unemployment is experienced. Both the financial impact and the impact on work identity and identity within the family tend to vary with the 'previous location within the labour market' (Ashton 1985). Workers who have been in routine and repetitive jobs can experience short-term unemployment as a relief, for instance, and housewives who also work full time may be able to use their domestic responsibilities to 'impose a temporal structure on their daily activities' if they become unemployed. It is working-class males who appear, from the evidence, to have the greatest difficulty in imposing a temporal structure on their day.

A considerable amount of evidence has been collected to show that there is a significant connection between the experience of unemployment and both physical and mental ill health. In reviewing the evidence gathered by a series of studies, Gallie and Vogler (1994) show that the unemployed suffer from a process of cumulative disadvantage and that their 'weak labour market position is accompanied not only by much greater financial difficulty, but by disadvantage in both health and housing'. It is widely believed that it is the fall in income which has the greatest impact on people's mental health followed by the removal of the socio-psychological factors identified by Jahoda. Burchell (1994), however, places particular stress on insecurity as a generator of psychological stress. His research showed little difference between the levels of stress among the unemployed and among those experiencing high levels of insecurity within work. He further shows that unemployed people who enter a secure job show much greater improvement in psychological well-being than those taking up insecure jobs.

The evidence from those cases where people appear to cope well with the experience of unemployment strongly indicates the importance of psychological factors and personal values. Warr (1983), for example, reports that the 'good copers' whom he studied all had financial difficulties but maintained high levels of emotional well-being. This was associated with 'considerable personal activity, driven by strongly held religious, social or political values'. Miles (1984) found that the psychological well-being of the sample of more than a hundred unemployed men he studied was better where there was involvement in such activities as voluntary work, team sport or part-time education. But he adds that the large majority of men failed to get much access to experiences which would meet socio-psychological needs; the signs of 'adaptation to unemployment' were 'very limited'. This is supported by the evidence gathered by Gershuny (1994) which shows that once they are unemployed people have far fewer opportunities of experiencing social interactions than the employed. This applies to men more than women, however.

The evidence indicates that the unemployed form, as Gallie and Marsh (1994) put it, 'a distinctive group at the bottom of the social heap'. This raises the question of whether members of this group possess or develop distinctive attitudes to work and employment in general. The studies gathered by Gallie, Marsh and Vogler (1994) show that only a minority of the unemployed studied were not seeking work or were inflexible about what work they were willing to undertake. There is little evidence of a 'culture of dependency' developing among the unemployed. Where there is inflexibility about opportunities it tends to be among those who are held back by their circumstances – age or being a single mother (Dawes 1993). A study of redundant steelworkers carried out by Westergaard, Noble and Walker (1989) suggests that it was much less worker attitudes and behaviour that led to success or otherwise in obtaining work as the qualifications of individuals and how this related to the level of demand for particular skills in the labour market. Commitment to the work ethic among these men was high and they were typically prepared to take jobs at a skill level lower than that for which they were qualified. Young unemployed people are similarly shown to want to find jobs. Research by Banks and Ullah (1988) shows this but it also shows how continuing unemployment created a sense of discouragement and reduced efforts to find work.

What is indicated by these considerations of work and non-work is that human beings' experience of work and their activity, experience and values outside work are closely connected. The choices to be made about the role of work in the future will have to take this interrelationship fully into account. The nature of these choices will be returned to later, especially in the final chapter. For the present, the focus will move away from individuals and their experience of work as such to look more closely at the variety of structural contexts in which this experience occurs. This is only a matter of emphasis, however, and sight of the individual will by no means be lost in the coming chapters.

■　　■　　■

Chapter 5

The structuring of work: occupations and the social division of labour

Introduction

If we seek some pattern underlying the work which people do in modern societies we will find that there are two basic principles which contribute to the structuring which can be observed. These principles are partly complementary and partly in a relationship of conflict and rivalry:

- *Administrative* – the structuring of work on a bureaucratic, administrative or 'formal organisation' basis. Emphasis is on the ways in which work tasks are designed by certain people who then recruit, pay, co-ordinate and control the efforts of others to carry out these tasks. These are the concerns of the next chapter.
- *Occupational* – the structuring of work on the basis of the type of work that people do. Emphasis is on the patterns which emerge when we concentrate on the way specific work tasks are done. Here we take as our starting point the carrying out of a specific type of work operation, say driving a lorry, cleaning a house, catching fish or running a business. We then concentrate on the social implications of there existing within society groups of people regularly doing similar tasks.

The implications of the existence of occupational groupings arise at various levels, as we shall see in this chapter. Occupations have implications in a number of ways:

- For society as a whole and for social change.
- For members of these occupational groups in so far as the groups become collectivities.
- For the individual engaged in a particular type of work.

It is important in defining an occupation to recognise that the concept is not simply a sociological tool of analysis but is also a notion used by the people whom the sociologist studies. A definition has therefore to take into account that whether or not any given work activity is to be regarded as an occupation depends in part on the decisions made by those doing the tasks and also by the wider public as to whether such an identity is to be bestowed.

Occupation

Engagement on a regular basis in a part or the whole of a range of work tasks which are identified under a particular heading or title by both those carrying out these tasks and by a wider public.

This conception of an occupation is wider than simply paid employment. Membership of an occupation may involve total independence of an employer, as in the case of a freelance writer, say, and it may mean that there is no direct financial reward from the work. In this latter case the individual will have to be supported by someone else. This will apply to the commercially unsuccessful poet and to the student, either of whom may receive a government grant.

Occupational and administrative forms of work structuring

Practically every person who works can be assigned to an occupation. But for many individuals, their location in a work organisation may be more salient than this occupational membership. In trying to place a stranger we may ask either 'what do they do?' or 'who do they work for?' Traditionally, we locate people in society by their occupation – tinker, tailor, soldier, sailor – but with the growth of bureaucratised work organisations the specific tasks in which a person is engaged and the skills which go with it become less relevant for many people than the organisation in which they are employed. It is not uncommon for one person to say of another 'I don't know exactly what he does but it's something with the council' and the nearest to any occupational specification which is often achieved with regard to the work of friends, acquaintances or relatives may well be along the lines that 'she does something in the offices' or 'it's some kind of factory job'.

For many people, then, the way they are seen by others and often the way they regard their own work is less in terms of the occupational principle than the organisational or administrative one. There are, however, two special cases where the *study* of people's work has tended to concentrate on the occupational principle:

1   Where the tasks associated with a job are particularly distinctive. This may be through

    • a degree of public visibility – policeman, teacher, actor;
    • their being somewhat peculiar or deviant – prostitute, undertaker, dope pedlar.

2   Where the tasks involved in a certain kind of work are such that control over the carrying out of those tasks can be sought by members of the occupation itself at the expense of control by an employer, government or clients. These will tend to be highly skilled 'trades' or, more especially, the 'professions'.

The twentieth-century study of particular occupations by sociologists has tended to veer between a fascination with high-status professionals and various low-status or deviant work activities. The history of western occupations has, however, been very much one of the rise and fall of the degree of occupational self-control maintained by various groups. The occupational principle is seen very clearly in the occupational guilds which were at their height in the thirteenth century. The guilds developed as part of the urban world which was growing within the feudal structure. They originally served as protective societies for merchants trading in Europe but were then taken up by groups of artisans within the cities as an organisational form to provide them in a similar way with mutual aid and protection.

With the guilds we see an example of that common tendency in social life and social change for people to form coalitions of interest. The guilds, as such coalitions, helped mediate between the trades people and the city authorities, thus providing in part a defensive role for the group. But they also acted in a more assertively self-interested manner by maintaining a tightly controlled monopoly in their trade. They not only controlled raw materials, and restricted entry to trades, but laid down work procedures which, whilst maintaining quality of the product or service, ensured that any job took the longest possible course with the effect that technical change and any move toward an increased technical division of labour was ruled out. The guild gave the occupation a stratified structure of master craftsman, journeyman and apprentice, thus providing in theory a career structure for the individual. However, groups tend to exist within interest groups and those who find themselves with relative material advantages tend to operate so as to maintain that advantage. Thus the master craftsmen began to operate as an élite within the guilds, often preferring to pass on their advantaged positions to their own children rather than to aspiring journeymen.

With the growth of the more competitive and market-oriented capitalism which was developing within and threatening the feudal order, master craftsmen were strongly tempted to break their guild monopolies and associate more with the growing class of merchant capitalists. These individuals helped break down the occupational principle of work organisation as they began to use former guild members as wage labour and as they made use of the former peasantry within the putting-out or domestic system of production. Later, of course, the development of factory production accelerated the dominance of the administrative principle, leaving the occupational form of organisation as a residual principle – a principle to be defended by groups whose trade skills were a resource sufficiently exclusive to allow them to maintain some autonomy.

The survival of the occupational principle among the growing working class was carried over into workshop and factory production in the first half of the nineteenth century in the form of a 'labour aristocracy' which retained an élite position 'through the force of custom, or combination and apprenticeship restriction, or because the craft remained highly skilled and specialised' (Thompson 1968). The growth of the new skills accompanying the rise of engineering created a potentially new occupational élite or labour aristocracy but by the late nineteenth century the growing predominance of the administrative principle was such that the more important bodies formed by groups like the engineers were the more *defensively oriented* trade unions. Throughout the twentieth century the trade or occupational basis of unions has become undermined as occupational groups have amalgamated to help in the primary union task of representing *employee* rather than occupational interests. The occupational principle of work organisation did not only survive the growth of industrial capitalism in the vestigial form represented by skilled trade unions, however. It has survived and indeed

See page 221 flourished in parts of the middle-class sphere of work in the guise of professionalism, as we shall see later.

Occupational structure

In contrast to the term 'organisational structure', which refers to the internal patterning in work organisations, the concept of occupational structure is used by sociologists.

Occupational structure

The pattern in a society which is created by the distribution of the labour force across the range of existing types of work or occupation.

Patterning may be sought, for example, by looking for both *hierarchical* and *horizontal* differentiating factors.

Horizontal and hierarchical patterning

A frequently used way of showing horizontal differentiation is to divide a workforce into three sectors:

- A primary sector – agricultural and extractive industries.
- A secondary sector – manufacturing.
- A tertiary sector – services.

This type of distribution, widely used by economists, has been used sociologically to study industrialisation processes. However, various sociologists have also looked for ways of grouping occupations other than hierarchically. The notion of *occupational situs* is the chief contribution here and this refers to a grouping of occupations which is differentiated from other groupings according to various criteria other than or in addition to those which imply status or reward-yielding capacity. Morris and Murphy (1959) took up this concept (which had first been applied to the occupational sphere by Hatt (1950)) using the criterion of 'societal function'. Hopper and Pearce (1973), who point out that the particular criterion used may vary with the purpose of the research being undertaken, classify occupations for their own purposes on the basis of economic function. They thus develop nine situs categories:

- Distribution
- Manufacturing
- Finance and insurance
- Agriculture
- Building and transport and communications
- Civil service
- Church, military and government
- Education
- Medicine and health

Occupational situs as a tool of analysis has been used far less than occupational status. This is perhaps not surprising, given that an individual's occupation is the key indicator of their social class and social status – as those concepts are generally used, inside and outside of sociology. As well as the prestige which one derives from a job, one's market position and relationship to the means of production is generally dependent upon the job which is held. As we saw in the last chapter, the hierarchy of jobs based on material rewards tends to coincide with that based on intrinsic rewards which contribute to job satisfaction, and both of these factors influence the general life-chances not just of the workers themselves but also of their dependants.

Sociological researchers often develop their own set of socio-economic categories or classes to help in their particular investigations, and a useful example is the scheme of class positions used in research on class mobility in Britain (Goldthorpe *et al.* 1980). The categories used here achieve differentiation in terms of both occupational function and employment status. Occupations are brought together in such a way that we can expect incumbents to share in 'broadly similar market and work situations' – these being taken to be the two principal components of class position. The groupings, somewhat simplified for present purposes, are as follows:

Class I: higher-grade professionals, administrators, managers and business people.

Class II: low-grade professionals, administrators and managers; higher-grade technicians and supervisors of manual employees.

Class III: routine non-manual, largely clerical, workers; sales personnel and other rank and file service workers.

Class IV: small proprietors; self-employed artisans and other non-professional own-account workers.

Class V: lower grade technicians and supervisors of manual workers.

Class VI: skilled manual wage-workers.

Class VII: skilled manual wage-workers; semi and unskilled workers.

Thus the study of occupational structure involves classifying occupations horizontally, vertically, or a mix of both of these. The categories developed can be used in various ways, including examining the numbers of people covered by certain sectors or socio-economic groups, the mobility of people between different categories, the characteristics of people in various positions in terms of such criteria as gender, race and age and, especially, the way these patterns change over time. These factors are central to understanding the social structure and processes of change occurring in society at large. We shall now look at some of the principal changes which have been suggested.

The changing division of labour: Durkheim and Marx

At the basis of the study of changes in occupational structures is a concern with the *division of labour* in society.

> **The division of labour**
>
> The allocation of work tasks to various groups or categories of individual.

Durkheim (1984, originally 1893) saw the division of labour as central to the nature of a society's solidarity – the way in which a society achieves integration. In a simple society there would be little occupational differentiation with, say, most of the women carrying out one basic task, most of the young men occupied in another general task and so on. A similarity of outlook would develop between people, most of whom are engaged in more or less similar activities. Social order and stability would thus be maintained through *mechanical solidarity*. However, in the vastly more complex industrialising world where a large range of specialised occupations have developed, each with distinctive ideas, norms and values, a similarity of outlook cannot be depended upon to hold society together. The source for stability is to be found, instead, in the inevitable interdependence of members of occupations one with the other. Bakers depend on butchers for their meat, butchers on the bakers for their bread, and so on. We thus have integration through *organic solidarity*.

Although Durkheim saw the occupational principle as offering a basis for integration in modern society in this way he nevertheless began to note how the increasing emphasis on material advancement and sectional interests of his own time tended to undermine social solidarity, leading, in particular, to the moral confusion and purposelessness which he conceptualised as *anomie*. But Durkheim treated such tendencies as pathological rather than as essential features of industrial capitalism. The more closely we look at Durkheim's assumed source of social order in modern societies – the organic solidarity achieved by interdependent occupations – the more we come to realise that the structure and dynamics of industrial capitalism can be better understood in terms of interests, power and control. The attachment of people to the prevailing social order is more realistically seen as deriving from their dependence on the material rewards to be gained from their relationship not to occupations but to bureaucratic work organisations; whether this relationship is more one of submitting to control within an organisation, exercising such control or servicing the organisation in some direct or indirect way. See page 51

Consideration of the division of labour in the Marxian tradition has seen the increasing specialisation of tasks which accompanies the capitalist labour process as essentially disintegrative. An important distinction is made between the general or *social* division of labour and the detailed or *technical* division of labour.

Social division of labour

The allocation of work tasks at the level of society, typically into trades and occupations.

Technical division of labour

Task specialisation within an occupation or broad work task.

The technical division of labour has generally been seen as involving a splitting down of tasks within a former craft at the initiative of employers or their agents in order to increase the efficiency of the enterprise – efficiency as conceived by those extracting a surplus (Braverman 1974). The dividing of tasks *within* occupations, with its alienating effects, is often seen as fundamentally different from the dividing of tasks *between* occupations – the latter constituting a healthy and necessary part of any human society.

The changing division of labour: convergence

The Marxian view of the changing occupational structure, which in its basic form looks to the ultimate polarisation of all former occupational roles into those of capitalist and proletariat, can be contrasted with those analyses which have focused on the nature of industrialism rather than capitalism. Implicit in many of the discussions of the type of occupational structure which develops with industrialisation is some attachment to the 'logic of industrialism' thesis discussed in Chapter 3. It is suggested that the technological changes basic to industrialisation lead to the growth of occupational structures which are bound to be more or less similar in all industrial societies at the equivalent level of development. In the work of such writers as Aron (1967), Kerr *et al.* (1973) and Moore (1965) we see suggested a number of trends which accompany industrialisation:

- The fall in numbers occupied in the primary sector and the rise in numbers employed in the secondary, and later, tertiary sectors.
- The increasing differentiation of occupations and the appearance of new ones.
- The general upgrading of skill levels with an increasing proportion of skilled workers.
- An increasing proportion of professional, scientific and managerial jobs.
- An increase in the mobility of labour both within and between occupations as a result of the ongoing changes in the occupational structure and the need to appoint people on the basis of ability rather than status.

Prior to the move of Central and East European socialist societies away from command economies after 1989, Kerr (1983) was insisting that the convergence thesis which he put forward two decades earlier continued to be valid. Convergence was always a strong likelihood because the desire for the goods and services of industrialism is so widespread and because the means by which these can be obtained are more or less fixed. From this, Kerr went on to suggest that if there was an upturn in economic growth in the world then convergence would tend to be towards the western version of industrialism with an emphasis on efficiency of production rather than equality. If growth were to be restricted, however, then the tendency would be towards the Soviet pattern, with an emphasis on the distribution of the limited goods and services available and towards equality. As events turned out, the shift which occurred followed the former rather than the latter pattern and a significant interpretation was made of this by Fukuyama (1992) and his 'end of history thesis'.

See page 87–8

The changing division of labour: post–industrialism

In the same way that sociologists have often observed a transformation occurring in occupational structures as societies industrialise, so have several writers in recent decades suggested a further transformation in some industrial societies which is thought to be significant enough to warrant recognition of the approach or the arrival of the *post-industrial society*.

Post-industrial society

A type of economically advanced social order in which the centrally important resource is knowledge, service work has largely replaced manufacturing employment and knowledge-based occupations play a privileged role.

Bell (1974) has made one of the most influential statements of this kind, suggesting that advanced industrial societies are entering a new phase in their development. This will make them as different from what we now know as 'industrial society' as such societies differed from 'pre-industrial' ones. The characteristic features of the post-industrial society are to be found in the spheres of technology, the economy and the social structure. The economy undergoes a shift from a predominantly manufacturing to a service economy; in technology the new science-based industries become central; in the social structure we see 'the rise of new technical elites and the advent of a new principle of stratification' (Bell 1974). The suggestion is that a new type of occupational structure develops in which white-collar workers outnumber blue-collar ones and in which the professional, scientific and technical occupations become predominant.

This trend follows from the essential principle underlying the new type of society: the emergence of 'theoretical knowledge' as the basis for innovation and policy-making. Post-industrial society is thus a 'knowledge society' and thus those occupations which possess theoretical knowledge will – on the principle that knowledge is power – come to exert a controlling influence on society. With the diminution of the manual working class a relatively stable order will follow as social and economic policy is rationally formulated and as individuals are tied into the social order through the operation of the meritocratic system of rewards which must accompany an occupational structure dependent on recruiting individuals with high ability. The potential for satisfaction at work is increased, it is claimed, by the increased opportunity created by the expanding service sector for people to relate to other people in their jobs rather than to machines.

Bell's assumptions about the changing nature of the work people *actually* do can be strongly questioned. Qualitative inferences about the nature of occupational life are made on the basis of statistical trends whereby tasks are allocated to official categories which tell us little about what people actually do in their work (Gershuny 1978). The greatest weakness in Bell's thesis, however, lies in his assumption that there is anything novel about the centrality of knowledge to economic and working life. The growth of industrialism and the rise of capitalism were both dependent on the increasing application of rational-calculative thinking to social life, as was argued in Chapter 3. Thus the growth of scientific and technical qualifications among the population is part of the rationalisation process which Max Weber saw as characterising western history over several centuries. As Giddens (1973) suggests 'modern technology is not "post-industrial" at all, but is the function of the principle of accelerating technical growth built into industrialism as such'.

The changes which are occurring as 'information technologies' play an increasingly significant role in people's lives have to be related to the specific forces to which they are related rather than to an alleged sea change in the way societies are organised. There are also various countervailing tendencies occurring alongside those which are empha-sised by advocates of a post-industrial perspective. In addition to the possibilities of a decentralisation of work and industrial structures and an increase in the quantity of information and knowledge, Smart (1992) observes, there are trends towards '(re)centralisation; an increasing privatisation and commercialisation of social life; a commodification of information and knowledge; and an extension of surveillance and control'. And, he goes on, these 'major transformations in social relations and forces of production' have been occasioned by the following developments:

- The multinational extension of corporate capitalism.
- An increasingly global labour market.
- Military and political preoccupations with command and control, national security and law and order.

Much of the kind of post-industrial analysis which continues to be generated by authors like Gorz (1985), Toffler (1983) or Bahro (1986) can be seen as sloppy, superficial and over-optimistic in its utopianism (Frankel 1987). There are, however, more pessimistic versions of post-industrialism. Advanced technology and the growth of educational institutions to train those who will apply and administer it does not necessarily have to be seen as a force for making society more stable, for example. Such changes can equally be taken to be a source of deep conflict in society. This was suggested by Touraine's version of post-industrialism (1971) which, as with Bell, was a 'knowledge society'. In this French view of the new type of society and occupational structure, the members of the predominating knowledge-based occupations (engineers, accountants, educators, skilled workers, etc.) form a new working class – one which is increasingly alienated, not by the way ruling groups economically exploit them, but by the way they involve them in *dependent participation*. The highly-skilled and the university educated are seen as resenting the way in which they are required to apply their skills and knowledge in a system which does not give them the discretion and autonomy they increasingly expect. The new working class can thus be expected to mobilise itself against prevailing ruling interests, not to challenge this 'exclusion', as did the old working class, but rather to challenge the way they are 'integrated and used' (Touraine 1971).

Touraine's prognostications about an emerging new working class have not been borne out by empirical research and the assumption which he shares with most other theorists of post-industrialism of the arrival of a post-scarcity society is wildly over-optimistic. However, the possibilities which he points to may yet become real. Analyses such as these should be seen less as exercises in prediction and 'futurology' and more as suggestions of possibilities which might come about.

Postmodernity and a changing world

A more recent attempt to label changes occurring in the world which have implications for the division of labour – between nations as well as between organisations, groups and individuals – has been the talk of a move into an epoch of *postmodernity*. This concept was introduced in Chapter 2 as part of an emerging strand in the analysis of work and industry. Discussions of postmodernity pay attention to various ways in which *fragmentation* of existing patterns can be seen to be occurring in the world – although there is also attention to some countervailing trends within this. As the association of a concept of postmodernity with *postmodernism* as a way of thinking about the world (explained in Chapter 2) would imply, a concern with changes in human knowledge plays a key role here, as it did with claims about post-industrialism. Lyotard's (1986) claim that the basis of legitimacy of 'modern' knowledge is withering away is crucial here. Postmodernity is associated with 'heterogeneity, plurality, constant innovation, and pragmatic construction of local rules and prescriptives agreed upon by participants, and is thus for micro-politics' (Best and Kellner 1991). The implications of claims like these for the way work is organised will be a concern of our final chapter. Here, though, we can identify some of the basic shifts identified by those who see sufficient change in the human world to imply that we have a new epoch of postmodernity:

- The nation state declines in importance either through breaking up into smaller units (as with the former USSR or Yugoslavia) or by combining into bigger units (the European Union, for example).
- Large political parties decline and are replaced by numerous social movements.
- Social classes fragment and are joined by other potential interests groups focusing on gender, ethnicity or sexual orientation.
- The pleasure principle and a drive to consume replace the work ethic as motivators to economic activity.
- Flexible and decentralised work organisation replaces big bureaucracies; employees are given autonomy and skill and use advanced electronic technologies to produce customised goods and services.

These claims are open to review by a consideration of changing trends across the world and attempts to do this by such authors as Crook, Pakulski and Waters (1992) show that, in different ways in different parts of the world, some such shifts are occurring. The final set of changes will be considered in the last chapter.

Dualism and labour market segmentation

In discussing post-industrialism, postmodernism and the convergence thesis, especially given the convergence thesis' assumption of a 'logic of industrialism', it is easy to forget our earlier insistence that modern western societies are best understood as industrial *capitalist* societies. As one of the main distinguishing features of a capitalist society is that labour, or 'labour power', is treated as a commodity to be bought and sold on the market, it is necessary to relate matters of occupational structure to the principles which underlie the operation of labour markets. It is also necessary to recognise the economic and political difficulties which are faced in industrialised societies generally, which put pressures on how work is organised and how the division of labour is 'managed'.

Goldthorpe (1985) accuses the theorists of convergence of failing to see the instabilities which are created for western capitalist societies by the 'generally damaging effects of interest-group activity on the operation of market mechanisms' and by the challenges and demands of organised labour. The most obvious manifestation of these problems was that by the 1960s western economies had become inherently inflationary. Instead of these problems leading to one generally-used type of solution which would leave us with some kind of convergence, at least within capitalist societies, there have been two divergent approaches to dealing with these problems. On the one hand, says Goldthorpe, there have been *corporatist* attempts where states have attempted to manage the economy.

Corporatism

A political system in which principal decisions, especially with regard to the economy, are made by the state in close association with employer, trade union and other pressure group organisations.

On the other hand, where this has been less politically or ideologically acceptable, there has been a greater move towards *dualism*.

Dualism

The effective division of an economy into two parts: typically a prosperous and stable 'core' sector of enterprises and jobs and a 'peripheral' sector which is relatively and systematically disadvantaged.

Whereas corporatism deals with the problems posed by economic interest groups, and organised labour in particular, in an 'inclusionary' way – by involving them in forming and implementing economic policy – dualism works on 'exclusionary' lines. Here, the increased power of organised interests is offset by the creating or expanding of groups of workers (and potential workers) who lack effective organisation or the potential to mobilise themselves. A principal source of dualism has been migrant labour which has provided employers with a flexible, tractable and generally quiescent source of labour supply. This acts not only as an 'industrial reserve army' but as a labour force susceptible both to market forces and the changing needs of employers and managers. Goldthorpe sees the trend towards dualism going further than this, however, and relates it to a general trend in western societies whereby production is subcontracted and various types of temporary and part-time labour are employed on terms which pushes them towards a 'secondary' category within the total labour market.

The concept of a *dual labour market* first appeared as part of an attempt to understand the phenomenon of racial discrimination in employment in the USA but it is now used to cover a wider range of issues, as we have seen.

Dual labour markets

The labour market dimension of *dualism* in which there is a relatively advantaged *primary* type of employment and a relatively disadvantaged *secondary* type of work and employment.

Labour markets, with their associated occupational groupings, are dichotomised into primary and secondary segments:

- In the primary sector, the work is characterised by good working conditions and pay levels, opportunities for advancement and fair treatment at work and, especially, stability of employment.
- In the secondary sector, workers are worse off in all these respects and their employment is associated with considerable instability and a high turnover rate (Doeringer and Piore 1971). The members of this secondary labour force will tend to be people who are easily dispensed with, possess clearly visible social differences, are little interested in training or gaining high economic reward and tend not to organise themselves collectively.

Given these features of the secondary labour market, and the social and cultural characteristics of the wider society, we tend to find recruitment to the secondary labour force drawing to a disproportionate extent on women, blacks, immigrants, unqualified teenagers, students seeking part-time work, disabled and handicapped persons (Piore 1979).

To explain the dual labour market phenomenon, a great deal of attention has been paid to the attempts of employers to come to terms with the uncertainties of economic life by developing *internal labour markets*.

Internal labour market

The creation by an employer of a stable and well-rewarded labour force through a policy of internal promotion and training.

The use of internal labour markets by employers in order to maintain consistent, appropriately skilled and motivated workforces, creates at a societal level a primary labour force. Employers which are less techno-logically advanced or which have less stable markets are correspondingly likely to encourage the growth of the secondary sector through adopting a more traditional hire-and-fire approach towards the less skilled and organised employees who are suitable to their purposes. A reaction to organised labour is also important here with an attempt to restore the flexibility lost with highly organised groups by using the 'buffer' of a weaker secondary labour group (Goldthorpe 1985; Piore 1980). This latter argument has been developed by Gordon *et al.* (1982) in a radical analysis of the role of segmentation in limiting both labour solidarity and the growth of class-consciousness among workers.

The Cambridge Labour Studies Group provides something of a check on the tendency of researchers such as Gordon to overemphasise the role of employers in bringing about dual labour market structures. Instead, it suggests, consideration must be given to the continual struggle for control between employers and employees. Worker strategies to secure advantaged work situations for their own particular groups are as important as the strategies of employers to divide and rule (Rubery 1978). In fact there is said to be a variety of causes of segmentation with a continual interaction occurring between technological factors, product markets, labour supply conditions and attempts to control the labour process itself (Rubery, Tarling and Wilkinson 1987). Research by the Cambridge group has shown that, although the pattern of jobs available is largely a matter of technological and structural factors independent of labour supply, an important role is played by social processes when it comes to supplying labour for secondary sector employment. It is such factors as the socially-influenced low expectations of women, youths, black and immigrant workers which encourage the pattern whereby the secondary types of occupations are disproportionately filled by people in these categories. And it is also the outcome of patterns of discrimination on such grounds as race or gender.

Light is thrown on how racial discrimination operates in employment processes by research such as that by Jenkins (1986), who showed that managers when recruiting employees do not simply apply technically appropriate criteria of *suitability* for posts. They also operate with notions of *acceptability* which cover attitude, manner, appearance, work history, age, marital status, speech style, personality and the likelihood of their 'fitting in'. Especially given the stereotypes of black people which Jenkins also shows to operate in Britain, these processes discriminate against the interests of ethnic minority workers. The racial and gender segregation which follows from processes such as these are intertwined with the 'fabric of work itself' not just in terms of the allocation of people to jobs but also in terms of the jobs and the organisation of the labour process, argues Tomaskovic-Devey (1993). He shows, in his US study, how processes of social closure operate against women and African Americans in different ways. A 'jobs for the boys' type of closure operates to disallow women from entering the higher paid and more secure types of job. Racial discrimination, however, operates to a greater extent at the lower levels of the labour market where whites with low skills have only their race to give them advantage over blacks. And these patterns of racial discrimination are further reinforced within the labour process itself where blacks play little part in the supervisory and managerial processes and are pushed towards the least skilled jobs.

Both race and gender are clearly important factors in how labour market segmentation occurs. And there are various similarities, in addition to employment experiences, between the phenomena of ethnic and gender discrimination. Nevertheless, it is possible to treat the gender aspect of the division of labour in societies as a separate matter. This, in fact, is necessary on two grounds:

- Having a gender identity is not a matter of belonging to a distinct social group as is the holding of a given ethnic identity.
- The differentiation both between people and between their occupations on the basis of their sex is a universal phenomenon transcending ethnic groups, societies and civilisations. It is a distinct and fundamental matter in human social and psychological existence.

The sexual division of labour

Women play a substantial part in the employed workforce of industrial societies and a conventional wisdom has arisen that the involvement of women in paid employment has been steadily rising for well over a century. This view has been strongly questioned by Hakim (1993) whose careful statistical analysis indicates that women's employment has, in fact, remained broadly stable for over a hundred years. And the 'much trumpeted rise in women's employment in Britain is found to have consisted entirely of the substitution of part-time for full-time jobs in the post-World War II period up to 1988'. She does, however, observe a sustained increase in women's full-time employment in Britain since this time. This, she believes, is remarkable – not least because it has occurred in a time of recession – and remains to be explained. It is a change of great significance and this significance should not go unnoticed as a result of its being connected to a 'long-standing myth of rising female employment'.

These observations have to be related to a more general pattern of occupational segregation by gender. Between 1911 and 1971, there was a reduction in the number of occupations which were exclusively, or nearly exclusively, filled by either men or women (Hakim 1979). Yet the separation between the sexes can be seen to have actually increased when one looks at people within the same broad categories. On the basis of Hakim's research, Oakley (1981) points out that in 1977 only 1 per cent of employed women fell into the category of skilled manual, professional and managerial occupations as compared to 62 per cent of employed men. She goes on to note that more than half of the employed women in Britain work in three service industries: the distributive trades (shops, mail order, warehouses); professional and scientific (typists, secretaries, teachers and nurses), and miscellaneous services (laundries, catering, dry cleaning).

An optimistic view of changes in gender segregation has been offered more recently by Crompton and Sanderson (1990) as they note the increasing number of women who are acquiring high level academic and professional qualifications. If this is coupled with the equal opportunities policies of employers and the general impact of feminist thinking, there are increasing opportunities for women to make inroads into previously male-dominated white-collar hierarchies. Their analysis focuses on pharmacy, accountancy, building societies, cooking and cleaning, but studies of other areas have questioned their optimism about the higher levels of these activities. Knights and Morgan (1990) in their study of the insurance industry show that when mainly female counter staff take on selling responsibilities, the older paternalistic branch managers react against this. Women end up handling minor transactions within the branch whilst bigger jobs like selling life insurance go to largely male sales staff outside the office. And Devine (1992a) suggests that Crompton and Sanderson have overstated the influence of feminism on men in industry. On the basis of her study of the engineering and scientific 'professions' she says that 'while there have been changes in supply and demand in the technical professions, the overwhelmingly "gendered" character of high-level technical jobs in industry will persist in the foreseeable future'.

These patterns cannot be accounted for without reference to patterns of active discrimination by men towards women in the employment sphere. Logically, the patterns could be explained by women's preference for the kind of work in which they are heavily represented and, undoubtedly, such preferences do play a part in certain kinds of work. However, there is strong evidence of discriminatory behaviour within employment processes as we showed in the previous section. Curran's (1988) study of recruitment into service sector jobs further supports this and she shows how both gender and 'a variety of personal attributes, social and tacit skills in which gender is embedded' are treated by employers as characteristics actually necessary for the job to be done well. This relates to more widely pertaining stereotypes about gender and Curran notes that some of the stereotypical assumptions made about the women service workers she studied were *positive* ones which saw women as particularly socially and tacitly skilled. Managers are keen to recruit what Jenkins (1986) calls 'predictable manageable workers' thereby both creating and being influenced by general patterns of gender discrimination. Detailed case study research by Collinson, Knights and Collinson (1990) shows the considerable extent to which private sector managers, often in defiance of legal and company equal opportunities policies, blatantly excluded women from what they saw as 'men's jobs' and seemingly shamelessly utilised rationalisations for this which focused on the allegedly greater reliability and ability of men. Women's biology, their temperaments and their unreliability in the face of domestic commitments all rendered them less desirable for certain jobs – regardless of evidence which might have indicated to them otherwise.

Discrimination occurs both in recruitment and in the later careers of women in all kinds of occupations. The very concept of a professional occupation, for example, is a 'gendered' one according to Witz (1992) and she demonstrates how strategies of *exclusionary closure* were used by medical men in the nineteenth century during the period in which the modern medical 'profession' took shape. Prior to this period, women had carried out tasks from which they were now being excluded. The professionalising process had a clear patriarchal dimension. Among the mechanisms and principles which are behind such exclusionary activity on the part of men, there are what Lorber (1985) calls 'ironic double binds' that virtually guarantee that women will not become fully accepted members of work communities which are dominated by men. If they are married, they are considered to be more committed to their family than their career and, if they are unmarried, they are considered 'unreliable or dangerous protegées and colleagues, because the assumption is that a sexual relationship is their prime property'.

A key theme in this discrimination is a constant reference back to the non-work aspects of women's sexual and gender roles and, especially, their roles as wives, mothers and homemakers. A study which skilfully illustrates the interplay of work and domestic identities is that of the development, manufacture, marketing and use of the microwave oven carried out by Cockburn and Ormrod (1993):

- In the microwave factory, the female 'home economists' have different inputs from male designers and, indeed, a degree of tension exists between these groups.
- In the shops, women shop assistants sell functional 'white goods' like microwaves whilst the entertainment-oriented 'brown goods' (hi-fis etc.) are sold by male assistants, this being based on the alleged affinities of women and men salespersons to the gendered interests of the respective purchasers of these two types of product.
- In the home, there is the gender politics of food preparation in which men tend to make use of the oven but only within understandings which leave the main food-providing responsibilities to women.

This underlines the existence of a very simple factor playing a leading part in the gender patterns which prevail in societies – male interests. If we note the traditional association of women with the less pleasant and the more onerous work tasks in the home and we put this alongside the fact that men in employment are more or less in control of the better rewarded and higher status jobs, we can see why men might be expected to want to 'keep women in their place'. Research among male managers, for example, shows a tendency for men to 'work late' not just to demonstrate how committed and important they are to the company, but also to avoid arriving home before the children have been fed, bathed and got ready for bed (Watson 1994a). And we can readily link this behavioural pattern to structural aspects of society if we remember that the people making the employment decisions within industrial capitalist (and indeed non-capitalist) societies are men. Through the use of the

See page 185 kind of dual labour market structure discussed earlier, both the interests of the employers as employers are furthered and the interests of men as men are defended.

The maintenance of women's secondary labour market position can be seen to function in three ways:

1   It provides employers with a relatively cheap and malleable labour force.
2   It reduces the number of potential competitors which aspiring males face in their work careers.
3   It avoids attracting too many women away from the domestic setting which would either leave men without wives or would require them to take on the dirtier and more boring household tasks.

This explanatory framework for examining how the sexual division of labour operates in industrial capitalist societies usefully relates occupational patterns back to the wider pattern of inequality which prevails between the sexes in society at large. What it does not do, however, is to help us to understand how male members of society came to achieve the kinds of advantage which it sees them having over women in the first place. To understand this is a much more challenging matter.

The first difficulty we have to overcome with regard to the problem of explanation is that of separating the particular pattern of male–female relations which exists in any one society or time from the more general patterns which run through all kinds of societies. In the particular case of an industrial capitalist society in which labour is bought and sold as if it were a commodity, we can use the notion of industrial reserve army (Beechey and Perkins 1985) or, as we have seen, the dual labour market. And the importance of considering the particularities of the basic form of economic organisation, in ways like this, is effectively illustrated by the case of the !Kung bush people of Africa. Draper (1975) observed that as these people changed from a nomadic foraging type of economy to a more settled pattern in which the women engaged in agriculture and the men in herding, so women lost the high degree of power and autonomy which they had held in the bush life. Whereas they had been mobile and independent workers in the bush, they were now less mobile and soon became tied to the home. There was an increase in domestic tasks to be done in the more settled existence and this became designated the province of the women. The men, however, developed an 'aura of authority' and distanced themselves from the domestic world. In place of the egalitarian pattern of childrearing followed in the bush came a more gender-differentiated pattern in which the lives of girls were more narrowly defined than those of boys. The girls' world was to be the domestic one.

Underlying this kind of 'particular' process we have to find some general factor, or set of factors, which encouraged these tribespeople to adopt this sexual division of labour or encouraged the corresponding pattern to be followed historically in Europe with the growth of industrial capitalism. An important starting point here can be found in the observation of the anthropologist Margaret Mead (1962) that a problem which faces all men, in all civilisations, is defining their role in a way which is satisfactory to them. Women have a key role which is defined by nature: childbearing. Men, on the other hand, have to create a role for themselves through culture which differentiates them from women. It is almost as if men have to compensate for the fact that they have no natural role as significant as that of bearing children and therefore feel the need to give themselves prestige and status through cultural institutions which award them a superior status.

It follows from this phenomenon that, although societies vary in the particular details of gender relations, there tends to be a general pattern whereby men take up certain occupational roles from which they exclude women – most typically roles in government, warfare and religion. And typically associated with this will be an awarding of high status to these exclusively male occupations and a tendency to downgrade the domestic tasks of women. These two tendencies are often linked by a 'super-structure of myths' (Pickford 1985) in which women's prime place in social life is seen as protecting, nurturing and fostering the growth of others and in which it is suggested that women's biology somehow makes them unfit to perform as, say, politicians, priests or generals. The concept of *patriarchy* stresses the interrelating of the variety of aspects of relationships between men and women – paid work, domestic work, male sexuality, male violence, state power – and how they amount to a fundamental pattern of inequality (Walby 1986).

> **Patriarchy**
> The system of interrelated social structures and cultural practices through which men exploit women.

Explanations of the tendency of males to want to assert dominance in most societies and in most social settings within any society can also be found in recent accounts of the psychology of childrearing. Chodorow (1978), for example, has argued that the social and psychological differences between men and women go back to the fact that male children, unlike female children, have to achieve their identity by breaking away from the mother who has nurtured them and by building an identity which is distinctive. This involves a rejection of feminine patterns of behaviour but also a fear of regressing to their earlier state. Masculinity has to be worked at and, as Chodorow says, because masculine identity is so 'elusive', it becomes important that certain activities are defined as masculine and superior. Control of these activities and 'the insistence that these realms are superior to the maternal world of youth, become crucial both to the definition of masculinity and to a particular boy's own masculine gender identity'.

See page 113 These are clearly fundamental matters of both human psychology and the ways in which, through culture, human beings try to come to terms with basic existential problems. To obtain any satisfactory understanding of the sexual division of labour of our own society, today and in the future, it is most important that we consider these underlying psychological and cultural factors as well as those relating to the specifics of the particular way in which we organise our economy.

Social class and the division of labour

Ethnic and gender factors are clearly important in differentiating human beings and in relating them to the general division of labour and the inequalities of opportunity and condition which are associated with it. And working with these factors to produce the pattern of social inequality in a society are the factors of class and status. The competition between social groups for access to scarce and valued resources becomes consolidated over time as some groups win out over others. Patterns of advantage emerge and these have traditionally been represented by sociologists as *social stratification*.

Social stratification

The patterns underlying the inequalities which exist between people in a society and form 'layers' on the basis of such factors as their class or status.

Different types of social structure are seen as having different characteristic forms of stratification. Feudalism has its estates, for example, whilst other societies may have groups stratified into castes or into slave and non-slave categories. The form of stratification to be found in industrial capitalist societies, however, is generally seen as a mixture of class and status differentiation, with social class predominating. This class and status stratification, together with ethnic and gender inequalities, makes up the structure of social inequality to be found in such societies.

The use of the term *class* in anything like its modern sense developed during the period following the industrial revolution (Williams 1976). Prior to this, terms like rank, degree and station had been used. The term 'working class' (and the use of 'middle class' to contrast with it) is closely associated from the start with the emergence of a category of landless wage labourers. Given that one of the key defining features of a capitalist society is the existence of such a group, it is clear that social class is, sociologically, a centrally significant feature of such societies.

Class

An individual's class position is a matter of the part which they play (or the person upon whom they are dependent plays) within the division of labour of a society and the implications which this has for their access to those experiences, goods and services which are scarce and valued in that society.

The concept of class, understood in this way, links one's occupational position and one's position in the general societal structure of advantage.

See page 69 Within sociology, there is a variety of different approaches to class analysis. In the basic Marxian model we have an image of capitalism relentlessly pushing towards what would eventually be just two classes: the property-owning bourgeoisie and the proletariat. The proletariat can subsist, given their lack of sufficient property, only through selling their labour power to those with property or capital. Marx recognised the existence of various other classes but he saw their status as transitional. This notion has been very influential in sociology, even among non-Marxist sociologists who have refused to accept the two-class model. A great deal of sociological debate – as we shall see shortly – has been about whether any given occupation, or a part of one, is moving towards an identity with the bourgeoisie or towards the proletariat. But perhaps most important in Marx is the emphasis that one's class position is not so much defined by one's income as by the part which one plays in the way wealth is created in society. Weber followed a similar approach in so far as he regarded property or the lack of it as a basic feature. But he differed from Marx in that he gave an emphasis to both markets and production where Marx had concentrated on production. He also insisted on there always existing a variety of classes.

Weber sees a class arising when a number of people share similar *life chances* in the market.

Life chances

The ability to gain access to scarce and valued goods and services such as a home, food and education.

This ability to gain access to these benefits derives from the 'amount and kind of power, or a lack of such, to dispose of goods or skills for the sake of income in a given economic order' (Weber 1968). The Weberian approach thus encourages us to differentiate between, say, a class of people who basically live off capital; senior and junior classes which manage, administer or provide professional services; a clerical and a shopkeeper class; and a manual working class. But precisely which classes exist at any one time in any one society is a matter for empirical investigation and not simply for abstract analysis alone.

Weber recognised that alongside the objective aspect of social inequality which can be understood as 'class' is a subjective aspect whereby people are located hierarchically in society in terms of prestige or status.

Status

That aspect of social inequality whereby different positions are awarded different degrees of prestige or honour.

People belong to both classes and 'status groups', membership of the latter giving a certain amount of socially estimated honour or prestige. In practice, says Weber, class and status positions tend to coincide, but he insists that this need not necessarily be the case and we can indeed see instances where some disjuncture occurs in the ethnic or religious status groupings which exist within industrial capitalist societies. For example, a successful entrepreneur of visibly different ethnic background from the main population may well not be placed in the same subjective or 'status' ranking as a member of the majority population who, by virtue of their being similarly placed in economic terms, has an identical class position.

In both Marx and Weber, social class is seen in terms of power rivalries and conflict. There is a dynamic dimension to social and economic inequality as a result of the struggles between different groupings in production and in markets. This contrasts with a popular 'common-sense' view of inequality which sees the different types of reward which are attached to different occupations as being simply a matter of what is needed to motivate people to do socially important kinds of work. Such an explanation of social stratification took an academic form in the *functionalist theory of social stratification* (Davis and Moore 1945). This suggested that occupational roles vary in terms of their importance to the functioning of society as a whole (or to the 'common good', if you prefer) and those which require of their members greater individual application, motivation and willingness to undergo long training are more highly rewarded, materially and in terms of satisfactions, comforts and status. Among the numerous problems with this theory is the basic one that it ignores the issue of power and the way occupations, 'professions' and trade unions struggle to achieve the level of status and reward which their members enjoy. It also ignores the extent to which efforts by these groups may be contested and resisted by other groups.

Figure 5.1 shows three possible models of class structure. The models each have some value and are not necessarily incompatible since their differences are based on which of the divides (the four horizontal lines in the diagram) we choose to emphasise. The divides stressed by each model do not necessarily exclude the relevance of those stressed in the other models.

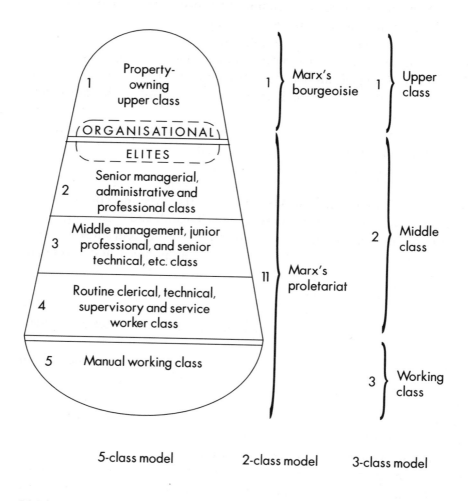

5-class model	2-class model 3-class model

FIGURE 5.1   Three ways of looking at class structure

Occupational analysis

So far in this chapter the emphasis has been on the way we can analyse societies and how they are changing through examining occupational patterns and the division of labour. This continues to be a concern but the emphasis moves more towards specific occupations or groups of occupations. The following questions can be asked when analysing any occupation:

1   How does the occupation fit into the broader structure of society?
2   How are people recruited to the occupation?
3   How are people socialised into the occupation?
4   What career paths are typically associated with the occupation?
5   What strategies, if any, have been followed by members of the occupation; have there been attempts to acquire the label of a 'profession'?
6   What culture and ideologies are associated with the occupation?
7   Does engagement with the occupation involve members in a broader occupational community?

The rest of this chapter is structured around this set of questions and the ways in which such questions have shaped research and theorising in the sociology of occupations. We turn, first, to the question of how occupations can be related to broader social, political and economic patterns.

The structural location of occupations

General principles

A great deal of sociological attention has been given to locating particular occupations within the dynamics of class relations in industrial societies with analysis varying according to the particular theoretical tradition the sociologists follow. Those working within the Marxist tradition, for example, are most strongly influenced by Marx's basic two-class analytical model and are concerned not just to locate occupations in the social structure for its own sake but to examine the state of progress towards the polarisation of classes which is expected to precede the eventual overthrow of capitalism.

Working in the Marxist tradition, Poulantzas (1975) examined occupations in terms of whether they provide 'productive' or 'unproductive' labour whilst Carchedi (1975) considered the changing fortunes of occupations according to whether they are contributing primarily to the 'surplus-value producing process' of monopoly capitalism as part of the *global functions of capital* or are contributing to the 'labour process' as part of the *collective labourer*. Another Marxist, Wright (1985), has gone beyond his earlier view of middle-class occupations as occupying 'contradictory class locations', in which people like managers are partly bourgeois (in that they are part of the control hierarchy) and are partly proletarian (in that they are propertyless in the same sense as the working class), to concentrate on the part played by occupations in processes of capitalist exploitation. He now accepts that middle-class occupations have a distinctive position of their own through their possession of professional credentials and administrative or 'organisational' assets. This allows members of such occupations to exploit others.

The recognition that the market position of occupations must be taken into account as well as their place in production when locating them in the social structure is a key one in analyses informed by the Weberian tradition. Parkin (1972), for example, suggests that the most important determinant of the rewards received by an occupation's members is their 'marketable expertise' and Giddens (1973) combines Marxian and Weberian insights to suggest that there are three principal classes in advanced capitalist societies:

1   An upper class involving the 'ownership of property in the means of production'.
2   A middle class involving 'possession of educational or technical qualifications'.
3   A working class involving the 'possession of manual labour power'.

Giddens follows Weber's preference for combining conceptual analysis with attention to the observable behaviour and the perceptions of the members of society at a particular time in his emphasis on processes of *class structuration*. In this he accepts that class consciousness and action do not automatically follow from the existence of economic divisions; the actual degree of structuration or 'classness' of a group depends on cultural and status factors as well as economic structure. Crompton (1993) stresses the importance of examining actual changes which are occurring within society and of incorporating gender and ethnic dimensions into the patterns which emerge. She also pays attention to the identities which people develop and how they seek to organise shared interests. In this spirit, Roberts *et al.* (1977) interpreted their study of class imagery in Britain as showing that the class structure of Britain was fragmenting and Marshall *et al.* (1988) argue that studies of class imagery such as this which suggest ambiguity, ambivalence and contradiction reflect objective characteristics of an increasingly 'opaque' contemporary class structure. Marshall *et al.* follow Weber in viewing the operation of the 'capitalist market' as the primary mechanism determining class processes and see three consequences for the class structure in changing patterns of investment and division of labour:

1   The ownership and control of capital is becoming more complex as family proprietorship gives way to pension funds, multinational companies, cartels and the like.
2   The differences between workers in various economic sectors are increasing as both the industrial structure and the labour force structure change.
3   The shedding of surplus labour during the recession has reinforced labour market segregation and in particular the boundary between those in relatively secure occupational or company careers and the unemployed and subemployed. As a result of this, the owners and controllers of capital are less concrete and more distant, the occupational structure is more complex and manual/non-manual distinction is becoming less salient both sociologically and among the population at large.

In spite of this complexity and growing 'opaqueness', it is still possible to locate occupations within the general social structure, not least as a way of understanding the structural changes which are occurring. It is possible to take insights from the various approaches to analysing social class which were discussed above to suggest that there are three basic factors which influence how an occupation fits into the societal division of labour and to the general pattern of rewards which is associated with it. These three factors, which are closely interrelated in practice, are as follows:

1   The contribution which an occupation makes to the carrying out of tasks which, if neglected, would undermine the general social order and, especially, the distribution of power and 'structure of advantage' associated with the social and economic system. This takes account of 'functionalist' arguments but replaces the social consensus emphasis of functionalist sociology with the important recognition of the part played by occupations in maintaining a specific structure of advantage. This factor has to be related to the next one, however.

2   The possession by the members of the occupation of a skill or other attribute which is scarce and marketable and which is more or less exclusive to the members of that occupation, or at least is believed to be exclusive in the relevant market. The way in which the occupation is controlled, through a professional body or a trade union, will be important here, not only in controlling and restricting supply but in persuading clients, employers or even the state that only the members of the occupation can or should apply the relevant skill or expertise. Associated with the latter aspect may be the third factor.

3   The existence of some traditional criterion of status or 'mystique' within the society's culture. This can be utilised by an occupation as in the case of undertakers or, especially, by the so-called professions where much is made of tradition by such groups as lawyers or clerics.

With these various principles and these specific three factors in mind, we can now briefly examine the societal location of several occupational groups and some of the issues which face them with respect to this. Before we do so, however, an important point has to be made. The See page 171 occupational principle, as was explained earlier, is only one of the two main principles of work structuring which operate in contemporary societies. It has to be seen alongside the administrative or 'organisational' principle which is the concern of the next chapter. Important factors which will influence the division of labour in the future and the fortunes of many occupational groups arise from the strategies of employing organisations, a central one being technological change.

Managerial and administrative occupations

Managerial, administrative and associated 'expert' occupations have been seen by many commentators as forming part of a new 'technocracy' and as playing an increasingly significant role in the control of enterprises as the *separation of ownership and control* has allegedly increased following the appearance of the joint stock company in the nineteenth century (Galbraith 1972). In the words of Burnham (1945), a *managerial revolution* is said to have come about. It is argued that the specialist knowledge and skills of managerial experts have become crucial to the successful running of the increasingly large and complex business corporations and public bureaucracies. The dominance of the owners of wealth is therefore undermined and a new class of professional salaried managers is said to be exercising significant control.

The 'managerialist' thesis, as it is sometimes called, claims a fundamental change in the division of labour and the structure of advantage.

Managerialism

A belief that the people who manage or 'direct' the corporations of modern societies have taken control away from those allegedly separate interests who own wealth.

But closer examination of both the claims about the separation of ownership and control assumption and those about managerial behaviour have not stood up to close scrutiny. The criteria of performance under which managers operate are, in practice, perhaps even more oriented to what have traditionally been seen as ownership interests than to any new or any less capitalistic ones. Nichols (1969) showed how more successful managers tend to be those who have internalised profit-oriented values and priorities and Pahl and Winkler (1974) showed, in their study of company directors, that the indicators of successful performance by professional managers are profits, growth and return on investment. They say that the essence of the professional manager, when compared to the owner-manager, is a rigorous and 'exclusive dedication to financial values'. The research suggests that such managers were more oriented to profit, and were more capable of obtaining it, than the traditional owner-managers.

This British evidence fits with the range of evidence from the USA and other countries assembled by Zeitlin (1989) who dismisses the thesis of the managerial revolution and establishes that the claim of a separation of ownership and control is well described as a 'pseudo fact'. He points out that 'growth, sales, technical efficiency, a strong competitive position are at once inseparable managerial goals and the determinants of high corporate profits'. These corporate profits are the prerequisites of high managerial income and status. The high status and material rewards which can be achieved by membership of a managerial occupation are dependent on the contribution made to profit achievement, or at least to the continued survival of the corporation in a context where too great a deviation from profitable performance would lead to collapse or takeover. The ownership of wealth and the control of work organisations are closely related, on the basis of this kind of evidence. It is the case, however, that ownership of enterprises is far more dispersed than it was in the past with the growth of an 'impersonal' structure of possession which has not, however, 'resulted in a loss of power by wealthy persons'; both managers and owners play their parts in the same 'constellations of interest' which are dominant (Scott 1979). McDermott (1991) argues similarly and uses the term 'ruling class' to cover the economic, cultural and political 'bloc' created by the alliances which arise between capitalist and middle-class managerial class interests. A part in this is inevitably played by interlocking company directorships whereby the 'pattern of meetings' which these involve are 'reinforced by a network of kinship and friendship' (Scott and Griff 1984). The importance of kin networks is shown by Marceau's (1989) research on European business graduates. She demonstrates how the 'international business élite' which she sees emerging uses kin networks as sources of prestige, information and finance. Power, managerial careers, wealth ownership and prestige are all closely interlinked in practice.

The growth of managerial and administrative occupations has not, then, had the degree of impact on the structure of industrial capitalist societies that some have claimed. However, it would be wrong to suggest that all managers, at all levels, simply share the interests of the owners of capital or that they are simply and unequivocally the agents of capital. A survey of over a thousand managers (Poole et al. 1981), questions both the managerialist thesis and the Marxian emphasis on managers straightfor-wardly controlling 'for capital'. Managers' interest in 'control' is much more pragmatically related to their own career and immediate interests. Opposition to industrial democracy or trade unionism, for instance, is less a matter of principled class action than a matter of defending their own freedom to manoeuvre in their everyday work as is strongly suggested by the evidence that personnel specialists within management hold distinctive attitudes in these two areas. We can infer that the presence of trade unions and any spread of industrial democracy can be seen as favourable to the particular occupational interests of personnel managers rather than threats to them.

Managers simultaneously carry out certain functions on behalf of capitalist interests whilst having to defend themselves against corporate capital (Carter 1985). This can be illustrated by Smith's (1990) study of middle managers in a US bank. A significant number of these managers clashed with the top management of the bank over organisational issues and implemented different measures from those which they were directed to take. Their defiance was not, however, anything to do with questioning basic corporate goals. Instead, their actions were 'shaped by an alternative sense of the corporate interest'. Watson (1994a) shows, similarly, how managers in a British company disputed the particular decisions and styles of their corporate headquarters on the grounds both of their own interests (a desire to be more involved in strategic decisions) and those of the 'business as a whole'. Managers are *agents* of the owners of capital and this kind of research suggests that they seek ways of operating which recognise an affinity between their personal or group interests and the interests of those who employ them. This means that managerial and administrative occupations have to be seen as holding a distinctive position in the division of labour and in the class structure which distinguishes them from both ownership and working class interests.

The notion of a 'service class' is one way of recognising this sociological principle (Goldthorpe 1982). This currently heterogeneous class contains several 'situses' and includes public service employees such See page 174–5 as civil servants, managerial, administrative and technical experts in private businesses, and employees in the social services. These people exercise power and expertise on the behalf of corporate authority yet they are 'proletarian' in that they are employees selling their services in the market. But their salaried employment is distinctively different from that of the wage-earning working class in three respects: they have relative security; they have prospects for material and status advancement; and their work involves a measure of trust and a 'code of service'. This class, says Goldthorpe, is growing and is becoming increasingly identifiable socio-culturally. Its role in future social and political development is likely to be significant given that it is unlikely to ally with the manual groups (over whom it will tend to defend its advantage) whilst it will have no 'necessary preference for capitalism' – it will go along with it only as long as it is a means to its maintaining its lot. Middle-class groups such as this may, however, become increasingly heterogeneous. Savage, Barlow, Dickens and Fielding (1992) identify three factors which influence the class circumstances of individuals within this broad category:

- Bureaucracy – their position within organisations. This varies with their positions as managers or 'professional' workers and whether they are in the public or private sectors.
- Property – position in the housing market is important.
- Culture – where different lifestyles, values and political orientations are found among different segments of the middle class.

This leads us on to consider the position of non-managerial middle-class workers of varying status levels.

Professional, supervisory and clerical occupations

It may seem extravagant to bring together such a broad range of occupational types into a single category, especially given that the notion of 'professionalism' will be dealt with later in its own right. The rationale for the present grouping is that these three occupational categories are often discussed sociologically in similar terms and, especially, in terms of whether or not they are becoming 'proletarianised'.

> **Proletarianisation**
> A trend whereby members of a 'middle-class' occupational group move downwards in the class and status hierarchy, finding themselves located in a position more like that of working-class than middle-class people.

Earlier we considered the 'post-industrial' view that advanced societies are increasingly becoming 'knowledge societies'. Such a view has led various writers to see society as increasingly 'professionalised' as the locus of power moves from commercial organisations to those occupations upon whom society is more and more dependent for specialised knowledge and its application. Freidson (1973), for example, portrayed post-industrial society as one in which the *occupational* principle of work control takes over from the *administrative* principle. In more recent work (Freidson 1994), he has remained 'optimistic' on the potential for professional strategies although he does see a more fragmented picture than previously and observes tendencies towards polarisation, whereby certain occupational groups gain and others lose within processes of organisational, technological and economic restructuring. He does not accept the 'proletarianisation thesis' associated with writers like Braverman (1974) and Oppenheimer (1973). This argues that professional work is increasingly devalued as increasing fragmentation of work associated with an extensive division of labour brings 'experts' more under administrative control and hence treats them more like the traditional wageworker. Johnson (1977) argued that both of these trends can occur simultaneously. Which way an occupation, or a part of one, goes is a matter of whether the knowledge or skills associated with it can be routinised, split down or taken over by machines and thus become identified with the 'collective labourer' or, alternatively, are such that the degree of uncertainty or 'indetermination' in the knowledge or skills is of a kind which cannot be routinised and devalued without interfering with the contribution it makes to the 'global functions' of capital.

See page 180

This kind of analysis valuably alerts us to the different kinds of changes which can occur to any occupation or branch of an occupation as a result of wider changes occurring within economy and society. In a study of technical workers, Smith (1987) shows that developments can 'go either way' even within a single occupation area and that this has implications for union activity. He shows an older pattern whereby draughtsmen felt a common craft culture with manual workers – whilst nevertheless being clearly 'staff' rather than 'works'. This gave them a 'proletarian' orientation towards union activity. These people worked alongside a newer type of graduate technical worker who was being recruited directly from higher education into technical and design work and who was less interested in 'pro-labour' styles of collective behaviour.

Divergences within a previously common occupational position are a possibility which can arise in all kinds of administrative, technical and 'professional' work with the occurrence of technological change. It would be possible, for example, for certain branches of the accountancy occupation to be downgraded through, say, the computerisation of routine operations whilst other branches might retain traditional advantages through their continued exercise of discretion and expert judgment at a strategic level in the management of capital. Similarly, in the spirit of science fiction, we might imagine the invention of a wonder medicine-machine which could cure all physical human diseases, disorders and injuries. This we can envisage leading to the rapid social and economic downgrading of medical practitioners whose expertise-dependent and critical role in the maintaining of the nation's health (and the health, therefore, of the labour force) had been severely curtailed. At the same time, it might be that the psychiatric branch of the medical profession, whose skills and mystique had not succumbed to technological change, continue to retain the prestige, income and occupational autonomy allowed to them through their role in the maintenance of a 'sane' population of producers and consumers of goods and services.

The possibility of movements in either direction, in terms of class location, have been considered with regard to clerical work by Crompton and Jones (1984). Their conclusion is pessimistic and white-collar work generally is seen as liable to proletarianisation in two ways:

1   As it becomes more involved in the actual processes of production rather than the purchasing of labour power to carry out that production.
2   As its involvement in buying labour power itself becomes routinised, deskilled and restricted by bureaucratic controls.

The seminal analysis of the class situation of clerical workers was Lockwood's (1958) study of the 'blackcoated worker'. Accompanying a re-issue of the book, Lockwood (1989) reviews the changes which have occurred in the intervening decades. The most significant shift has been that whereby clerical work has moved away from being a heavily male occupation to being three-quarters female. He shows that rewards and working conditions for women clerks are superior to those of manual women workers and argues that the increasing coverage of routine tasks by women leads to a situation where young male clerical workers are experiencing very good promotion opportunities. There is a high degree of occupational mobility – through promotion or (women) leaving to start families – and little evidence of a general lowering of skill levels. A simple proletarianisation thesis is not therefore supported.

Foremen and supervisors are a further group whose location is seen as problematic sociologically. The industrial foreman emerged out of the role of the labour contractor or piecemaster in the late nineteenth and early twentieth centuries (Littler 1982). This emergence was not straightforward, however; some contractors became integrated into the organisation as a directly-employed foreman whilst others simply became workers or ended up as chargemen or leading hands. In spite of being a paid employee rather than a contractor the traditional foreman hired, fired, set wages, planned and allocated work. This made him, says Littler, 'the undisputed master of his own shop', yet the role's 'power started to be eroded almost as soon as it had emerged from the decay of internal contract'. Incursions were soon made by various technical experts, inspectors and rate-fixers. This was followed by erosion by production engineers, personnel managers and the rest so that supervisors became reduced to a role as 'the man in the middle' (Roethlisberger 1945) in which they owe locality to both management and workers and yet are part of neither. Alternatively, the supervisor has been seen as the 'marginal man' of industry (Wray 1949) – the one who is held accountable for work carried out but who is excluded from managerial decision-making.

A study of supervisors by Child and Partridge (1982) shows that supervisors generally felt that they were undervalued by their managerial superiors and that the managerial aspect of their work was under-emphasised. These authors argue that this situation is problematic from the wider managerial point of view in that it leads to lower efficiency and worse shopfloor relations than might be possible were the supervisors better integrated into management. And, because the downgrading of supervisory work is increasingly seen as having these negative implications from the employer point of view, we cannot expect to see a simple continuation of the marginalisation of supervisors in the future. Such processes will undoubtedly occur, especially where the role can be eroded by technical changes or by movements towards self-management by workgroups. Yet in other situations, where a direct managerial presence at the point of production is seen as necessary, we can expect to see some upgrading. This may mean the growth of what Dunkerley (1975) has called the 'middle-class foreman', who may well be a graduate employee in training for later promotion up the management career ladder. Increasingly, supervisors are being replaced by 'team leaders' and research yet has to show the extent to which these roles – and the career potential which is associated with them – differ from those associated with the foremen and supervisors of tradition.

Manual occupations

At first sight, the structural location of manual workers is straightforward: as members of a working class they sell to an employer their capacity to work in return for a wage since they neither own capital upon which they could live nor possess qualifications and other 'cultural capital' as do middle-class individuals. They therefore have in common a type of work situation and a market position which locates them in an inferior position in the societal structure of advantage to that of upper-class and middle-class people. However, it has been widely recognised that manual workers do not, in practice, form anything like as homogeneous a social group as this common economic categorising suggests. To the despair of those who have believed that the emergence, in Marx's terms, of a revolutionary 'class for itself' out of a logical 'class in itself' was ever a possibility, manual workers have retained a differentiated pattern of structuration, refusing, for example, to vote solidly or en masse for a 'labour' party and organising themselves in sectional trade and union groups. Although some writers have pointed to the significance of the existence of an historical skilled aristocracy of labour, it can be argued that the role of skill differences in the structuration of the working class has been greatly underestimated.

Penn (1985) argues that the study of British class structures has been weakened by a widely accepted model of a fairly homogeneous 'traditional' working class and by a 'Marxisant' concern with class-consciousness or the lack of it. This has led to the 'cart being put before the horse' in class analysis with commentators assuming that the working class 'has existed in some sort of pristine fashion'. In a thoroughly Weberian fashion, Penn suggests that the existence of a coherent working class is a matter for empirical investigation and, on the basis of his historical study of cotton and engineering workers in Rochdale, he argues that an 'internal division of the manual working class around the axis of skill has been a central feature of market and work relations' in Britain since the mid-nineteenth century. Trade union organisation has been associated with a 'battle for skill' which involves skilled groups not only retaining rules over the exclusive use of machinery but also maintaining economic differentials. Penn's consideration of marriage patterns leads him to conclude that this pattern of 'closure' did not spill over into the social sphere within the broader working class and he draws the sociologically and politically important conclusion that occupation and skill have been 'far more central to the everyday activities of manual workers' in the industries studied than has 'class per se'. It is suggested that the skilled/non-skilled divide is sociologically and historically 'central' and Penn (1990), in a wider review of evidence from Britain and the USA, stresses the continuing significance of occupational identities within manual work.

Domestic work

In the previous chapter, consideration was given to the ways in which men and women share, or do not share, the work tasks which are done in the home. But, as that discussion showed, the amount of such work, especially if there are children, is too great to be treated as marginal to people's lives. For this reason there are considerable numbers of people for whom housework, or domestic labour, is a full-time occupation. See page 160

Domestic labour

Household tasks such as cooking, cleaning, shopping and looking after dependent young, old or sick members of the household.

The majority of full-time domestic workers are women who are located in the social division of labour with the title of 'housewife' and, as Williams (1988) observes, the definition of 'domestic labour' which dominates the literature is one of the 'unpaid work undertaken by women in their own households'. Since this is not a paid or employee occupation and since housewives experience widely varying social and material conditions in line with the varying economic positions of their spouses, it is far more difficult to locate economically and sociologically than most occupations. Members of the women's movement have been concerned to come to terms with this problem, however, and considerable use has been made of Marxian concepts within what has come to be known as the 'domestic labour debate'.

Most of the protagonists in the debate agree that housewives not only work for the sake of their husband and family but also work to contribute to the maintenance of the capitalist economic system by 'reproducing' the labour force through childbearing and by 'maintaining' the labour force through caring for husbands and children. The dispute tends to be over such matters as whether or not housewives supply 'productive labour' or create 'surplus value'. Whether or not one finds such conceptual detail of importance, one is drawn by the debate towards a recognition of the considerable importance to the economy as a whole of the unpaid work which is done by the, predominantly female, houseworkers.

The danger which arises with too much attention to the contribution to capitalism of women's work in the home is that the crucial sexual politics of housework are played down. To deal with this, Delphy and Leonard (1992) argue that a distinction should be made between the industrial mode of production within which capitalist exploitation occurs and the domestic mode of production which provides the basis for patriarchal exploitation. Marriage is equivalent to the labour contract within employment and the husband can be seen as appropriating the labour power of his wife just as the employer appropriates that of the worker. This kind of conceptualisation assumes the validity of Marxist assumptions about work and exploitation whilst expanding the category of 'work' to include emotional, cultural and sexual/reproductive work as well as directly economically productive work. But a recognition of the problems which arise in the experiences and meanings of those engaged in full-time housework are not dependent on an acceptance of such assumptions. The work of housewives was analysed by Oakley (1974) as if it were an occupation like any other. She reported three-quarters of her sample of women as dissatisfied with their role and noted its loneliness, its monotony, its repetitiveness, its long hours, its low status, and the fact that tasks never seemed to be complete. A more recent study by Bonney and Reinach (1993), however, found a majority of houseworkers 'endorsing' the role. Women with young children experienced more of the negative features of the role than others. As these researchers say, their research stresses the need 'to appreciate the diverse, as well as the common, experiences of incumbents of the role of full-time houseworker'.

It remains to be seen how the activity of domestic labour, and how it is seen in society, will adjust to two of the changes looked at in Chapter 3 – the increase in the numbers of 'house husband' domestic workers and the numbers of people brought into homes as paid domestic workers (Gregson and Lowe 1994a).

Dirty and deviant occupations

In any society there are various jobs which have a clear and often necessary function within the division of labour but which are seen by the public as 'dirty' – either in a literal way or figuratively in that they are regarded as somehow morally dubious by the public (Hughes 1958).

Dirty work

An occupational activity which plays a necessary role in a society but which is regarded in some respects as morally doubtful.

Thus the work of people like mortuary attendants, sewage workers, prison guards or even police officers can create problems for their members with regard to how they are received and accepted socially. Their position is a paradoxical one in that they play a part in servicing the social order generally approved of by the same people who often prefer to avert their eyes from such occupations – or from their members. And the same could be said of other pursuits of a more dubious or even illegal nature, with pornographers, prostitutes, and 'exotic dancers' helping to cope with sexual tensions which might otherwise threaten the respectable institution of marriage. These are often termed *deviant occupations*.

Many of the anxieties which arise for members of marginal occupations such as these may be seen as weaker versions of those which are experienced by people in more mainstream or 'respectable' occupations. It is not unknown, for example, for an estate agent, an undertaker or even an accountant to be as coy about their occupation in a social gathering as a lavatory cleaner or sewage farm worker. In the following See page 58 sections of this chapter the lead of the Chicago school in the sociology of work will be followed by taking a number of illustrations from marginal or deviant occupations to illustrate principles applying to occupations in general, recognising that, as Hughes (1958) puts it, 'processes which are hidden in other occupations come more readily to view in these lowly ones'.

Occupational recruitment and socialisation

The effect of occupational socialisation and the ways in which people 'learn the ropes' of particular occupations has been a key theme of writers in the interactionist tradition and Becker *et al.* (1961) in their classic study of medical students showed how groups facing common problems and situational pressures tend to develop certain common perspectives or 'modes of thought and action'. A peer group pressure on the individual's orientation to work is thus created.

Occupational socialisation

The process whereby individuals learn about the norms, values, customs and beliefs associated with an occupation which they have joined so that they are able to act as a full member of that occupation.

Most people's work socialisation is not as specifically 'occupational' as that of medical students, however. A large proportion of people are recruited into work and trained by an employing organisation. Although this may emphasise a 'trade' or a type of 'professional work' it is much more likely to concentrate on the specific organisational tasks in which they will engage rather than on occupational characteristics of the work. The occupational principle nevertheless retains sufficient force for us to recognise the existence of various patterns of recruitment and socialisation which are essentially occupational rather than organisational.

Occupational recruitment

The typical processes and routes of entry followed by members of an occupation.

Certain occupations will restrict their entry in terms of the recruit's age. This may be a trade stipulation relating to the requirement of an apprenticeship, which serves as a protection for members of that occupation by presenting a barrier to sudden or uncontrolled recruitment into the occupation. The stipulation of youth may also help with the problem of socialising new members of the occupation, not only in terms of learning skills but in order to aid the acquisition of appropriate attitudes and values. This is as likely to apply to a professionally oriented occupation as to a trade-based one. In some cases the age requirement may relate to the physical attributes necessary in the occupation as would be the case with professional sportsmen, dancers, models, or flight attendants (Hochschild 1985).

Associated with age requirements may be certain educational or qualification barriers to occupational entry. These may be specific to the skills to be developed in the occupation – the requirement of some certification of mathematical ability in the case of engineering apprentices for example – or may have far less specific functions. Dalton (1959), in his study of industrial managers for example, pointed out that the 'total experience of going to college' may be more relevant to occupational success than the technical content of what is learned. The future executives learn, as students, how to analyse their teacher's expectations and manoeuvres, how to utilise social contacts, how to cope with competition, meet deadlines, co-operate with others, cope with intangibles and ambiguities and make rapid adjustments to frequently encountered new personalities and situations. There equally may be a degree of occupational *pre-socialisation* in this sphere. This is suggested by Marceau's (1989) study which observed how common it was for her European business graduates to have been infused with business values and aspirations and to be inspired by the examples of their successful relatives. The majority of these graduates of a leading and prestigious European business school had fathers or grandfathers who had held senior business positions.

The relevance of educational background for entry to élite occupations and the social class and family implications of attendance at prestigious schools and universities has been widely demonstrated. Salaman and Thompson (1978) closely examined the behaviour of officers engaging in recruitment for commissions in the British Army and noted the 'inevitable residue of flexible ad hoc practices' which takes place within what is claimed to be an objective and scientific selection procedure. These practices ensure that class and cultural factors intrude into the apparently 'neutral' procedure so helping the 'legitimised perpetuation of a social élite' in this occupational élite. But family background is not only relevant to the way individuals are recruited into high status occupations, as we saw in Chapter 3. Further to this, Hill (1976) showed how the kinship system of labour recruitment survived intact in the London docks and how, at least in the past, the family networks in this occupation were encouraged by employers who were able to look to the family connections between dockers to cope with problems of training and the maintenance of discipline.

It is clear that a variety of patterns of occupational recruitment exists, ranging from the very formal to the very casual. The casual nature of the recruitment process is stressed by Skipper and McCaghy (1970), for example, in the case of striptease dancers. Occupational entry here is 'spontaneous, nonrational, fortuitous, and based on situational pressure and contingencies'. The appeal of monetary reward urged upon them by agents, friends and others encourages them to move on from work as singers, dancers, models and the like, to stripping. People may well 'end up' in an occupational setting simply because they have found no alternative. Gabriel (1988) shows this to be the case for most of the workers in his study of catering; they had 'an instrumental orientation *thrust upon* them by unrewarding jobs and the lack of alternatives due to the economic slump'. Few had systematically looked for alternatives; 'Age, lack of qualifications and training, poor command of the language, the chores of housekeeping and the need to look after children outside school hours, all compounded the feeling that "there is no alternative".'

Despite the fact that individuals may frequently appear to drift casually into a particular occupation, and stay within it because they see little alternative, the social scientist may nevertheless observe patterns at the wider level of occupational structure when it comes to the various characteristics of people who enter certain types of occupation. The dual labour market model is particularly useful for analysing the way women See page 185 and certain racial groups are the predominant recruits in certain occupations. Dualism can cut through firms, industries and industrial sectors (Barron and Norris 1976) in such a way that a particular occupation can be seen to draw on its own dual labour markets. Thus the occupation of teaching, for example, will draw more on men and on whites for higher status or 'advanced' work than it will on women and blacks, who will tend to be employed more predominantly in the nursery or other lower-status areas of teaching. It is interesting to note that many service occupations tend to draw to a large extent on the secondary labour market, most notoriously the catering industry referred to above. This suggests significant qualifications to the optimism seen earlier to prevail among theorists of the post-industrial or 'service' society.

Once the typical pattern of recruitment to a given occupation has been noted attention can be turned towards the way in which the individual 'learns the ropes' (Geer *et al.* 1968) of the particular milieu which has been entered. Richman (1983) shows how traffic wardens really learn the ropes once their formal training is over and they begin to collect 'a repository of information and collective wisdom' by means of an accumulation of 'stories from the street'. The more coherent and socially self-conscious is the occupation the more likely is there to be an initiation ceremony at some turning point in this socialisation process and the more pressing will be the need to learn the special language, formal and informal rules, and attitudes of the group as well as the technical skills involved in the work.

The informal rules, values and attitudes associated with an occupation are of great importance in helping the newcomer to adjust to the exigencies of the occupation which has been entered. Becker and Geer (1958), for example, observed the way in which the low status of the medical student within the hospital setting was adjusted to by the students through their suspension of the idealism with which they entered their training and its replacement by a relative cynicism which pervaded the student culture. The idealism which re-asserted itself later as the students moved closer to graduation and professional practice is consequently a more realistic one than had previously existed – an idealism which would not have helped the practitioner cope with difficulties to be confronted in the real world of medical practice.

A significant element of cynicism developed by the socialisation process is also suggested by Bryan's (1965) study of the 'apprenticeship' of call girls – an apprenticeship which has little to do with skills and is aimed at developing appropriate values and rules. Central to these values are those which stress the maximisation of gain for a minimum of effort and which evaluate people in general and men in particular as corrupt (the prostitute thus becoming defined as no more reprehensible than the public at large). Rules which follow from this include the regarding of each customer as a 'mark' and avoiding emotional involvement or pleasure with the client. As Roberta Victor, the 'hooker', says in Terkel's collection of interviews, *Working* (1977), 'You always fake it. You're putting something over on him and he's paying for something he didn't really get. That's the only way you can keep any sense of self-respect.' We see here a significant *emotional* element to the socialisation process and this is also stressed in Hill's (1992) study of people becoming managers. This, she says, is 'both an intellectual and emotional exercise' with the managers being as 'desperate for help in managing the new position's emotions and stresses' as for help in solving business problems.

The socialisation process which the occupational entrant both undergoes and participates in will contribute to the extent to which the individual identifies with and becomes committed to the occupation. Becker (1960) uses the term investment to conceptualise the processes by which commitment can come about. This can refer to the investment in time, effort and self-esteem which the individual makes in his or her job and in acquiring the relevant skills but it also covers a series of 'side bets' which are external to the occupation itself but which discourage movement out of the job which might break up friendship networks, disturb children's schooling, and so on. A factor which may either encourage or discourage individuals' commitment to an occupation is the career structure which they find associated with it.

Occupational careers

As was suggested in the previous chapter, where the emphasis was on the individual's experience of work, we can understand the way in which people achieve a sense of coherence in their working lives through the use of the idea of the subjective career. It was pointed out that the structural context which influences that processual self-view may be the objective career pattern provided by either an occupation or an organisation. These two are frequently related but, here, we are concerned with the occupational dimension.

Occupational career

The sequence of positions through which the member of an occupation typically passes during the part of their life which they spend in that occupation.

Different positions within an occupation generally involve different levels of prestige and give varying levels of reward of various other material and psychological kinds. We therefore tend to see careers in terms of the upward, downward or horizontal movement which they imply for the individual. It is commonplace to observe that many professional and administrative occupations provide career structures of a 'ladder' type – a series of positions of improving status and reward through which the successful individual can expect to move – but other occupations involve quite different career patterns. For many manual workers there may be little change in the work done over the whole of a working career and although a certain status may accrue from 'seniority' in later years, it is just as likely that rewards may decrease as physical strength falls off.

It is an important part of the analysis of any given occupation to note just what shape the typical career, or variety of careers, may take. We may note, for example, the following characteristics:

- The relative shortness of the typical career of the sportsperson, dancer, soldier, or police officer.
- The insecurity of the typical career of the actor.
- The risks involved in certain entrepreneurial careers.

These are all factors which must seriously influence the orientation to work of the occupational member. Involvement in the occupation of lorry driver, for example, holds promise of advancement from initial shunting work to tramping and then to trunking but is later likely to return to the earlier lower-status shunting work (Hollowell 1968). Of course, any one occupation can offer more than one typical career pattern, depending on certain characteristics of the individual and various other career contingencies (what Ritzer (1972) defines as 'chance events which occur at critical points in a career'). The high-class call girl, for instance, may progress to work as a madam, given the appropriate abilities and opportunities, or she may be reduced to the status of a street-walker – the difference between these two 'career grades' of prostitution being graphically illustrated by Roberta Victor in Terkel (1977) as equivalent to the distinction between an executive secretary and somebody in the typing pool. In the former role 'you really identify with your boss' whereas in the latter 'you're a body, you're hired labour, a set of hands on the typewriter. You have nothing to do with whoever is passing the work down to you. You do it as quickly as you can.'

Professionalisation and occupational strategies

The work which people do is, we have seen, bound up with the distribution of power and resources of society at large. Most individuals are not in a position to defend or improve their location in the wider structure of advantage on their own. Some form of collective action to defend or further individuals' interests is inevitable. A variety of ways in which people attempt to control the extent of their autonomy in work will be looked at in Chapter 7 but our present concern is with the way the members of any identifiable occupation form an association for such purposes *by virtue of their membership of that occupation* rather than on the basis of commonly experienced problems arising from their position as employees.

As was suggested earlier, the trade union as an *occupational* association is of decreasing significance as former trade groups increasingly amalgamate to deal with the more crucial problems experienced by people as employees or organisational members rather than as holders of specific skills and knowledge. The trade union strategy, traditionally associated with working-class values and interests, is essentially defensive. It is a coalition of interest arising from the recognition of a common problem of defending individuals' implicit contracts where the other party to that contract, the employer, tends to treat the rewards offered to employees as a cost to be minimised. But where the members of an occupation recognise in their skills, expertise or knowledge a potential basis for their own monopolistic control over their work they may look towards an alternative strategy; one which draws their eyes towards the traditionally middle-class symbol of *professionalism*. This, in contrast to the trade union strategy of seeking power through an amalgamation of occupational groups (following what Parkin (1974) has called a *solidaristic* attempt at social closure), is a move towards *exclusivity*, involving, in Weber's (1968) terms 'the closure of social and economic opportunities to outsiders'. It is the members of the occupational group, not a group of employees, who define who is an outsider.

Those occupations, like law and medicine, widely recognised as professions, can be seen as forms of work organisation which gave a place within industrial capitalism to those doing high status work whilst keeping them in part outside and above those processes which were bringing the work lives of so many people under the administrative control of employers.

> **Professions**
>
> Occupations which have been relatively successful in gaining high status and autonomy in certain societies on the basis of a claimed specialist expertise over which they have gained a degree of monopoly control.

The increasing influence of the work ethic in the developing industrial capitalist society meant that those upper-class practitioners in such areas as medicine, law and university teaching who had formerly seen their efforts as gentlemanly pursuits rather than as labour needed to redefine their position. We thus see the decline of what Elliot (1972) calls status professionalism and the rise of occupational professionalism. Those who had previously been 'above' having an occupation (the upper class being in many ways a leisure class in principle if not always in practice) now embraced the occupational principle as a way of engaging in work without becoming contaminated by industrialism and commercialism. The ideology developed by such high status groups existed beyond these specific occupations, however, being found among the military and senior civil servants and propagated in the universities and new public schools. This ideology of liberal education, public service and gentlemanly professionalism was elaborated, as Elliot (1972) stresses, in opposition to the growth of industrialism and commercialism: 'it incorporated such values as personal service, a dislike of competition, advertising and profit, a belief in the principle of payment in order to work rather than working for pay and in the superiority of the motive of service'.

The essence of the idea of a profession is *autonomy* – the maintenance of the control over work tasks by those doing these tasks. It should not be surprising therefore to find groups of people who operate within formal organisations or within other restricted settings looking to the traditional high status 'free' professions to find ways of developing strategies to oppose control over them by others. The concern of so many sociologists with the occupational strategy of professionalisation is justifiable because it represents one of the principal ways in which the prevailing mode of work organisation and control has been and will perhaps continue to be challenged. The possibilities of the occupational principle developing so as to reduce the conflicts and excesses of capitalism have been suggested by both classical and more recent sociologists (Durkheim 1984; Halmos 1970). In recent years there has been a powerful and sceptical reaction to this approach. Crompton (1990), however, points to the danger of an 'either/or' approach to assessing 'professional' occupations; seeing them on the one hand in G. B. Shaw's famous phrase as 'conspiracies against the laity' or, on the other, as 'islands of occupational altruism in a sea of self-interested commerce'. She suggests, instead, that we see these occupations as incorporating elements which 'reflect the contradictory tendencies underlying the division of labour' in modern societies. They are clearly involved in furthering the projects of 'dominant interests' in a capitalist market context. At the same time, they express certain norms of what Merton termed *institutionalised altruism*; 'experts and professionals have protected the weak as well as the strong, sought to restrain and moderate the excesses of the market'. Crompton relates this to the fact that market capitalism is 'simply not viable in its own terms'. Without accompanying norms of trust and reciprocity (Fox 1974) and some defence of what Durkeim calls the 'non-contractual aspects of contract' the system would collapse.

It is clear that in a society where the majority of people work as employees rather than as independent fee-paid practitioners, any given group strategy – involving whatever mixture of self-interest and concern for others may be the case in particular circumstances – is likely to involve some mixture of elements from both the trade union and the professional ideal types of strategy. Hence we see the high-status medical profession using, from time to time, trade union tactics in its relations with the government which, in Britain, mediates between the professional and the client. Sociological analysis of occupations has often sought to identify the extent to which any given occupational group is able to act as an occupational collectivity, that is, on the professionalisation model. This has involved identifying the conditions which influence the capacity of any group to act in this way. Before we do this, however, we must clarify what we mean by the process of professionalisation.

> **Professionalisation**
>
> A process followed by an occupation to increase its members' status, relative autonomy and rewards and influence through such activities as setting up a professional body to control entry and practice, establishing codes of conduct, making claims of altruism and a key role in serving the community.

Traditionally, professions have been identified by the extent to which they have certain features, the following six being the most commonly cited (Millerson 1964):

- Skill based on theoretical knowledge.
- The provision of education and training.
- The testing of member competence.
- The existence of a professional body.
- Adherence to a code of conduct.
- An emphasis on altruistic service.

However, the position taken here is that there is no clearly definable category of occupations which can be recognised by their possession of a series of traits or elements of professionalism. There is, however, what Becker (1971) has called a *symbol of professionalism*. This is a 'folk concept' or image based on traditionally independent occupations like law and medicine and, as Becker puts it, the 'professions' are 'simply those occupations which have been fortunate enough in the politics of today's work world to gain and maintain possession of that honorific title'. To acquire the professional label and the prestige and economic benefits associated with it, any given occupation will, *to the degree to which its material situation allows it*, organise itself on a basis resembling the traditional élite occupations. An occupation following the professionalisation strategy will therefore tend to stress a claim to esoteric competence, the quality of which it will argue must be maintained for the sake of client and society, and will accordingly seek for its licensed members the exclusive right to do work in its sphere of competence whilst controlling who enters the work, how they are trained, how they perform their work tasks and how this performance is checked and evaluated. The fact that many occupations by their very nature can never approach the level of autonomy traditionally associated with lawyers and physicians does not prevent occupations as varied as industrial managers, estate agents and embalmers getting together and pursuing some elements of the professionalisation strategy.

A view of professionalising processes as a form of occupational market strategy which seeks monopoly control over an area of activity so guaranteeing an advantaged position within the class structure was central to the influential analysis of Larson (1977). Larson (1991) has more recently said that her earlier work, in concentrating on Anglo-American cases, gave undue emphasis to the *market* aspect of professionalisation. In Britain and the USA it may have been the distinctive 'inaction of the state' which prompted 'professional leaders to take the initiative in organising mechanisms of closure and protection around their fields'. Alternative processes of mobilisation around expert knowledge can occur in other circumstances. She argues, therefore, that we should move away from trying to develop a general theory of the professions and focus instead on the more important theme of 'the construction and social consequences of expert knowledge'. The concept of profession or professionalisation, however, is still pertinent, she argues, to the 'relatively high levels of formal education and relatively desirable positions and/or rewards in the social division of labour'. Education is thus the linking mechanism between occupational 'expertise' and social class advantage.

An emphasis on professionalisation as a process of occupational closure and control is retained by Freidson (1994) but, within this, he emphasises how attempts are made to 'institutionalise' specialist skill and expertise in occupational and organisational forms so that they become a *resource* to be used to the social and economic advantage of those engaged in the professionalisation strategy. Abbott (1988), however, attempts to change the direction of analysis away from professional structures and onto the *work* undertaken by professionals. He observes that there is a *system of professions* operating in any given society. Professions evolve through their interactions with each other; they compete with each other for *jurisdiction* over *abstract knowledge*. It is not control over technique which gives a group professional advantage (that can be delegated) but it is control over a 'knowledge system governed by

·abstractions' that allows members of an occupation to defend themselves from interlopers or 'seize new problems' (as medicine has seized alcoholism, according to Abbott). For his purposes, he says, motor mechanics would be a profession if they were able to develop a form of abstract knowledge about the repair of internal combustion engines. Were they to do this, they would assert their role within the 'competitive system' of professions and would take over or 'contain' what are currently sections of the engineering profession.

The value of this emphasis on competition between members of occupational groups for jurisdiction over abstract knowledge is that it brings together issues about the power and advantage of people's labour market position with the changing nature of knowledge, technology, markets and political contexts. As global markets change, new technologies emerge and governments react to or attempt to shape these shifts, so certain groups within the division of labour will mobilise themselves to defend or further their interests. This takes us back to the earlier concern with the ways in which members of occupations may find themselves either losing or gaining in both the potential for autonomy in the work situation and broader class and status position in society.

See page 142

Occupational culture and ideology

Throughout social life we see human beings forming coalitions of interest and to justify or legitimate shared interests to both members and relevant outsiders a set of ideas is frequently developed and propagated, thus creating a *group ideology* (Watson 1982). An occupational ideology is an example of this.

> ### An occupational ideology
> A set of ideas developed by an occupational group, and especially by its leaders, to legitimate the pursuit of the group members' common occupationally related interests.

The ideology associated with an occupation is a component of the wider occupational culture.

> **Occupational culture**
> The set of ideas, values, attitudes, norms, procedures and artifacts characteristically associated with an occupation.

The tasks in which an occupation is involved, the occupational culture and the ideological component of that culture are all closely inter-connected. Bensman and Lilienfeld (1973) argue, for example, that the specialisation of occupational members in handling certain materials creates 'habits of mind, attitudes and loyalties' and that these craft attitudes interlock with interests and attitudes which are based on the historical success of the occupation in developing its professional acceptance and claims in the society at large.

Occupational cultures and ideologies are to be found in occupations of varying status levels. Among the higher status occupations (and many other less prestigious but aspiring ones) the symbol of professionalism is frequently drawn on. It is an invaluable ideological resource which typically assists occupational members and spokesmen in seeking legit-imacy for their claim to exclusive involvement in certain tasks and in justifying the high rewards which are felt to be appropriate. This is accomplished by pointing out how it is in the interest of clients and, especially, of society at large for the tasks to be carried out on the occupation's terms. An occupational claim is 'ideological' regardless of the truth of the claim. Doctors may or may not be right in arguing on the grounds of patients' interests against the licensing of rival osteopaths to carry out treatments, and solicitors may or may not be justified on similar grounds in their insistence on an exclusive right to do conveyancing work. Either way, the claim made is an illustration of professional ideology in action. Self-interest and altruism may often clash in the politics of work but this is by no means necessarily the case. The best way for a group to serve its self-interest may well be to do the best for others.

At the lower status levels the occupational culture is less likely to be expressed in ideological form by any official group 'leader' as is frequently the case with professionally organised types of occupation.

Any occupational member (as in all groups) is likely to articulate the culture when talking about his or her work in a way which will vary with the audience (again, as with all groups). With the more lowly type of occupation, however, the content is more likely to function in a defensive way – helping occupational members cope with problems created for them by the disadvantageous or threatening environment in which they operate. Pringle's (1989) Australian study of secretaries illustrates this, showing how women have managed to move definitions of their occupational role away from that of the 'office wife' of the pre-1960s and 'sexy secretary' of the 1960s and 1970s towards some recognition of their being a member of the management team in their own right (and not as an appendage of a man). To understand the varieties of function and emphasis found in different occupational cultures we can look at further examples found in studies of both 'professional' and deviant occupations.

A study of two occupational groups involved with the treatment of cancer (Elliot 1973) observes how different positions are taken up by doctors on the one hand and scientific researchers on the other with regard to how the disease is to be approached. The two leading positions are related to and bound up with the occupational situation of each group. The occupational and organisational positions and problems of the doctors are reflected in their adherence to a 'therapy ideology' whilst the different situation and career interests of the scientists influence their adherence to a 'basic science' ideology. This research illustrates the need for the public, as consumers of occupationally created goods and services, to be sensitive to the ideological accounts given by occupational members. It is an important question of public policy as to how resources should be allocated to dealing with diseases like cancer. In relying on the experts to whom lay persons must turn for advice it may be vital to take note of the occupational interests behind the advice which is given as to how resources should best be allocated. However sincere occupationally related advice or actions may be, they are unlikely to take a form which undermines the career investments which practitioners have made in their occupation.

Certain features of the occupational culture of prostitutes were discussed earlier when we considered some of the values and associated rules which are met in the process of occupational socialisation. The defensive function of aiding the occupational members' retention of self-respect was important here. O'Connell Davidson (1995) provides a powerful account of the daily work of one self-employed prostitute and few would read this without seeing the need which such a worker might have for personal defence mechanisms. But such mechanisms are not simply personal or psychological ones. They have to relate to wider cultural norms because

> prostitutes and clients alike are socialised into a world where particular meanings are attached to human sexuality..., a world in which it is widely held that the only legitimate sex is between men and women who love each other and that 'money can't buy you love'.
>
> (O'Connell Davidson 1995)

For this reason, there need to be cultural devices available to handle the sex worker's 'deviance' from these norms. The legitimatory function of certain ideas upon which prostitutes typically draw is also illustrated in interviews with ten Soho prostitutes (James 1973), all of whom 'felt they were helping people in some way by providing a service'. This might involve the following:

- Giving 'paid consultations'.
- Acting as a 'psychological doctor'.
- 'Helping society' by providing an alternative to rape.
- Generally 'keeping down the number of sex crimes'.

The echoes of professionalism here in what is often ironically called the 'oldest profession' are quite apparent. Similar attempts at rationalisation and enhancement of the occupational image are reported in studies of strippers who may alternatively stress the quality of their work as entertainment, sex education or therapy for men who would otherwise be lonely and sexually frustrated (e.g. Salutin 1971).

Occupational communities

We can expect an occupational culture to be especially strong and to spill over into areas of members' lives outside the work sphere itself in occupations where the work and non-work lives of its members are closely related. This tends to be particularly the case with what some sociologists have described as occupational communities.

Occupational community

A form of local social organisation in which people's work and non-working lives are both closely identified with members of the occupation in which they work.

The notion of the occupational community is implicit in the analysis of Kerr and Siegal (1954) who suggested that the high propensity to strike of such groups as miners, longshoremen, sailors and loggers could be related to their living in an 'isolated mass': the communities found in the 'coal patch, the ship, the waterfront district, the logging camp, the textile town' are all seen to have 'their own codes, myths, heroes and social standards'. The notion was further developed by Lipset, Trow and Coleman (1956) to characterise the interlinked work and non-work life of printers, and Blauner (1960) followed up their arguments in his discussion of factors which can contribute to job satisfaction. Blauner suggests that the essential feature of the occupational community is that workers socialise more with persons of their own occupation in non-work hours than they do with members of other occupations. To this he adds that participants tend to 'talk shop' in their off-hours and that the occupational community constitutes a 'little world' in itself. It follows from this that its members regard it as their key reference group in such a way that 'its standards of behaviour, its system of status and rank, guide conduct'. Blauner suggests that occupational communities arise either where there is spatial isolation or where communal identity is encouraged by the kind of shifts worked by some printers, by steel workers, firemen and railway workers.

It is clear from the above discussion that the concept of occupational community implies more than the geographical proximity of members' homes. The concept of community in sociology implies a type of relationship between people which need not, in a society with relatively developed means of communication, necessarily involve geographical identity. The essence of community is an integrated set of social relationships, a system which provides its members with a sense of common identity and a shared values system. Goode (1957) suggested that professions constitute communities in this sense, an argument which encouraged Salaman (1974) to propose that we can usefully talk of two types of occupational community:

- A community based on the occupation as a whole.
- A community based on a common geographical location.

Salaman suggests that both the architects and the railwayworkers he studied can be seen as members of occupational communities and he notes that both were strongly and positively involved in the work they did, gaining satisfaction from carrying out their work tasks, using their valued skills or from the responsibility or autonomy intrinsic to the work they do.

The suggestion that occupational communities may be important sources of job satisfaction, as Blauner and Salaman argue, is one important reason why occupations should be examined in such terms. The presence or otherwise of a sense of occupational community is also relevant to understanding certain dynamics of political and industrial conflict behaviour as well as occupational and professionalisation strategies. Filby (1987) observes how the 'independence in relations with employers' is sustained by racing lads working in the Newmarket stables by a 'vibrant occupational culture'. In spite of 'disagreements, competition, divisions and contradictions' among the lads 'the occupation of the racing lad provides a basis of a community of shared forms of discourse, understanding, experience and affectiveness'. Membership of an occupational community need not, however, necessarily lead to an oppositional 'them and us' class conflict view on the part of manual workers. Moore (1975) has pointed out that coalminers have on various occasions recognised a market situation shared with supervisors and employers in their particular industry. Elements of this became very relevant in attempts to resist state rundown of the British mining industry in the 1980s and early 1990s with events during and after the 1984–5 mining dispute showing a powerful mixture of class-related oppositional action and community-oriented solidarity in the face of attacks on a whole occupational identity (Beynon, Hudson and Sadler 1991; Warwick and Littlejohn 1992).

Occupational communities tend to be associated with more 'traditional' occupation activities. Care needs to be taken over this, however, as any examination of the very modern technologies used in contemporary coal mines would show. A study of the fishing industry by Thompson (1983b) shows how that industry is not, and never has been, a 'traditional' one – in spite of the fact that it is often carried on by people living in seemingly traditional communities. It was, in fact, one of the first industries to be developed within an international capitalist market. Recent developments in the British fishing industry have shown, however, that the distinctively capitalist institution of labour employment can undermine the effectiveness of the industry. The 'modern' capitalist trawler fleets of the big ports – which depend on wage labour and therefore suffer from all the problems which accompany standard industrial employment practices – have been failing. In contrast, and working within a set of values which combine egalitarianism, social independence and individuality, the northern Scottish fishermen, in their co-operatively-owned boats which may be worth more than half-a-million pounds, flourished. It is, says Thompson, to the community-oriented, co-operative and family-based approach of the fisher people of the Moray Firth and the Scottish islands that we can look for ideas on work organisation and patterns of ownership for the future. This may, however, be over-optimistic and the community-orientation of these areas may be more significant, as it was in mining areas, as sites for resistance to state-mediated (or state-initiated) occupational decline.

In the light of the questions which are raised here about both the decline and the survival of elements of occupational community and the questions which this, in turn, raises about the necessary superiority of modern forms of work organisation and employment, we now move on in the next two chapters to examine these modern patterns of organisation and labour employment and some of the problems associated with them. In the final chapter we shall return to the question of alternatives.

■　■　■

Chapter 6

The structuring of
work: organisations

Introduction

The administrative or organisational principle of work structuring partly complements and partly comes into conflict with the occupational principle examined in the previous chapter. The structuring of work in the form of administrative institutions or 'formal organisations' is the dominant and currently prevailing aspect of work patterning in industrial capitalist societies. The forms in which the occupational principle still survives – in certain trade-based trade unions, in certain 'professional' groups and in public perceptions of certain distinctive types of job – must be seen in the light of this.

> **The occupational principle of work structuring**
> emphasises the way in which people with similar skills, traditions and values co-operatively conceive, execute and regulate work tasks.

> **The organisational principle of work structuring**
> emphasises the ways in which some people conceive of and design work tasks in the light of certain ends and then recruit, pay, co-ordinate and control the efforts of other people who do not necessarily share those ends, to fulfil work tasks.

To analyse sociologically any given area of life, such as work organisations, we have to meet the very basic requirement indicated in Chapter 1 of fully recognising the interplay which occurs between the patterns, regularities or structuring of social life and the varied interests, initiatives and values of the individuals which create and operate within this structuring. To understand formal work organisations sociologically, therefore, we need to see them as general patterns of regular behaviour which include the whole range of informal, unofficial and even illegitimate actions and arrangements which occur. It is highly inappropriate and *partial* (in both senses of the word – inadequate and biased) to see organisation structures as just the formal arrangements which are portrayed in the management's organisation chart, rule book and official operating procedures. This all too often happens in standard organisation and management writing and teaching and, as a way of conceptualising organisations, it is as unhelpful to those who are interested in managing organisations as it is to those who simply wish to study how they work. Some careful attention to how we define organisations is therefore vital.

Following this, consideration will be given to some of the basic formal design principles which underpin the way work is organised in the twentieth century. The bulk of the chapter will then examine the various ways in which there are seen to be limits to these principles and to show how different research and theoretical traditions have gone beyond the assumptions of the 'classical' attempts to generalise about formal work organisations. Consideration of particular changes which have been observed in patterns of organisation and the management of work are not central to the present chapter. It is more concerned with the basic underlying principles of work organisations and how they are analysed. Changing organisational and managerial practices are a key concern of the final chapter but they are also an issue in the next chapter when managerial initiatives in handling problems of control and conflict are explored.

The nature and definition of work organisations

The concept of 'organisation', used in a general sense, is fundamental to sociological analysis. A basic insight of the discipline is that life is socially organised in various ways; it displays certain patterns and exhibits regularities. Indeed the occupational aspect of working life and the social division of labour are as much a part of this general social organisation as is the administrative component which we are examining in the present chapter and which is often referred to as *formal organisation*. It therefore needs to be made clear that in the ensuing discussion the terms 'the organisation' and 'organisations' are being used to refer to just one aspect of the wider social organisation of society. Reference is to institutions which have been deliberately set up at some historically distinguishable point in time to carry out certain tasks and which, to do this, make use of various administrative or bureaucratic techniques. Organisations thus include banks, firms, hospitals, prisons but exclude families, tribes, social classes and spontaneous friendship groups.

What ultimately distinguishes formal organisations, however ramshackle they may become and however diverse and confused may be the interests and concerns of their members, is some initially inspiring purposiveness. Important in this is the existence, at least in the organisation's early history, of some kind of relatively explicit charter or programme of action. Organisations are pieces of human social structure which are much more deliberately or consciously designed than are any of the other forms of human association. And the increasing pervasiveness in modern history of organisations is to be understood as part of the wider trend of increasing rationalisation looked at in Chapter 3 which underlies the development of industrial capitalism: the process identified by Max Weber whereby deliberately calculated means are adopted in the pursuit of consciously selected ends.

Organisations are being portrayed, then, as specifically purposive and characteristically rational constructs. But this is a characterisation which can be accepted only if two massive qualifications accompany it:

- The tendency within social life towards human conflict and, related to this,
- The tendency towards structural contradictions and unintended consequences.

Social structures reflect the institutionalising by dominant social groups of the advantages which they have with regard to scarce and valued resources. The stability of social structures – seen as a 'pattern of advantage' in this way – is constantly threatened by social conflict, where less advantaged groups and individuals resist or challenge the current order. This occurs in formal organisations as much as in society as a whole as does the second tendency, that towards structural contradiction. In this, the institutionalised means chosen to achieve certain purposes tends to develop unintended consequences which may undermine the achievement of the ends for which they were designed. As we shall see, this tendency is central to the functioning of organisations.

The fact that, relatively, organisations are more purposively conceived than other social forms has led to a degree of emphasis on their 'rationality' which has seriously exaggerated the extent to which, in practice, they operate as machines or systems efficiently pursuing specific purposes. Such an exaggeration has permeated business and management thinking but has also been present in much organisational sociology. This is revealed by the tendency of many writers on organisations to define organisations in terms of organisational goals. A leading textbook on organisational behaviour, for example, defines organisations as 'social arrangements for the controlled performance of collective goals' (Huczynski and Buchanan 1991).

The danger in focusing on goals in this way is that attention is drawn away from the sociological fact that organisations, in practice and despite any clarity of purpose of those in charge of them, involve a wide range of people who have a range of different goals or purposes. As well as the co-operation which must occur for an organisation to survive there will be considerable differences and conflicts of interest. What common purpose there is in the typical modern work organisation is as likely to be the outcome of the power behaviour of those in charge and of compromises reached between differing interest groups as it is of any consensual recognition of 'neutral' or collective organisational goals.

A definition of organisations is required which recognises the existence of a multiplicity of interests and of a power structure in the typical organisation whilst nevertheless accepting that organisations are essentially purposive or task-based.

Work organisations

Social and technical arrangements in which a number of people come or are brought together in a relationship where the actions of some are directed by others towards the achievement of certain tasks.

This definition encourages a view of the organisation less as a pregiven

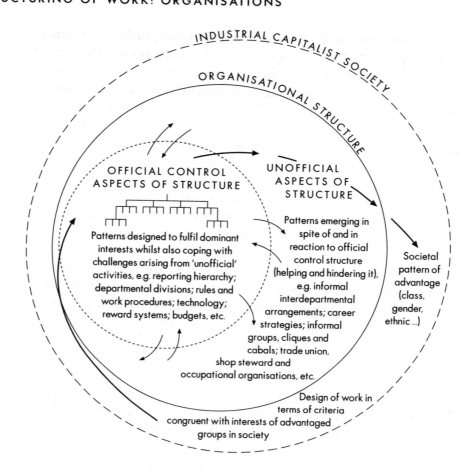

FIGURE 6.1 A sociological model of the modern work organisation

structure into which people are 'slotted' and more as an ongoing and ever-changing coalition of people with quite different and often conflicting interests and purposes who are willing, within rather closely defined limits, to carry out tasks which help to meet the requirements of those in charge. The organisation involves both 'formal' and 'informal' activities and these are represented in Figure 6.1 as the intimately interrelated *official control structure* and the *unofficial aspects of structure*. This covers the range of micropolitical activities, the fixes and fiddles and the arrangements such as trade union and professional groupings, which emerge against the grain of the official structure. These two elements of organisation structure are best seen only as conceptually or analytically distinct aspects of what is really one general organisational structure. The two are dialectically related in that they are influenced by each other and in that activities in one encourage activities in the other. For example, a payment system devised by officials to increase output may invite unofficial strategies among workgroups who choose to resist pressure to speed up their work. At the same time, however, it may also lead to some redesign of the official structure in the form of, say, the following:

- Changes in the supervisory arrangements.
- New arrangements to maintain and improve levels of quality.
- The introduction of a plant employee relations officer.

The model being offered also complies with the key criterion of a distinctly sociological perspective which was introduced at the beginning of this book: that whatever is studied is ultimately related back to the way society as a whole is organised. Hence we see the outer circle in Figure 6.1 and the recognition that organisations are simultaneously outcomes of the wider pattern of advantage in society and contributors to it. Organisations are generally designed to further the interests of those who are better placed in society, if only because these tend to be the people with sufficient resources to establish and develop organisations. In this way they tend to reflect the wider social structure. But once they are in operation, organisations tend to support or 'reproduce' this structure through rewarding on a differential basis those who contribute to them, so contributing to the allocation of people to different positions in the class, gender and ethnic patterns of inequality 'in society'.

Modern work organisations: basic design principles

Although to understand organisations sociologically we need to see them as involving both formal and informal practices, the heart of any work organisation will be the *official control apparatus* which is designed and continuously redesigned by those 'managing' the enterprise.

The official control apparatus of an organisation
The sets of roles, rules, structures and procedures managerially designed to co-ordinate and control work activities.

In designing the organisation, the management makes the following decisions:

- How the tasks to be done within the chosen technologies are to be split into various jobs.
- How these jobs are to be grouped into sections, divisions and departments.
- How many levels of authority there are to be.
- The nature of communication channels and reward structures.
- The proportions of supervisors to supervised.
- The balance of centralisation to decentralisation and authority to delegation.
- The degree of formalisation and standardisation of procedures and instructions.

The most basic set of principles which underlies the formal aspect of organisational design in the twentieth century are those of *bureaucracy*. We can consider what this entails first, and then go on to examine two prescriptive 'schools' of organisational thinking, classical administrative principles and Taylorism, which have provided managements with design guidance, respectively, for the organisation as a whole and for the part of the organisation most directly involved with productive tasks.

Bureaucracy

The main design principle of modern formal organisations — central to which is a hierarchical structure of authority in which specialised office holders fulfil specified responsibilities according to codified rules and procedures.

As has already been emphasised, the bureaucratisation of work has to be seen as part of a wider set of historical processes in western industrial capitalist societies whereby more and more aspects of life were being subjected to more instrumental or calculative styles of thinking. This See page 66 rationalisation process involved the rapid development of scientific and technological thinking and, with regard to work organisation, it was increasingly felt that by carefully calculating the most appropriate way of achieving tasks and then basing on this formalised roles, procedures and arrangements within which people would be rewarded only in terms of their contribution to officially-set tasks, the efforts of large numbers of people could be co-ordinated and controlled and large and complex jobs done.

The appeal of bureaucracy was twofold:

- *Fairness* in the distribution of posts and rewards, particularly in the sphere of public administration, this increasingly being expected in the democratising societies of Europe and America. By the following of procedural neutrality and impartiality, the old evils of favouritism, nepotism and capriciousness would be removed.
- *Efficiency* was an associated appeal, both in state administration and in industrial enterprises. Great promise was seen in terms of output and quality if large organisations could be administered on the basis of clear procedures, expertise and co-ordination.

To help analyse the process of bureaucratisation, which he saw as central to modern societies, Weber in *Wirtschaft und Gesellschaft*, published after his death in 1921, presents a model of what a bureaucracy would look like if it existed in a pure form. In doing this he used the device of the *ideal type*. Weber's ideal type of bureaucracy is often taken to be the conceptual starting point in organisation theory and much of the effort expended by sociologists and other social scientists to understand organisations has been an attempt to refine or take issue with what Weber was taken to be implying in its use.

In ideal-type form (in an imagined pure case of the phenomenon, that is) bureaucracy has the following features:

- A hierarchy of offices whose functions are clearly specified.
- Office holders subject to a unified control and disciplinary system.
- Officials appointed on a contractual basis after being selected because of their specific expertise.
- Officials' posts constituting their sole employment or career and officials rewarded by a money salary paid according to their position in the hierarchy.
- Officials promoted up the hierarchy at the discretion of their hierarchical 'superiors'.

Weber's ideal type of bureaucracy is in no sense a model of what he thought *ought* to be the case administratively. It is a device to help us analytically.

Weber's ideal type of bureaucracy

is, in effect, a sketch of an impossibly pure and unachievable structure against which reality can be compared.

Weber was concerned to contrast characteristically modern forms of administration (which he saw based on a *legal-rational* form of authority in which orders are obeyed because they are seen to be in accord with generally acceptable rules or laws) with earlier forms (based on traditional or *charismatic* authority). As we shall see in the next main section of the present chapter, Weber was in no way advocating bureaucracy, nor was he addressing himself to the managers of organisations. The bureaucratic principle which he was analysing in his historically-based political sociology was put into prescriptive form by a number of writers who were probably quite unaware of Weber's existence and who can be grouped together as the advocates of classical administrative principles.

Classical administrative principles

Classical administrative principles
Universally applicable rules of organisational design widely taught and applied, especially in the first half of the twentieth century.

Largely drawing on their own experiences and reflections, writers such as Fayol (1916), Mooney and Riley (1931) and Gulick and Urwick (1937) attempted to establish universally applicable principles upon which organisational and management structures should be based. Fayol can be seen as the main inspirer of this approach and the following suggestions for practice can be found among the mixture of exhortations, moral precepts and design principles which make up his writings:

- There should always be a 'unity of command' whereby no employee should have to take orders from more than one superior.
- There should be a 'unity of direction' whereby there should be one head and one plan for a group of activities having the same objective.
- There should be regular efforts to maintain the harmony and unity of the enterprise through the encouragement of an *esprit de corps*.

The advocates of principles like these for the designers and managers of work enterprises vary in their sophistication and in the extent to which they see their principles as relevant to all conditions. However, there is a pervasive underlying principle of there always being a 'one best way'. This can be seen in the suggestion that there should always be a differentiating of 'line' and 'staff' departments (those directly concerned with producing the main output of the organisation and those who support this process) and in the various attempts to fix a correct 'span of control' (the number of subordinates any superior can effectively supervise). This kind of universalist prescribing is of importance because

See page 250

it has influenced a great deal of twentieth-century organisational design. Yet, as we shall see later, more recent research and practice has shown the limits of such a search for rules which can be applied to all organisational circumstances.

Taylorism or 'scientific management'

See page 44–5

Whilst the classical administrative writers were advocating what amounts to a set of basic bureaucratic design principles for work organisations as a whole, F. W. Taylor and his associates were putting forward principles for job and workshop design which would apply to the 'lower parts' of these organisations. The details of the Taylorist 'scientific management' approach are provided in Chapter 2 and it is easy to see how Weber came to see in these principles the most extreme manifestation of the process of work rationalisation and the 'greatest triumphs in the rational conditioning and training of work performances' – 'triumphs' he anything but admired but which he saw as fulfilling its 'dehumanising' potential.

Although Taylorist principles of work organisation can be understood as part of the general rationalising process hastening the bureaucratisation of work organisations after the turn of the present century, it is very important to note that these principles are only partly to be understood as bureaucratic. This is pointed out by Littler (1982) who notes that the 'minimum interaction model' of the employment relationship implied in Taylorism contrasts with the career aspect of the principle of bureaucracy. An official in a bureaucracy has the potential to advance up the career hierarchy but a shopfloor worker, under scientific management, has no such potential. Different conditions therefore apply to people employed in the lower half of the industrial organisation's hierarchy than apply to those located in the upper part – which is therefore more fully bureaucratic. And this has considerable implications for the way in which formal organisations are implicated in the social class structure of society as a whole.

The logic of work deskilling which is central to Taylorism is by no means an invention of the scientific managers. They were only developing in a particularly systematic way principles of work organisation which were first written about by Adam Smith in his *Wealth of Nations* in 1776.

Smith recognised that part of what was later to be seen as the industrial revolution was a move beyond the principle of a general or social division of labour into crafts and occupations (as examined in our previous chapter) into what can be called a detailed or 'technical division of labour'. Smith recognised that enormous gains in efficiency were to be obtained if what might be seen as a 'whole' task such as the making of pins could be split up into a number of smaller scale and less-skilled tasks or jobs. Each job would be easy to learn and each operation readily repeatable. The employer would benefit enormously from the increased dexterity of the worker, the reduction of time spent in preparation and changeover from one operation to another and from the possibilities which were opened up for further mechanisation. But it was Charles Babbage, in 1832, who pointed out that this kind of deskilling also reduced the cost of labour. If 'whole' tasks were carried out then you had to pay each worker a rate which was appropriate to the most skilful or physically demanding element of the task. You could, however, 'by dividing the work . . . into different degrees of skill and force . . . purchase the precise quantity of both that is necessary for each purpose'.

Fordism

To some observers, the growing significance of the assembly line alongside the spreading influence of Taylorism is sufficient to warrant the recognition of a set of work design and management principles which exist in their own right. Henry Ford, in his car factories, is seen as introducing what amounts to a development of Taylorism in one respect and a departure from it in another.

Fordism

A pattern of industrial organisation and employment policy in which

(a) mass production techniques and an associated deskilling of jobs is combined with

(b) treatment of employees which recognises that workers are also consumers whose earning power and consumption attitudes — as well as their workplace efficiency — affect the success of the enterprise.

'Fordism' follows such scientific management principles as the use of a detailed division of labour, intensive management work-planning and close supervision and, in fact, extends these considerably in the close attachment of the individual to the work station and in the mechanising of work handling. But it goes beyond Taylorism, which tends to treat labour strictly as a commodity, in making a connection between labour management policy and attention to markets. Fordism is essentially a mass production process which recognises that the people which it employs are part of the market for its products. It therefore recognises the necessity of taking an interest in the lives of workers as consumers as well as producers.

The connection between production and consumption in Fordism is stressed by Aglietta (1979) who points to Fordism's recognition of the need to develop working-class 'social consumption norms' which stabilise the markets for the products of mass production industries. The mass consumption market has to be created and stabilised to fit the mass production organisation of the factory. It is in this context that we can understand Ford's particular innovation of the Five Dollar Day – a relatively high wage level which could be obtained once the worker had a minimum of six months continuous service and as long as they complied with certain standards of personal behaviour. Ford's policies in this latter respect are simply one example, appropriate to their time and place, of a more general feature of what has been labelled Fordism: the recognition that the workforce should be treated as more than a commodity to be dealt with at arm's length whilst, nevertheless, keeping it under the close control and instructions of the management in a machine-paced environment.

Having considered some of the principles which underlie modern work organisation and how it is designed at various levels, we can now consider how both theorists and organisational practitioners have come to recognise the limits within which these principles can be applied.

The limits of bureaucracy

Modern employing organisations, all of which are more or less based on the bureaucratic principle, use various rational calculative techniques as means towards the ends pursued by their controllers. They also use the work efforts of human beings in this way – as if they were a resource, a means, a device. However, human beings are assertive, creative, and initiating animals. They differ fundamentally from other animals in their capacity to develop conceptions of alternatives about how they live. This potential means that they are always problematic when used as instruments, as the means to other people's ends, as is typically the case in work organisations in industrial capitalist societies. Every organisation is thus confronted by a basic paradox.

A basic paradox of organisations

The means used by the controlling management of the organisation to achieve whatever goals they choose or are required to pursue do not necessarily facilitate the effective achievement of these goals since these 'means' involve human beings who have goals of their own, which may not be congruent with those of the managers.

This paradoxical reality not only accounts for many of the 'motivational' and 'industrial relations' problems which organisational managements continually experience in their work but also provides the starting point for explaining many structural features of organisations themselves. It provides the key to explaining the growth of the following:

- Quality and auditing functions within organisations.
- Management services departments.
- Personnel and industrial relations departments.

It also accounts in part for the existence of government and quasi-government agencies involved in regulating the activities of employing organisations. These are all involved in coping with potentially destructive contradictions.

This view of organisations caught up in a paradox is very much in the spirit of Weber's view of modern society and is developed from his key distinction between formal and material rationality, explained in Chapter 2. Yet, ironically, many sociologists and organisation theorists – who frequently refer back to Weber as the founder of organisation theory – completely miss the point of Weber's view of bureaucracy. They assume that when he wrote of the high degree of formal rationality achievable by bureaucratic organisation he was claiming that it is necessarily 'efficient' in its meeting of goals. As Albrow's (1970) important reappraisal of Weber's position shows, Weber did indeed recognise, in pointing to the high formal rationality of bureaucracies, their 'technical superiority' and their virtues of calculability, predictability and stability. But he was nevertheless well aware that although these were necessary conditions for 'efficient' achievement of goals, they in no way constituted a sufficient guarantee of such success. Formal rationality (choice of technically See page 66 appropriate means), as was argued earlier, does not guarantee material rationality (achievement of the original value-based goal). In the light of this argument it is indeed ironic that attempts to refute Weber's imputed belief in the efficiency of bureaucratic organisations have provided a key motivation behind much organisational sociology. At this point we can introduce some of the key studies undertaken in this tradition, noting that their mistaken intention of 'correcting Weber' does not in itself invalidate their findings. In a sense they are extensions of the Weberian view rather than refutations. The basic mistake made by many writers on organisations is to take Weber's ideal type of bureaucracy as a prescription of what an efficient organisation should be.

One of the first sociologists to point to negative aspects of bureaucratic administration was Merton, who concentrated on certain of what he termed *dysfunctions of bureaucracy* – a dysfunctional aspect of any system being some aspect of it which undermines the functioning of that system. Merton (1957) argued that the pressure put upon the individual official by bureaucracy, which encourages accountability and predictability through the use of rules, could encourage a counter-productive inflexibility on the part of the officials themselves. Rules and operating procedures thus become ends in themselves rather than means towards organisational goal achievement. Here may develop the 'bureaucratic personality' whose existence as such was questioned earlier but who inhabits contemporary folklore as the 'jobsworth' – the petty official who if asked to interpret any rule flexibly (such as unlocking a door half a minute before the appointed opening time of a building) characteristically responds with the words 'it's more than my job's worth'.

See page 155

Selznick (1966) observed an equivalent form of *goal-displacement* arising from a different source. The sub-units or departments resulting from delegation of authority within organisations may set up goals of their own which may come to conflict with those organisational purposes behind the setting up of that sub-unit. Responses to such problems involving the setting up of further departments to cope with these difficulties only exacerbate the situation as further sectional interests or goals are created.

Gouldner's classic factory study *Patterns of Industrial Bureaucracy* (1964) illustrates in a corresponding way how attempts to cope with contradictory tendencies within the organisation may merely set up a vicious circle of increasing organisational dysfunctions. Impersonal rules in the workplace contribute to control and predictability in task performance and they also function to reduce the visibility of the power relations between supervisors and workers. But the tendency of rules to be interpreted as minimum standards of performance may in certain circumstances reduce all activity to an apathetic conformity to this 'official' minimum. Should this happen there is likely to be a managerial response whereby rules are tightened or direct supervision increased – with the effect that power relations become more visible and overt conflict between managers and managed is increased. Through this the achievement of managements' goals is increasingly threatened as their control is challenged.

The rules, procedures and administrative devices shown in these studies to create problems for those in charge of organisations, are all means by which power is exercised. The so-called 'dysfunctions' arising within organisations are, in effect, limitations on the successful exercise of power within the organisation. We shall later note some of the unofficial ways in which managers attempt to cope with these problems. However, the problems which arise with bureaucracy have not just been a concern of sociologists wishing to deepen an analytical understanding of bureaucracy. An attack upon bureaucracy has been central to newer managerial discourses which place an emphasis on innovation and enterprise. Bureaucratic modes of organisational governance – in both the public and private sectors – are seen as 'inefficient and ineffective because they fail to open up and incite people's personal involvement and ideas' (du Gay 1994). The assumptions behind this are questioned by du

See page 155 Gay (see also the critique of the 'organisation man' notion). He draws on Weber's observation that the 'impersonality' of the bureaucratic role is an alternative to the pre-bureaucratic situation in which office-holders could readily do their work in a way which prioritised their private advantage. Bureaucracy is thus defended by du Gay as 'an important ethical and political resource in liberal democratic regimes because it serves to divorce the administration of public life from private moral absolutisms'. This is not to deny the advantages of reducing the size and costs of certain bureaucratic bodies but to remember that in part bureaucracy is a 'positive political and ethical achievement'.

Contingency thinking and the limits of universal design principles

Sociologists like Merton, Selznick and Gouldner raised problems about the practical functioning of bureaucracies in general. Other researchers have raised doubts about the universally relevant prescriptions of the kind suggested by Fayol and others. The classical administrative writers offered universally applicable guiding principles on the best vertical and horizontal span of hierarchies, the best degree of specialisation, formalisation, centralisation, delegation and the like. In place of this it is increasingly suggested that managements should seek the most *appropriate* shape of organisation to achieve their purposes given prevailing situational *contingencies*.

The so-called *contingency approach* to the design of the official control aspects of organisational structures has grown in popularity in organisation theory since the late 1950s. Two studies which were particularly important in establishing this new flexibility in thinking were those of Woodward (1965) and Burns and Stalker (1994, 1st edn 1961).

Woodward's study of a hundred manufacturing firms in Essex started with an interest in seeking relationships between successful business performance and organisational structure. However, it was only when the variable of technology was introduced into the researchers' thinking that sense could be made of the variations which were found in such features as the spans of control within firms, the number of levels in the hierarchy, and the extent to which communications were verbal or written. When firms were examined in terms of their place on a scale of complexity of production technology (a scale ranging from unit and small batch production, through large batch and mass production to process production) it became clear that different structural configurations were appropriate to different technologies. Thus it would be appropriate for, say, a petro-chemical company to have a relatively tall and narrow hierarchical shape whilst a firm turning out custom-built perambulators might be better suited to a short and wide configuration.

Burns and Stalker's study can also be taken to show the importance of technology as a contingent factor, although technology itself is emphasised here less than is the environment to which the technology relates. The authors observed that a different organisational pattern is likely to be appropriate in an industry like textiles where the environment is relatively stable compared to the pattern appropriate to an industry like electronics where the environment produces a constant pressure for innovation. To cope with pressures for innovation an *organic* structure will be appropriate. The structure here will be loose and flexible with a relatively low degree of formalisation and task prescription. Where conditions are more stable, however, *mechanistic* structures may be more appropriate, these approximating far more to the ideal type of bureaucracy and the prescriptions of the classical administrative writers.

Contingent factors of *technology* and *environment* are stressed in these studies but other contingencies are emphasised by later contributors. Researchers at Aston University (Pugh and Hickson 1976; Pugh and Hinings 1976; Pugh and Payne 1977), for instance, argue that Woodward's analysis does not sufficiently take into account the *size of the organisation*. The Aston studies are interpreted by their authors as indicating that Woodward's generalisations about organisational shape and technological complexity may apply only in smaller organisations and in those areas of larger organisations close to the production process itself. Generally valid organisational principles may well be applicable, it was argued, at the higher levels of management. Thus, once you move away from the 'shopfloor' or operating level of any organisation the structural pattern will be more influenced by the organisation's size and its degree of independence from other organisations (within and without a parent group).

Lawrence and Lorsch's (1967) work has concentrated on environmental contingencies, stressing the influence of the degree of certainty and diversity in the environment on ways in which organisations are structured in terms of *differentiation* and the *integrating* mechanisms used to cope with problems arising from the operation of differentiated units. Perrow (1970b), on the other hand, has argued for the centrality of technology, which he conceptualises in a much wider way than have other writers. Perrow concentrates on the nature of the 'raw material' processed by the organisation, whether this be a living material as in an educational organisation, a symbolic material as in a financial institution or an inanimate material as in manufacturing. These raw materials clearly differ in their variability and hence their processing will create different problems to be faced by the organisational structure. The more routine such materials processing is the more a formal centralised structure is appropriate – and vice versa.

There are many valuable insights to be derived from the studies briefly examined above. There are a number of difficulties which arise, however, not least of which is the tendency for the various studies to rival each other in the particular contingency which they emphasise. An overview of the contingency literature does suggest that a variety of contingencies are likely to be relevant to any given organisation. Even if we accept this, we are still left with the problem of incorporating the insights of this literature into a general sociological theory of organisations which sees organisational structure as arising out of the interplay between official and unofficial activities within what is an essentially humanly initiated and political competitive process. To help us here we can turn to Child's influential critique and refinement of the contingency approach.

Child (1972) stressed the dangers of seeing organisational structures as automatically reacting to or being determined by contingent factors like environment, size or technology. He pointed out that those effectively managing the organisation, whom (following Cyert and March 1963) he calls the *dominant coalition*, do have a certain leeway in the structures which they choose to adopt in their strategic directing of the organisation. In pointing to the *strategic choices* made by a concrete group of motivated actors as part of an essentially political process, Child is indeed providing a 'useful antidote to the sociologically unsatisfactory notion that a given organisational structure can be understood in relation to the functional imperative of "system needs" which somehow transcend the objectives of any group of organisational members'. There will clearly always be a range of contingent factors limiting the decision-making of senior managements but, as Child argues, their strategic choices are not limited to establishing structural forms. They also include the manipulation of environmental features and the choice of relevant performance standards.

In a review of the factors which lead to different levels of organisational performance, Child (1984a) suggests that there are a range of relevant *task contingencies* which bear on the structural patterns adopted and which fall under the following headings:

- Environment
- Diversity (e.g. product diversification)
- Size
- Technology
- The type of personnel employed

This last factor is an important one and takes into account the fact that managements, in the structural arrangements made, need to take into account the expectations and perceived needs of their employees if they are to achieve their purposes. To qualify the importance of all these contingencies, Child cites research which suggests the importance of factors which may be relevant over and above the various contingent factors. Particularly important is the degree of consistency between elements of the organisational structure, both in themselves and with the general philosophy of management. He also suggests that we should add to the task contingencies of the traditional contingency approach a consideration of various *political contingencies* which may apply to an organisation. These include the following:

- The general political context of the society in which the organisation is situated.
- The managers' own preferences.
- The relative power of managers and employees.

Work redesign and the limits of Taylorism and Fordism

See page 52

The human relations movement represented an important questioning of many of the assumptions of scientific management as the account given earlier indicates. This movement not only produced a theoretical approach to understanding work behaviour but provided a managerial ideology more fitted to the US inter-war period when trade union representation of employees was increasing (Bendix 1963). The common tendency to describe the human relations approach as rediscovering the social aspects of work which scientific management is said to ignore is quite mistaken. Taylor understood well workgroup behaviour and in place of his attempts to destroy workgroup solidarity the human relations approach prescribes an alternative tactic: integrating the workgroup so as to control it better.

See page 54

Human relations ideas played a role in countering trade unionism in the USA and were especially influential in its encouragement of the use of personnel counselling (Madge 1963). Despite the systems element of the human relations stance, the prescriptions provided by it tend not to involve structural redesign within organisations. The most important manifestation of human relations thinking within organisations has perhaps been in the form of supervisory and junior management training schemes. These schemes, which are very popular across a range of contemporary organisations, tend to emphasise the importance of 'communications' and the careful 'handling of people'. Instead of altering work organisation, existing structures are marginally humanised through more sensitive 'people management'.

See page 46

The writings of the more directly social-psychological *democratic humanists* discussed earlier are also very popular in contemporary management training. This approach, however, in its concern to create conditions in which employees can achieve self-actualisation, does suggest a need for structural modification. Hence, for example, we find advocacy of *job enrichment* following from the 'motivation-hygiene' theory of Herzberg (1966).

Job enrichment

The expansion of the scope of jobs by such means as

- the reintegration of maintenance or inspection tasks,
- an extension of the work cycle, or
- an increased degree of delegation of decision-making opportunities for employees.

Structural implications are also found in the work of Likert, another proponent of so-called participative styles of management. Likert (1967) advocates integration of individuals into the organisation through groups which are, in turn, integrated into the organisation's official structure of decision-making by their being made to overlap by means of their continuing 'linking pin' members who belong to more than one group.

Among the variety of approaches to job redesign one of the more theoretically sophisticated is that developed by the Tavistock Institute of Human Relations in London. This approach encourages a view of the organisation as a *socio-technical system*.

The socio-technical systems perspective

stresses that to achieve the organisation's 'primary task' most effectively, the technical and the social components of the system must be designed to take each other into account.

One does not design a technology and then fit a social organisation to it but devises one alongside the other in order to jointly optimise the two. It is assumed that the precise technical form required to achieve tasks is variable, as is the social structure to accompany it. Both can therefore be chosen to get the best fit, one with the other. Trist *et al.* (1963), in their influential study, showed how technical innovations introduced in post-war British coal mines failed to give either the social and psychological satisfactions traditionally expected by miners or the levels of productivity and uninterrupted working sought by management. This was because the technical pattern of, for example, new occupational roles and the shift arrangements associated with new machinery took away the relative autonomy of workgroups and removed the opportunity for the coal miner to use a variety of skills. The researchers devised a different approach to the use of new machinery which allowed retention of some of the traditional features of the social and cultural arrangements preferred by miners. A better *fit* having been obtained between the social and technical arrangements, there was said to be a marked improvement in productivity, worker–management co-operation and absenteeism levels.

Probably the most important single innovation of the Tavistock researchers is that of the semi-autonomous workgroup.

Semi-autonomous workgroup

The grouping of individual jobs to focus work activities on a general 'whole task', with work group members being given discretion over how the task is completed.

Work tasks are grouped together to form a logical 'whole task' which can be performed with minimal interference. The work designer attempts to devise 'a group consisting of the smallest number that can perform a whole task and can satisfy the social and psychological needs of its members' this being 'alike from the point of view of task performance and of those performing it, the most satisfactory and efficient group' (Rice 1958). A parallel movement towards devising workgroups organised around 'whole tasks' which can be carried out relatively autonomously was a 'group technology' approach increasingly initiated by work engineers. Typically, shopfloors (or offices) were rearranged so that machines (or desks) are grouped together not on the basis of similar work (drilling, grinding, invoicing or whatever) but on the basis of a contribution to a certain product or service. Thus a group of people all involved in making, say, small turbine blades or dealing with house insurance are brought together in such a way that greater integration is obtained and a greater degree of job satisfaction is facilitated by members' greater relative autonomy and through their productive co-operation with colleagues.

In the 1970s and early 1980s there was a tendency to consolidate many of the work redesign ideas which had emerged over previous decades and present them as part of a social movement which would improve the 'Quality of Working Life' of people in industrial societies (Rose 1985). Littler and Salaman (1984) identified five principles of 'good' job design which they believed typified the QWL movement's alternative to scientific management. These principles helpfully bring together the challenges which have been presented to traditional industrial approaches to work design by reformers working with a variety of different purposes.

Leading job redesign principles

1 The principle of closure whereby the scope of the job is such that it includes all the tasks necessary to complete a product or process, thus giving the individual a sense of achievement.

2 The incorporation of control and monitoring tasks whereby the individual or group assumes responsibility for its own quality and reliability.

3 Task variety whereby the worker understands a range of tasks so as to be able to vary the daily work experience.

4 Self-regulation of work speed and the allowance of some choice over work methods and sequence.

5 A job structure which allows some social interaction and the possibility of co-operation among workers.

Practical interest in job redesign by some employers has developed less perhaps from a social concern with the quality of employees' lives than from more pragmatic worries about the *costs* of standard job design principles in terms of, for example, the following factors:

• The willingness of employees to be reliable in their attendance at work.

- The degree of care showed by employees towards service and product quality.
- The amount of task flexibility employees are willing to undertake.
- The extent to which employees are prepared to show necessary initiative.
- The growing costs of a control, monitoring and trouble-shooting apparatus of quality, production planning and control and industrial relations departments.

A European survey in the 1970s suggested that the key motives for job redesign were shown to be improving quality or reducing labour turnover and absenteeism (Wild and Birchall 1975). And an international study in the 1980s of job redesign experiments suggested that managements were generally gaining from redesign through an improvement in the time and effort devoted to production, this often involving a loss of jobs at the same time as leading to improvements both in work experience and extrinsic rewards for those who kept their jobs (Kelly 1982). Kelly interprets this research to argue that job redesign efforts do not represent a substantial departure from the basic principles of work design which have applied throughout the twentieth century. He claims that job specialisation as such is less important to Taylorism than is the general intensification of effort through increasing the managerial control over labour. This could, at times, involve making tasks less specialised rather than more so. Consequently, Kelly divides job redesign efforts into three main types and is able to claim that a large proportion of these are quite compatible with Taylorism:

- In flowline reorganisation, the individualisation of tasks or the breaking up of a sequence of work interdependencies fits perfectly with Taylor's interest in replacing the emphasis on the group with emphasis on the individual and the trend towards vertical role integration.
- Where workers take over tasks previously done by the more senior inspectors, supervisors and the like (as long as these are not 'managerial' tasks) this accords with Taylor's principle of giving as much work as possible to the cheapest category of labour.
- Only the third type of job redesign, that involving the introduction of flexible workgroups (on the socio-technical and 'group tech-

nology' lines discussed earlier) represents a move away from Taylorist principles. And this is because the flexible workgroup enables managements to 'cope more effectively with production variations'.

In the 1990s there has been a rethinking of the significance of many of these innovations. Although various commentators in the 1970s argued for the need for these changes to be related to broader organisational design and cultural changes if they were to have a significant impact, they were 'expressed at a time when their implications were seen as inappropriate, unrealistic or unacceptable by many managers' (Buchanan 1992). However, over the following decade, the arguments for a more comprehensive approach to work design were 'set in a new context, by developments in product markets, changing trading conditions and new technological possibilities'. Buchanan draws out the distinctiveness of the new, more comprehensive approach to work design by contrasting the QWL techniques of the 1970s with the 'high performance' approach of the 1990s, for example:

- Whereas the 1970s concern was with reducing costs of absenteeism and labour turnover and increasing productivity, the 1990s concern is with improving organisational flexibility and product quality for competitive advantage.
- Where the QWL advocates argued that increased autonomy improves quality of work experience and employee job satisfaction, the 1990s argument is that increased autonomy improves skills, decision-making, adaptability and use of new technology.
- Where changes in the 1970s had little impact on the management function beyond first line supervision, 1990s changes involve attention to organisation cultures and the redefinition of management functions at all levels.

These changes in approach to work design are, then, elements of broader shifts occurring in the organising and managing of work. The concern with organisational cultures will be taken up later in this chapter and the concept of 'human resource management', to which these shifts also relate, will be considered in Chapter 7. The general pattern of change, and especially the focus on increasing 'flexibility', will be covered in Chapter 8.

Labour process and work organisation

The labour process perspective in industrial sociology represents an attempt to link issues such as work design and managerial control over labour to the political economy of the society in which they arise. It is stressed that organisational practices within capitalist economies cannot be fully understood without considering the implications of capitalism itself for managerial and work design practices.

The capitalist labour process

is one in which the interests of the capital-owning class are represented by managements whose basic task is to design, control and monitor work tasks and activities so as to ensure the effective extraction of surplus value from the labour activity of employees.

This follows Marx's view of capitalist employment as essentially exploitative in attempting to take from working people the 'value' which they create through their labour and which is properly their own. In managing the labour process to fulfil this function, managers are following the logic of the capitalist mode of production whereby the need for capital accumulation demands employers' constant attention to subjugating labour in order to extract enough profit from it to enable the employer to survive within the capitalist market economy.

A central role in stimulating the application of this kind of analysis of modern work activity was played by Braverman's (1974) application of it to various trends in work design. The Braverman thesis is that the pursuit of capitalist interests has led to a general trend towards deskilling, routinising and mechanising of jobs across the employment spectrum, from manufacturing to retailing and from design to clerical work. Industrial engineers are seen as going from strength to strength as they apply the deskilling logic of Taylorism to work tasks. They are helped along in this by the personnel and human relations experts who act as fellow manipulators and as a 'maintenance crew for the human machinery' rather than as a check upon or reaction to work degradation. Braverman links these work design processes to class analysis by reference to Marx's argument that the working class will become increasingly homogeneous. He suggests that, through the process of deskilling and work degradation, all employees are finding themselves in a more and more similar position and distinctions between blue-collar and white-collar, technical and manual, production and service workers are becoming increasingly blurred. Taylorism is said to be rampant in the later twentieth century and is aided and abetted by modern electronic techniques which are continually reducing the need for capitalist employers to depend on human skills and hence reducing their need to reward employees in any but a minimal and straightforwardly economic way.

The 'labour process debate' which followed the publication of Braverman's book has centred upon the extent to which Braverman's claim of a single and universal trend towards the deskilling of work is true (Wood 1982; Sturdy, Knights and Willmott 1992). There have been some considerable criticisms of Braverman. His approach, and that of people who have followed his lead, has been criticised on various grounds including the following:

- Portraying management as much more omniscient and united than it really is.
- Exaggerating and romanticising the skilled craft worker of the past.
- Underplaying the role of organised labour in defending workers against managerial strategies.
- Failing to recognise that managements may, in certain circumstances, see it as advantageous to upgrade rather than downgrade jobs.
- Paying insufficient attention to the subjective experience of those working within labour processes.

Much of this criticism has come from writers not unsympathetic to a radical analysis of work relations and considerable attention has been paid to refining labour process theory (Knights and Willmott 1989a) and doing fuller justice to the role of human agency and subjectivity. Some of the research emerging from this development was reported in Chapter 4. See page 126 Thompson (1989) points to the continuing need to develop this work and to attempt to explain why it is, for example, that workers 'defend their skilled identities even after "technical" deskilling' or why it is that workers get 'attached to routines that are seemingly devoid of self-expression'. Attention to matters such as these can help avoid the two dangers which can arise with process analysis:

1   The danger of labour process theory coming to represent a mirror image, albeit with a radical critical intent, of orthodox organisation and management theory in which the organisation is seen very much as the rationally and consciously constructed 'tool' of the owner or manager. Those in charge of organisations can too easily be seen as carefully, consciously and ruthlessly adopting policies which will produce profits and capital accumulation. To question the validity of this is not to say that, in capitalist societies, managerial decisions are not in some ultimate sense related to the profit criterion which underpins the political economy. It is to suggest that organisational and employment decisions are often made for a variety of reasons not immediately connected with profit – or even efficiency. To such factors as the maintenance of traditional practices for 'social value' reasons and the preserving of jobs and practices by managers who are looking to their own sectional interests we have to add 'muddling through', the following of habitual practices and the general ability of employers and managers alike to make mistakes.

2   The danger of exaggerating the extent to which the managers of organisations focus on employment and work design issues. Such exaggeration can result from operating within a politically radical perspective which is centrally concerned with issues of class conflict and economic exploitation. To put it more crudely: there is a danger of assuming that managers and employers give much more time to considering 'what to do about the workers' than they really do. Decisions about the way work is organised are best seen as just one element of the range of decisions which are made about finance, investment, technological change, market policy and so on. And these decisions are made within the internal politicking processes of organisational management.

A concern with labour processes continues to be significant in industrial sociology and many of those using it are conscious of these dangers. Thompson (1989) points a way forward for labour process analysis by arguing for its informing, and being informed by, a 'critical social psychology'. He has also argued for its moving away from a close integration with Marxism as a 'totalising narrative'. He suggests a more modest version of labour process analysis but retains within what he proposes as a 'core theory framework' a recognition that 'there is a logic of accumulation which forces capital constantly to revolutionize the production process'. This arises from the 'competition between capital and labour that is unique to capitalism as a mode of production'. He also stresses the need to recognise that there is always a 'control imperative' because 'market mechanisms alone cannot regulate the labour process'. In this way organisational and managerial initiatives are related back to wider issues of social, economic and political structures and processes. This is a vital requirement of any properly *sociological* approach to studying issues of work and work organisation.

Micropolitics, careers and unofficial management practices

The micropolitical perspective within organisational sociology focuses on the 'upper' part of organisations and sees the organisation as a political arena in which people co-operate and compete both as individuals as well as in a series of groups and coalitions. Organisational members are seen 'to form alliances, do deals with each other, plot the downfall or the promotion of colleagues, or mobilise coalitions' (Sims, Fineman and Gabriel 1993).

Micropolitics

The political processes which occur within organisations as individuals, groups and organisational 'sub-units' compete for access to scarce and valued material and symbolic resources.

Vertical aspects

Noting that 'interests, influence and the resulting politics ... are the very stuff of decision-making in organisations', Hickson (1990) asks, 'How else could it be when organisations are made up of so many people with diverse viewpoints and are surrounded by so many people who have a stake in what they do?' But organisational politics do not come about simply as a result of the diversity of human interests in an organisation. A sociological analysis of politicking examines how it is related to the broader structures and processes of which it is a part. It can be seen as an inevitable outcome of the way organisations are designed.

The bureaucratic structure of organisations, as a reading of Weber's ideal type of bureaucracy would reveal, provides not only a control mechanism but a potential career ladder and thus a reward mechanism for individuals. Burns (1961) in early and influential work on micro-politics pointed out that organisational members are 'at one and the same time co-operators in a common enterprise and rivals for the material and intangible rewards of successful competition with each other'. The bureaucratic structure thus has both an integrative and a disintegrative aspect. The fact that the career rewards available to individuals are necessarily scarce means that those who are officially intended to work co-operatively are likely to find themselves in conflict with each other. Although a certain amount of competition between individuals may be 'functional' for the organisation, it equally may create organisational problems. And individuals' political behaviour readily takes a group form as coalitions, cliques and cabals arise. Sectional interests may be served at the expense of those of senior management. Burns (1955) notes the tendency for two types of group to arise:

- *Cliques* which develop norms and values contrary to the dominant organisational ones, especially among older managers who lack promotion prospects and feel a need to act defensively.
- *Cabals* which develop among younger managers whose individual interests may be better served by compliance with dominant norms and values.

The managers working in modern organisations are seen by Jackall (1988) as the 'paradigm of the white-collared salaried employee' and in his study of managers in several US corporations he portrays them as experiencing the corporation as 'an intricate matrix of rival and often intersecting managerial circles'. He says that 'the principal role of each group is its own survival, of each person his own advancement'. Individuals are forced to surrender their personal moralities when they enter the world of the bureaucratic career and the meaning of their work – especially if they are ambitious – 'becomes keeping one's eye on the main chance, maintaining and furthering one's own position and career'. In this pessimistic view of organisational politics all higher moral principles retreat in the face of a logic of bureaucratic priorities and the self-interests of those who seek careers in them. Such a view can be contrasted with the points made earlier about the ethical basis of bureaucracy as a form of governance.

See page 250

The provision by organisations of career advancement as a motivational inducement is frequently systematised in administrative procedures such as 'career development' programmes, annual assessments, promotion boards and the like. Yet again Weber's 'paradox of consequences' manifests itself since such systems may well create unrealistic expectations of advancement with consequential demotivating results when these expectations are not met (Watson 1977). The potentially disruptive effects of internal promotion procedures are well illustrated in Burns's (1977) study of the BBC where promotion procedures are so highly stressed that the corporation appears to put a 'positive value on careerism, on the energetic pursuit of promotion' with the effect that performing well at appointment boards becomes more important than actually being successful in one's job.

Officially, the criteria for career advancement are meritocratic ones but since there are often no clear technical criteria to make unambiguously achievement-based appointments possible, unofficial factors inevitably come into play. Advancement is likely to be based in part on the basis of what Offe (1976) called 'peripheral' characteristics. Dalton (1951) showed the importance of extrafunctional promotion criteria in the organisations which he studied where particular importance was attached to membership of the Masonic Order, not being a Roman Catholic, being Anglo-Saxon or Germanic in ethnic origin, belonging to the local yacht club and affiliated to the Republican Party – in this order of importance. Coates and Pellegrin's (1962) investigation of factors relating to the promotion of managers and supervisors indicates the importance not of 'native ability', hard work or the 'demonstration of ability' in the explanations given by interviewed individuals of their career success or failure but of what the authors recognise as varying normative orientations. Such factors as cultural and educational background together with early career experiences lead individuals to 'adopt attitudes, values and behaviour patterns which function as important positive or negative influences in subsequent career progress and occupational mobility'. Burns (1977) again provides research illustrations of this. He shows how individuals attempt to appear as 'BBC types' through carefully managed impressions of self, thus contributing to 'a latent system of approved conduct and demeanour'. Although this was by no means uniform, it was nevertheless 'always consonant with the prevailing code by which individuals . . . were selected and gained approval and promotion'.

Horizontal aspects

We have to take care here not to stress the interpersonal career competitions and the striving for individual power outside the context of the departmental structures in which people are located. Research on the horizontal dimension of organisational power activity has attempted to explain why it is that departments or organisational 'sub-units' are rarely equally powerful – in the sense of the access they allow to scarce and valued resources. In eleven of the twelve industrial firms studied by Perrow (1970a), managers felt the sales department to be the most powerful. Perrow explains this in terms of the 'strategic position with respect to the environment' of these sales departments. In line with this argument we find various authors arguing that coping with organisational uncertainties may be the key to power within organisations. This was stressed by Thompson (1967) who sees leadership within organisations going to those who deal with the sources of greatest uncertainty for the organisation and by Crozier (1964) who identifies power with the ability to resist the removal by others of uncertainty in one's sphere of activities. Thus, in this sense, maintenance workers in a factory will have more power than those who operate the machines which they maintain. Similarly the personnel manager in an organisation where labour is in short supply or where trade unions are well organised will be more powerful than the personnel specialist in an organisation where the resource of labour is less problematic.

The above type of insight has been developed and applied by Hickson and his colleagues (1971) to produce a *strategic contingency theory of power*. This theory suggests that the power of a department depends on three elements:

1   The extent to which it is *central* to the workflows between sub-units (other sub-units have to wait for it to complete its tasks).
2   Its not being *substitutable* by any other sub-unit.
3   The part it plays in coping with *strategically important uncertainties*.

This analysis suggests that if any individual or departmental grouping within an organisation wishes to increase its access to the material and qualitative rewards available within the organisation, a successful claim must be made to being independent of other parties, irreplaceable by other parties, and capable of dealing with whatever uncertainties face the dominant interests within the organisation in the pursuit of its goals.

The location of individuals within the administrative structure clearly influences their relative autonomy and their access to rewards but it is important to note that these structures are not pregiven patterns into which people are simply slotted. Organisational structures are the outcomes of an interplay between official and unofficial influences. The organisational structures within which individuals both contribute to organisational performance and pursue sectional interests are in part the outcome of their own initiatives. Pettigrew (1973) shows in his study of organisational decision-making, 'by their ability to exert power over others, individuals can change or maintain structures as well as the norms and expectations upon which these structures rest'. Pettigrew's study shows how the head of a management services department is particularly able to influence key organisational decisions on computerisation through being in a 'gatekeeper' role – one which enabled him to bias the information which reached the formal decision-makers.

Some organisational sub-units contain functional or 'professional' specialists and these may act in particular ways to enhance the influence of their specialism and, hence, improve their personal careers. A study of industrial relations specialists by Goldner (1970) examines how several labour relations departments in US companies developed to cope with uncertainties facing those companies with regard to employment issues.

This was not an automatic process, he observed – individuals sought out uncertainties and thus created roles for themselves. It is, he says, 'advantageous to an individual's career to find such activities if they are not already apparent'. Research in the British personnel management field also observed how it is possible to watch personnel departments 'expand ("empire build") as career advantages and structural uncertainties are brought together by individual personnel specialists who see the need for a job evaluation manager today and a remunerations manager the next' (Watson 1977).

The efforts of groups within British industry, like these personnel managers, who have embraced the 'professional' label in attempts to further occupational interests have been looked at critically by Child *et al.* (1983). They consider the possibility that the growth in influence of these would-be professional groups within British managements may have reduced the influence of the more 'core' or central activities, like production, at the expense of organisations' economic performance. Similar issues have been tackled by Armstrong in a series of studies of 'professional' functional groups such as engineers, accountants and personnel managers (1986, 1993). Armstrong makes the 'structural uncertainties' which provide these groups with opportunities to increase their influence more specific than other theorists and ties them into the interests of 'capital'. He interprets his own and others' research in this area as suggesting that 'there is a link between certain aspects of organisational politics, the process of professionalisation of managerial occupations and changes in the nature and intensity of the crises confronting capitalist enterprises'. That link, he says, is 'the need for capital to control the labour process' (Armstrong 1986).

Unofficial practices and bureaucratic dysfunctions

See page 248–50

Not all unofficial or informal managerial behaviour is primarily concerned with sectional interests. Because of the contradictions and dysfunctions of bureaucratic structures managers often depart from formal or official procedures to help fulfil rather than compromise the goals of the interest dominant in the organisation. To illustrate this we can again refer to Gouldner's classic study (1964) which was used earlier to illustrate the dysfunctional aspects of rule-conformity. The same study illustrates how, conversely, unofficial rule-breaking may in fact help meet the ends which those rules were originally intended to serve. Gouldner noted the existence of an *indulgency pattern*:

Indulgency pattern

The ignoring of selected rule infringements by supervisors in return for the those being supervised allowing supervisors to call for co-operation in matters which, strictly speaking, they could refuse.

Here supervisors avoided the potentially negative effects of workers taking certain rules as minimal performance standards by their own demonstrating of flexibility in conniving at the breaking of certain other rules by subordinates. Such a pattern is very common and industrial supervisors frequently find that one of the few devices left to them to obtain flexible and more than grudging co-operation from those they supervise is to be willing to turn a blind eye to illegally extended tea-breaks, late arrivals at work and various other minor rule infringements.

A study of two government agencies by Blau (1963) reveals what he calls the *dynamics of bureaucracy* through observing the various ways in which employees avoid what could become 'dysfunctional' aspects of official procedures. 'Procedural adjustments' constitute one form of adaptation in which the officials when faced with alternative courses of action choose that more congenial to themselves, typically justifying this choice as the one more in the interests of successful organisational performance. Law enforcement agents, for instance, justified their preference not to obey the rule of officially reporting bribes which were offered to them on the grounds that keeping the offer to themselves gave them a psychological advantage over the offender which would help them complete their investigations. Another tactic is to redefine a rule or procedure in a way which 'deliberately sacrifices the original objective of a procedure in order to achieve another organisational objective more effectively' as in the case of the employment agents who more or less abandoned counselling clients in order to concentrate on getting them speedily placed in jobs. In reaction to this type of unofficial activity, Blau observes, managerial attempts are made to elaborate or 'amplify' procedures. These, in turn, lead to further unofficial adjustments. Here we see an ongoing dialectical relationship between what is here called the official and the unofficial aspects of the organisation. In the end all this helps the functioning of the organisation through accommodating the interests and preferences of employees to the wider purposes of those in charge of the organisation.

Ambiguity and decision processes

It is increasingly being recognised by organisation theorists that social scientists are prone to see far more rationality in organisational activities and arrangements, in the sense of fully-calculated goal-oriented and purposive thinking, than is justified. As Perrow (1977) puts it 'a great deal of organisational life is influenced by sheer chance, accident and luck'; that most decisions are ambiguous and 'preference orderings incoherent'; that sub-systems are very loosely connected and that 'most attempts at social control are clumsy and unpredictable'.

A theoretical starting point for this kind of thinking is often found in the suggestion of Simon (1957) that human rationality is bounded.

> ### Bounded rationality
> Human reasoning and decision-making is restricted in its scope by the fact that human beings have both perceptual and information-processing limits.

Human beings can only 'take in' so many data and can only mentally manipulate them to a limited extent. As Weick (1979) expresses it, there is little viewing of all possible circumstances and a criterion of 'sufficiency' is applied with people dealing with the 'here and now in a way which involves least possible effort'. This kind of insight was incorporated into the 'behavioural economics' of Cyert and March (1963) where 'search procedures' are shown to be essentially 'simple-minded' (in that the search for a new solution to a problem stays close to the old solution) and as taking place within the process of coalition-manoeuvring which constitutes the norm in organisations.

March and Olsen (1976) emphasise the ambiguity of organisational situations, arguing that there is typically ambiguity about the following matters:

- What objectives are meant to be set.
- The nature of the technologies which are used.
- The state of the environment.
- Knowledge about the past – much history is being reconstructed or twisted.
- The involvement of the individuals working in the organisation – their attention varies and the pattern of participation is uncertain and ever-changing.

Because individuals have a range of interests of their own, they come to use decision-making situations or 'choice opportunities' as occasions for doing much more than simply making decisions, say March and Olsen. Decision processes are occasions which people may use in a variety of ways:

- To fulfil duties.
- To meet commitments.
- To justify themselves.
- To distribute glory and blame.
- To exercise, challenge and reaffirm friendships.
- To seek power and status.
- To further personal or group interests.
- To simply have a good time and take pleasure in the decision-making process.

On the basis of their study of US universities, which they describe as 'organised anarchies', Cohen, March and Olsen (1972) developed their 'garbage can model of organisational choice'. The decision opportunity operates like a dustbin because the eventual outcome is a result of what happens to have been thrown into the bin. The following 'garbage' may be included:

- Problems which are around at the time.
- Solutions which are available and might be attached to those problems.

- The people who happen to be around and the amount of time those people have available.

On decision-making occasions we therefore get choices looking for problems, issues and feelings looking for decision situations, solutions looking for issues and decision-makers looking for work. Because there are so many types of garbage being thrown in, conventional rational and analytical processes will have difficulty in coping. Hence, March and Olsen (1976) advocate supplementing the 'technology of reason' with a 'technology of foolishness'. In this, organisational participants relax the normal rules and 'playfully' experiment.

Conceptual work of this kind can be seen to fit with the findings of those who have empirically examined the nature of the work which is done by managers in organisations. Carlson (1951) showed that his sample of managing directors were rarely alone and uninterrupted for periods long enough to engage in systematic analysis and thought. On the basis of a review of this kind of study, including a series of his own, Mintzberg (1973) argued that the manager's job is not one which 'breeds reflective planners'. Instead it produces 'adaptive information manipulators who favour a stimulus-response milieu'. Hence, managers gravitate towards the current, the specific and the well-defined and they prefer 'gossip, hearsay, speculation to routine reports'. Managerial work is thus seen as opportunistic, habitual and almost 'instinctual' but, as the research of Kotter (1982) suggests, this may not reflect an inappropriate fondness for simply muddling-along but indicates a managerial recognition that their key concern has to be with developing and maintaining a network of relationships with other people in order to obtain the level of co-operation needed to get the job done. Managerial work is essentially social rather than fundamentally analytical.

Organisations, environments and effectiveness

Sociological perspectives typically focus on the social and class environments of organisations. However, when those managing organisations think about their own organisational environment in a day-to-day sense they are much more likely to focus on the threats and opportunities which they perceive in the behaviour of other organisations, be these competitors, suppliers, the state, trade unions, pressure groups or the communication media. All of these can create the kinds of uncertainties which were discussed in the above analysis of intra-organisational power. Organisational leaders do not simply react passively to problems in the environment but, as Child argued in his critique of contingency theory, actions are taken as an outcome of internal political processes within management and 'strategic choices' are made with regard to the environment. Organisations adopt *external domination strategies* (McNeill 1978) to achieve a degree of administrative predictability in the face of the inherent unpredictability of the market logic of the capitalist market environment. Consequently, we observe the managements of large organisations seeking to influence governments, legislatures and local authorities and we see them attempting to manipulate the affairs of smaller or weaker organisations as well as influencing their clients and consumers in ways ranging from advertising to bribery. See page 252

One way of considering the relationship of organisations to other organisations in the environment is to regard them as involved in a process of natural selection: a fight for survival within the ecological system of which they are a part. This line is taken as part of the *population ecology* approach (Carroll 1988; Morgan 1990). Here, organisations are seen as adapting and evolving in order to survive within the organisational population of which they are a part. They go through both planned and unplanned 'variations' in their form, and, largely through processes of competition, the environment 'selects' the form which best suits the organisation. Organisations then 'retain' the form which best suits their particular 'niche' or 'domain', this retention process including all those normal organisational practices – from the use of operating manuals to socialisation activities – which organisations follow to maintain stability.

With *resource dependence analysis* (Pfeffer and Salancik 1978; Watson 1986) and in the *strategic exchange* perspective (Watson 1994a) the determinist and biological problems of the above approach are avoided whilst the essential idea of organisational strategies being ultimately to do with a fight for survival is retained. Organisations are not seen here as simply competing with others but as depending on a whole series of other organisations (state, client bodies, pressure groups, trade unions and so on) as well as on various managerial and employee internal constituencies for the supply of resources upon which their continued life depends.

Internal micropolitical and industrial relations processes are thus inter-twined with market and other macropolitical processes.

In the strategic exchange perspective, organisational effectiveness is seen, not as the making of profits, the curing of patients, the educating of pupils *per se*, but as the satisfying of the demands of resource-supplying constituencies to the level below which the constituencies would with-draw resources from the organisation and thus threaten its survival. At particular times particular groups would have more pull than others so that managements have to deal first with the currently most 'strategic constituency'. Thus a manufacturing organisation located in a capitalist political economy in which investors demanded profits of a certain level before they would continue their investment would be effective only if it produced those profits, although it would also need to pay employees enough to get the required level of performance, comply with the state and local laws, and so on. However, a similar enterprise in a command economy in which ruling groups demanded output at any cost, would be effective, however inefficiently it performed, as long as it kept those groups happy and did not lose the support of other resource suppliers. Effectiveness is thus a contingent matter and not an essential quality which an organisation either possesses or lacks.

This approach has the virtue of recognising the interplay between human initiatives and structural constraints vital to the sociological perspective. It also successfully relates the 'micro' or small-scale pro-cesses of organisational functioning to the 'macro' or political-economic dimension of societal processes. And it puts a very necessary stress on the power dimension of all social life. What now needs to be added to the attention given to political processes in social life is attention to the ways in which people create meaning for themselves and others in the world and develop cultures.

Organisations, meanings and culture

An important strand in sociological analysis is that which, instead of looking at social or organisational structures as systems, puts the emphasis on the socially significant actions of individuals and groups and upon the patterns of interaction between people. Especially influential in arguing for this type of approach in the sociology of organisations has been Silverman (1970, 1994) and the basic insight drawn upon is that which conceives of social arrangements – be they societies, organisations or groups – not as pregiven structures into which people are slotted but as the outcome of the interactive patterns of human activity. Organisations are often experienced as if they are 'things' which exist outside and prior to human activity but what are really being experienced are institutional processes. And the human actor is always implicated in those processes rather than existing merely as a passive object upon which the process works.

The organisation can be seen as being continually negotiated and renegotiated by the inter-subjective relating of its members to each other. It is, in Silverman's (1970) words, 'the outcome of motivated people attempting to resolve their own problems' and is better seen, according to Bittner (1974) as a common-sense construct of ordinary people than as a scientific concept to be used unproblematically by the social scientist. According to this ethnomethodological position, the social scientist has to be careful about confusing topic and resource. What have to be studied are the human processes whereby organisational meanings are created rather than organisations as solid entities. Thus, for example, organisational rules or procedures are not simply followed by people because 'the organisation' requires it. Rather, people more or less comply with rules because they recognise a set of expectations that they should, with a greater or lesser degree of willingness, obey. But they typically do this in a way which, as far as possible, suits their own current purposes or projects. *Institutional theories* of organisations (Perrow 1986; Dimaggio 1988) examine how organisations take the shape they do because people draw from the culture around them value-based notions of how things should be organised. Thus human culture and value-oriented interpretations are more significant factors in shaping organisations than either contingencies like size or technology or pressure from the organisation's ecological (or resource dependent) context.

The pattern of expectations is not to be seen as a politically neutral matter. Meyer and Rowan (1977) point to the significance in the modern world of the *rational myth* of the organisation, whereby rules in organisations are institutionalised in a form where they appear to be neutral technical matters. Their connection to values or interests is thus obscured. This 'institutional approach' emphasises the extent to which common understandings in the culture outside the organisation come to be 'culturally embedded' within the organisation (Zucker 1988). The meanings and expectations which prevail in *any given organisational setting* are partly imposed upon organisational members by those holding power and are partly negotiated between the variety of parties involved in that situation. Those with power, and especially the organisation's management, attempt to create definitions of situations among the employees which make the prevailing pattern of power, and distribution of scarce and valued resources, acceptable. In Weber's terms, power is made legitimate and thus converted to 'authority'. Hence, managerial work is very much involved in the creation of meanings for organisational members although these are not meanings which can ever be unilaterally imposed. All realities are to some extent negotiated but a very significant trend in management thought in the latter part of the twentieth century has been one in which managers and employers are persuaded that the most effective or 'excellent' organisations are those which have strong cultures – patterns of meaning which enable employees to make their own lives significant through working towards the purposes of their employers.

A definition of organisational culture can be developed from the general definition of human culture offered in Chapter 3:

Organisational culture

The system of meanings which are shared by members of an organisation and which defines what is good and bad, right and wrong and what are the appropriate ways for the members of the organisation to think and behave.

In practice, the culture of any organisation can be either

- clear, tight and coherent or
- muddled, loose and vague.

And it can be either

- oriented towards the official and dominant purposes of those in charge or

- function as an oppositional ethos encouraging a clash between the expectations and purposes of senior members and the rest.

The potential for the performance of an organisation, in terms of the interests of the senior organisers, of an organisational culture which is both clear and coherent and which is oriented towards the preferences of these senior members has been increasingly recognised by management researchers and by managements themselves. A theoretical interest in organisational cultures can be traced back to Selznick's (1949, 1957) contrast between the mechanical idea of an 'organisation' and the more culturally developed 'institution' (an idea which also influenced the institutional theorists considered above). Organisations are set up to act as tools to meet certain purposes, he argues, but a process of *institutional-isation* occurs whereby the organisation becomes a more responsive and adaptive social organism with an identity and a set of values. These integrate the organisation in such a way that it has significance for its members which is far greater than simply being involved in fulfilling the tasks for which it was originally designed. The management is centrally involved in moulding what Selznick calls the 'character' of the organis-ation. Although Selznick does not formally use the concept of 'culture', his thinking was taken up by the authors of one of the most widely-read management books of all time, Peters and Waterman (1982), who argued that the US business organisations which they identified as outstanding or 'excellent' were characterised by several key features. These were not, as many might have expected, the rigorous use of techniques of organisational design, of financial planning, or of computerised control systems. Outstanding business success came, they argue, from reliance on simple structures, simple strategies, simple goals and simple communi-cation. And the key to managing in a basically simple way in what are often large and potentially complex organisations is the use of a clear and 'tight' culture. The stronger the culture, in which shared values would be communicated through 'rich tapestries of anecdote, myth and fairy tale', and the more it was directed towards the marketplace, the 'less need there was for policy manuals, organisation charts, or detailed procedures and rules'.

These ideas had a substantial impact upon management thinking so that, by the mid-1990s, it became almost normal for the managements of the larger organisations in Britain and the USA to frame their restructuring activities in terms of 'changing culture' or 'managing through values'. Where close research on organisations adopting such approaches has emerged, the picture looks far more complex than the widely-read prescriptive managerial texts would suggest. A study of managerial processes in a British telecommunications manufacturing plant shows how a 'discourse' of culture change, personal development and employee 'development' came to clash with alternative discourses which reflected corporate interests in cost controls and tight corporate control (Watson 1994a, 1995b). The 'progressive' culture-based ideas in fact became counter-productive as the expectations which they created came to be undermined by corporate policies leading, for example, to regular redundancies among employees.

A similarly ethnographic study of an organisation attempting to 'mould' its culture and its employee (Kunda 1992) looks in detail at processes of 'normative control' through which attempts are made to win the deep commitment of technical workers to corporate goals and values. Kunda expresses strong concern about what he sees as managerial attempts to channel people's feelings, thoughts and ways of seeing the world. Yet he does show how individuals tend to balance an absorption of some of this with a degree of personal distancing from the corporate embrace. Casey (1995) shows a degree of this too in her study of another US company she calls Hephaestus, one which promoted an 'official discourse' defining an 'ideal Hephaestus person' who worked within 'values of diligence, dedication, loyalty, commitment and the ability to be a good team-player, to be adaptive and flexible, and to be a good, somewhat conservative, citizen'. However, in spite of limited evidence of resistance and 'defence of self' among employees, Casey notes a 'homogeneity of view and values and a conformity of self presentation'. As the language practices and values 'become everyday parlance and employees act out the desired characteristics most come to own these practices and roles of the ideal Hephaestus employee'.

Employers and managers engaging in these ways with issues of employees' self-identities and the values through which they judge the rights and wrongs of their daily lives must be a matter of serious concern. To attempt to mould cultures – given that culture in its broad sense provides the roots of human morality, social identity and existential security – is indeed to enter 'deep and dangerous waters' (Watson 1994a). The 'guiding aim and abiding concern' of what Willmott (1995) calls *corporate culturism* is to win the 'hearts and minds' of employees and Willmott expresses deep anxiety about corporate attempts to 'colonise the affective domain' and to achieve 'the governance of the employee's soul'. The US research of Kunda and Casey perhaps gives grounds for this pessimism. The British evidence, which is still limited however, suggests a greater degree of scepticism. The employees of ZTC (Watson 1994a) were cautious about, although not universally dismissive of, the management's 'winning culture' and the workers in a British company taken over by a US organisation dismissed the new management's corporate culture campaign as 'yankee bullshit' and 'propaganda' (Collinson 1994).

Such issues of resistance and the way processes of work and its organisation involve both co-operation and conflict, resistance and control are a central concern of the next chapter.

■　■　■

Conflict, challenge and control in work

Introduction

To do justice to the subtlety and the complexities of the phenomena which it studies, sociology has to take account of the interplay which occurs in social life between initiative and constraint, involving recognition of the importance of both structural factors and the experiences and intentions of individuals. The emphasis in the preceding two chapters has been on tendencies towards structure, in the form of occupations and organisations. The accounts given of these tendencies towards a patterning in work life did not, however, reify these structures, giving them a concrete existence over and above the human efforts which create them. These structural tendencies were, rather, seen as the outcomes of various human processes of initiative, power-seeking and negotiation.

Occupational and organisational structures reflect to a large degree the greater success of some social groups compared to others in securing control over their own lives and over parts of the lives of others and hence in gaining access to scarce and generally desirable rewards. The emphasis of the present chapter will be on various reactions to these efforts to control and, inevitably – given the continuous dialectic which occurs between initiative and structuring – on the resulting institutionalisation of these reactions, giving us once again patterns or structures. We will not be looking so much at something different from the earlier concerns with occupations and organisations as at a different aspect of them. Whereas, for example, the emphasis in our discussion of work organisations was on attempts of dominant interests to exert control over work and its products, we shall now give greater emphasis to the efforts and accommodations of the subordinate, the disadvantaged and the aspiring. The view from above, so to speak, will be complemented by the view from below. But efforts to control from above continue to play their part, as we see managerial efforts to manage conflict and to handle potentially rival challenges to control.

Much of the present chapter will be concerned with the area of academic study which takes the title 'industrial relations'.

> **Industrial relations**
> The activities and institutions associated with relationships between employers and groups of collectively organised employees.

A sociological interest in conflict at work goes beyond the territory of the typical industrial relations specialist in two respects, however:

1   It sets specific conflicts and activities in the wider context of the structure and dynamics of the type of society in which they occur.
2   It looks to the opposite end of the spectrum to consider the unofficial, the informal and the relatively spontaneous activities of conflict, challenge and defence in work.

Since the experience of work for the majority of people in industrial capitalist societies occurs in an employment relationship, employer–employee conflicts will be central to our concerns. These conflicts are indeed the most crucial ones and they provide the context in which many other work conflicts occur. Edwards (1986) characterises the basic conflict of interests between capital and labour in terms of *structured antagonism*. Each side to the employment relationship 'depends on the other while also having divergent wants'. This means that 'conflict is intertwined with cooperation: the two are produced jointly within particular ways of organizing labour processes'. However, employer–employee conflicts are by no means the only conflicts which occur, although the context for other divergences of interests will be the more basic patterns of 'structured antagonism'. Within this context, people at work come into conflict not only with their bosses and their subordinates but with their peers, their customers and their clients. Divergence of interest and orientation between individuals and groups in the course of their work experience is our concern here and justice must be done to the range of these divergences and to the variety of ways in which they are manifested in the different contexts and at the different levels at which people work.

Understanding conflict at work

Conflict and co-operation

For social life to proceed at work as in any other sphere, be it leisure activity or political life, there must be co-operation between people. Co-operation is vital not only for necessary tasks to be achieved, it also gives stability to daily life. The minimising or controlling of differences of interest between people required by it suggests some positive psychological significance for co-operative activity. Co-operation is comfortable, we might say. From this it is not difficult to make the leap to the suggestion that co-operation is 'good' and conflict 'bad'. But co-operation and conflict cannot really be opposed in this way, either ethically or theoretically. Conflict and co-operation are omnipresent and inevitably co-existent in social life. Given the scarcity of humanly valued goods in the world and the competition which tends to follow in order to obtain access to these, we find that co-operation with one interest group may automatically imply conflict with another. Conflictful activities are as much part of life therefore as 'co-operative' ones.

Conflict and co-operation are two sides of the same coin. Yet there is a common tendency in everyday thinking about social life to see examples of co-operation as healthy and conflicts as pathological. This no doubt relates to the psychologically comforting overtones of the notion of co-operation. But it is none the less a nonsense. Co-operation cannot *of itself* be evaluated as good or healthy any more than conflict *per se* can be seen as bad or unhealthy. We can judge it only by the ends to which it is related. Co-operation with a murderer would be as widely deprecated, for example, as conflict with a rapist would be applauded. By the same token, to enter into conflict with one's employer (or one's employee) cannot of itself – without reference to the point at issue – be judged right or wrong, desirable or undesirable, healthy or unhealthy. Yet in our contemporary society such judgments do tend to be made. This probably results from the effects of various ideologies combined with the negative psychological overtones of the idea of 'conflict'. This tendency presents a substantial barrier to the understanding among academics and laymen alike of work conflicts and 'industrial relations' activity. For sociological analysis of these spheres to proceed, issue has to be taken with a formidable array of conventional wisdoms and everyday evaluative tendencies.

Frames of reference

To come to terms with some of the difficulties of analysing issues of work conflict and to deal with the frequent confusions of description and prescription which characterise this field, it is helpful to look at the various frames of reference which are typically used in discussions of employment relations issues. Following the approach of Fox (1973, 1974) we can note the existence of three analytical frameworks which are available to us: the unitary, the pluralist and the radical. Each of these stresses particular aspects of work relations:

1   The *unitary* framework assumes a fundamentally common interest between all of those operating in the workplace or in society at large.
2   The *pluralist* view recognises a variety of interests but sees these as more or less balancing each other out in practice.
3   The *radical* perspective recognises the basic inequalities and power differentials characterising industrial capitalist society and relates work conflicts to these structural patterns.

These three frames of reference are clearly rivals as tools for analysis. But our problem in evaluating them is made particularly complex by the fact that these three perspectives not only tend to describe the world differently but are frequently used to support arguments for how the world should or should not be. In other words, these analytical models also function as ideologies. Our consideration of these three approaches will primarily be concerned to judge their relative analytical utility.

Unitary thinking

In what Fox characterises as the unitary frame of reference (1966, 1973) the employing organisation is seen as being based on a community of interest. The management is the best qualified to decide how these common interests are to be pursued. Hence employee opposition is irrational and 'industrial action' on the part of the employee is generally misguided and frequently the outcome of the successful agitation of troublemakers or 'politically motivated' individuals. The ideological value of such a perspective to the owner or manager of the work organisation is clear to see; the employee who questions the authority of the manager can readily be compared to a disloyal family member or to a footballer who challenges his team captain. In this way the employee challenge is rendered dishonourable or misguided.

At the national level, the unitary frame of reference makes much use of the concept of 'national interest', a notion which is popular with government representatives – whose task is not dissimilar at times to that of the manager in the work enterprise – in a way directly analogous to the industrial manager's talk of football teams, families and the like. The effectiveness of such appeals is questionable in practical terms. Nevertheless some general legitimacy given to them in the culture at large is suggested by the popularity in everyday talk of references to trade unions or groups of workers 'holding the country to ransom'. As Fox (1973) points out, the unitary framework offers a variety of ways of questioning the legitimacy of trade union activities suggesting, alternatively, that unions are historical carry-overs, no longer needed in an age of enlightened management; that they are outcomes of sectional greed; or that they are vehicles for subversive political interests.

There is no denying the sense behind the advocacy by leaders of enterprises or governments of 'team spirit' or community of interest. All leadership requires legitimacy and this involves ideological utterances. Where such utterances become a threat to the understanding of what is the case is when prescription and description become confused. Managers or politicians are as likely to be misled as the rest of us if they come to believe their own propaganda. To attempt to run an organisation or a government on the assumption that there are no fundamental conflicts of interest between employers and employees, producers and consumers and so on would be folly indeed. Hence the increasing popularity, at least among academics, of viewing both industrial and political issues through a pluralistic frame of reference.

Pluralist analyses

Pluralism as both an ideology and an analytical perspective has been the subject of extensive debate among both political scientists and industrial relations analysts. At the level of the work organisation this perspective recognises the existence within the enterprise of various different and indeed conflicting interests. However, these differences are not such that they cannot be accommodated. The benefits of collaboration between these fairly evenly balanced interests are such that compromises can be achieved to enable collaborative activity to proceed – to the benefit of all parties. Employees do have to surrender autonomy at work and recognise certain managerial prerogatives. This should not be seen as unreasonable or as reflecting any basic inequality, since management has to accept corresponding constraints. These involve recognition of a right on the part of employees to organise themselves to 'loyally oppose' and bargain over rewards and procedures. In this view, trade unions and the mechanisms of collective bargaining are necessary for the 'managing' of the conflicts of interest which exist between employers and employed and whose existence it is naive and foolish to deny. At the national level the state tends to be seen becoming involved as only one among the range of different stakeholders or as the protector of the public interest where that may be threatened by any one interest group becoming too powerful. This pluralist doctrine was supported by the Donovan commission on industrial relations in Britain which argued in 1968 for the continuation of the British voluntaristic tradition whereby managements and unions are left to settle their differences, as far as this is possible, on their own terms.

The pluralist frame of reference became almost an orthodoxy among British industrial relations experts in the 1960s, but for a variety of reasons it became increasingly subject to critical scrutiny in the 1970s. This was largely as a result of its being found to be inadequate *sociologically*. As has been pointed out by one of those who became a leading critic of the pluralist perspective, which he had once advocated, the pluralist framework offers a fairly appropriate set of working assumptions for those involved in the practical world of industry and politics, given that 'irrespective of personal philosophy, a working acceptance of the basic structure, objectives, and principles which characterise industry is usually a condition of being able to exert influence towards reform' (Fox 1973). Nevertheless, it is felt that the radical alternative, as well as offering what Fox sees as a 'necessary stimulus and guide to the pursuit of more fundamental change', also has 'greater intellectual validity'.

Radical perspectives

The sociological reaction to pluralist analyses of industrial conflict and 'industrial relations' helped shape industrial sociology more broadly and, says Brown (1992), provided a 'favourable context' for the new interest in labour processes which was to emerge. The reaction to pluralism was based upon the recognition of various 'crucial limitations' (Brown 1983):

See page 260

- Pluralist analyses fail to recognise the extent and persistence of 'marked inequalities of condition and opportunity' in society at large. This means that there is a playing down of the extent to which settlements ultimately rest on the power of some groups to impose outcomes on others in a society which lacks what Goldthorpe (1974) called 'any principled basis for the distribution of income and wealth'.
- The extent to which the state has to become involved in industrial relations is underestimated.
- Too little attention is given to problems in the societal 'infra-structure' which is so diverse and differentiated that there is no basis for the growth of a formalised and centralised set of institutions for the regulation of industrial conflict.

Given that a basic characteristic of sociological thinking is that it ultimately relates whatever it is studying to the way society as a whole is organised, it is not surprising that sociologists who have been sensitive to the structured inequalities of modern societies baulked at industrial relations analyses which might imply some degree of power equality between the various parties in industrial conflicts. However, some of the radical critics of pluralist thinking may have exaggerated the extent to which pluralists have assumed such equality. Hugh Clegg (1975), a key figure in British industrial relations research and practice, defended his own 'pluralism', denying that he assumed any equality of power. And Batstone (1984) has pointed out that a radical such as Hyman (1978), in attempting to provide evidence for such a criticism, is unable to quote pluralist writers in a way which 'unequivocally indicates such a belief'. What is more accurate, says Batstone, is to see a fear in the pluralists' minds that attempted moves to greater equality might 'end up in dictatorship and poverty'. Because they highly value liberal principles, they are prepared to tolerate a degree of inequality.

Radical analyses of industrial conflict, in the sense of analyses which go beneath the surface phenomena to the underlying 'roots' of issues and stress the importance of basic inequalities, need not necessarily involve a rejection of pluralist values. Fox (1979) has pointed out that one can argue that a country like Britain has deep social inequalities, and is not therefore adequately liberal and pluralist, whilst still believing in liberal pluralism as a means of action and a desirable goal. Because there is a tendency to question all forms of liberal pluralism within Marxism, as Fox points out, it may be helpful to use Crouch's (1982) distinction between Marxist analyses and radical (or, more properly, 'radical pluralist') analyses.

A radical pluralist frame of reference

recognises the plurality of groups and interests in society (and welcomes social pluralism *in principle*) whilst observing the more basic patterns of power and inequality which tend to shape, and be shaped by it.

As Crouch says, in applying these frames of reference to questions about the nature and role of trade unions, the Marxists go a stage further than the radicals. Whereas the radicals differ from the pluralists in generally 'digging deeper into the social structure to find their explanatory variables', the Marxists are more specific in taking as the cornerstone of their analyses the class relationship between capital and labour as 'the major determinant of social relations'. The concept of contradiction, however, is one which is used by both Marxists and non-Marxists as a device for examining the structural patterns which underlie the surface phenomena of work conflicts.

Contradictions and conflicts

To talk of contradictions in social, economic and political structures is to discuss the ways in which the various principles which underlie social organisation are inconsistent or clash with each other. To analyse contradictions is to locate internal tensions or strains which exist within 'systems' and which may lead to either collapse of that system or some kind of adaptation of it by those wishing to retain the basic features of the system.

The notion of contradiction, in one form or another, is widely used throughout sociology and it can be applied to some fundamental issues arising within industrial capitalism as was demonstrated in Chapter 3. The close correspondence between the Marxian notion of contradiction and structural-functionalist ideas of 'strain' (structural-functionalism having been seen by many as the most conservative brand of sociological theory) is pointed out by Lipset (1976) who cites Eisenstadt's (1973) observation that 'both Durkheim and Weber saw many contradictions inherent in the very nature of the human condition in society in general, and saw them articulated with increasing sharpness in the developments of the modern order in particular'. These sociologists, says Eisenstadt, were far less optimistic than Marx about overcoming the ubiquitous and continuous 'tensions between the creative and restrictive aspects of modern life, of potential contradictions between liberty and rationality, between these on the one hand and justice and solidarity on the other'.

In stressing the idea of structural contradiction we are drawing attention away from the specific conflicts which may arise between different actors or groups in social life to the general problems which give rise to these. For example, within the Marxian perspective it is not the particular conflicts which happen to take place between capitalists and workers that are crucial but the more basic contradiction between the collective production of wealth and its private appropriation. A basic sociological issue is thus raised: are the organisational principles of collective production and private consumption compatible in the long run? Such questions correspond to those raised by Weber's notion of a 'paradox of consequences' in social life. In the long run can the formally rational *means* such as wage-labour, advanced technical division of labour, and instrumental motivation serve the materially rational *ends* of those who devised them? The answer may well be no because of the constant tension between formal and material rationality in social life.

See page 66

The particular strain or contradiction with which Durkheim has commonly been associated is that whereby social inequalities lead to a situation in which certain goals are stressed by the culture but to which access for many is systematically denied. Durkheim's observation of industrial capitalism in action led him to an increasing awareness that persisting inequalities threatened the social solidarity which he thought to be possible within the 'organic division of labour' which characterises modern economic life. For economic life to be regulated there needed to be some moral basis underlying it, otherwise anomie would prevail, but he could not see how such a 'normative order' could be achieved whilst inherited inequalities of opportunity and condition existed. Industrial capitalist society, with its basic class inequalities, has to impose order, and, to the extent that this is so, 'fundamental discontent and unrest persist if only in latent form' (Goldthorpe 1974). From his reading of Durkheim, Goldthorpe infers the futility of trying to bring lasting 'order' to industrial relations activity, on the lines advocated by pluralist thinkers, whilst substantial inequalities of wealth and opportunity persist in society at large.

On the basis of the various discussions of structural contradictions, and the centrality to them of a concern with the implications of structured inequalities, we can draw together certain basic factors in the structure of industrial capitalist society which give rise to conflicts in work. Industrial capitalist society involves the buying and selling of people's labour capacity. These transactions are not made on a basis of equality between the parties. Inequality itself does not create a problem; the threat to the stability of industrial capitalism arises from it in two indirect ways:

1   Instability arises from the fact that industrial capitalism has been historically dependent on a rhetoric of social equality and of rewards based on achievement, a rhetoric which conflicts with the actual or effective distribution of rewards and opportunities for advancement in society. This gap between claims and 'realities' is less likely to be visible during periods of economic growth and changing occupational structures than when growth slows down or stops. Inequalities of distribution, for example, are more likely to become contentious when there is a 'cake' of fixed size to share out, than when this cake is growing.

2   Instability arises from the fact that in a culture where individual freedom, choice, independence and autonomy are central values,

the great majority of people in their work experience find themselves coming under the control and instruction of others to a degree which potentially clashes with cultural expectations.

Many of the conflicts which arise between employers and employees can be seen as paradoxical outcomes or unintended consequences of the actions and means which have been chosen by employing interests themselves in the course of the history of industrial capitalism. Collective resistance to employers could not have arisen had not employers brought together employees in single workplaces, for example. Further, the instrumental and calculative approach to work of many employees which employers frequently bemoan reflects the logic of employers' own policies as much as anything else: 'the first generation of factory workers were taught by their masters the importance of time: the second generation formed their short-time committees in the ten-hour movement; the third generation struck for overtime or time-and-a-half' (Thompson 1967). The low level of moral involvement of junior employees can also be seen as reflecting the very way their work is designed. Whilst employees are given narrowly restricted tasks, are closely and often coercively supervised by 'superiors' and are treated as dehumanised factors of production, managements can expect little more than grudging compliance.

Untrusting management policies and control techniques are likely to be reciprocated with low trust employee attitudes and behaviour. What results from this is what Fox (1974) characterises as 'low trust industrial relations' in which we see the very familiar features of bargaining on a win–lose basis, attempts to bring the other side under closer prescription and control, and a screening and distortion of communication between bargaining parties. Managements often recognise this danger and therefore attempt to build trust relationships. This reflects their involvement in the central contradiction that

> the function of labour control involves *both* the direction, surveillance and discipline of subordinates whose enthusiastic commitment to corporate objectives cannot be taken for granted; *and* the mobilisation of discretion, initiative and diligence which coercive supervision, far from guaranteeing, is likely to destroy.

But to build trust relations within employment is expensive, observes Armstrong (1989), and takes them back to the pressure to substitute 'performance monitoring and control' for trust. This creates a contradiction: 'because trust is expensive there arises a contradiction between its indispensability and employers' economic interest in substituting for it'. Out of this contradiction Armstrong sees arising a 'historical dynamic within capitalist organisations' whereby some managerial groups attempt to wrest from others a role in building trust on behalf of the employers for whom they are acting as agents. In this way the specific type of 'micropolitical' rivalry between managerial groups which we considered earlier is understood within the more structural dynamics of the basic See page 263 employer–employee antagonism.

The logic of this type of analysis, with its radical concern to 'go to the roots', is fundamentally sociological. It not only questions the validity of many of the assumptions upon which the pluralist frame of reference is based, it also inevitably takes issue with many of the simplistic and psychologistic common-sense beliefs which are held about industrial conflict by numerous men and women in the street and by many politicians and contributors to the communication media.

Conflict and society

Strikes, go-slows, restrictions of output, sabotage, managerial politics, etc. are seen sociologically not so much as the outcomes of greed, bloody-mindedness or envy but as partly logical reactions and inititatives of people living in a certain type of society and economy.

It is now necessary to link into this consideration of general concepts and broad patterns of social organisation the situation of the working individual to his or her structural context. We can do this by focusing on the implicit employment contract.

Effort bargains and implicit contracts

The relationship between the employee and the employer and the fundamental conflict which exists between them is central to the important insights (Edwards 1986) offered by Baldamus (1961): 'As wages are costs to the firm, and the deprivations inherent in effort mean "costs" to the employee, the interests of management and wage earner are diametrically opposed.' This conflict of interests is manifested in the struggle which takes place to achieve 'wage disparity' in the favour of either the employer or the employee. In certain circumstances the employees may achieve an improvement in the amount of reward which they gain for a certain effort but, more typically in a capitalist economy, the tendency is towards disparity in the favour of the employer, for the following reasons:

- Partly because employees have been socialised into accepting a certain level of work obligation 'as a duty', thus conceding some effort to the employer 'free of compensation'.
- Probably more crucially, the employer, in the context of a capitalist market economy, simply cannot afford – in the long run – to concede wage disparity in the favour of employees. The capitalist context obliges the employer to intensify the work effort derived from the employee at a given cost.

Baldamus' concern with the ongoing conflict over what Behrend (1957) called the *effort bargain* tends to emphasise the material rewards available from work and concentrates on the factory shopfloor situation. The concept of the *implicit contract* offered here attempts to make more widely relevant some of the insights offered by Behrend and Baldamus. Something similar to shopfloor wage and effort bargaining goes on in all types of employment and over a wide range of issues, it is suggested. Building on the earlier explanation of the idea of implicit contract the following framework is put forward:

See page 138

1   In a world where valued resources are scarce, people form coalitions of interest to help in the pursuit or defence of interests with regard to these resources.
2   Over time, some groups win out over others in the competition for

scarce resources and attempt to consolidate their advantage through their control of institutions and through the propagation of ideologies.

3   Industrial capitalism emerged as 'bourgeois' groups became successful in pursuing their interests in certain societies, but the advantages which accrue from their use of such formally rational means as bureaucracy, technical division of labour, wage-labour, advanced technology and the rest are constantly threatened. The threat comes not only from challenges on the part of less privileged groups but also as a result of various contradictory tendencies in the industrial capitalist system itself.

4   The relationship between the employer and the employee centres on an *implicit contract*. This is an agreement between unequal parties in which the employee, in the light of his or her particular motives, expectations and interests, attempts to make the best deal possible, given his or her personal resources (skill, knowledge, physique, wealth, etc.). The bargain which is struck involves a certain relationship (in part explicit but largely, owing to its indeterminacy, implicit) between the employee inputs of effort, impairment and surrender of autonomy and employee rewards of cash payment and fringe benefits, job satisfactions, social rewards, security, power status, career potential.

5   The bargain is essentially unstable, especially as a result of the market context in which it is made. Market viability on the part of the employer creates a constant pressure to minimise costs – this in turn leading to a pressure to either cut the rewards or increase the efforts of the employee – either way to the employees' disadvantage. However, employees are bound to defend themselves, especially since they buy goods and services on the same market. Paradoxically, the advertising and marketing efforts of employing organisations create a pressure on their employees to increase, or at least hold stable, their rewards (employees and customers being ultimately the same people). The contradictory pressures operating on the employment relationship here are illustrated in Figure 7.1.

6   To increase efficiency or market viability, employers introduce various organisational and technological changes, but any such change, however minor it may seem, potentially invites opposition from employees whose implicit contracts may be seen to be

threatened. This may be because of a tendency to reduce 'rewards' like job satisfaction or the opportunity to use craft skills or because of a tendency to call for increased employee 'inputs' in the form of increased effort or a further reduction in the amount of autonomy which the employee has at work. Potential conflict, we can see, arises with practically any kind of managerial initiative in employment situations.

7 Both to improve their market position and to defend themselves, employees tend to form various coalitions of interest to present the kind of group challenge which is necessary to have any effect in the face of the greater power of the employer (the exception here being where the individual employee has unique skills or knowledge on which the employer is dependent). Thus we get, within employing organisations, trade union organisation, 'professional' group mobilisation and 'informal' office and shopfloor groupings. All of these present challenges to the managerial prerogative.

8 In every workplace there is a constantly renegotiated agreement about what goes on and what rewards accrue. Only a fraction of this negotiating process is formal and much of the agreement is tacit. External conditions are never constant and therefore there are always threats to the stability of arrangements. The underlying conflicts of interest between employer and employee may become overt and apparent at any time and will tend to centre on two main issues: the amount of material rewards available to the employee and the extent of control over employees conceded to the employer.

9 We can say that a grievance situation arises whenever a particular implicit contract is perceived to go out of balance. The grievance may lead to any of a range of employee reactions, from striking to absenteeism and from obstructive behaviour to resigning. A grievance can be settled or accommodated not only by a return to the prior status quo but by a rebalancing of the implicit contract in a new form; an increase in cash being agreed to compensate for a loss in autonomy resulting from a technical change, for example.

Here we have a frame of reference which can be used to analyse conflict in the widest possible range of employment situations. Having established this framework we can now turn to the variety of ways in which

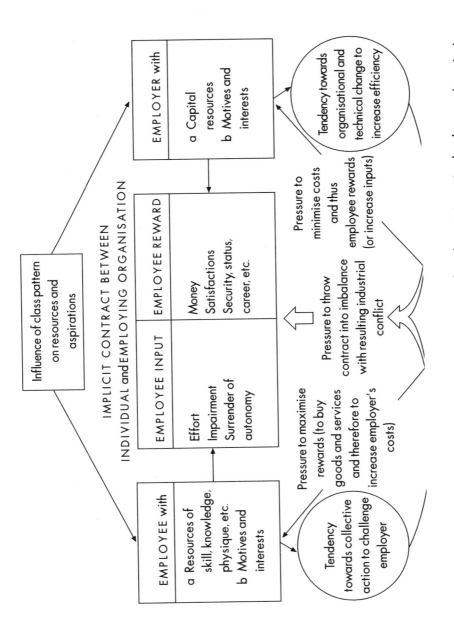

FIGURE 7.1 The implicit contract between employer and employee in its societal and economic context

people adjust and defend their interests and their very selves in their work situation.

Adjustment and defence

When individuals take up employment, they inevitably surrender a certain amount of autonomy. In effect, all employees are *made use of* in some sense when they submit to the control of others in the work setting. We now consider how people adjust to the variety of ways in which they are made use of in the employment situation. We will see that individuals adjust to being made use of in different but corresponding ways in service occupations where adjustment has to be made to being made use of by customers or clients as well as or instead of by employers.

Accommodation, subjectivity and values

The 'adjustments' to be considered here all, in one way or another, involve a degree of resistance to the patterns of power in which the workers find themselves. This resistance involves a degree of 'defence of self' – an attempt to maintain individuals' sense of personal integrity. Paradoxically, it is precisely the key concern of these 'oppositional practices' with the 'self' and with adjusting to circumstances that reduces the extent to which what is done is significant resistance (Collinson 1992). Attention and effort is deflected from changing those circumstances and existing patterns of power are, in effect, reproduced.

It is important to recognise that when we are talking about people defending their sense of self in the face of more powerful 'others', there is not a fixed 'self' which is wholly separate from its structural context. Self-identities 'are always in process' (Jermier, Knights and Nord 1994) and power 'provides the conditions of possibility' for the self-formation of identities, 'a process involving perpetual tension between power and resistance or subjectivity and identity'. We also must remember that a person's self-identity involves them in holding values and beliefs which will always in part differ from those implicit in the 'subjectivities' which are pressed upon them in the discourses current in their employment See page 126–8 setting (see Chapter 4). This is illustrated by O'Connell Davidson's

(1994) research in a recently privatised public utility. Clerical workers' resistance to changes being made by the management to emphasise profitability at the expense of service to the public, as these employees saw it, related to the 'subjective state' of these workers and this, says O'Connell Davidson, was shaped not simply by their immediate work situation but also by 'their commitment to supplying a socially useful service'. Similarly, opposition to corporate policies by managers in ZTC was shown to be related not just to a sectional interest in keeping open the plant in which these managers worked but also to personal values and notions of personal integrity – these often being articulated in terms of 'the sort of person I am' (Watson 1994a).

Withdrawal, instrumentalism and the management of boredom

One of the most direct ways of reacting to the deprivations of a given work situation is to leave the job. Indeed, levels of 'labour turnover' in employing organisations are often taken to be useful indicators of the level of conflict within that organisation. It was shown in a study of navvies, for example, that 'jacking suddenly and for little or no reason was regarded as a demonstration of freedom and independence of the employer' (Sykes 1969). The importance of the idea of 'jacking' in the navvies' occupational ideology reflects the men's strong desire to feel and be seen as independent of any particular employer and as indicating a basic hostility to employers in general.

The same grievances or dissatisfactions which are reacted to by people leaving their job may equally take the form of absence from work or the collective application of formal sanctions. Even accidents may reflect industrial discontent (Nichols 1975). But care has to be taken in regarding different manifestations of conflict as straightforward alternatives for employees. Edwards and Scullion (1982) stress that the different forms of conflict behaviour which they studied, ranging from absenteeism to strikes and effort bargaining, have to be understood in the context of the specific work control structures of which they are a part. They show, for example, how the absenteeism among a set of women workers was acceptable to their management. These same managers, however, would have found a similar level among male workers – who were much more directly and intensely controlled than the women – far less acceptable. Absenteeism itself is not an issue; the issue is what it means given the control structure context in which it occurs. As Turnbull and Sapsford (1992) observe in the case of the British docks, where there is a considerable conflict across the workplace 'frontier of control', absenteeism is especially likely to be an 'expression of industrial conflict' rather than a matter of separate individuals choosing to take time off without reference to wider norms of that workplace. Here, absenteeism is more a social than an individual act as is seen elsewhere where there exists a 'subculture' of absenteeism (Edwards and Whitson 1989).

One very significant way in which the employee may come to terms with work deprivations is by taking his or her identity not so much from the occupation but from their home life. Thus, for the 'instrumental privatised worker' (Chapter 4), it is the non-work life which forms the central life interest. Work deprivations are coped with by being rationalised as necessary means to other ends. Here, for instance, we find manual workers accounting for their acceptance of the negative aspects of work by pointing to the way that their income is enabling them to give their children a better 'start in life'. In addition to or as alternatives to deriving vicarious satisfactions from children's advancement people may daydream at work about the material goods or the holidays which their work enables them to buy and this may be extended into fantasising about the delights of, say, winning the national lottery.

See page 121

In their discussion of what they call the 'hidden injuries of class', Sennett and Cobb (1977) argue that for people to accept a circumstance whereby they are constantly given orders by others they may have to adjust by viewing themselves in a self-disparaging way and even by feeling secretly ashamed of what they are. Purcell (1982) argues that a key reaction of the women factory workers whom she studied to such 'hidden injuries' is one of fatalism. And this is manifested in their daily interest in horoscopes, fortune-telling and superstitions. She argues that this is stronger among women than among men. Women at work, as in their biological and domestic lives, have to adjust to 'things happening to them' more than do men.

Perhaps the simplest expedient for getting through an unfulfilling day's work is for the individual to allow themselves to be 'drawn along' by the technology which they are operating – what Baldamus (1961) calls 'traction'. Nevertheless the typical seven- or eight-hour shift represents a long period of time for the manual worker to pass in this way. For long periods of unchallenging work to be psychologically manageable, the experience has to be structured and broken down into manageable components. This type of structuring is illustrated in Roy's (1952) classic participant observation study of a group of machine operators who alleviated the monotony of their daily routine by creating games and rituals within the workgroup and by devising a series of work-breaks: coffee time, peach time, banana time, window time, and so on. An alternative strategy is for workers to devise ways of imposing their own pacing on even the most mechanically paced of jobs. On the car assembly line, for example, the individuals may work 'back up the line' to 'build a bank' (by completing operations before the car reaches their station on the line) and hence buy time for themselves (Walker and Guest 1952).

Joking, cursing and horseplay

Joking and horseplay can play a leading role in people's adjustment to work circumstances. Humour covers a variety of activities.

Workplace humour

All forms of communication occurring in the work situation which create within people feelings of amusement and a predisposition to express that emotion through laughter.

Workplace humour may be seen as a way of simply inserting a degree of leisure into the working day. However, its functions go beyond this and a parallel can be drawn between joking at work and behaviour patterns noted by anthropologists in other settings. The classic discussion of the so-called joking relationship in social life is that of Radcliffe-Brown (1965). He points out how playful antagonism and teasing may help individuals in a potentially conflictful situation to accommodate each other thus enabling them to co-operate and interact successfully. Such relationships are typically seen to develop in families between new spouses and their various 'in-laws'. Bradney (1973) has shown how such relationships and associated humorous behaviour developed between sales assistants in a London department store. It was in the interest of each assistant to increase her own sales, something which put her in conflict with colleagues. To avoid hostility and strain, joking was regularly resorted to. For example, a new assistant seen to be working too hard and seriously was told by an old hand 'You want to sell up the shop today, don't you?' Bradney notes that this was said 'in a friendly joking manner even though it did conceal a reprimand'.

A study of construction workers suggests that 'kidding and horse-play' simultaneously channel hostility and elicit feelings of friendship and solidarity (Applebaum 1981). This corresponds to the suggestion in Boland and Hoffman's (1983) machine-shop study that humour serves a dual function; helping people accept a structure whilst avoiding their surrender of self. Thus, jokes are played on new members to teach them their 'place', but later jokes are allowed which reverse this 'place' – building them up again. Humour thus helps maintain an organisational culture. Again, subversion and resistance help existing structures reproduce themselves. As Linstead (1985), puts it, humour has the capacity both to 'resist a dominant formulation and also to accommodate to it'. Indeed managers themselves frequently use humour to achieve their purposes. Far from sabotaging organisational purpose, 'humour is instrumental in pursuing it' (Barsoux 1993). Managers, says Barsoux, use humour in two ways:

1 As a sword, to influence and persuade, to motivate and unite, to say the unspeakable and to facilitate change.
2 As a shield, to deflect criticism, to cope with failure, to defuse tension and to make their working lives more bearable.

In the workplace the dominant mode of making sense of events is what Mulkay (1988) calls the 'serious mode'. Subordinate to this, but always likely to break through it, is a 'humorous mode' and Barsoux (1993) shows how the 'serious, structured, rational side of business provides a poignant backdrop' for humour. Humour is born out of incongruity and a key incongruity in organisations is that between this serious side of life and the 'pettiness, chaos, fallibility and uncertainty of any human endeavour'. We often laugh at work, then, as we attempt to come to terms with the contrast between the earnestness of the tasks we are meant to undertake and our human shortcomings. Laughter helps us 'cope emotionally with that which could frighten us into madness: the fragility of our identities and the contingency of our social locations' (Watson 1994a).

Much of workplace joking can hardly be seen as riotously funny, and the humour indulged in by Roy's subjects (1952) in his 'banana time' article is funny only in its pathos. One of the men's standard themes, for example, was to ask each other 'how many times did you go poom-poom last night?' The perfunctory nature of much workplace communication is recognised by Meissner (1976) who portrays workplace humour as a rather alienated form of activity in itself, as opposed to a brave resistance to alienation. Such a suggestion is clearly made when he claims that the obscene joking frequently observed among female manual workers is participated in more 'as a matter of defence against male presumption and dominance than for fun'. If it is at all funny, he notes, it is only in a 'self-destructive sense'.

In contrast to this, Willis (1977) emphasises the ways in which manual workers 'thread through the dead experience of work a living culture which is far from a simple reflex of defeat'. He notes how in the shopfloor situation and in the classroom situation of boys destined for the shopfloor there is the same kind of informal groupings with the same counter-cultural 'complex of chauvinism, toughness and machismo'. He argues that the attempts of 'the lads' to control their own routines and life spaces at school parallel their fathers' informal control strategies at work. He also notes continuities between the attitudes to conformists and informers ('earoles' and 'grassers') in both situations as well as their common 'distinctive form of language and highly intimidating humour', where many of the verbal exchanges which occur are 'piss-takes', 'kiddings' or 'wind-ups'. The way in which the working-class counter-culture can be seen as a reaction to middle-class culture is illustrated by the fact that the shopfloor 'abounds with apocryphal stories about the idiocy of purely theoretical knowledge'. A story is told, for example, of the book enthusiast who sent away for a book which he has yet to read – it arrived in a wooden box which he is unable to open!

Whether one chooses to see shopfloor humour and practical joking (which, as Willis notes, is, indeed often 'vigorous, sharp and sometimes cruel') as a manifestation of work alienation or as a creative reaction to it, it clearly contributes to group solidarity in various ways. In our earlier discussion of occupational socialisation and occupational cultures (Chapter 5) we noted how norms are developed which help protect the autonomy and self-respect of lower status workers. The strong emphasis on masculinity in many workgroup subcultures may help provide male employees with the 'counter-culture of dignity' (to borrow a phrase from Sennett and Cobb 1977) needed by males whose potency is symbolically threatened by their being 'under the thumb', so to speak, of employer and supervisor.

The cursing and obscene language which typify many workplace subcultures are usefully seen in the context of the connection which exists between sexuality, potency and autonomy in contemporary western culture. But such language does not always exist in isolation from the technical component of work group life. Meissner (1976) notes the double meanings of many words which are used in the workplace. His own research on the sign language used by workers in the very noisy setting of a sawmill illustrates this well. Meissner notes that the same sign is used for 'pin' as is used for 'fuck' whilst the rubbing together of index finger and thumb may alternatively signify a requirement to advance a log a little bit or stand as a reference to sexual intercourse (as in 'going home to get a little bit'). In this way the language and subcultural practices provide both a technically necessary form of communication and a way of breaking the routine of repetitive and demanding work.

The multiple purposes which humour may serve in the manual work situation is illustrated by Collinson's (1992) study which highlights 'three aspects of the joking culture':

1   As a medium to help develop 'collective solidarity to resist boredom, the organisational status system and managerial control'.
2   To reinforce the central values of 'working-class masculinity' so that workers were 'required to show a willingness, for example, to give and take a joke, to swear, to be dismissive of women, white collar workers and managers' and to retain their domestic authority.
3   To control those perceived to be 'not pulling their weight'.

Cheating, fiddling and breaking things

The counter-cultures which grow up in work settings in part represent a challenge and an opposition to dominant interests and values, but in the end these cultures often enable the less privileged simply to adjust to their lack of freedom and privilege at work. To this extent they provide an integrative mechanism within work organisations. As was argued in the previous chapter, organisations are constituted by the interplay between official and unofficial practices of participants. Even those activities which are 'against the rules' or are illegal in the narrowest sense can often be seen as integral to the way work is organised rather than as aberrant and constituting an unambiguous threat to dominant interests.

If we examine the type of pilfering and fiddling which Mars and Nicod (1984) observed among hotel waiters, it is clear that the money made – which is seen as 'a part of wages' – is a form of theft from the employer. Yet we need to bear in mind that these losses by theft may constitute very reasonable 'costs' from the employers' point of view. This is not only because they enable wage rates to be kept low but also because they constitute a form of reward which is not conducive to official negotiation. Because of this, unionisation is unlikely. By maintaining a particularly individualistic form of activity, the potential for collective organisation and opposition to managerial control is effectively reduced. Ditton's (1977) participant study of bread salesmen also shows how illegal gains can become part of the implicit contract of the employee. Here it is the money 'fiddled' from customers which makes up the wage and Ditton (1974) interprets the way 'the firm's entry and training procedures are explicitly geared to teaching recruits how to rob the customer regularly and invisibly' as indicating how the fiddle helps solve certain managerial problems.

The officially deviant behaviour in the above cases is very much tied into the implicit contract between the individual and the employer. In other cases the illegal activity may be more clearly group-based as happens in the case of dockers (Mars 1974). Here the illegal activity and its control contributes to group solidarity, which may indeed contribute to its oppositional potential. Yet it is also likely, given the particular technology involved, to increase their technical efficiency, and hence the meeting of official goals. The social functions of illegal activity in the workplace have been strongly emphasised by Henry (1978), who argues that the general trading in pilfered goods which goes on in many workplaces and which constitutes a 'hidden economy' involves deals which 'often have less to do with the material worth of the goods and more to do with fulfilling the expectations and moral obligations of the friendly relationship'. To obtain for a colleague something which 'fell off the back of a lorry' is as much to 'do a favour' for that colleague as it is to make money, we might say.

The extent and variety of workplace fiddles is enormous. In a survey by Mars (1982) fiddling is shown to be 'woven into the fabrics of people's lives' but in ways which vary with their occupation:

- *Hawks* are the entrepreneurs and professionals.
- *Donkeys* are those highly constrained by rules at the cashier's desk or beside a machine.
- *Wolves* operate in packs in places like the docks.
- *Vultures* operate in highly individualistic and competitive ways as befits their work as we see, for example, with travelling sales representatives.

These fiddles represent activities designed primarily to benefit individuals and groups at work. They may or may not threaten the dominant interests in the work organisation but, if they do, this is not their key purpose. With sabotage, however, such a purpose is more central.

Sabotage
The deliberate disruption of work flows within an organisation or the undermining of the conditions whereby dominant management purposes are readily achieved.

Destructive physical workplace behaviour is perhaps the most obvious form of sabotage. Such acts should not, however, be seen as meaningless. Taylor and Walton (1971) identify three types of physical sabotage, each with a different degree of immediate disruptive intent:

- Attempts to reduce tension and frustration – the shipbuilders who, about to be sacked on completion of a ship, got drunk and smashed the royal suite, for example.
- Attempts to facilitate or ease the work process – 'tapping' nuts into place in aircraft assembly, for example.
- Attempts to assert control – the 'collective bargaining by riot' indulged in by the Luddites, for example.

Thus, even literally destructive behaviour can be seen as a part of the process whereby realities are negotiated, interests are defended, and the problems of 'getting through' the day at work are coped with. The most apparently senseless acts of vandalism have a rationale – a rationale which can be appreciated only as long as we note not only the conflicts but also the element of reciprocity between employer and employee expectations which develop in many 'low-trust' employment situations. This reciprocity is illustrated in the comments of a former shop steward in a car industry press shop who suggested that workers tend to feel that if they are treated like children they can act like children and hence behave irresponsibly (Brown 1977).

Sabotage should not be associated with low status work alone and may take forms other than engaging in physical destruction. Where managers and technocrats find themselves subjected to the types of control normally associated with manual workers, LaNuez and Jermier (1994) observe that we may find them acting in the following ways:

- Letting machines break down.
- Allowing quality to fall.
- Withholding critical information.
- Revealing information to competitors.
- Denigrating the product.
- Speaking negatively about the organisation to employees.
- Falsifying data.
- Actually engaging in physical destruction, for example, destroying information.

LaNuez and Jermier suggest five macro-level forces which can lead to this:

1 Mergers and organisational restructuring.
2 Increased use of monitoring and other control strategies.
3 Technological changes that have replaced highly skilled with less skilled labour.
4 Deskilling and deprofessionalisation.
5 Displacement due to technological obsolescence.

To understand sociologically deviant behaviour at work, we clearly need to locate it in the social structure and culture of the setting in which it occurs. Quinney (1963) also makes this point when he shows how the level of prescription violations committed by retail pharmacists depends on the way the individual deals with a particular 'role conflict' built into the occupation: between an orientation to professional values on the one hand and business values on the other. In effect, the extent to which those activities which are labelled 'deviant' are ultimately oppositional in society at large is questionable. 'Fiddling' can be seen as sharing many features with business and legitimate commerce itself and, like selling, it can be said to epitomise the 'capitalist spirit' (Ditton 1977). In the jargon of the deviance theorists, much workplace deviance is subcultural rather than contra-cultural: it reflects dominant values and norms as much as or more than it opposes them.

Rule manipulation

Supervisors and managers are necessarily implicated in many of the manifestations of conflict at work which we have considered here. Conflict and co-operation are two sides of the same coin and, at all levels, the breaking of official rules designed to help achieve official goals may, paradoxically, be necessary to meet these goals. In the previous chapter we saw how supervisors operate an 'indulgency pattern' whereby rule-breaking is connived at to achieve employee co-operation and we noted how bureaucratic procedures are sometimes broken or modified to get See page 269–70 the job done.

Writers who have used the insights of ethnomethodology in studying organisations have questioned the common assumption that rules determine behaviour. It is argued, instead, that individuals frequently use rules as *resources* or as means to be employed in dealing with whatever situations arise and have to be coped with. Thus, Bittner (1973) shows how the police officers operating on skid-row do not simply enforce the law – even when they invoke it. Instead they 'merely use it as a resource to solve certain pressing practical problems in keeping the peace'. Zimmerman (1973) has shown how reception personnel in a public assistance organisation similarly draw on official rules and procedures to explain or justify the way they happen to cope with the day-to-day pressures and circumstances of their jobs.

People cope with the conflicts and contradictions of their work situation through what Zimmerman (1973) calls 'the practicalities of rule use'. This is illustrated in Manning's (1977) discussion of the contradiction between

- the 'myth' of police work which sees it as controlling crime and
- 'the reality' in which they maintain order (often without invoking the law) and help out people in trouble.

In the end, street-based police officers have to use their discretion and decide how they should apply general rules to particular situations. In this way, the individual working police officer finds a source of relative freedom from control by superiors. The 'fractional bargaining' indulged in by industrial supervisors (Kuhn 1961) and the condoning of prisoner rule-breaking by warders (Morris and Morris 1973) can be seen in a similar light.

Service work and defence of self

Given the strong cultural value put upon independence, autonomy and self-expression, problems are as likely to arise for many of those in work which involves taking instructions from customers or clients as they are for people who take orders from bosses. The strategies used by prostitutes to maintain their self-respect in such situations were noted earlier and similar strategies can be seen across the range of service occupations. The more potentially demeaning the service given might be to the service worker, the more there is the tendency for contempt for the client to become an element of the particular work culture. Hence a variety of depersonalising titles are used for the client: the mark, john, patsy, trick or punter. In all of these is an implication of naivety on the part of the client and hence an implied superiority on the part of the worker, one which compensates for his or her superficial subservience.

See page 229

Labelling of clients is not simply a mechanism used by service workers to maintain their self-respect in the face of implied servant status. The refining of the labelling process and the development of typologies of clients can play a useful technical role and help the individual cope with the exigencies of the job. Taxi-cab drivers, for instance, find that their livelihood depends on how accurately they can 'size up' the ability of potential customers to pay. Hence, as Davis (1959) observes, they may utilise a typology of customers which ranges from the generously-tipping 'sport' through the 'blowhard', the 'businessman' and the 'live ones' to the 'stiffs' who give no tips and are passionately disliked. Correspondingly, Spradley and Mann (1975) describe the complex typology of customers used by cocktail waitresses (jocks, animals, regulars, bitches, annies, zoos, pigs, johnnies, etc.) and note how, in particular, the most potentially antagonistic relationship which exists within the bar, that between waitresses and female customers, is reflected in the way 'bitches' almost becomes a synonym for 'women'.

Every service occupation has its own types of 'awkward customer' and develops strategies to deal with them, whether it be the handing out of large quantities of low value coins in the change of the shop assistant's over-choosy customer, or the adoption of ludicrously jargon-ridden language by the car mechanic dealing with a know-all motorist. Sanctions play an important role in the achieving of client control; an integral element of service work, as Richman observes in noting how bus staff tend to train their passengers into 'the correct attitude' (1969) and how traffic wardens accrue to themselves or lose honour through the 'street bargains' which they make with motorists (1983). The warden who bargains successfully with the motorist transforms them into a 'client', 'instilling a sense of social responsibility' towards the warden's purposes.

The mobilisation of interests

Coalitions and interests

The typical employee in an industrial capitalist society, unless they have especially marketable personal skills or attributes, rarely has the capacity to defend themselves against attempts of employers to alter the balance of the implicit contract in the employer's favour – let alone improve the conditions or rewards of work. A concerted challenge coupled with the threat of a general withdrawal of effort can create such a possibility, however. We therefore see a general tendency within the world of work for groups to form around common interests and for collective action to be taken to defend or further those interests.

In the discussion of occupational strategies and cultures in Chapter 5 we saw how such mobilisation may occur around a common *occupational interest* and particular attention was paid to the professionalisation process. Here we are particularly concerned with situations where the common interest primarily arises, although not always exclusively, from the individuals' statuses *as employees*. Groups of employees located at all levels tend to form groups to defend or further their interests. Groups of employees can be seen to make claims to professional status even when they are primarily administrators (Watson 1976). And we have seen how managers form themselves into defensive cliques or assertive cabals, depending on how they perceive their career interests within the organisation. However, it is at the lower levels, where autonomy and discretion is lower, that defensive groups are most necessary. It is here that we have traditionally seen the strategy of unionisation.

See page 264

Trade unions and collective bargaining

Trade unions can be seen as necessary defensive mechanisms which have developed among employees in industrialising societies.

Trade union

An association of employees formed to improve their ability to negotiate working conditions and rewards with employers and, sometimes, to represent common interests within the political sphere beyond the workplace.

Trade unions developed in industrialising societies as the typical employment relationship changed from a traditional one based on a *status contract* – a relatively diffuse master–servant relationship with an implication of longer-term mutual commitment – to one based on a *purposive contract* where 'the emphasis is on a transitory arrangement for limited and specific performances' (Fox 1974). Given the low-trust type of economic exchange associated with this form of contract, collective defence of the employees' position becomes necessary. It would be wrong, however, to view the history of trade unionism simply in terms of necessary and inevitable reactions of a purely calculative kind. Trade unionism, particularly in Britain, has always been associated with the idea of a labour movement, something which has provided an ideology over and above the legitimation of sectional interests.

Labour movement

A coming together of such bodies as trade unions and associated political parties to represent the interests which employed people as a whole are believed to hold in common.

Views of what the purposes of trade unions should be have varied between intellectuals both on the political left and on the right, this reflecting the importance of unions to society given, first, unions' ability to give a voice to worker groups and, second, the potential power to be wielded through strike action (Martin 1989). The political potential of trade unions, varying from vehicles of revolutionary potential in association with revolutionary political groups to acting more pragmatically to improve the welfare of working-class people has been a matter of radical political debate from the time of Marx (Moses 1990). It is unlikely, however, that a political dimension to trade union activity can arise separately from a concern with the daily circumstances of people's employment situations. To mobilise people to act collectively, a fairly clear and direct link has to be established in their minds between the proposed political action and the specific circumstances of their lives which may be changed by that action. And the specific circumstances to which group leaders and their representatives typically have to look are connected with the implicit contract with the employer. To appeal to generalised ideal interests in the absence of a clear link between these and specific local advantage is unlikely to be effective given the essentially calculative ethos of the industrial capitalist workplace. There is a basic contradiction characterising many trade unions which leads to a need to somehow combine an essentially capitalistic function – negotiating a price for labour – with socialist principles and ideals. Trade unions exist within a tension between their possible role as elements of labour movements and their role in collective bargaining.

> **Collective bargaining**
>
> A method of agreeing work conditions and rewards through a process of negotiation between employer representatives and the representatives of collectively organised employees.

Trade unions, as their name implies, have their origins among manual workers. With the growing rationalisation of work organisations and the spread of low-discretion direct-control work tasks among white-collar groups, unionism has spread to groups higher and higher up the organisational and occupational hierarchy. An increasing application of what Baldamus (1961) calls 'administrative instruments of effort intensification' on the part of employers later led to a shift from status to performance criteria and hence union-like initiatives among groups like teachers and doctors (Eldridge 1975). Increasing stress on the cash nexus and the erosion of the 'moral obligations which are traditionally embedded in the idea of vocation' (Eldridge 1975) was reflected in the spread of what Goldthorpe and Lockwood (1969) term 'instrumental collectivism' and hence the spread of collective bargaining among non-working-class workers.

A social class dimension still exists within these trends, however. Crompton and Jones (1984) argued that one of the important factors in the expansion of white-collar trade unionism was 'the objective change in the class situation' of such workers. These result from pressures on labour costs which lead to the rationalisation and deskilling of white-collar work and an accompanying decline in job security and in their conditions of employment relative to manual workers.

Various studies over the years have suggested that the orientations of trade union activists go beyond a simple instrumental concern with job-related problems (Fosh 1981; Fosh and Heery 1990). The relationships between trade unions and their members more generally have moved through three phases in Britain (Heery and Kelly 1994; Kelly and Heery 1994):

- From the 1940s until the mid-1960s a 'largely passive membership was serviced by a cadre of professional negotiators'.
- After the mid-1960s this was partially displaced by a participative

relationship in which 'the function of union officialdom was to facilitate self-servicing and participation in decision-making by members'.

- Since the mid-1980s this organisational model has given way to a new servicing relationship in which members are viewed as reactive consumers whose needs must be researched and responded to using the techniques of strategic management.

These changes have to be set in the context of wider cultural changes in society, say Heery and Kelly, and they point to the values associated with the 'enterprise culture' – possessive individualism and the 'celebration of consumer sovereignty'. They also suggest that changing modes of organising work among employers are having an influence on trade union organisation; union officers are absorbing 'current organisational styles'. This analysis suggests the sensitivity of trade union officers and leaders to members' expectations and to the pragmatic circumstances in which they find themselves working (Watson 1988). A great deal of the academic debate on the role of union officers has for many years taken as a focus the question of 'trade union democracy'. The starting point for this debate has been the claim made by Robert Michels in 1915 (1949) in his 'iron law of oligarchy' that the direct democratic control by the members of labour organisations is bound to be compromised by the interests of the officials who have to be appointed once the union gets beyond a certain size and degree of complexity. This occurs because the officials become indispensable and have the capacity to manipulate situations to suit their personal and career interests. The members can never know enough to challenge successfully the leadership who, anyway, have control of the channels of communication.

Legislation in Britain was passed in an attempt to increase 'union democracy' and this provided an opportunity for research to examine the widely held belief that trade unions are made 'more democratic' if they use, or are compelled by law to use, secret ballots in the election of officials or prior to taking industrial action. The simplistic nature of popular assumptions is well shown by a study by Undy and Martin (1984) which showed, for example, it not to be the case that the increased participation in national leadership elections which results from the holding of postal balloting necessarily leads to the kind of 'swing to the right' which was intended by legislators. Other factors such as the general state of the national economy and the perceived abilities of the candidates play a leading part in who is elected. More generally, it is argued that while ballots can appear to 'increase democracy' by obtaining a higher level of voting than might otherwise occur, they might equally undermine it through, say, reducing the ability of executive officials, who are frequently being submitted for re-election, to check the power of a general secretary who, being a better known figure, is better able to survive election battles.

When considering evidence such as this, it is vital to recognise that national cultures and systems of political ideologies inevitably play important contextual roles in how trade unions and their members behave (Poole 1986; Bean 1994). Fox (1985) shows how a series of features of British history lay behind the unrevolutionary nature of British trade unionism, for example. In addition to the role of a non-interventionist state, a period of economic growth and a reluctance on the part of employers to engage in an all-out battle with trade unionism, there was an employer recognition of the part that 'respectable' trade unions could play as a safety valve for class conflict. On the employee side, the pre-industrial religious and political movements left a legacy of differentiated groupings which precluded the evolution of a general and united confrontational consciousness. Yet a low-trust adversarial approach to collective bargaining within enterprises did develop in Britain which Fox contrasts with the more consensual German approach, which emerged from a different set of historical and cultural factors again. Studies by Gallie and Lash (1984) have further shown the importance of national differences in attitudes related to trade union membership and behaviour with Lash stressing the role of the histories of France and the USA in giving the one country a relatively political and class-conscious style of trade unionism and the other an apolitical and economically oriented 'business unionism' approach.

These differences are still apparent in patterns of strike activity. In spite of the fact that there was a general reduction in such activity during the 1980s there were nevertheless countervailing trends in countries in which strikes rates had generally been lower – Germany, Netherlands, Sweden and Norway (Shalev 1992). In general, however, changes occurring in the occupational structures and the social compositions of labour forces across the world have been 'largely detrimental to union organisation' and, in particular, the growth of new occupational groups with scarce skills (which may lead to a preference for individual, rather than collective, labour market strategies) makes it difficult for unions to recruit such workers, while the growing numbers of employees in private services with low-paid and insecure jobs may lack the resources and cohesion to undertake collective action.

(Bean 1994)

The increasingly competitive nature of product markets, high levels of unemployment and state initiatives to reduce trade union 'power' (Martin 1992) have all added to what Visser (1994) describes as a 'cascade of decline'. The post-1979 British governments were especially zealous in an assault of trade unions, introducing a series of acts which, for example, first restricted and later removed all legal basis for closed shops, made secondary picketing illegal, made the sacking of strikers possible, required secret ballots before strikes and later for approval of political contributions, and required the regular re-election of main union leaders by secret ballot. This is often attributed to 'Thatcherism' but, as Marsh (1992) points out, the strategic intent behind this was not as clear as many have assumed and, indeed, the trend had continuities going back to earlier periods.

If union power is looked at in terms of outcomes, we see, in the British manufacturing case, that real wages grew less slowly and productivity more rapidly in non-unionised plants (Martin 1992). This is also noted by Brown who observes that less than half of private sector employees in Britain in the 1990s are covered by collective bargaining; trade union membership is not above a third of employees; industry-wide bargaining is almost gone and old centralised systems are being broken up (Brown 1994). Millward *et al.* (1992) observe a pattern in the results of the series of Warwick Industrial Relations Surveys carried out since 1980:

- In 1980 unions represented employees in 'clear majority of work-places' and through a variety of channels.
- In 1984, union bargaining power was severely reduced but unions were still a 'core element' of the industrial relations system.
- By 1990 much of this had changed and 'key elements of the system of collective bargaining had faded or been transformed'.

In spite of pressures and falling memberships, most British trade unions survived this period in a reasonably healthy state. But continuing pressures and the low subscriptions paid (they are a lower proportion of average earnings than in 1950) must necessarily push unions to a less competitive approach over recruitment practices in the future (Willman, Morris and Aston 1993). To survive as a significant force, however, unions will have to find ways of influencing wider national economic policies. Specifically, as Visser (1994) says, 'unions' power and legitimacy will continue to erode unless they find a way of promoting a feasible and creative policy of full employment'.

Workgroup power and job control strategies

A tension which has long existed within the trade union movement is between the need for large-scale representation across a wide con-stituency and the need for the defence of interests of individuals and groups in specific or 'domestic' work settings. And it was this tension which can be understood as lying behind the growth of the shop steward movement in Britain during the First World War. This movement was motivated in part by radical and syndicalist ideals (Hinton 1973) but the more contemporary importance of the workplace representative (known in different settings as shop steward, office representative, father of chapel, corresponding member, for example) has a more pragmatic basis. The spread of payment-by-results schemes, the high demand for labour, the inappropriateness of the district (rather than plant-based) organis-ation of union branches, and the decline of employer associations all contributed to the tendency for the workplace itself to become the point at which the implicit contract was to be protected or improved.

Shop stewards can usefully be regarded then as a group representative.

Shop steward

A worker representative and 'lay' trade union official who rep-resents to management the interests of fellow employees who elect the representative as their workplace spokesperson.

This implies far more than shop stewards being a 'mouthpiece', however. It sees them playing the part of articulating the common objective interests of the group, thereby creating subjective interests and willingness to mobilise. This equally readily may mean encouraging members to desist from immediate and spontaneous action as it might the opposite and, as Batstone *et al.* (1977) show, the 'leader' type of steward, who tries actively to shape group activity, is more successful than the 'populist' steward who tends to follow group instructions. The stronger links of these 'leaders' with other stewards and the respect which they obtain from the management not only enables the more effective defence of employee interests in the face of managerial control and the improvement in wages but also aids management by ensuring a greater predictability of shopfloor behaviour and fewer strikes.

The effectiveness of group mobilisation in the workplace cannot, however, be seen as entirely dependent on the leadership skills of shop stewards. The technology used in a particular situation and the skills of the workers associated with it clearly create important conditions which are relevant to the potential for mobilisation (Sayles 1958). Darlington (1994) identifies a broad pattern over time in the relationship between shop stewards and British managements in which in the 1970s the approach of stewards was relatively *conflictual* and in the 1980s more *consensual*. A range of factors influenced this but Darlington's detailed case study research suggests the importance of managements' approach to stewards and their tendency to switch back and forth between a 'hard line approach' and a more co-operative 'soft line . . . aimed at incorporating them into accommodative relationships'. Within this there will be specific factors shaping the potential influence of stewards in particular work situations. The insights of the strategic contingency theory of organisational power discussed earlier are helpful here. Batstone *et al.* (1978) have taken such an approach and locate four 'sources' of power:

See page 267

- The extent to which workers have skills which cannot easily be replaced.
- The extent to which the position occupied is crucial to the production process.
- The immediacy with which a group can disrupt the company.
- The extent to which a group can create or cope with uncertainty in the production process.

Whether or not a role is played in them by these 'lay' union representatives, we can observe a variety of different group strategies followed by employees to protect their relative autonomy *vis-à-vis* management and generally to defend their implicit contract with the employer. These are *job control strategies* or, more pejoratively, restrictive practices. A particularly significant activity here, given the constant pressure on employers to rationalise their methods and improve their efficiency, is the tendency towards resisting change.

Resistance to change on the part of lower status employees is frequently regarded as neurotic behaviour or an irrational conservatism. In practice, it can be seen as highly rational. This becomes clear only once we recognise that any change in work organisation, payment scheme, technology or whatever, contains a potential threat to the implicit contract between employer and employee. Unless the employee can clearly see that there is not going to be a disparity in the favour of the employer (and a consequent loss to the employee), the safest action is to resist the change. The charge of irrationality often arises, however, because managers tend to see resistance occurring to changes which they believe will benefit the employee as well as the employer. In the low-trust atmosphere which characterises so much of contemporary industrial relations, it is most unlikely that employees will 'take the management's word for it'. When employees have any kind of countervailing power whatsoever they are likely to draw on it and insist on negotiating over any managerially initiated change which may threaten their current implicit contract. A case study in which a serious dispute almost occurred over management's attempt to stop factory workers making tea on the shopfloor shows that behind this seemingly trivial concern was a perception of the management's intention to interfere with established break-time practices as a very serious infringement of their general autonomy (Watson 1982). The workers' implicit contract was threatened by the management's apparent intention to increase the sphere in which it exerted control over employee behaviour. As many employees explicitly stated, this was a matter of principle. Ultimately this issue was conceded by the company and a number of other fairly costly concessions had to be made in the course of negotiations before union co-operation with the introduction of changes was secured. The whole shopfloor strategy was based on a sensible, rational and wisely sceptical approach to defending the existing implicit contracts of employees.

One form of job control strategy which has received a great deal of attention over the years has been the practice of workgroups paid on an incentive scheme to restrict their output to a level which they find See page 45 acceptable. Taylor called this 'systematic soldiering' and saw it as an abuse which scientific management would remove. The human relations investigators, noting such behaviour in the bank wiring room, did not stress the rationality of the fixing of a norm of a 'fair day's work' and the defence of this norm by the sanctioning of 'ratebuster' and 'chiseller' behaviour (going above and below the norm, respectively) but interpreted the phenomenon in terms of an assumed social need and the necessary defence of a psychologically supportive group social system.

Later studies of the way incentive schemes are 'fiddled', especially those of Roy (1952, 1953, 1954) and Lupton (1963) have laid emphasis on the rationality behind them, however. Lupton argued that the 'systematic manipulation of the incentive scheme' was an effective form of worker control over the job environment. The 'fiddle' not only gives a measure of control over the relationship between effort and reward but protects the workers against the effects of management shortcomings, defends them against rate cuttings and helps stabilise earnings. The widely followed practices of 'cross booking' and 'banking' of work helps hide high bonuses when these are earned and enables workers to carry over and spread earnings. This activity of 'making out', in US terminology, can also give workers an opportunity for self-expression and the enjoyment of an

> 'exciting game' played against the clock on the wall, a 'game' in which the elements of control provided by the application of knowledge, skill, ingenuity, speed and stamina heightened interest and lent to the exhilaration of 'winning' feelings of 'accomplishment'.
>
> (Roy 1952)

Burawoy (1979) who found himself doing research in the same factory that Roy had studied years earlier, observes however, that in developing these strategies of seeming independence, the workers were also accommodating to the established pattern of power and ownership in the factory, a pattern in which they were the relative losers – in political economy terms, they were manufacturing their own consent.

The management of conflict and the pursuit of control

The institutionalisation of conflict

As a result of the actions and initiatives which we have looked at so far in this chapter, structures and institutions arise to regularise and cope with potentially disintegrative conflicts of interest. These institutions range from highly informal 'understandings' and accommodations in the workplace to more formal collective bargaining arrangements and to state involvements in employment relationships through methods as diverse as employment legislation, industrial policy and the placing of informal pressures on employers and trade unions. Although it is most often applied to institutions of collective bargaining, the notion of the *institutionalising of conflict* can usefully be applied to this very wide range of arrangements. All of these institutions function to help maintain and reproduce a particular type of social order, that associated with industrial capitalism.

The basic reason, beyond general issues of 'human nature', why conflicts arise within the work institutions of industrial capitalist societies is that employers in effect 'use' employees for various purposes of their own whilst employees, in turn, (though from a weaker position) use their employment for their own various purposes. For the employment relationship to exist at all there is clearly a range of common interests, which provides the co-operative dimension to employment, whilst the remaining divergence of interests provides the considerable conflict dimension. Industrial capitalism, we can say, is dependent on the three intertwined institutions of *the employment and rational organisation of free labour* (Watson 1986):

- The institution of *formally free labour* – labour which is not 'unfree' like that in slavery or serfdom and which, in principle, involves choices on the parts of workers about where and how they are going to work.
- The institution of *employment* whereby some people sell their capacity to work (labour power) to others.
- The institution of *rational organisation* which subjects work activities to processes of close calculation, a detailed division of labour, a bureaucratic hierarchical control structure.

A basic contradiction arises from the relationship between these three institutions, however. It is a contradiction between the following principles:

1   The principle of *control* of human beings implicit in the institutions of employment and rational organisation.
2   The principles of *freedom and autonomy* implicit in the institution of formally free labour.

The more specific institutions of conflict management and accommodation in industrial capitalist societies all relate to this basic structural pattern and contradiction.

Managerial accommodations within collective bargaining

The trade union organisation of employees has often suited employers, not least because having employee representatives to negotiate for employees simplified the negotiating and communication channels which otherwise would have been necessary (Marchington 1992). This is not to suggest that employers always welcomed unionisation of employees – far from it. Union initiatives are likely to be welcome to employers only once the degree of organised employee opposition has reached a point where it is seen as needing to be contained and institutionalised. The shop steward system in Britain has been shown, however, to have been a joint creation of employees and managers and not something simply imposed on employers (Willman 1980). Managers contributed to the growing importance of the shop steward not only because of managerial deficiencies of procrastination and inconsistency of policy within and between plants but because of the value to a management of there being an individual to speak for a group of employees on day-to-day work control issues (Goodman and Whittington 1973). It was a system in no sense initiated by managers but once it became a significant reality it could be encouraged and utilised as a means of managing relationships and conflicts.

A similar pattern can be seen with regard to the institution of the closed shop, which has now become of more historical than contemporary interest.

> ## The closed shop
> An arrangement whereby work in a particular setting is exclusively carried out by members of a specified trade union. Pre-entry closed shops required workers to be union members before they could be recruited whereas the new worker could join the union after entering the job in the case of the post-entry closed shop.

The closed shop was seen to be encouraged by managers to achieve 'order, cohesion, and a sense of authority in the workplace' (Taylor 1982) and, prior to state initiatives to outlaw the closed shop, Dunn and Gennard (1984) showed managers having reservations about closed shops whilst nevertheless being concerned about the degree of uncertainty which might be introduced into industrial relations if the closed shop were removed.

The initiatives of the British state in the 1980s were intended to increase managers' powers and 'right to manage'. In many ways they were an attempt to bring back a nineteenth-century *laissez-faire* element to employment relations (MacInnes 1987). In the light of this, questions can be raised about the extent to which the decline in trade union influence has led to 'better management' in the way some of those keen to see such changes hoped. There has been a significant reduction in strike activity but, says Brown (1994), no other improvement in competitiveness. He observes that 'few employees have any mechanism though which they can contribute to the operation of their workplace in a broader context than that of their own job'. Without such a presence, employers 'manage labour less well'. He therefore argues that attacks on collective bargaining have been in large part mistaken and that attempts should be made to recreate an 'articulate workforce, able to respond intelligently to the strains of innovation and able to put pressure on employers to manage labour efficiently'. This is a plea for a return to a model of British industrial relations in which trade unions, in effect, play a role in the management of work.

It can be argued that the state has been more anxious to reduce trade union influence in employment than have many employers. And the survey evidence does not indicate that there has been as much replacing of manager-union communication channels with new forms of consultation, communication and employee involvement as many have believed (Millward *et al.* 1992). There has been no rush to re-recognise unions with managements preferring simply to take advantage of the weakness of union representation in current circumstances. Where there have been attempts to *exclude* unions this has not been part of any concerted anti-union movement but a matter of an 'extreme reflection of a much wider shift in the frontier of control *within* collective bargaining' (Claydon 1989). Nevertheless, exclusion can be a viable option and the conditions in which this may be the case are suggested by Smith and Morton (1990) in their analysis of such exclusion in the provincial newspaper industry. Here the following conditions were identified:

- A stable and profitable product market.
- Access to capital.
- Investment in new production facilities and systems.
- A 'history of union strength overlaid by contemporary weakness'.

This is not to say that any employer experiencing this set of conditions would automatically attempt to exclude trade unions. It only indicates situations in which such a possibility is a viable one.

Employer control strategies

In attempting to generalise trends in how employers handle industrial conflict issues, it is very important to recognise that different employing organisations are likely to follow different approaches. Attempts have been made, however, to identify patterns underlying the variety of different approaches taken by employers. Particularly influential has been the typology of employee relations styles developed by Purcell and Sisson (1983):

- The *traditionalist* in which managements directly enforce their wishes.
- The *sophisticated paternalist* in which various benefits are given and welfare measures adopted so as to discourage the desire for union involvement.
- The *sophisticated modern* where unions are given a role in the

handling of issues either in a 'constitutionalist' way where strong collective agreements form the basis of relationship or in a 'consultative' way whereby a less formal relationship is fostered so that many issues are dealt with before they reach the stage of a formal dispute.

- The *standard modern* in which it is recognised that management and employees have different values and purposes and where, in the absence of a formalised industrial relations approach, industrial relations interventions occur only when disputes arise and make them necessary.

Having recognised that managements may follow different control strategies with regard to their employees, we are left with the question of which circumstances lead to the adoption of which general type of strategy. One approach to answering this question has been developed by theorists in the labour process tradition who wanted to develop a more See page 260 subtle and 'dialectical' approach to analysing capitalist labour processes which affords much greater recognition of the challenge offered to employers by organised labour than was the case in Braverman's (1974) seminal work. It is argued that managerial activity should be understood not as straightforwardly imposing upon employees the work tasks 'required by capital' but as engaging in a competition for control with employees, albeit in the same long-term interests of the owner of capital. Friedman (1977) shows how some employees are better able than others to resist managerial controls, and hence deskilling. Here the emphasis is on the longer-term aspect of the capitalist profit motive and it is stressed that the managerial treatment of labour and the way jobs are designed may vary according to the circumstances. Working on the assumption that managements operate in the ultimate interests of long-term profit- ability, he offers an insight which is partly compatible with orthodox contingency thinking. He suggests that management may choose See page 250 between the following:

- A *direct-control strategy* which is consistent with Taylorist deskilling policies.
- A *responsible autonomy strategy* in which employees are allowed a degree of discretion and responsibility in their work. Job redesign policies would fit in here.

This latter approach is followed where management fear that the introduction of Taylorist controls would risk a loss of what they see as necessary goodwill. Workers who are *central* to long-term profitability, in that they have skills, knowledge or union power which renders their opposition dangerous, have to be treated carefully and are therefore candidates for responsible autonomy treatment. *Peripheral* workers, on the other hand, who are less critical to longer-term profitability, can be more directly controlled. Their work is much more liable to deskilling and 'degradation'.

This type of analysis was developed by Edwards (1979) who suggests that the simple employee control strategies of early competitive capitalism were gradually found wanting as the trend towards modern monopoly capitalism developed. As class resistance towards 'simple' managerial controls grew and as the centralisation of capitalist organisation increased, various alternative approaches to control were tried. However, experiments with scientific management, welfare policies and company unionism were not successful, as Edwards attempts to show with his analysis of a selection of notable US companies. The shift, instead, was towards more 'structural' approaches to control in which there would be less dependence on the personal power of employers and managers and more on the effects of the physical and social structure of the enterprise. There are two of these:

1   A *technical control strategy* depending on the discipline of assembly line and similar types of technology.

2   *bureaucratic control strategies* which emerged as problems arose with the technical control approach. Central to this strategy is the role of internal labour markets within organisations (cf. Burawoy 1979). These involve career structures and relatively high levels of job security are offered to privileged sections of the labour force. The effect of this is to gain commitment of employees to employer purposes and to encourage 'reasonable' and predictable levels of performance. Again, there are elements of a contingency approach in Edwards' analysis and this is particularly visible when he points out that the three forms of control strategy (simple, technical and bureaucratic) exist at the same time. Simple control, for example, can be found in small businesses and 'core' sectors of the economy will use different strategies from 'peripheral' ones.

Labour process thinking has been inclined to attend to large-scale underlying trends in the political economy of capitalism on the one hand and to fine details of workplace organisation and job design on the other. Too little is said about the intervening levels of social structure and, especially, about how the labour process relates to wider existing inequalities in society. Edwards' analysis usefully considers this middle ground by building on the dual labour market type of analysis. He argues See page 184 that there is a particular type of labour market associated with each of his three control strategies. Thus, corresponding to simple, technical and bureaucratic control strategies are the following labour markets:

- The secondary labour market (covering lowly paid and insecure jobs like cleaning, portering, and other casual service work).
- The subordinate primary labour market (including traditional unionised working-class and clerical employment in 'core' forms).
- The independent primary labour market which includes pro-fessional, managerial and craft work.

This analysis relates gender and ethnic as well as class inequalities to organisational and work design practices.

One way of examining the broad direction taken by employing organisations towards their employees is to use the concept of *employment strategy* (Watson 1986). This was developed in an attempt to go beyond the tendency to see such matters as industrial relations, job design, personnel management style, organisational culture or organisational design as separate matters in the strategic shaping of work organisations in dealing with influences on managerial choice of strategy.

Employment strategy

The general direction followed by an organisation in the way its management handles the problems created for performance and long-term survival by the range of employee constituencies and other constituencies concerned with employees.

The employment strategy of any organisation may or may not be explicit and formally stated. Strategies with regard to employment issues are rarely based on a clear, integrated and explicit *plan* (Rose 1994). Strategies can be perceived as a pattern which arises over time, however (Mintzberg 1994). In this sense, we can perceive employment strategies emerging in organisations in conjunction with market strategies, financial strategies, technological strategies and so on. The employment strategy concept covers the whole range of issues discussed in this and the previous chapter in so far as they relate to the employment relationships:

- The official structure of the organisation (relatively centralised or decentralised, for example).
- The organisational ethos or 'culture'.
- Matters of job design, leadership style, pay system, training, redundancy, communications, consultation and welfare provisions and so on.
- The role of personnel or 'human resource management' specialists in the organisation.

The employment strategy of any organisation will be the outcome of managerial choices and these are influenced by the following factors:

1   The micropolitical and value preferences of the dominant management constituency.
2   The extent to which this key coalition perceives varying contingent factors as making employee constituencies *relatively problematic or unproblematic to organisational survival and performance.*

See page 273 In terms of the resource dependence thinking discussed earlier, this latter perception is a matter of how 'strategic' the employee constituencies are perceived to be. And the perception is likely to vary with certain contingent circumstances:

- The prevailing labour market.
- The role of the state.
- The technology used.
- The organisational size.

These contingencies have no direct influence on the employment strategy chosen. They are mediated by the interests and values of the managerial groups involved.

This model would lead us to expect to see a relatively employee-centred or 'progressive' employment strategy if human resourcing specialists had penetrated the dominant management group in an organisation. But, at the same time, we would expect this to be more likely if the employee constituencies looked more strategic (and hence 'problematic') to the management generally through their being male, white, skilled, unionised, expensive, aspiring and difficult to replace. A less 'progressive' type of strategy would be likely, on the other hand, if the employee constituencies were generally female, black, unskilled, non-unionised, cheap, unambitious and in plentiful supply. The adoption of one employment strategy rather than another is thus understood theoretically in terms of an interplay of matters of structural condition and human agency, as should properly be the case in sociological analysis.

Various of the key contingent circumstances and some of the basic managerial philosophies which potentially influence employment strat-egies have changed in Britain in ways which affect most employing organisations as we have seen. There have been high and increasing levels of unemployment, government legislation aimed at improving the strength of employers relative to that of organised labour, technological possibilities which can reduce labour skill or quantity and a general recognition of the need for business organisations to be more competitive and public organisations to be more cost-saving. These and other factors have influenced the broad patterns of change which are emerging in the way work is organised, managed and experienced and which we now review in the final chapter.

■   ■   ■

Chapter 8

The restructuring
of work
and employment

Introduction

Sociology studies the relationships which exist between people, the patterns of social organisation within which people live and the trends and contradictory tendencies which provide the ever-shifting context of people's lives. A key role for sociology is that of informing the social, political and economic choices which people make and sociology still has the same part to play in social thought which it had in its early days: helping people come to terms with the implications of living in a particular type of society – an industrial capitalist society. In the preceding chapters a relatively open view of history has been taken which stresses the importance of human agency, effort and interests in the processes of social change and which opposes any tendency to see abstract determining forces pushing history along. However open a view of human nature and history we might prefer to take, sociology has nevertheless, by its very nature, to pay close attention to the constraints and circumstances which limit human choice and initiative, not least because one social group's freedom and one group's advantage is inevitably dependent on another group's disadvantage.

The industrial, technical and bureaucratic developments which have taken place in industrial capitalist societies have given social advantage to those whose prime initiatives brought them about. And the continuing legitimacy of this relative advantage has been maintained to a large extent through the achievement of a general economic growth. This growth in western economies enabled most social groups to improve their condition and allowed concessions to be made to the less advantaged in political, educational and welfare spheres. But unintended consequences are ever present and contradictory tendencies emerge. For example:

- Technological developments have the potential to threaten employment levels and undermine the expectations people have traditionally had of a specific occupational identity.
- The search for greater efficiencies through a stronger emphasis on

market forces can increase insecurity and employee commitment.

- The lack of clear principles underlying the distribution of rewards or the availability or otherwise of secure work opportunities can threaten social cohesion and general economic confidence.

In addition to this are problems of pollution and the depletion of natural resources and there are fundamental issues raised by the substantial changes which are occurring in the world economy as the international division of labour changes and corporations increasingly operate across national borders. These factors constrain the human choices which can be made as well as create opportunities for innovation. Sociological analysis can, however, play a significant role in informing our understanding of these matters, and how we make our livings in the future will in part depend on the extent to which such analyses are used. In this final chapter we shall examine some of the principal ways in which work and associated aspects of social life are becoming restructured in a world seeing substantial changes in the pattern of economic activities and in the technologies which are emerging.

The dynamic nature of industrial capitalist economies

Industrial capitalist economies are *essentially* dynamic ones. Their mainspring is technical and organisational innovation in a context of sectional interest groups, competition and the pursuit of material human improvement. Because of the enormous promise of industrialisation, society after society has followed the industrial lead taken by Britain in the late eighteenth century. France, Germany and the USA industrialised in the nineteenth century and in the twentieth century not only have avowedly socialist societies followed the industrial path, but aggressively capitalist nations have emerged as leading industrial forces in recent decades in the Far East. At the same time, oil-supplying nations have shown a capacity to shake the foundations of economies throughout the world. All of this has presented substantial challenges to established economies whose institutions and practices have become more settled. Such societies are highly vulnerable to competition or pressure from economies which are less settled and which are more geared to commercial innovation.

The recent newcomers to the front of the industrial capitalist stage such as Japan, South Korea, Singapore or Taiwan have had the significant advantage of being able to learn from what they would see as both the achievements and mistakes of western economies, organisations and technologies. This has enabled them to construct a set of social institutions and priorities, at state and organisational levels, which gives them a massive commercial and technological thrust which has powerfully challenged western economies. But western economic interests have not simply attempted to reorganise on their own territory to handle these changes in other nations. They have engaged in the emergence of enormous multinational and global corporations. Thus western owning-interests have often been parties to the moving of resources and production efforts to foreign settings where cheaper or more flexible labour is available. In this way, the inhabitants of the established industrial societies have faced a combined challenge to their economic way of life from nations pursuing aggressive international national competitive strategies and from economic interests within their own borders who invest abroad.

The effect of these broad international economic trends, together with problems of economic recession and changing political ideologies at the state level, on work and employment in western societies has been considerable. International competitiveness and trade threats have forced both employing organisations and states to seek ways not only of increasing the cost-effectiveness of labour *per se* but of increasing the total capacity of the organisations within which that labour is used to innovate at a rate which will enable them to produce goods and services which are competitive in the international context. Work and work experience are widely seen to be caught up in processes of restructuring.

The restructuring of work

The changing patterns of work experience and occupational activity resulting from economic, political and cultural changes unfolding across the world.

Restructuring within the older economies has involved a move away from traditional heavy industry activities such as steel-making, textiles and mining towards, on the one hand, service industries and, on the other, the production of both consumer goods and capital products using advanced electronic technologies. Employment has shifted accordingly and white-collar employment has grown as manual work has decreased. Increasing numbers of jobs are part-time or short-term and accompanying this have been persistently high levels of unemployment with governments, whether nominally of the political left or right, tending towards tight control of public spending and the freeing of labour markets from tight controls. Industries previously controlled by the state have been privatised or 'put into the market', especially in central and eastern Europe and in Britain. There has nevertheless been considerable variation in the policies of different nation states with Britain, for example, pursuing a distinctively more deregulatory approach than other nations within the European Union. Nation states and blocs such as the European Union necessarily operate, however, within the broader patterns of global change.

Globalisation and changes in the international division of labour

Globalisation is a concept which is increasingly used to label changing ways in which different parts of the human world relate to each other.

Globalisation

A trend in which the economic, political and cultural activities of people in different countries increasingly influence each other and become interdependent.

It is important to stress that changing world relationships are not wholly a matter of economics, in spite of the fact that every other influence has a significant economic dimension. *Political* initiatives, at the level of political-economic blocs and at the level of worldwide institutions such as the United Nations or World Bank have a background in attempts to overcome the types of international conflict, war and exploitation that occurred in the past. And the *cultural* dimension of international changes is stressed by Robertson (1993) who defines globalisation as 'the compression of the world and the intensification of consciousness of the world' and analyses the ways in which the trend towards global consciousness develops at local levels as people look outwards towards the world. He questions the thesis that globalisation represents a growing domination of the world by western rationality. The considerable role of religious movements across the globe, examined by Robertson, is strong evidence of the powerful 'local' level of consciousness which exists alongside the international popularity of various forms of entertainment and the ubiquity of certain fast-food 'outlets'. A world becoming culturally globalised in a total sense would neither see the growth of religious fundamentalism in the USA or Islamic countries nor witness the fervour of nationalism in countries emerging from communist blocs.

Economic forces are clearly not the only factor shaping a changing world. Markets and international competition are central to global changes but there has been a general tendency to overemphasise the role of the market in our thinking about economic and business behaviour according to Lazonick (1991). He argues that market economies are not organised on the basis of impersonal market relations between atomistic traders and businesses. Market factors operate within networks of existing and changing institutions and the pursuit of innovation within business organisations is not to be understood simply as a matter of the pursuit of market advantage.

If there were full economic globalisation, national governments would become powerless in the face of the international market and national and local élites would lose their power and influence to international 'capital'. Multinational corporations – with a base in a particular country – would be replaced by transnational corporations whose management is internationally recruited and who move business activities about the world regardless of interests in any one country. However, it is clear that the world's leading business corporations are still located in particular countries. Although large corporations move investments about the world and build international markets, they are still recognised as being 'Japanese companies' or 'American corporations'. On the basis of a review of trends here, Whitley (1994) comments that, given the 'continued importance of national political, financial, labour and cultural systems in structuring economic relations within and across market economies', the 'separation of an international level of economic organisation has not developed'. It is not, he adds, likely to do so 'as long as national and regional institutions remain significant and different'. And while nation states themselves increasingly manage their economic activities with regard to global factors, they nevertheless look towards alliances within economic blocs rather than operate as independent 'players' on a global playing field. National, regional and ethnic identities are significant factors continuing to influence national political-economic policies as can be seen in the former USSR, or the arguments within members of the European Union.

In spite of this, the increasing movements of capital across the world do put considerable limits on what nation states can do. Such trends, say Lash and Urry (1987), lead to a 'disorganisation of capitalism' as economic activities within a nation state become decreasingly amenable either to state management or to working-class-based political initiatives. The claim of these authors that there is a general move from an era of 'organised capitalism' to one of *disorganised capitalism* has a cultural element as well as an economic one, however, and relates to the notion of postmodernism which we met earlier. Lash and Urry observe the 'disorganising' effects of a postmodern culture, with its fetishising of cultural images which they see as tending to fragment people's cultural or class identity.

See page 183

One of the most powerful theoretical analyses of the forces bringing about economic globalisation has been that often labelled the 'new international division of labour' thesis. This is most systematically represented by Frobel *et al.* (1980) and it focuses on how the logic of 'capital accumulation' moves production about the world, especially in pursuit of lower labour costs. It is the logic of capitalist economics which is the key force here and not 'the result of changed development strategies by individual countries or options freely decided upon by so-called multinational companies'. This analysis is criticised by Henderson (1989) for its 'devaluing of the role of nation states, classes, and other social forces (racial or ethnic groups, for instance)' in the ways different countries develop. The thesis is criticised both theoretically and in the light of Henderson's study of the international pattern of the production of 'high technology' goods. He shows how the economic activities of various countries wishing to become semiconductor producers cannot be understood as a simple submission to the logic of global capital accumulation. Whilst, as the 'new international division of labour' theorists stress, governments have taken initiatives to attract foreign investment, this has not occurred at the 'behest' of international capital but 'rather has been a product of their own development priorities'.

Information technologies and their potential for transforming work

The above discussion of claims about a trend towards globalisation involves a rejection of *economic determinism* in explaining trends across the world. Yet, clearly, economic factors and especially those associated with the principles of capitalism are centrally significant. They have to be seen as operating in conjunction with political and cultural dimensions of the efforts of human beings to shape their world. Similar arguments arise when we look at technology and, as we saw in Chapter 3, it is important to avoid any kind of *technological determinism*. Yet, as we saw earlier, technological factors do play a role within social processes which make them seem at times as if they are a determining force. Technology in itself can make no difference to human history. It is what human beings can do with the technologies which they develop that has the potential to transform the ways in which they live. In sociological terms, it may not be appropriate to speak of computers and other aspects of the new information technologies bringing about a *revolution* in the way we live. For such a term to be appropriate, there would need to be a movement beyond the present industrial capitalist mode of life. It is more likely, however, that the new information technologies will modify substantially how we live and work. These changes are occurring, however, within the same set of basic principles which underpin our present society and economy. In fact, some of their basic characteristics make them an ideal 'engine' for the future development of industrial capitalism. There is a fit between the basic dynamics of industrial capitalism and the potential of information technologies to effect the following:

- Reduce production costs.
- Accelerate innovation in products and services and innovation in the ways these are produced and delivered.
- Increase flexibility in production and service provision methods.

The broad term 'new technology' can embrace a range of technical developments of which the new information technologies are just one type, albeit that which at present seems to have the greatest potential for changing people's lives (developments in the biological sciences and technologies may come to have a similar impact).

Information technology

The combination of microelectronic and computing technologies with telecommunications potentially to transform the way in which human information is manipulated and, hence, radically alter the way both production and consumption activities are shaped.

The key characteristic of modern information technology is the linking of advances in microelectronics with innovations in telecommunications (Gill 1985) and, with its associated developments in computer science, software engineering and system analysis, it can 'dramatically increase the ability to record, store, analyse, and transmit information in ways that permit flexibility, accuracy, immediacy, geographic independence, volume, and complexity' (Zuboff 1988). IT has a unique capability, as Zuboff says, to 'restructure operations that depend upon information for the purposes of transaction, record keeping, analysis, control, or communication'.

The idea of computerising and automating tasks is, of course, not new. What is new about the microprocessor-based innovations, however, is the potential impact which they can have as a result of their cheapness, speed, reliability, smallness, and, above all, breadth of application. Information technology is having an increasing impact on the various aspects of work and its adminstration, in particular on the following:

- *The products* which people can buy, from home computers through to 'chip-controlled' car engines or domestic appliances.
- *How goods are developed*, since products can be speedily designed on computers and rapidly tested by electronic simulations.
- *How products are made*, through the use of robots and computer-controlled machine tools and transfer devices.

- *How work is administered* through its applications in word-processing, information storage and retrieval, electronic mail and computerised data analysis.
- *How goods and services are distributed*, where, in retailing for example, barcoded products are priced at the 'point of sale' and are stock-controlled and monitored by computers. Other service applications are seen in financial institutions where innovations ranging from cash dispensers to 'electronic funds transfer' are appearing and in legal and medical work where 'expert systems' can help the practitioner rapidly tap vast electronic banks of information and the accumulated recordable judgments and diagnoses of countless human experts.

Perhaps the greatest impact of information technologies may come not from discrete developments of this kind as from the *integrating of what have previously been treated as separate areas*. Electronic networks (and, later, optical-fibre networks) will be able to connect different organisations and to link their component parts so that processes of learning, research, design, manufacturing, administration, product and service delivery can be closely linked. This will make possible the abolition of existing distinctions between office and factory, works and staff, training and doing and even home and work, through the development of electronic 'outworking'. It can also, in certain fields, undermine the distinction between worker and manager. In fact, a large proportion of currently existing managerial and administrative jobs could disappear as machines are used for the co-ordination and monitoring of tasks and the processing of information. Zuboff (1988) explains how information technology can be used to do far more than 'routinise, fragment, or eliminate jobs'; it can be used to 'increase the intellectual content of work at virtually every organisation' level and, hence, 'challenge the distinction between manual and mental work as it has evolved in the industrial bureaucracy'. This potential exists because information technology (IT) can do far more than automate. It also *informates*.

> **Information technology *informates* work**
>
> IT 'records' and hence can 'play back' or make visible the processes behind the operations that were once deep in the minds of the people doing that work.

As Zuboff expresses it, IT-based automation 'extends the body' like machines have always done but it is different in that it 'simultaneously generates information about the underlying productive and administrative processes through which an organisation accomplishes its work' and thus provides 'a deeper level of transparency to activities that had been either partially or completely opaque'. This is the potential of such technological development. But how far it is being realised in practice is quite another matter. We shall return to this question below when we look in more detail at IT at the level of work organisation.

At this stage, we are concentrating on the potential for change which is inherent in these new technologies. Henderson (1989) contends that 'industrialisation (or reindustrialisation) based on new technologies takes a different form, and may well have different consequences from previous rounds of industrialisation, based as they were on steel, engineering, automobiles, shipbuilding, textiles and the like'. He distinguishes four elements which distinguish electronics industries from those which formed the basis of the 'initial industrialisation of the core economies':

1   They utilise the distinctive raw material of knowledge.
2   Because electronic products have a fundamental task of processing information and 'because all social relations are predicated on the need to communicate' then these products have 'a singularly important utility to almost the entire realm of human activity'.
3   It generates technical and social divisions of labour quite different from those of other manufacturing industries. It employs, on the one hand, a large number of skilled engineers and technicians (who tend to be male) and, on the other hand, a large amount of unskilled manual labour (which tends to be young, female and often migrant).
4   Because its labour process can be 'technically disarticulated' (as,

indeed, can textiles and car assembly), different parts of the production process can be allocated to different parts of the world. If this fact is combined with the potential of modern tele-communications and transport systems, the potential for the *world factory* emerges.

As Henderson's study shows, these factors, together with the types of national state initiative mentioned earlier when looking at the global-isation thesis, help explain various specific and local transformations. These include the famous establishment of 'Silicon Valley' in the USA, the industrialisation of previously non-industrial areas of 'core' societies such as those along the English M4 corridor or around Toulouse in France, the reindustrialising of what were becoming deindustrialised areas of 'core' societies such as those in central Scotland, as well as the industrialisation of various 'peripheral' societies such as those of East Asia. Changes like these are, however, sometimes seen as part of more fundamental shifts in the way work is being organised and as part of a new era in work organisation.

From Fordism to post-Fordism?

See page 245–7

The realisation of the potential of IT is seen by some theorists as closely related to broad historical patterns in both production and consumption which are related to failures in the older type of 'Fordist' industrialism. According to Blackburn, Coombs and Green (1985), for example, the economic recession of the 1970s and 1980s was part of a general economic downswing associated with a crisis in the Fordist approach to production and consumption. An upswing becomes possible, however, if information technology is exploited to break out of these difficulties and is allowed to enable 'the mechanisation, at high levels of productivity, of more flexible production of a higher level of variety of products'. This would involve work redesign and an upgrading of jobs. The work of different organisational sub-units would be integrated by electronic methods and there would also be a change in the pattern of consumption, especially in the service industries. In this way IT helps to sever 'the Fordist link between mass-production and economies of scale' by allowing 'the production at lower costs of smaller but still economic batches of both goods and, most significantly, services'. The physical concentration of workers in large units would no longer be necessary to enable cost-effective production to occur.

The possibilities for this 'neo-Fordist' or, more usually, *post-Fordist* way of organising both production and consumption are suggested by various sets of commentators and theorists (Hirst and Zeitlin 1991; Gilbert, Burrows and Pollert 1992). Post-Fordism can be defined in simple terms:

Post-Fordism

A pattern of industrial organisation and employment policy in which skilled and trusted labour is used continuously to develop and customise products for small markets.

Regulation theory (Aglietta 1979; Lipietz 1987; Boyer 1988) uses this concept in a particularly developed way and relates it to the ways in which particular 'regimes of accumulation' in capitalist societies are supported by specific 'modes of regulation'. It claims that a different relationship emerges between these two structural elements as Fordism begins to fail and is replaced by post-Fordism.

- The *Fordist regime of accumulation* in which standardised products for price-competitive mass markets are mass produced with largely semi-skilled labour is supported by a *Fordist mode of regulation* in which there is state macro-economic regulation, public welfare provision and the institutionalising of collective bargaining.
- The *post-Fordist regime of accumulation* replaces the Fordist one with an emphasis on quality-competitive production for shifting and differentiated markets using qualified and highly skilled flexible labour and is supported by a *post-Fordist mode of regulation* in which there is reduction in state intervention in labour markets, a shift of responsibility for welfare provision from the state to employers or private individuals and a more flexible and varied approach to employment relations.

Sociologically, this theory is useful in that it relates specific manifestations of 'restructuring' to broader structural trends and, in relating in neo-Marxist terms the regime of accumulation to the mode of regulation which supports it, it suggests a possible relationship between institutions of work and industry and broader societal ones. The theory suffers from a similar tendency towards economic determinism to that which we saw earlier with the similarly neo-Marxist theory of the new international division of labour. It is helpful, however, in drawing attention to possible links between the economic and the political spheres – as long as these are not seen as too mechanistic and as operating in only one direction (Hyman 1991). The theory is, however, also vulnerable to criticisms of oversimplification because of its dualistic style of analysis and this criticism is sometimes linked to the more concrete one that there is little sign of mass production dying out in the contemporary world (Sayer and Walker 1992; Williams *et al.* 1987). Also, when we look at more detailed and local studies of restructuring such as that of Bagguley *et al.* (1990) who examined restructuring in two particular towns, there is less evidence of changes being 'driven by capital' than the neo-Marxist theories would suggest. These researchers argue that although economic factors are central to what they saw occurring, they are far from the whole story. Local, ethnic, political, gender and class factors play a significant role.

An alternative approach to the way work is or might be restructured which also focuses on a move away from Fordism is that which uses as its central concept *flexible specialisation* (Piore and Sabel 1984; Piore 1986). This is close to the definition of post-Fordism given above but extends the idea in several ways.

Flexible specialisation

An approach to employment and work organisation which offers customised products to diversified markets, building trusting and co-operative relationships both with employees, who use advanced technologies in a craft way, and with other organisations within a business district and its associated community.

Those identifying a trend towards flexible specialisation see the breakdown of the mass markets associated with Fordism leading to a use of computer-controlled production equipment for the small batch production of high quality, customised products for discrete or specialised market niches. The speed and economies possible with microelectronic technology allow firms to respond rapidly to changes in demand and to combine low unit costs with non-repetitive manufacturing. For this to succeed, workers have to be competent across a range of tasks and be prepared to switch between these as demand requires. Recomposition of tasks leads to reskilling of labour and the revival of craft traditions. Co-operative relationships are developed not only with the employees, however, but with other organisations and institutions within the firm's business district. Collective services relating to training of labour, low cost finance, marketing and research and development are developed in the district in such a way that firms both co-operate and compete with one another.

Patterns of flexible specialisation in this sense have arisen in districts of Germany and Italy and its advocates see a potential for its principles spreading into larger organisations as these perceive a need to react to changes in consumer demand. The picture painted by Piore and Sabel has been criticised as over optimistic, of giving an oversimplified account of the alleged period of mass production and of underestimating the costs of computer controlled production (Williams *et al.* 1987). It has been argued that British traditions and general approaches to business are not conducive to this approach (Lane 1985; Hirst and Zeitlin 1991) and case studies of firms introducing technical innovations and work reorganisation carried out by Tailby and Whitson (1989a) suggest that the outcome for workers has been 'job losses, more oppressive supervision and higher levels of stress' this leading them to comment that the 'alleged universally beneficial results of flexible specialisation, to say nothing of the idea of the newly autonomous worker, are questioned by such findings'. In spite of this, there is growing evidence that these broad principles are having an impact and are, as Starkey and McKinlay (1989) put it, 'being widely appropriated by manufacturing managements in their diagnosis of product market segmentation and work organisation'.

A theme running through much of the thinking on the alleged shift towards post-Fordism is employers taking a more *flexible* approach to the organisation of work. The language of flexibility is widely and frequently used among employers as well as among academic commentators. But what precisely is it that is being pursued in the much discussed search for more flexible ways of working?

The pursuit of flexibility

Given the international dynamics of modern industrial capitalism, the shifting patterns of demand for goods and services and the innovative potential of information technologies, it can be argued that those economies and those work organisations which will perform relatively well in terms of generally accepted industrial capitalist criteria will be those whose work and employment institutions are the more responsive or *flexible* and are thus better able than their rivals to innovate. However, the concept of flexibility has been so widely used, applied to such a wide range of different phenomena and used to give ideological legitimacy to certain employer practices that there has been a backlash against its use. The main critic of the concept has been Pollert who writes of the 'fetish of flexibility' (1991). Her main case is that the concept 'obscures' a variety of changes in the management of labour, such as job enlargement, effort intensification and cost controls by 'conflating them into flexibility'. Criticisms are also made of the tendency to oppose new patterns of flexibility in work and employment practices to the inflexibilities of Fordism on the grounds that Fordism clearly had its own elements of flexibility. It is pointed out that flexibility was indeed central to the basic principles of Taylorism. It is inherent in the principle of the dispensability of labour and seen in the numerical flexibility resulting from short training periods and the routinisation of jobs (Wood 1989).

However, many of these problems are avoided if we recognise that there are two types of flexibility which have been emphasised in different ways and in different setting at different times. The type of flexibility sought under Taylorist or Fordist regimes may not be the same as that being sought in the spirit of post-Fordism, for example. We need to recognise that there is *flexibility for predictability* and *flexibility for adaptability*, the former to give employing organisations greater predictability and tighter control over their circumstances, and the latter to give them adaptability and a capacity to innovate (see Figure 8.1).

Type of flexibility	Flexibility for predictability and tight control	Flexibility for adaptability and innovation
Associated flexible practices	Centralised and top-down control with a mix of (a) low-skilled labour force which is readily obtainable or dispensible (b) buying-in of services otherwise provided by employees	Relatively autonomous operating units with a mix of (a) high-skilled individuals given security and regular learning opportunities (b) buying-in of services otherwise provided by employees

FIGURE 8.1   Two types of flexibility

To varying extents, employers will emphasise

1   Flexibility for predictability – involving structures and staffing policies which will enable labour to be taken on, dispensed with or moved about to suit changing circumstances.
2   Flexibility for adaptability – involving the encouragement of those people whose work involves either technical complexity or the handling of crises to 'think for themselves' and take initiatives without waiting for orders.

The emphasis on one type of flexibility or the other, and the balance of the mix which will be attempted in many organisations, will vary with the circumstances and policies of each employing organisation. These circumstances are likely to be those which were examined in Chapter 7 See pages 327–9 when consideration was given to the factors which influence the type of employment strategy followed by an employer. The implication of this would be that an organisation with a simple technology, a stable market, a steady supply of labour, and so on, would be more likely to seek flexibility for predictability. If, however, the nature of the product, technology, market situation and the rest were such that long-term survival depended much more on the active commitment and initiative-taking of employees then the emphasis would be on flexibility for adaptability. However, it is likely that any organisation will experience pressures for both types of flexibility and will need to handle the tension between them. This tension can be very significant. In the study of a telecommunications company (Watson 1994a), for example, the high-tech nature of the business meant that a series of measures were pursued to achieve the latter type of flexibility and gain the long-term commitment and creative enthusiasm of employees. However, the corporation owning the business closely monitored costs and regularly insisted on reducing the numbers of employees to achieve certain accounting ratios. The effect of this kind of flexibility for predictability was to undermine the flexibility for adaptability because it tended to create a sense of insecurity and to undermine the trust relations upon which flexibility for adaptability depends.

One way in which an employing organisation might handle the tension between the two types of flexibility would be to organise itself in accordance with the model of *the flexible firm*.

The flexible firm

A type of employing organisation which divides its workforce into *core* elements which are given security and high rewards in return for a willingness to adapt, innovate and take on new skills and *peripheral* elements who are given more specific tasks and less commitment of continuing employment and skill enhancement.

See page 186

Trends are becoming clear in which measures to achieve flexibility for adaptability (involving what we have seen earlier characterised as primary labour market jobs) may be accompanied in the same organisations by labour flexibility measures of the other type. These are measures whereby some jobs are designed to be a secondary labour market type and are such that the employer can 'switch on' and 'switch off' labour supply as circumstances change. Studies by the Institute of Manpower Studies (Atkinson 1985, 1987) suggest that a new employment model reflecting such trends is emerging. This *flexible firm* maintains the following categories of employees:

- A core group of permanently employed primary labour market staff of skilled workers, managers, designers, technical sales staff and the like. These will share a single status (abolishing the works–staff distinction) and, in return for their relatively advantageous work, reward and career conditions, will be flexible in the work they do and be willing to retrain and shift their careers within an internal labour market as required.

- A first peripheral group of secondary labour market type will also consist of full-time employees, but their security and career potential will be less. They will do clerical, assembly, supervisory or testing jobs which can more easily be filled from external labour markets.

- A second peripheral group of part-timers, public-subsidy trainees and people on short-term contracts or job-sharing arrangements.

- In addition to these three categories of employees, a range of specialised tasks like systems analysis and simple tasks like cleaning are 'put out' through the use of agency temporaries, subcontracting and other 'outsourcing' practices such as 'teleworking' or 'networking', whereby people work from home and are linked by computer into the organisation.

This model is perhaps best seen as an attempt to locate some pattern in changes which are occurring in a piecemeal way across employing organisations. If we see strategic change in employment practices *as a pattern in outcomes* rather than as a deliberate and concerted plan then 'the See page 328 evidence, though not overwhelming, does suggest that important changes are taking place' (Procter *et al.* 1994). Research suggests that specific initiatives are opportunistic, pragmatic, derived from 'higher level' business pressures, and in accord with traditional attitudes to labour (Hakim 1990; Hunter and MacInnes 1992). This does not mean, however, that the sociological observer of trends and patterns in the structuring and managing of work should not perceive a clear direction, or strategic pattern, in the attempts of employers to increase the flexibility of their operations.

Emerging patterns in organisation and work design

See page 277

The need to balance *flexibility for predictability* with *flexibility for adaptability* is reflected in thinking about the way organisations are structured as a whole and, in particular, on the development of 'decentralised' structures which retain a strong degree of 'centralisation' in certain key respects. This follows from the influential analysis of Peters and Waterman (1982) who suggest that 'simultaneous loose-tight controls' will increasingly be developed whereby a basic simple structure (probably divisional) and a strong organisational culture will be combined with a tendency to 'chunk' the organisation into 'small-is-beautiful' units, 'cabals' and other problem-solving and implementation groups. Information technology can play a leading part in the similar trend which Deal and Kennedy (1982) envisage for the future in which small task-focused work units are bonded like molecules into a 'strong corporate whole'. The need to achieve this bonding through integrated business and manufacturing *systems design* is central to Drucker's (1992) analysis of management in the future and of the *postmodern factory*. Where the traditional factory was seen as a battleship, says Drucker, the new enterprise will be more like a *flotilla* – 'a set of modules centred around stages in the production process or a set of closely related operations'.

Trends such as these across all types of employing organisations have been brought together using the notion of postmodernism. The *postmodern organisations*, according to Clegg (1990) will be 'more organic' and 'less differentiated ... than those dominated by the bureaucratic designs of modernity'. He suggests the following definition:

- Where modernist organisation was rigid, 'postmodern organisation is flexible'.
- Where modernist consumption was 'premised on mass forms, postmodernist consumption is premised on niches'.
- Where modernist organisation was influenced by technological determinism, postmodernist organisational practice is premised upon 'technological choices made possible through "de-dedicated microelectronic" equipment'.
- Where modernist organisation and jobs were highly differentiated, demarcated and deskilled, postmodernist organisation and jobs are highly de-differentiated, de-demarcated and multi-skilled.

- Employment relations, influenced by the constraints of large-scale organisation, 'give way to more complex and fragmentary relational forms, such as subcontracting and networking'.

However these changes work out, information technology is likely to play a key role in the structures which are chosen. It is, however, compatible with both recentralisation and decentralisation of organisations. Child (1984b) points out that it has, on the one hand, the potential to help centralisation through getting comprehensive and current information directly to senior management and through an ability to simplify management structures and so reduce senior managers' span of control. On the other hand, it has the potential for decentralisation through more effective delegation whereby sub-units are put into an information network with other sub-units, so enabling them to make acceptable decisions without checking with the centre. Decentralisation is also assisted by the opportunities which computerised analytical tools offer for the enhancement of the capacity of local units to make 'sound' judgments.

This latter aspect of the decentralising potential of information technologies clearly relates to issues of job design. The analyses of certain labour process writers, we saw earlier, suggest a significant underlying See page 260 trend towards deskilling in capitalist societies. Deskilling strategies are bound to be attractive to managements in certain circumstances. Considerable *flexibility for predictability* can be achieved if new technologies are used to reduce the work efforts of employees to machine-minding and machine-feeding. Predictability and tight control become possible, the older ideals of the scientific management movement are approached and the bulk of discretion is given to the managers who tightly control a limited workforce which can be cheaply employed, easily trained, readily recruited or dispensed with and who have limited bargaining power. Yet in many circumstances, this would be to risk compromising the second kind of flexibility, that whereby employees are encouraged to think for themselves and to take initiatives to cope with crises or technical problems which cannot be designed out of the work context.

Evidence has been put forward of circumstances which are associated with movement in one direction or the other. In the area of computer numerically controlled (CNC) machines we find Noble (1984), in his social history of this form of automation, claiming that its development at the Massachusetts Institute of Technology was closely tied to a desire to produce a technique which would suit its military customers and was less influenced by a cost-minded business logic than by one of avoiding methods of production being left in the hands of skilled workers rather than in the hands of management or programmers. On the other hand, we find studies of CNC technology by Jones (1982), Rosenbrock (1982) and Wilkinson (1983) showing that removing control over machine processes from the hands of the workers is not the only possibility. Managements may alternatively choose to involve the operators in the implementation of the new system and can choose to retrain and reskill them so that they play a part in programming the machines which they use. Research in a variety of technological contexts by Boddy and Buchanan (1986) shows that new technology decisions can either 'distance' employees from their tasks and limit the positive contribution which they make or can bring about 'complementarity' between the employee and their job. In the latter case, much fuller use is made of both technical capabilities and human skills. But what comes about is unlikely to follow directly from what is pre-planned. For example, negotiations and accommodations which accompany the introduction of changes may lead to actual outcomes which differ from those originally intended by management (Rose and Jones 1984). Certain circumstances, however, may be more conducive to deskilling and others to reskilling. Child (1984b) shows, for example, how a greater degree of initiative appears to be left to workers in circumstances where there are frequent batch changes, a high incidence of new work and where variability in materials or physical conditions creates a 'requirement for flexibility at the point of production'. And, in the politics of real organisational life, the relative power which the workforce enjoys prior to its work being changed is an important factor operating alongside managerial choices. A study of various service sector contexts (Child et al. 1984) shows how some workers are better able than others to resist degradation of their work through the following means:

- Their being collectively organised.
- Their scarcity in the labour market.
- Their key position in the production process.

The interests and motives of managers themselves are also inevitably relevant to directions followed in the upskilling of employees and the 'pushing down the hierarchy' of responsibilities and decision-making. Earlier, we considered Zuboff's (1988) analysis of the potential of IT in this area. However, her studies in a number of US organisations show substantial resistance to the realisation of this potential coming from managerial staffs. Her case studies revealed no case of an organisation 'fully succeeding in exploiting the opportunity to informate' work and hence significantly increase workers' understanding of processes and the amount of discretion they exercise. The main force resisting such change she takes to be the anxieties and insecurities of managers whom she portrays as unnerved by the concept of workers taking initiatives and engaging in creative thinking. The managers thus lean more towards the automating potential of IT, the promise of which 'seemed to exert a magnetic force, a seduction that promised to fulfil a dream of perfect control and heal egos wounded by their needs of certainty'. Organisations which use IT to automate work – which implies a deskilling of remaining workers – are, according to Zuboff, 'likely to find themselves crippled by antagonisms from the work force and the depletion of knowledge that would be needed in value-adding activities'.

See pages 339–42

What both theorising and research suggests is that there are forces at play pressing towards both deskilling and upskilling. Where attempts have been made to throw light on the general trends through survey studies such as that by Marshall *et al.* (1988) there appears not to be a general trend towards deskilling. And a review of the range of evidence available for Britain by Gallie (1996) suggests that the main trend has been towards upskilling in all classes, apart from among non-skilled manual workers. Although there appears to be a cost in terms of a significant intensification of work, workers are finding greater variety in their work and are being given opportunities to develop themselves through skill enhancement. In the case of male workers this is accompanied by the decentralising of responsibility for decisions about the immediate work task. Such a shift does not appear to be occurring with regard to women workers – in spite of the fact that the general trend towards upskilling appears to apply to them as well as to men. The gender aspect to cultural beliefs and managerial philosophies is seen as significant here. Such patterns are not peculiar to Britain it would appear. Lane's (1985) review of the German experience in the office context, for example, suggests that a range of more challenging tasks does come about with computerisation but that such high-discretion jobs are lower in number than was the case prior to technical change and tend to be filled by men. The routine office work was largely done by women, who complained of an increase in both mental and physical strain after office computerisation.

Japanisation, teamworking, TQM and HRM

In very general terms, it would appear that many of those who are staying in employment in the advanced industrial societies are both doing more skilled and varied work than previously and working harder. The range of pressures considered in this chapter so far is influencing this pattern. The competition presented to established manufacturing enterprises by Japanese corporations has, however, provided a symbolic focus for many of the changes which have come about, both within the private manufacturing sector and beyond it. Hence, the concept of *Japanisation* has been used as a label for several interrelated trends in workplace change.

Three main uses of the term Japanisation are identified by Ackroyd *et al.* (1988):

1   'Direct Japanisation' whereby Japanese firms move into the economy and industry of another society.
2   'Permeated or full Japanisation' whereby a whole economy would be modelled on the Japanese example.
3   'Mediated Japanisation', perhaps the most common use, which includes two variants: 'attempts to incorporate the best of Japanese practice and to integrate the new with the old in appropriate ways' and an 'appeal to Japanese efficiency' as a way of 'legitimating the introduction of indigenous changes that are seen as necessary or desirable'.

There is little evidence of full Japanisation – the second of these theoretical possibilities – but various commentators have seen a significant influence being exerted in various countries as a result of the entry of Japanese corporations – the first of these potential developments. The concept of Japanisation itself is questioned by Mair (1994) who nevertheless uses his study of Honda to argue that Honda is playing a significant role in world level change by introducing what he calls the *global local corporation*. This involves a 'westernisation' of Japanese management techniques, rather than the other way round as Honda adapts for plants around the world the principles it uses in Japan. All of these 'local' organisations are linked together though a worldwide learning network involving the sharing of experiences derived from local initiatives.

The key principle which differentiates the Japanese approach from Fordist mass production, according to Kenney and Florida (1993) – who say it amounts to a new form of labour process – is the use of team commitment and effort to achieve *innovation mediated production*. Team pressure not only encourages people to work harder but continuously to improve both products and processes, as well as develop new ones. This type of change is central to efforts which fit Ackroyd *et al.*'s middle category of 'mediated Japanisation'. In this usage the term functions as a shorthand for an interrelated package of developments and principles. A concept to relate these theoretically is suggested by Oliver and Wilkinson (1988): 'high dependency relationships'. Such relationships between the various parties within the work organisation process are necessary to support two specific elements of 'Japanisation' – just-in-time (JIT) and total quality management (TQM). The JIT element of production means that there are no buffer stocks held in the factory, with materials and components being delivered only immediately before they are required. This means that production is vulnerable to disruption and makes necessary the maintenance of stable employment relations and flexible and co-operative behaviour on the part of workers. TQM, to which we will return shortly, involves a commitment to continuous improvement of processes and the quality of the product, which makes the manufacturing system further dependent on employees.

A variety of terms other than Japanisation have been used to bring together the emerging new approaches to production. Womack *et al.* (1990) use the idea of *lean production*, for example, to describe what they say amounts to a 'new way of making things' through a combined use of multiskilled worker teams and flexible automated technology which is changing the world. Storey (1994b) uses the broad term of *new wave manufacturing* to cover what he sees as a 'systemic break with conventional mass Fordist production' involving key characteristics of 'flexibility, teamworking, continual improvement and adaptation, and integration'. There is, he says, a set of keywords: 'flexibility, quality, teamworking, just-in-time delivery, right-first-time production, elimination of waste and non-value-added activity, zero defect and continual improvement which, taken separately, are arguably not new. What is different, however, is the way the NWM approach brings these principles together into 'a new, mutually reinforcing, whole'. Hence, JIT 'places a premium on right-first-time' and the continuous improvement theme of TQM 'requires involvement from everyone and some form of teamworking'. Teamworking, in turn, 'implies a need for flexibility, while flexibility means a better trained and more competent workforce'.

See page 257 The principle of people working in teams, with varying degrees of autonomy or independence from direct management control, arises throughout the variety of changes occurring in the organisation of work. It is far from a new concept as we saw in the earlier review of work design principles and takes various forms. The Japanese practice of forming teams to act as 'quality circles' or 'problem-solving teams' is different from the 'semi-autonomous' type of team which carries out basic work operations within the organisation and is given a degree of discretion about how tasks are shared and carried out (Buchanan 1994). Perhaps the most significant use of teamworking is within the principle of modular or cellular work organisation, in which people and machines are grouped around information or product flows and in which these 'cells' are, to a greater or less extent, integrated into the type of postmodern factory identified, as we saw earlier, by Drucker (1992), alongside statistical quality control, strategic manufacturing management accounting and a 'systems approach to the business of creating value'. In this approach, sometimes labelled MSE (manufacturing systems engineering), cells have a degree of independence from each other and from the organisation as a whole which not only reinforces identification of the team with its own product or service but also increases the flexibility of the organisation as a whole.

Total quality management can be seen as playing a key role in this pursuit of flexibility. It is a less piecemeal aspect of Japanisation than new supplier relations, JIT or quality circles, according to Hill (1991).

Total quality management

An approach to the production of goods and services in which employees at all levels focus on 'satisfying customers', use statistical and other techniques to monitor their work and seek continuous improvement in the processes used and the quality of what is produced.

Hill sees TQM as the key to understanding how 'flexibility' is being managed (the management of flexibility being an important and neglected dimension of economic restructuring) and 'as exemplifying the ways firms are restructuring'. He defines it as 'a holistic system of management which is a synthesis of a number of discrete principles of managing into a discipline intended to promote continuous business improvement' so that companies may achieve the following developments:

- Become more innovative by anticipating and creating new market opportunities and devising new products and better ways of producing.
- Increase efficiency by economising on costs whilst also improving product quality.
- Respond more rapidly to change.

Hill's research leads him to argue that quality management addresses the 'twin issues of how large corporations may increase the entrepreneurial propensity of their managers and debureaucratize their organisations'. However, many of the innovations in the area of quality improvement have been primarily associated with detailed changes of practice at the level of production processes – with what Wilkinson *et al.* (1992) call the 'hard' or 'systems and tools' side of TQM. Their full implications emerge, as these authors point out, only when they are linked to broader changes in organisational cultures and personnel management practices. This takes us onto the alleged shift in this area towards a new style of employment management known as human resource management (HRM).

The concept of HRM as a different way of approaching the

employment aspects of work organisation originated with various US academic commentators (Tichy, Fombrun and Devanna 1982; Beer and Spector 1985; Walton 1985) and was later taken up by British academic researchers (Storey 1989, 1992; Hendry and Pettigrew 1990; Guest 1991). Sisson (1994) sees a 'simple message' behind the advocacy of HRM. It is 'to copy the Japanese' by combining flexible specialisation types of work organisation and TQM approaches to production with employment management practices with the following aims:

- The 'development of a highly committed and adaptable workforce willing and able to learn new skills and take on new tasks'.
- The elevation of 'the management of people' to a strategic level of organisational decision-making.
- An emphasis on trust rather than rules and procedures.
- The encouragement of managers to become leaders and facilitators of cultural change by 'harnessing the co-operation and commitment of others'.
- A move away from hierarchical organisations with a number of tiers of management, separate functions and tightly defined job descriptions to much 'flatter' and more 'federal' organisations.
- An emphasis on the flexibility of function, task, time and reward and on teamworking and 'single status' terms and conditions of employment.

Many of these aims we have seen already under various of the fashionable labels which different commentators have put on changing practices in work organisation and management. The managers who are involved in bringing about these changes appear to need to identify ideas with management 'gurus' (Huczynski 1993) and to package them as management 'fads and fashions' or 'flavours of the month' (Watson 1994d). It is clearly important to search behind the claims which are made for 'new paradigms' and the like and to examine what is actually happening in employment and work organisation. With regard to HRM, Sisson (1994) comments that in only a small number of cases have the 'significant changes which are taking place' amounted to a transformation in the direction of the 'HRM organisation which so many pundits have proclaimed'. There is, however, a 'substitution of individualism for collectivism', and an 'assertion of management freedom from constraints'. On the basis of his own surveys of trends, Storey (1994a) observes that there is a 'flurry of initiatives' but that 'it is probably fair to say that the mainstream organisations have not rigorously and consciously pursued "Japanisation", HRM, or any other coherent model'. And the same author (1994b) concludes that a large number of organisations are 'at an early stage' of coming to terms with the broad range of 'new wave management' innovations. They have engaged consultants and embarked on 'educational, awareness-raising and training programmes'. This means that the common language of the new methods has been learned but the extent to which it is put fully into practice has yet to be seen.

On the basis of his close study of six British organisations, Bratton (1992) concludes that a 'transformation of work based on the Japanese-type manufacturing paradigm is evident among non-exceptional UK manufacturing organisations'. However, when we look at studies of specific innovations, it is common to find a pattern whereby the full potential of the changes are not realised – as we saw earlier in Zuboff's (1988) consideration of the potential of IT. A study of cellular manufacturing innovations in one factory by Buchanan and Preston (1992) illustrates the range of factors which inhibit the realisation of the 'radical potential' of self-regulating, multiskilled teamwork, the transformation of the role of first line supervision 'from policeman to coach', and for a movement towards a high employee involvement management style. Central to these inhibitors was a failure to recognise the

> Human Resource Management dimension of such changes and, particularly, the need to involve human resourcing expertise, to get away from inflexible company-wide agreements on rewards and job gradings, to improve training and more clearly work out a strategy for the transition of the role of the foreman.

A common pattern in research like this last study is a recognition that changes in one aspect of work organisation and employment tend not to be integrated into changes in other aspects. This reduces the likely transformation of enterprises into some new general 'type' of work organisation. Sociologically, we may question whether any such fundamental transformation is possible, given that the basic political economy of work relations stays the same. Whatever changes may be evolving, the basic employment relationship 'remains a market transaction in which respective actors are assumed to utilise their respective resources in order to optimise their returns from the exchange process' (Keenoy 1991). Securing managerial legitimacy and employee commitment is a continuing issue for employers and, as Keenoy puts it, any talk of a new paradigm 'which abandons this analytical touchstone seems premature if not self-deceptive'.

As this observation recognises, initiatives such as those in quality management are 'embedded in social institutions' (Wilkinson and Willmott 1994) and, as Kerfoot and Knights (1994) note, whilst quality management principles claim to give an enhanced role to employees, workers tend neither to be 'treated as equals nor even consulted when companies decide to adopt programmes of quality management: they are often merely trained in its practices once the programme has been adopted by the senior management'. Such a view is borne out by case study research like that of Dawson and Webb (1989) who show how an increase in discretion and autonomy among the workforce at the job level did nothing to extend 'to any substantive control over business strategy or the dispersal of profits'. And Sewell and Wilkinson (1992) argue that TQM and JIT, when connected with the potential of information technologies and computers to monitor human performance, enable managements to achieve the benefits 'that derive from the delegation of responsibility to teams while retaining authority and disciplinary control through ownership of the superstructure of surveillance and the information it collects, retains and disseminates'. In the light of analyses such as this, the term *social Taylorism* is suggested by Webster and Robins (1993) to cover what they see as a development within an era of 'post-Fordist capitalist reconstruction' leading to the 'management of ever more aspects of social life which presume close monitoring as a requisite of action'. This claim may well exaggerate both the interest and the capacity of those in societally advantaged positions to pursue deliberate strategies of social control, but it does valuably make the point that changes in work activities have to be considered in relation to broader changes in society as a whole. Webster and Robins see an appeal in the potential of information technologies not just to employees, but to consumers or voters, 'in terms of empowerment and decentralisation of responsibilities'. But that potential exists alongside a situation in which individuals, as citizens, consumers or workers, are 'more closely surveilled as a means of better exercising greater plan and control'.

Changing work and changing societies

From manufacturing to service work?

It has been argued, as we saw in Chapter 5, that societies are changing from industrial to post-industrial societies. The term deindustrialisation is frequently used when figures are produced in western industrialised societies to show falling numbers of people employed in organisations identified with manufacturing. The increasing numbers of people appearing in these statistics under headings of 'services' has encouraged talk of a move towards a new type of post-industrial society. The assertion that a move from secondary sector employment (manufacturing) to tertiary sector employment (services) indicates a basic move from an interest in goods to an interest in the consumption sphere, as commentators like Bell would suggest, has been seriously questioned by Gershuny (1978). See page 180

Much of the apparent increase in service employment (increases in numbers of managers, technologists and other professionals) is, according to Gershuny, associated with an increase in activities aimed at improving the efficiency of systems of material production. This is not to say that people are not looking for increased services, however. Gershuny's essential point is that service requirements will often be met by increased production by manufacturing industry. For example, we do not take washing to a laundry, so creating laundry service employment, but we purchase washing machines, thus putting demand on the manufacturing sector. What we have is a developing self-service economy, and technological developments may be such that those service occupations proper whose increased numbers have been part of the growth of the tertiary employment sector – education and health occupations – may in the future be replaced by technically-supplied services used more directly by the consumer (televised and videotaped educational services, for example).

It is clear that secondary and tertiary employment sectors are far more closely bound up with each other than is often realised and that it would be wise to abandon the old categories – which often confuse or conflate economic sectors and occupational types. People with a job making tea are in a 'service' occupation, for example, but if they serve tea to factory workers then they are in the manufacturing rather than the service sector of the economy. On the other hand, if they are serving tea to tourists they are in the service sector of the economy as well as in a service occupation. It therefore becomes difficult to disentangle what is being claimed when people refer to increasing 'service work' in the future.

In spite of these definitional difficulties, there is a pattern whereby people are more likely to work in areas like retailing, distribution, state employment, leisure, telecommunications and financial services than in factory-based manufacture. However, each of these is under pressure from the general competitive environment which has affected manufacturing and much of this work is similarly vulnerable to the impact of information technologies. The automation of retail checkouts and stock control, as well as electronic funds transfer at the point of sale, has considerable potential for limiting job increases in retail and distribution, for example. The pressures on state employment in many western countries have been towards a considerable reduction in employment in recent years and, on top of this, there will considerable potential for job reduction through the application of new technology to administration, tax collection, health (hospital monitoring devices and expert diagnostic systems, for example), education ('distance learning') and so on.

Leisure industries can be highly labour intensive – insofar as they involve actors, musicians, waiters, tourist guides and the like. But for every opportunity for work like this to be created we can envisage a lost opportunity where electronics provides alternatives ranging from the whole gamut of electrical entertainment devices to automatic vending facilities. Telecommunications are a substantial potential growth sector in economic terms, but it is possible to envisage increases in work here arising more in the producing of the devices than in their use. Even though we can envisage increased service work involving telecommunications in such areas as data gathering and the programming of information systems, it is easy to imagine this being grossly outweighed by other, and related, work losses. These could be in postal sorting and delivery, as electronic messages replace written ones, and in transport occupations as people engage in teleconferencing or personally communicate through video links rather than travel to meet each other. It is difficult to envisage precisely what will occur in many of these spheres, not least because a great deal depends on consumer preferences in matters of personal service (preferring singers to records or waiters to vending machines, for example).

However these changes work out in any particular society, there is an important argument that it is very damaging for an economy to be allowed to lose its manufacturing industry. A high performing economy cannot be sustained on the basis of the service sector alone – with manufactured goods being imported. Apart from the basic economic question of whether service industry, separated from manufacturing, can generate sufficient revenue to pay for these experts (Rowthorn and Wells 1987), it is argued that a significant manufacturing presence is vital to an economy because of the role it plays in sustaining a capacity to innovate, to develop skills and to design new products and methods. If there is no manufacturing setting for such skill development to focus on, the specialist services which are alleged to be able to take its place would be denied the skills they would need to do this (Cohen and Zysman 1987).

This argument for a continuing central role for manufacturing in modern societies depends on a belief that work in manufacturing enterprises is different from that in other sectors. The strongest element of this argument is that which sees a manufacturing interest being vital to sustaining a capacity to develop and deal with advanced technologies. If there is a difference between manufacturing and services in this respect, there is an equally powerful argument that the differences are often much less at the level of the workplace. The fast-food restaurant is a prime example of principles of industrial manufacturing being applied to service work. Taylorist principles underpin the operation of the fast-food restaurant. Labour in such restaurants is 'highly rationalised, and the goal is the discovery of the best, the most efficient way of grilling a hamburger, frying chicken, or serving a meal' (Ritzer 1993). As Ritzer comments, McDonald's, the best known fast-food business, did not invent these ideas, but combined them with the principles of bureaucracy and the assembly line 'to contribute to the creation of McDonaldisation'. It is claimed by Beynon (1992) that industrial manufacturing principles of mechanisation, rationalisation and routinisation are applied not only to fast-food service work but also to banking, retailing and other services work in a way which means that service work is tending to extend 'manual industrial labour' rather than erode it.

In contrast to these claims about the continuity between manufacturing and service, Allen and du Gay (1994) concentrate on the ways in which service work differs from manufacturing work. It is a 'hybrid' type of activity in that it combines with its *economic* function a *cultural* one (culture being involved with the 'production of distinct meanings'). Thus, a profitable service relation 'is one in which distinct meanings are produced for the customer' and service work can be seen as developing its own technologies – 'soft' technologies of 'interpersonal and emotion management'. This means that service work has its own characteristic types of skill, involving predispositions and capacities which are aimed at making it possible for them 'to win over the "hearts and minds" of customers'. This argument is helpful in enabling us to recognise service work as distinct and existing in its own right, so to speak, rather than always being subordinated conceptually or evaluatively to the 'real work' of manufacturing. However, it needs to be pointed out that a great deal of work in manufacturing organisations, especially in the managerial and marketing spheres, involves precisely these kinds of skills and dispositions. And a key principle of the 'total quality management' movement within manufacturing is that all workers, at all levels, should treat other members of the organisation as if they were customers.

Work in and beyond employment: the death of the job?

Central to the very nature of modern or industrial capitalist societies, as we saw in early chapters, is the institution of the 'job' as an ongoing relationship between the individual and an employer, with the latter paying a wage or salary to the former for performance of tasks which draw on a set of occupational skills which more or less remain constant over the period of employment. Thus, for a period of history covering perhaps less than a century, people have expected to leave school and 'get a job' with an employer which, with a degree of career advancement in some cases, could keep them occupied until their retirement. This pattern was supported by the existence of a 'work ethic' which motivated people to seek and sustain involvement in this institutional pattern.

Work ethic

A set of values which stresses the importance of work to the identity and sense of worth of the individual and which encourages an attitude of diligence, duty and a striving for success in the mind of the worker.

As we saw in the discussion of unemployment there is little evidence that See page 167 such an interest is widely diminishing among those with difficulty in finding employment. And a broader review of trends by Rose (1985, 1988a) leads him to reject the thesis that the work ethic is being abandoned. A process is under way, however whereby the more educated and highly trained have been 'modifying the interpretation' of the work ethic whilst not 'repudiating it as a scheme of values'. A new pattern of work meanings is emerging among the more educated and trained which contains elements of the traditional work ethic combined with a concern with self-fulfilment, the obtaining of 'just treatment' and the developing of 'more humanly rational economic organisation and technology'. It also involves an anti-authoritarianism in which people will be systematically suspicious of those giving orders. The adoption of these 'post-bourgeois values' is likely to be encouraged, says Rose, by such structural changes as the growth of service work (where employers will experience a tension between wanting tight control and avoiding the danger of disaffected employees alienating clients) and the attraction to public service work of those more educated people who believe that they can here better follow a 'service ethic'. The new values will also be supported by the continuation of 'commercial hedonism' (taking the waiting out of wanting, as the advertisers put it) and by the, as yet limited, renegotiation of family and gender roles.

All of this suggests a culture in which the majority of people expect and are seeking jobs of the type described above – a type which emerged with modern industrial capitalism. But will such jobs continue to be available? There will continue to be work, of course, but, as people have come to expect in advanced societies, will most adults have opportunities to be employed full-time over long periods to carry out tasks of a particular occupational nature? This is looking increasingly unlikely. As this chapter has shown so far, there is a series of restructuring pressures occurring across the globe in which there is a common theme of increasing competitiveness, efficiency and organisational 'leanness'. The implications for industrial capitalist societies are not yet clear. But we can look briefly at three main areas to begin to identify what is happening and what might happen:

- The implications of large-scale unemployment and the potential within this for 'informal economy' work activities.
- The rise of self-employment, small business, homeworking and 'teleworking'.
- The erosion of 'jobs' and occupational identities among those still employed.

Patterns of unemployment vary across the globe but it has been argued that more people are unemployed in the world in the 1990s than at any time since the 1930s. This is suggested by an International Labour Organisation report (ILO 1995) which describes almost a third of the international workforce as either unemployed or underemployed. Analyses of the causes of this vary – as we saw when considering the globalisation issue earlier in this chapter – but there is a common concern among those analysing international differences in employment and general levels of economic activity with a need for international agreements on both trade and labour market standards (Michie and Grieve Smith 1995). The challenges here are massive, given the competitive thrust of so much international business behaviour and the increasing difficulties of states to impose controls.

As a consequence of these pressures, many societies face coming to terms with the social and cultural, as well as the economic, implications of large-scale unemployment. In the USA, a combination of de-industrialisation elements of economic restructuring and existing patterns of ethnic segregation is creating a social category of the 'ghetto poor' (Wilson 1987; Massey and Denton 1993) and in Britain there is also evidence of a 'ghetto poor' developing, as illustrated in Byrne's (1995) close study of an industrial city in which he shows how the 'benefit-dependent and the irregularly and poorly employed live together in the same social areas'. Examination of school performance data for this area leads Byrne to suggest that this segregation will become 'reinforced over time by the absence of access for the children of the ghetto locales to favoured location in the labour market which increasingly depend on the acquisition of formal qualifications'. This trend towards a long-term poor means that certain social groups are disproportionately paying the price for the ongoing restructuring of work and economy, with all its implications for social justice, crime and social integration.

It has been suggested at various times that those people experiencing unemployment would tend to ameliorate their material situation by working in the informal economy (also known as the 'black', 'hidden', 'subterranean' or 'irregular' economy).

The informal economy

An area of economic exchange in which work, legal or illegal, is done for gain but is not officially 'declared' for such purposes as taxation.

There have been many types of argument about the extent and nature of the 'hidden economy' and the level of confusion which exists leads Harding and Jenkins (1989) to question the basis of the distinction between the formal and the informal. Insofar as these both exist, however, they are interdependent as well as separate. This is illustrated in Pahl's (1984) studies in the Isle of Sheppey which showed that the benefits gained from the various kinds of informal economic activities occurring in this not untypical part of Britain accrued to those households in which there were already incomes from formal employment. This is clearly seen in 'self-provisioning' activities where the employed were much better able to brew their own beer or do their own decorating than the unemployed – who were less able to afford the materials. As in the formal business world, money is needed for investment before work is created, whether this be 'do-it-yourself' work or 'moonlighting' activities where tools, transport and raw materials are often needed to enable one to earn extra money 'on the side'. If this evidence is right, and it is supported by French evidence, as Gallie (1985) mentions, then the informal economy is to be seen as functioning to reinforce a polarised pattern of 'haves' and 'have nots' in society rather than promising to undermine it.

A cultural theme given great prominence by the British state during the 1980s in its attempts to restructure the economy along more market-oriented lines was that of *enterprise*. This broad concept was given a 'narrowly economistic' meaning (Selden 1991) and a 'small business revivalism' (Ritchie 1991) played a key role in state exhortations to people to engage in economic activity on their own behalf rather than through employment with an existing organisation. The link assumed in this particular rhetoric of economic reconstruction between 'being enterprising' and running a small business is a doubtful one, given that the majority of small businesses involve little by way of innovation or creativity (Curran and Burrows 1986; Watson 1995a). A review of the growth of self-employment in Britain concludes, indeed, that

> the sudden rise in self-employment in the 1980s could be explained as much by employers pursuing a strategy of subcontracting more tasks and functions (either to individual self-employed or to independent companies) as by a resurgence of the enterprise culture finding expression among new recruits to self-employment.
>
> (Hakim 1988)

A reworking of survey evidence by Curran and Burrows (1988) for this period leads the authors to stress the need to distinguish between small business owners (who may or may not create 'employment' by taking on employees) and the growing number of people who are simply taking on paid work tasks other than through being engaged by an employer. The validity of this point is shown by a study reviewing the position in the 1990s which reveals that, although the number of self-employed in Britain had grown to 13 per cent of the total workforce by 1994, the numbers employing at least one person in addition to themselves had fallen to 28 per cent compared to the 39 per cent of a decade earlier (Small Business Research Trust 1995). Nevertheless, the survey does show that one in five of the small firms which did employ people had increased the numbers employed. This was at a time when large companies were regularly announcing job losses. The emerging pattern appears to be that small businesses are not substantial generators of employment in an absolute sense, but are nevertheless more significant job creators than large employers. This is not, however, to say that the people 'taken on' by these enterprises will retain their jobs in the long term. The trends towards flexibility and 'outsourcing' considered earlier in this chapter could lead us to conclude that small firms are, in effect, taking on labour *on behalf of larger organisations who would previously have employed them themselves*. And, following the logic of flexibility which is behind such shifts, these smaller employers may 'lay off' this labour when demand changes as readily as they took it on.

What occurs in the sphere of self-employment and small business is intimately connected with the wider, indeed global, patterns of work restructuring. The activities of the small businesses, subcontractors and homeworkers who make up so much of the British clothing industry, for example, are shown by Phizacklea (1990) to be shaped both by the processes of globalisation and the pursuit of profitability through cheap labour, on the one hand, and the domestic ethnic and labour market structures on the other. Competitiveness is problematic because of overseas competition and because of the inability to afford the computer-aided equipment used by bigger firms. The consequence of this is low wages and insecurity for large numbers of ethic minority women. Again broader social patterns and patterns of economic and employment activity are seen to be closely interrelated.

The link between work forms and wider social patterns is also seen in Allen and Wolkowitz's (1987) study of a range of homeworking activities. This suggests that the bulk of such work in Britain is, in effect, wage work in disguise. The homeworkers, who tend to have regular relationships with the businesses which bring work to their houses, lack the legal protection and benefits of the properly employed yet still experience the pressure of deadlines, productivity rates, piece-work systems, and fragmented work tasks. Allen and Wolkowitz regard this work not only as reinforcing gender patterns of inequality (given the predominance of women homeworkers) but as an employment strategy of capitalist firms which lowers both their labour and capital costs. This gives a firm following this strategy an advantage over those convention-ally employing people. And these competitive pressures, in turn, re-inforce the tendency to casualise the work of those they employ as in-workers. The type of work considered in this study is close to traditions which existed before the industrial revolution and the spread of the factory system. The use of computers and information technology may, however, see a new variant of the old theme emerge.

It has been widely forecast that homeworking among clerical and 'professional' workers will increase as more people engage in 'tele-working', 'telecommuting' or 'networking', where computers are used to link the home and the client organisation. This does not yet appear to have had a substantial impact. Most of those working on this basis are involved in the computer industry itself and the majority of the British workers contacted and interviewed by Huws (1984) were women who had gone freelance to meet more easily their domestic, and particularly child-rearing, responsibilities. These representatives of what has been seen as the 'cottage industry of the future' experienced an enhanced quality of life but had sacrificed sickness, holiday and pension rights and had reduced their income by leaving conventional employment. Reasons for the slow growth of this type of activity are suggested by Wilson (1991) who gives particular attention to the problems which managers in companies using the system have found in operating it. Managers have found difficulties in both monitoring and rewarding the efforts of the skilled professional workers who currently form the majority of those working in this way. Wilson also reports that companies found it necessary to invest time and effort in maintaining the involvement of such workers with the organisation. Taken together, this range of factors meant that using the services of skilled teleworkers was neither as simple nor as relatively cheap as many had envisaged. A study by Stanworth and Stanworth (1992) reinforces a view of teleworking as something which will develop only slowly and patchily and they show that the preferred working pattern among the teleworkers they studied was one in which people followed a combination of home and office working. This gives individuals the benefits of flexibility in their own lifestyle whilst avoiding a sense of isolation from others in the world of work.

Finally, in this review of how work is changing in and beyond employment, we turn to those who will be employed in what we saw earlier as the 'core' elements of work organisations – those with security of employment and a relatively high level of rewards which they receive in return for being flexible, not just in the tasks they take on, but in the skills which they acquire and use. One implication of a trend in this direction, combined as it is likely to be with the growth of teamworking and a commitment to philosophies of 'continuous improvement' and involvement in the values of a corporate culture, is what Casey (1995) calls *the demise of occupation*. In her study of the Hephaestus corporation she shows how its former specialists in mechanical and electrical engineering, in computing science, in chemistry and maths were 'crossing former professional demarcations and performing a range of duties in the team structure that promotes team responsibility for product development'. Casey claims that there has not yet been a full recognition of the social and self-identity implications of the decline of specialist occupations as 'persons from expert professions along with those from trade and service occupations are being transformed into multifaceted, pan-occupational team players in the new corporate organisation'. The social bondings which were provided by occupational status are being taken over by 'the identificatory processes of the new corporation'.

This trend takes increasing numbers away from having a job in what is clearly becoming an especially historically specific sense of the term 'job' – a sense in which the individual has an ongoing relationship with an employer who pays a wage or salary for the performance of tasks which utilise a set of occupational skills which more or less remain constant over the period of employment. The trend, says Bridges (1995) is towards the *dejobbed organisation* and those who, in the changing patterns of work organisation, remain in employment will increasingly 'work full-time under arrangements too idiosyncratic to be called jobs'. A 'redeployment manager' of a company producing microprocesssors is quoted as saying that they 'no longer look at a job as a function or a certain kind of work [but] as a set of skills and competencies'. This is similar to what was observed in a study of a British telecommunications company in which the very word 'job' was deliberately being removed from the corporate vocabulary (Watson 1994a). According to what Bridges calls the 'new rules' of work organisation, everyone is a *contingent* worker, not just the part-timers and contract workers; everyone's employment 'is contingent on the results that the organisation can achieve' and individuals will tend to work in project teams made up of people with different backgrounds. This experience is one in which

> workers must be able to switch their focus rapidly from one task to another, to work with people with very different mindsets, to work in situations where the group is the responsible party and the manager is only a co-ordinator, to work without a clear job description, and to work on several projects at the same time.

This image of the dejobbed organisation is based on trends observed in a range of high technology organisations. We can only speculate how far such a trend will extend across the range of what Bridges calls the 'slower moving industries', the 'traditional professions' and 'government service'. He believes that the patterns of reorganisation occurring in these areas does reveal, however, their moving towards the 'new rules' and the general demise of 'the job' as we have known it. If we look back over the range of trends reviewed in this chapter, and especially the pressures on businesses and other employers to pursue flexibility both for predictability and for adaptability in the face of global and technological change, we can see that this view fits with a great deal of what is generally happening. It appears that a high proportion of those in the world who wish to work will remain unemployed. It appears that a growing proportion of those who find work will experience it as a casual, part-time, temporary and contingent activity. In the light of this, it is perhaps not surprising to find that those with the advantage of full-time continuing employment are likely to experience a degree of discomfort and stress within their privilege.

■   ■   ■

Glossary

Action/social action Action is behaviour which has meaning or purpose. Social action, which Max Weber put forward as the fundamental concept in sociology, is behaviour which, through the meaning which is attached to it by individuals, takes account of the behaviour of others and is thereby oriented in its course. Thus, normal breathing would not constitute action – or social action. But if a person were to breathe heavily in a social situation to make a point then this would be social action (p. 14).

Action research A form of combined research and consultancy in which the client receives help with problem-solving whilst the researcher/consultant is able to contribute the knowledge gained in the process to the academic community (p. 34).

Alienation A state of existence in which human beings are not fulfilling their 'humanness'. They are living at a 'lower level' than they potentially might, as a result of their circumstances (p. 115).

Anomie A form of social breakdown in which the norms which would otherwise prevail in a given situation cease to operate (p. 51).

Authority Power which has been 'legitimised' or made acceptable to those subject to it. *See* **Power**.

Automation The application of machinery which is controlled and co-ordinated by computerised programmes to tasks previously done by direct human effort.

Bourgeoisie A Marxist category which includes all of those in a capitalist society whose ownership of capital enables them to subsist without selling their labour power (their capacity to work). The term is sometimes used in a more general way to refer to a 'middle class' (p. 7).

Bureaucracy The main design principle of modern formal organisations – central to which is a hierarchical structure of authority in which specialised office holders fulfil specified responsibilities according to codified rules and procedures. Weber's ideal type of bureaucracy is, in effect, a sketch of an impossibly pure and unachievable structure against which reality can be compared (pp. 241, 242).

Capitalism A type of political economy in which ownership and control of wealth (and therefore the means of production) is in private hands, a free market operates, the pursuit of profit motivates economic activity and the capacity to work of those without capital is 'sold' to those who own capital – or to their agents (p. 96).

Career A sequence of social positions filled by a person throughout their life. **Subjective career** is the perceived pattern which emerges as individuals make sense of the way they move through social positions in the course of their life (p. 127).

Class, social An individual's class position is a matter of the part which they play (or the person upon whom they are dependent plays) within the division of labour of a society and the implications which this has for their access to those experiences, goods and services which are scarce and valued in that society (p. 195).

Class-consciousness A state of awareness of their common interests and situation by the members of an objectively existing social class.

Class imagery The ways in which people perceive their own class position and how this relates to other class positions (p. 153).

Classical administrative principles Universally applicable rules of organisational design widely taught and applied, especially in the first half of the twentieth century (p. 243).

Closed shop An arrangement whereby work in a particular setting is exclusively carried out by members of a specified trade union. Pre-entry closed shops required workers to be union members before they could be recruited whereas the new worker could join the union after entering the job in the case of the post-entry closed shop (p. 323).

Closure, social The process whereby a group seeks to gain or defend its advantages over other groups by closing its ranks to those it defines as outsiders.

Collective bargaining   A method of agreeing work conditions and rewards through a process of negotiation between employer representatives and the representatives of collectively organised employees (p. 313).

Community   Often used synonymously with 'society'. The word generally implies a smaller entity than does 'society', however. The essence of the idea of community is that people are strongly aware of belonging to it and accept its traditions. It is small-scale and intimate and is characterised by face-to-face relationships (p. 231).

Concepts   The building blocks of models and theories – working definitions of factors playing a part in a scientific analysis (p. 27).

Conjugal roles   The parts played in the household by husbands and wives.

Contingencies   In organisation theory, those circumstances which influence the ways in which organisations are structured. Examples are the size of the organisation, the nature of the technology used or the state of the organisation's environment (p. 250).

Contradictions   These arise within a social structure when certain principles on which the structure is based clash with each other in a way which undermines that structure (p. 107).

Convergence thesis   Proposes that societies which industrialise become increasingly alike in their social, political and cultural characteristics as well as their work organisations (p. 86).

Co-operatives   Work enterprises jointly owned and controlled by those who work in them.

Corporatism   A political system in which principal decisions, especially with regard to the economy, are made by the state in close association with employer, trade union and other pressure group organisations (p. 184).

Cultural capital   The various linguistic and social competences derived from and certificated by the education system and manifested in a certain manner, ethos, know-how and set of aspirations.

Culture   The system of meanings which is shared by members of a human grouping and which defines what is good and bad, right and wrong and what are the appropriate ways for members of that grouping to think and behave (p. 12, 113).

Deskilling   An approach to the redesign of jobs which involves a lowering of the skill levels required from those filling the job than had previously been the case.

Determinism   A way of thinking in which the causal factors behind whatever is being considered are seen to lie outside human agency.

Deviance   All social life is characterised by the existence of rules, standards or norms. Deviance is simply the failure, deliberate or otherwise, of people to comply with the standards of any group to which they belong.

Dialectic   The interplay between two potential opposites which leads to a third possibility. For example, the interplay between individual initiative and social constraint (which are often seen as opposing phenomena) can be seen as leading to a third phenomenon – 'society'.

Differentiation   The process in which a society or an organisation is divided into specialised parts which contribute to the functioning of the whole.

Dirty work   An occupational activity which plays a necessary role in a society but which is regarded in some respects as morally doubtful (p. 213).

Discourse   A set of concepts, statements, terms and expressions which constitute a way of talking or writing about a particular aspect of life, thus framing the way people understand and act with respect to that area of existence (p. 75).

Division of labour   The allocation of work tasks to various groups or categories of individual. **Social division of labour** is the allocation of work tasks at the level of society, typically into trades and occupations. **Technical division of labour** is task specialisation within an occupation or broad work task (p. 177, 178).

Domestic labour   Household tasks such as cooking, cleaning, shopping and looking after dependent young, old or sick members of the household (p. 212).

Dominant coalition   The grouping of individuals within an organisation who effectively have greater influence over events than any other grouping.

Dualism   The effective division of an economy into two parts: typically a prosperous and stable 'core' sector of enterprises and jobs and a 'peripheral' sector which is relatively and systematically disadvantaged (p. 185). *See* **Labour markets**.

Effort bargain   *See* **Implicit contract**.

Embourgeoisement   The adoption by working-class people of the attitudes and lifestyle of middle-class groups.

Emotional labour   A type of work activity in which the worker is required to display particular emotions in the course of providing a service (p. 130).

Empirical enquiry   That part of the social scientist's endeavour which involves observation, experiment or other forms of data collection as opposed to the conceptual, theoretical and interpretative work which is also carried out.

Employment strategy   The general direction followed by an organisation in the way its management handles the problems created for performance and long-term survival by the range of employee constituencies and other constituencies concerned with employees (p. 327).

Ethnic group   A group of people sharing a language, customs and traditions. This is increasingly used to replace the idea of the 'racial group' which many social scientists feel to be based on questionable biological assumptions.

Ethnography A method of social science research in which the subjects are directly observed in their normal setting and in their normal pattern of living.

Ethnomethodology A form of sociological analysis which focuses on the everyday and commonplace practices of people and concentrates on how they go about creating a sense of reality and normality for themselves (p. 61).

Flexibility The achievement in work organisation and employment practices of managerial manoeuvrability in two forms: (a) flexibility for predictability and tight control; and (b) flexibility for adaptability and innovation (p. 347).

Flexible firm A type of employing organisation which divides its workforce into *core* elements which are given security and high rewards in return for a willingness to adapt, innovate and take on new skills, and *peripheral* elements who are given more specific tasks and less commitment of continuing employment and skill enhancement (p. 348).

Flexible specialisation An approach to employment and work organisation which offers customised products to diversified markets, building trusting and co-operative relationships both with employees, who use advanced technologies in a craft way, and other organisations within a business district and its associated community (p. 344).

Fordism A pattern of industrial organisation and employment policy in which (a) mass production techniques and an associated deskilling of jobs is combined with (b) treatment of employees which recognises that workers are also consumers whose earning power and consumption attitudes – as well as their workplace efficiency – affect the success of the enterprise (p. 246).

Function In simple terms, an action or an institution has a function within a social system if it contributes towards the maintenance or adaptation of that system. A 'dysfunction' exists when the effect is one 'harmful' to that system.

Functionalism An approach within sociology which concentrates on how the institutions or the 'parts' of a social system contribute to that system (be it a group, organisation or society) as a whole. Emphasis tends to be given to functions instead of causes.

Gender The social and cultural dimension of being male and female, which usually, but not always, coincides with having a biological sex of male or female.

Globalisation A trend in which the economic, political and cultural activities of people in different countries increasingly influence each other and become interdependent (p. 335).

Historicism   Sociologists generally use this term in the sense suggested by Karl Popper to refer to an approach to history which sees it as following laws (p. 88).

Human relations   The term is used by sociologists almost exclusively to refer to a 'school' of industrial sociology and to managerial styles which follow its general recommendations. The school is that associated with the Hawthorne experiments carried out in the pre-war years in the USA. Its emphasis is on the ways in which workers' 'social needs' are or are not met in the work situation (p. 52).

Humour, workplace   All forms of communication occurring in the work situation which create within people feelings of amusement and a predisposition to express that emotion through laughter (p. 301).

Ideal type   A model of a phenomenon or a situation which extracts its essential or 'pure' elements. It represents what the item or institution (capitalism, bureaucracy, instrumental work orientation, for example) would look like if it existed in a pure form (p. 37).

Ideology/group ideology   A set of ideas which are located within a particular social group and which fulfils functions for that group. It helps defend, justify and further the interests of the group with which it is associated.

Implicit contract   The tacit agreement between an employer and the employee about what the employee will 'put in' to the job and the rewards and benefits for which this will be exchanged (p. 139).

Incorporation   The process of directing the political and economic activities of groups who may threaten a social order or system so that they operate within that order instead of threatening it. This is often associated with the 'institutionalising' of conflict (p. 321).

Indulgency pattern   The ignoring of selected rule infringements by supervisors in return for the those being supervised allowing supervisors to call for co-operation in matters which, strictly speaking, they could refuse (p. 269).

Industrial capitalism   Large-scale or complex machinery and associated technique is widely applied to the pursuit of economic efficiency on a basis whereby the capacity for work of the members of some groups is sold to others who control and organise it in such a way that the latter groups maintain relative advantage with regard to those resources which are scarce and generally valued (p. 97).

Industrial relations   The activities and institutions associated with relationships between employers and groups of collectively organised employees (p. 283).

Informal economy An area of economic exchange in which work, legal or illegal, is done for gain but is not officially 'declared' for such purposes as taxation (p. 367).

Information technology The combination of microelectronic and computing technologies with telecommunications potentially to transform the way in which human information is manipulated and, hence, radically alter the way both production and consumption activities are shaped. Information technology has the potential to **informate work** because it can 'record' and hence can 'play back' or make visible the processes behind the operations that were once deep in the minds of the people doing that work (p. 339, 341).

Institution, social A regularly occurring and therefore normal pattern of actions and relationships (p. 12).

Instrumentalism An attitude to work which regards it as a means towards ends other than ones to do with work itself. It usually suggests a primary concern with the money to be earned.

Interpretive conceptions of social science These see social science as requiring different procedures from physical sciences. The social world is regarded as a reality only accessible through the meanings developed by social actors. *Understandings* of social processes and the patterns within them are sought rather than *explanations* of social behaviour (p. 24).

Job enrichment The expansion of the scope of jobs by such means as the reintegration of maintenance or inspection tasks, an extension of the work cycle or an increased degree of delegation of decision-making opportunities for employees (p. 255).

Job redesign principles Include (1) the principle of closure whereby the scope of the job is such that it includes all the tasks necessary to complete a product or process, thus giving the individual a sense of achievement; (2) the incorporation of control and monitoring tasks whereby the individual or group assumes responsibility for its own quality and reliability; (3) task variety whereby the worker understands a range of tasks so as to be able to vary the daily work experience; (4) self-regulation of work speed and the allowance of some choice over work methods and sequence; (5) a job structure which allows some social interaction and the possibility of co-operation among workers (p. 257).

Labour market, internal The creation by an employer of a stable and well-rewarded labour force through a policy of internal promotion and training (p. 186).

Labour markets, dual The labour market dimension of *dualism* in which there is a relatively advantaged *primary* type of employment and a relatively disadvantaged *secondary* type of work and employment (p. 185).

Labour movement   A coming together of such bodies as trade unions and associated political parties to represent the interests which employed people as a whole are believed to hold in common (p. 312).

Labour process, capitalist   One in which the interests of the capital-owning class are represented by managements whose basic task is to design, control and monitor work tasks and activities so as to ensure the effective extraction of surplus value from the labour activity of employees (p. 260).

Leisure   Activities which people pursue for pleasure and which are not a necessary part of their business, employment or domestic management obligations (p. 163).

Life chances   The ability to gain access to scarce and valued goods and services such as a home, food and education (p. 196).

Management   The set of roles in an organisation and the activities associated with them which are primarily concerned with directing the organisation rather than with carrying out the tasks which make up the main work of the organisation.

Managerialism   A belief that the people who manage or 'direct' the corporations of modern societies have taken control away from those allegedly separate interests who own wealth (p. 203).

Methodology   A term often misused to refer to research techniques and which, more properly, refers to the philosophical issues raised by the attempt to investigate the world scientifically.

Micropolitics   The political processes which occur within organisations as individuals, groups and organisational 'sub-units' compete for access to scarce and valued material and symbolic resources (p. 263).

Mobility, social   The movement of people between different positions in the pattern of inequality of any society. It may be intra-generational (the individual changes their position within their own life career) or inter-generational (where the individual moves into a position which differs from that of their parents). Movement may be upwards or downwards.

Models   Analytical schemes which simplify reality by selecting certain phenomena and suggesting particular relationships between them (p. 26).

Negotiated order   A view of social or organisational patterning as the *outcome* of interactions between people and their mutually developed meanings (p. 61).

Norm, social   Part of the underlying pattern of social life – the standards to which people are expected to conform or the rules of conduct whose infringement may result in sanctions intended to encourage conformity (p. 12).

Occupation   Engagement on a regular basis in a part or the whole of a range of work tasks which are identified under a particular heading or title by both those carrying out these tasks and by a wider public (p. 171).

Occupational career   the sequence of positions through which the member of an occupation typically passes during the part of their life which they spend in that occupation (p. 219).

Occupational community   A form of local social organisation in which people's working and non-working lives are both closely identified with members of the occupation in which they work (p. 230).

Occupational culture   The set of ideas, values, attitudes, norms, procedures and artifacts characteristically associated with an occupation (p. 227).

Occupational ideology   A set of ideas developed by an occupational group, and especially by its leaders, to legitimate the pursuit of the group members' common occupationally-related interests (p. 226).

Occupational principle of work structuring   Emphasises the way in which people with similar skills, traditions and values co-operatively conceive, execute and regulate work tasks. To be contrasted to the organisational or administrative principle of work structuring (p. 234).

Occupational recruitment   The typical processes and routes of entry followed by members of an occupation (p. 215).

Occupational socialisation   The process whereby individuals learn about the norms, values, customs and beliefs associated with an occupation which they have joined so that they are able to act as full members of that occupation (p. 215).

Occupational strategy   An action taken by the members of an occupation to advance or defend their common interests as occupational members (p. 220).

Occupational structure   The pattern in a society which is created by the distribution of the labour force across the range of existing types of work or occupation (p. 174).

Organisation man   An allegedly existing type of male executive employee whose whole life is moulded by the corporation for whom he works.

Organisational culture   The system of meanings which are shared by members of an organisation and which defines what is good and bad, right and wrong and what are the appropriate ways for the members of the organisation to think and behave (p. 276).

Organisational principle of work structuring   Emphasises the ways in which some people conceive of and design work tasks in the light of certain ends and then recruit, pay, co-ordinate and control the efforts of other people who do not necessarily share those ends, to fulfil work tasks. To be contrasted to the occupational principle of work structuring (p. 234).

Organisational structure   Sociologically, this would include all those relatively stable aspects or regularities in behaviour within an organisation, whether they be formally or 'officially' sanctioned or not. Writers on organisations often use the term, however, to refer only to the set of officially designed roles, procedures, groupings and hierarchies which are represented by the 'organisation chart' or the official manuals. Sometimes these are referred to as the 'formal' aspects of organisational structure and the remaining category as 'informal'. The terms 'official and unofficial aspects of structure' are preferred here (p. 238).

Organisations, work   Social and technical arrangements in which a number of people come or are brought together in a relationship where the actions of some are directed by others towards the achievement of certain tasks (p. 237).

Orientation to work   The meaning attached by individuals to their work which predisposes them to both think and act in particular ways with regard to that work. The work orientation perspective takes the employee's own definition of the situation as an 'initial basis for the explanation of their social behaviour and relationships' (Goldthorpe, Lockwood *et al.* 1968) (pp. 118, 121).

Paradigm   A 'model' in the very broadest sense in science which includes basic ideas about how investigation should proceed as well as what assumptions are made about the relationships between phenomena.

Paradox of consequences   Human actions often have unintended consequences which may be quite different from or even in direct opposition to what was intended. This is because their fulfilment typically depends on the actions of others who will have their own interests, interpretations and priorities (p. 65).

Paradox of organisations   The means used by the controlling management of the organisation to achieve whatever goals they choose or are required to pursue do not necessarily facilitate the effective achievement of these goals since these 'means' involve human beings who have goals of their own, which may not be congruent with those of the managers (p. 247).

Patriarchy   The system of interrelated social structures and cultural practices through which men exploit women (p. 194).

Phenomenology   In sociology, this covers those approaches which concentrate on the role of human subjectivity in everyday social life and upon human consciousness. Ethnomethodology is an example of this type of approach.

Pluralism   Social scientific perspectives which emphasise the multiplicity of interest groups which exist in societies. It is often, unreasonably, used to refer to what is properly seen as just one type of pluralist perspective in which the various interest groupings in society are seen as being more or less equally powerful. A **radical pluralist** frame of reference recognises the plurality of groups and interests in society (and welcomes social pluralism *in principle*) whilst observing the more basic patterns of power and inequality which tend to shape, as well as be shaped by it (p. 286).

Political economy Social scientific approaches which emphasise the power dimensions of social life and how these, together with the ways in which production is organised, influence whatever particular phenomena are being considered.

Population ecology A type of organisation theory which concentrates on how organisations adapt and evolve in order to survive within the general population of organisations of which they are a part (p. 273).

Positivism Generally used to refer to a position which sees social science and the natural or physical sciences as equivalent and therefore as amenable to the same basic investigative procedure. It sees the social world as an objective reality external to those who study it and seeks explanations in the forms of general theories or 'covering laws' which can be used to make predictions. To some, the essence of the positivist stance in the social sciences is a view of social science as being socially useful in that it can help in the prediction and therefore the control of social phenomena and events (p. 23).

Post-Fordism A pattern of industrial organisation and employment policy in which skilled and trusted labour is used continuously to develop and customise products for small markets (p. 343).

Post-industrial society A type of economically advanced social order in which the centrally important resource is knowledge, service work has largely replaced manufacturing employment and knowledge-based occupations play a privileged role (p. 180).

Postmodernism A way of looking at the world which rejects attempts to build systematic explanations of history and human activity and which, instead, concentrates on the ways in which human beings 'invent' their worlds, especially through language and cultural innovation (p. 74).

Postmodernity A state into which the world is moving which departs from the key organising principles of modernity (p. 76).

Power The capacity of any group or individual to affect the outcome of any situation in such a way that access is achieved to whatever resources are scarce and valued within a society or a part of that society.

Problematic This is similar to a paradigm (above) but the term emphasises the role of certain problems or issues which give a focus to the process of selecting phenomena on which to concentrate. A problematic is thus a set of linked concepts focusing on particular problems or issues.

Process, social Regularities or patterns in social behaviour, observed in movement (p. 12).

Professionalisation A process followed by an occupation to increase its members' status, relative autonomy and rewards and influence through such activities as setting up a professional body to control entry and practice, establishing codes of conduct, making claims of altruism and a key role in serving the community (p. 224).

Professions Occupations who have been relatively successful in gaining high status in certain societies on the basis of a claimed specialist expertise over which they have gained a degree of monopoly control (p. 222).

Proletarianisation A trend whereby members of a 'middle-class' occupational group move downwards in the class and status hierarchy, finding themselves located in a position more like that of working-class rather than middle-class people (p. 207).

Proletariat This category, in the basic Marxist scheme, includes all of those who lack sufficient capital upon which they can subsist and who, therefore, are forced to 'sell their labour power' (capacity to work) on the market.

Psychologism A tendency to explain social behaviour solely in terms of psychological characteristics of individuals (p. 17).

Rationalisation A trend in social change whereby traditional or magical criteria of action are replaced by technical, calculative or scientific criteria (p. 66).

Rationality and change The criterion of rationality involves submitting actions to constant calculative scrutiny and produces a continuous drive towards change (p. 103).

Rationality, bounded Human reasoning and decision-making is restricted in its scope by the fact that human beings have both perceptual and information-processing limits (p. 270).

Reification An error in which an abstraction is treated as a 'thing'. It is committed when one talks of 'society' or an 'organisation' making one do something. This is regarded as an error by many social scientists because it implies a denial of the human agency or choices which are, in fact, bringing about this behaviour.

Responsible autonomy An approach to the design of work tasks which gives discretion to those doing the work on the understanding that they will choose to accept the managerial trust put in them and perform the tasks in accordance with managerial priorities (p. 14).

Restructuring of work The changing patterns of work experience and occupational activity resulting from economic, political and cultural changes unfolding across the world (p. 334).

Role, social People are said to be playing a role in social life whenever they act in a situation according to well-defined expectations (p. 11).

Sabotage The deliberate disruption of work flows within an organisation or the undermining of the conditions whereby dominant management purposes are readily achieved (p. 306).

Science A formal, systematic and precise approach to building up a body of knowledge and theory which is rigorous in testing propositions against available evidence. Sociology is a science because it makes generalisations as systematically as possible in the light of available evidence (p. 20).

Scientific management An approach to workplace organisation and job design associated with F. W. Taylor which is based on the principle of giving as much initiative about how tasks are done as possible to managerial experts who define precisely how each detailed aspect of every job is to be carried out (p. 44).

Self-actualization 'To become more and more what one is, to become everything that one is capable of becoming' (Maslow 1943) (p. 48).

Self-identity The conception which each individual develops of who and what they are (p. 126).

Semi-autonomous workgroup The grouping of individual jobs to focus work activities on a general 'whole task', with work group members being given discretion over how the task is completed (p. 256).

Shop steward A worker representative and 'lay' trade union official who represents to management the interests of fellow employees who elect the representative as their workplace spokesperson (p. 317).

Socialisation The process whereby individuals learn about the norms, values, customs and beliefs of a group, occupation, organisation or society.

Sociology The academic study of the relationships which develop between human beings as they organise themselves and are organised by others in societies (p. 2).

Socio-technical systems perspective Stresses that to achieve the organisation's 'primary task' most effectively, the technical and the social components of the system must be designed to take each other into account (p. 255).

State That set of institutions which, in a modern society, typically includes government, parliament, civil service, educational and welfare apparatuses, the police, military and judiciary.

Status That aspect of social inequality whereby different positions are awarded different degrees of prestige or honour (p. 197).

Stratification, social The patterns underlying the inequalities which exist between people in a society and form 'layers' on the basis of such factors as their class or status (p. 195).

Strike The collective withdrawal from work of a group of employees to exert pressure on the employer over any issue in which the two sides have a difference.

Structuration   The ongoing process whereby individual initiatives are inter-woven into the patterns of human interaction which sometimes constrain and sometimes enable those initiatives (p. 11).

Structure, social   Regularities or patterns in social behaviour, observed as 'frozen in time'.

Symbolic interactionism   Studies social interaction through a focus on the ways in which people develop their concept of *self* through processes of communication in which symbols such as words, gestures and dress allow people to understand the expectations of others (p. 59).

Systems thinking   Social entities such as societies or organisations can be viewed as if they were self-regulating bodies exchanging energy and matter with their environment in order to survive (p. 55).

Taylorism   *See* **Scientific management.**

Technological implications thinking   The technology being used deter-mines, or at least closely constrains, the way in which tasks are organised which, in turn, significantly influences the attitudes and behaviour of workers (p. 148).

Technology   The tools, machines and control devices used to carry out tasks and the principles, techniques and reasoning which accompany them (p. 91).

Theory   Theories, in the most general sense, are ideas about how phenomena relate to each other and, especially, about how particular events or actions tend to lead to others. Theorising is about generalising and is at the heart of all scientific endeavour (p. 21).

Total quality management   An approach to the production of goods and services in which employees at all levels focus on 'satisfying customers', use statistical and other techniques to monitor their work and seek continuous improvement in the processes used and the quality of what is produced (p. 357).

Trade union   An association of employees formed to improve their ability to negotiate working conditions and rewards with employers and, sometimes, to represent common interests within the political sphere beyond the workplace (p. 311).

Unionateness   A measure of how committed the members of a trade union are to the traditional principles of trade unionism and the labour movement.

Value freedom   The idea that social scientific work can be done which is not unduly compromised by the values of the social scientists carrying it out (p. 64).

Values   Notions of what is good and bad, right and wrong, within a society or a part of a society (p. 12).

Work   The carrying out of tasks which enable people to *make a living* within the environment in which they find themselves (p. 113).

Work ethic A set of values which stresses the importance of work to the identity and sense of worth of the individual and which encourages an attitude of diligence, duty and a striving for success in the mind of the worker. It makes work the essential prerequisite of personal and social advancement, of prestige, of virtue and of self-fulfilment (pp. 115, 365).

■   ■   ■

Bibliography

Abbott, A. (1988) *The System of Professions: an essay on the division of expert labour*, Chicago: University of Chicago Press.

Abercrombie, N. and Warde, A. (eds) (1992) *Social Change in Contemporary Britain*, Cambridge: Polity.

Aberle, D. F. and Naegele, K. D. (1961) 'Middle-class fathers' occupational role and attitudes towards children', in Bell, N. W. and Vogel, E. F. (eds) *A Modern Introduction to the Family*, London: Routledge.

Ackroyd, S., Burrell, G., Hughes, M. and Whitaker, A. (1988) 'The Japanisation of British industry?', *Industrial Relations Journal*, 19(1): 11–23.

Aglietta, M. (1979) *A Theory of Capitalist Regulation: the U.S. experience*, London: New Left Books.

Albrow, M. (1970) *Bureaucracy*, London: Macmillan.

Albrow, M. (1994) 'Accounting for organisational feeling', in Ray and Reed (eds).

Allen, J. and du Gay, P. (1994) 'Industry and the rest: the economic identity of services', *Work, Economy and Society*, 8(2): 255–71.

Allen, S. and Truman, C. (eds) (1993) *Women in Business: perspectives on women entrepreneurs*, London: Routledge.

Allen, S. and Wolkowitz, C. (1987) *Homeworking: myths and realities*, London: Macmillan.

Alvesson, M. and Willmott, H. (eds) (1992) *Critical Management Studies*, London: Sage.

Anthony, P. D. (1977) *The Ideology of Work*, London: Tavistock.

Anthony, P. (1994) *Managing Culture*, Milton Keynes: Open University Press.

Applebaum, H. A. (1981) *Royal Blue: the culture of construction workers*, New York: Holt, Rinehart & Winston.

Arendt, H. (1959) *The Human Condition*, New York: Doubleday.

Armstrong, P. (1986) 'Management control strategies and interprofessional competition: the case of accountancy and personnel management', in Knights and Willmott (eds).

Armstrong, P. (1989) 'Management labour process and agency', *Work, Employment and Society*, 3(3): 307–22.

Armstrong, P. (1993) 'Professional knowledge and social mobility: postwar changes in the knowledge-base of management accounting', *Work, Economy and Society*, 7(1): 1–21.

Aron, R. (1967) *Eighteen Lectures on Industrial Society*, London: Weidenfeld & Nicolson.

Ashton, D. N. (1985) *Unemployment under Capitalism: the sociology of British and American labour*, Brighton: Wheatsheaf.

Ashton, D. N., Maguire, M. J. and Spilsbury, M. (1990) *Restructuring the Labour Market: the implications for youth*, London: Macmillan.

Atkinson, J. (1985) 'Flexibility: planning for an uncertain future', *Manpower Policy and Practice*, 1: 25–30.

Atkinson, J. (1987) 'Flexibility or fragmentation? The UK labour market in the eighties', *Labour and Society*, 12(1): 87–105.

Badham, R. (1984) 'The sociology of industrial and post-industrial societies', *Current Sociology*, 32(1): 1–94.

Baechler, J. (1975) *The Origins of Capitalism*, Oxford: Blackwell.

Baechler, J., Hall, J. A. and Mann, M. (eds) (1988) *Europe and the Rise of Capitalism*, Oxford: Blackwell.

Bagguley, P. *et al.* (1990) *Restructuring: place, class and gender*, London: Sage.

Bahro, R. (1986) *Building the Green Movement*, London: Heretic Books.

Baldamus, W. (1961) *Efficiency and Effort*, London: Tavistock.

Banks, M., Bates, I., Breakwell, G., Bynner, J., Emler, N., Jamieson, L. and Roberts, K. (1992) *Careers and Identities*, Milton Keynes: Open University Press.

Banks, M. H. and Ullah, P. (1988) *Youth Unemployment in the 1980's: its psychological effects*, London: Croom Helm.

Baritz, L. (1960) *The Servants of Power*, New York: Wiley.

Barker, D. L. and Allen, S. (eds) (1976) *Dependence and Exploitation in Work and Marriage*, London: Longman.

Barron, R. D. and Norris, G. M. (1976) 'Sexual divisions and the dual labour market', in Barker and Allen (eds).

Barsoux, J-L. (1993) *Funny Business: humour, management and the business culture*, London: Cassell.

Batstone, E. (1984) *Working Order: workplace industrial relations over two decades*, Oxford: Blackwell.

Batstone, E., Boraston, I. and Frenkel, S. (1977) *Shop Stewards in Action*, Oxford: Blackwell.

Batstone, E., Boraston, I. and Frenkel, S. (1978) *The Social Organisation of Strikes*, Oxford: Blackwell.

Baumann, Z. (1992) *Intimations of Postmodernity*, London: Routledge.

Bean, R. (1994) *Comparative Industrial Relations*, London: Routledge.

Bechhofer, F. (1973) 'The relation between technology and shopfloor behaviour', in Edge, D. O. and Wolfe, J. N. (eds) *Meaning and Control*, London: Tavistock.

Becker, H. S. (1960) 'Notes on the concept of commitment', *American Journal of Sociology*, 66.

Becker, H. S. (1971) 'The nature of a profession', in *Sociological Work: method and substance*, London: Allen Lane.

Becker, H. S. and Geer, B. (1958) 'The fate of idealism in a medical school', *American Sociological Review*, 23.

Becker, H. S., Geer, B., Hughes, E. C. and Strauss, A. L. (1961) *Boys in White*, Chicago: University of Chicago Press.

Beechey, V. and Perkins, T. (1985) 'Conceptualising part-time work', in Roberts *et al.* (eds).

Beer, M. and Spector, B. (1985) 'Corporatewide transformations in human resource management', in Walton and Lawrence (eds).

Behrend, H. (1957) 'The Effort Bargain', *International Labor Relations Review*, 10.

Bell, D. (1974) *The Coming of Post-Industrial Society*, London: Heinemann.

Bell, D. (1977) 'The return of the sacred? The argument on the future of religion', *British Journal of Sociology*, 28: 4.

Bendix, R. (1963) *Work and Authority in Industry*, New York: Harper & Row.

Bendix, R. (1965) *Max Weber: a Sociological Portrait*, London: Methuen.

Bensman, J. and Lilienfeld, R. (1973) *Craft Consciousness*, New York: Wiley.

Berger, P. L. (1973) *The Social Reality of Religion*, London: Penguin Books.

Berk, R. and Berk, S. F. (1979) *Labor and Leisure at Home*, New York: Sage.

Best, S. and Kellner, D. (1991) *Postmodern Theory: critical interrogations*, London: Macmillan.

Beynon, H. (1984) *Working for Ford* (2nd edn) Harmondsworth: Penguin.

Beynon, H. (1988) 'Regulating research: politics and decision-making in industrial organisations', in Bryman (ed.).

Beynon, H. (1992) 'The end of the industrial worker?' in Abercrombie and Warde (eds).

Beynon, H. and Blackburn, R. M. (1972) *Perceptions of Work*, Cambridge University Press.

Beynon, H., Hudson, R. and Sadler, D. (1991) *A Tale of Two Industries: the contraction of coal and steel in the North East of England*, Milton Keynes: Open University Press.

Bittner, E. (1973) 'The Police on Skid-row', in Salaman and Thompson (eds).

Bittner, E. (1974) 'The concept of organisation', in Turner, R. (ed.).

Bjorn-Anderson, N., Earl, M., Holst, O. and Munford, G. (eds) (1982) *Information Society: for richer for poorer*, Amsterdam: North Holland Publishing Company.

Blackburn, P., Coombs, R. and Green, K. (1985) *Technology, Economic Growth and the Labour Process*, London: Macmillan.

Blackburn, R. and Mann, M. (1979) *The Working Class in the Labour Market*, London: Macmillan.

Blau, P. M. (1963) *The Dynamics of Bureaucracy*, Chicago: University of Chicago Press.

Blau, P. M. (ed.) (1976) *Approaches to the Study of Social Structure*, London: Open Books.

Blauner, R. (1960) 'Work satisfaction and industrial trends', in Galenson, W. and Lipset, S. H. (eds) *Labor and Trade Unions*, New York: Wiley.

Blauner, R. (1964) *Alienation and Freedom*, Chicago: University of Chicago Press.

Blyton, P. (1993) *Managing the Flexible Workforce*, Oxford: Blackwell.

Blyton, P. and Morris, J. (eds) (1991) *A Flexible Future?*, Berlin: de Gruyter.

Blyton, P. and Turnbull, P. (1994) *The Dynamics of Employee Relations*, London: Macmillan.

Boddy, D. and Buchanan, D. (1986) *Managing New Technology*, Oxford: Blackwell.

Boland, R. J. and Hoffman, R. (1983) 'Humor in a machine shop: an interpretation of symbolic action', in Pondy *et al.* (eds).

Bonney, N. and Reinach, E. (1993) 'Housework reconsidered: the Oakley thesis twenty years later', *Work, Employment and Society*, 7(4): 615–27.

Bottomore, T. B. (1985) *Theories of Modern Capitalism*, London: Allen & Unwin.

Bowles, S. and Gintis, H. (1976) *Schooling in Capitalist America*, London: Routledge & Kegan Paul.

Boyer, R. (1988) *The Search for Labour Market Flexibility*, Oxford: Clarendon.

Bradney, P. (1973) 'The joking relationship in industry', in Weir (ed.).

Brannen, J. and Moss, P. (1988) *New Mothers at Work: employment and childcare*, London: Unwin Hyman.

Bratton, J. (1992) *Japanisation at Work: managerial studies for the 1990s*, London: Macmillan.

Braverman, H. (1974) *Labor and Monopoly Capital*, New York: Monthly Review Press.

Bridges, W. (1995) *Jobshift: how to prosper in a workplace without jobs*, London: Brealey.

Brown, G. (1977) *Sabotage*, Nottingham: Spokesman Books.

Brown, R. K. (1983) 'From Donovan to Where? Interpretations of industrial relations in Britain since 1968', in Stewart, A. (ed.) *Contemporary Britain*, London: Routledge & Kegan Paul.

Brown, R. K. (1992) *Understanding Industrial Organisation*, London: Routledge.

Brown, R. K., Brannen, P., Cousins, J. and Samphies, M. (1973) 'Leisure in work', in Smith *et al.* (eds).

Brown, W. (1994) *Bargaining for Full Employment*, London: Employment Policy Institute.

Bryan, J. H. (1965) 'Apprenticeships in prostitution', *Social Problems*, 12.

Bryman, A. (ed.) (1988) *Doing Research in Organisations*, London: Routledge.

Bryman, A. (1989) *Research Methods and Organization Studies*, London: Routledge.

Buchanan, D. A. (1992) 'High performance: new boundaries of acceptability in worker control', in Salaman (ed.).

Buchanan, D. (1994) 'Cellular manufacture and the role of teams', in Storey (ed.).

Buchanan, D. and Preston, D. (1992) 'Life in the cell: supervision and teamwork in a "manufacturing system engineering" environment', *Human Resource Management Journal*, 2(4): 155–76.

Burawoy, M. (1979) *Manufacturing Consent*, Chicago: University of Chicago Press.

Burchell, B. (1994) 'The effects of labour market position, job insecurity and unemployment on psychological health', in Gallie, Marsh and Vogler (eds).

Burman, S. (ed.) (1979) *Fit Work for Women*, London: Croom Helm.

Burnham, J. (1945) *The Managerial Revolution*, Harmondsworth: Penguin.

Burns, T. (1955) 'The reference of conduct in small groups', *Human Relations*, 8.

Burns, T. (1961) 'Micropolitics', *Administrative Science Quarterly*, 6.

Burns, T. (1962) 'The sociology of industry', in Welford *et al.* (eds) *Society: problems and methods of study*, London: Routledge & Kegan Paul.

Burns, T. (1977) *The BBC: public institution and private world*, London: Macmillan.

Burns, T. and Stalker, G. (1994) *The Management of Innovation* (2nd edn), Oxford: Oxford University Press.

Burrage, M. and Torstendahl, R. (eds) (1991) *The Formation of Professions*, London: Sage.

Burrell, G. (1984) 'Sex and organisational analysis', *Organisation Studies*, 5(2): 97–118.

Burrell, G. (1992) 'The organisation of pleasure', in Alvesson and Willmott (eds).

Burrows, R. (ed.) (1991) *Deciphering the Enterprise Culture*, London: Routledge.

Byrne, D. (1995) 'Deindustrialisation and dispossession: an examination of social division in the industrial city', *Sociology*, 29(1): 95–115.

Campbell, C. (1987) *The Romantic Ethic and the Spirit of Modern Consumerism*, Oxford: Blackwell.

Cannon, I. C. (1967) 'Ideology and occupational community', *Sociology*, 1.

Carchedi, G. (1975) 'On the economic identification of the new middle class', *Economy and Society*, 4.

Carey, A. (1967) 'The Hawthorne Studies: a radical criticism', *American Sociological Review*, 32: 403–16.

Carlson, C. (1951) *Executive Behavior*, Stockholm: Strombergs.

Carroll, G.R. (ed.) (1988) *Ecological models of Organisations*, Cambridge, Mass.: Ballinger.

Carter, R. (1985) *Capitalism, Class Conflict and the New Middle Class*, London: Routledge & Kegan Paul.

Casey, C. (1995) *Work, Self and Society: after industrialism*, London: Routledge.

Cavendish, R. (1982) *Women on the Line*, London: Routledge & Kegan Paul.

Child, J. (1972) 'Organisational structure, environment and performance', *Sociology*, 6: 2–22.

Child, J. (ed.) (1973) *Man and Organisation*, London: Allen & Unwin.

Child, J. (1984a) *Organisation* (2nd edn), London: Harper & Row.

Child, J. (1984b) 'New technology and developments in management organisation', *Omega*, 12: 3.

Child, J. and Partridge, B. (1982) *Lost Managers*, Cambridge: Cambridge University Press.

Child, J., Fores, M., Glover, I. and Lawrence, P. (1983) 'A price to pay? Professionalism and work organisation in Britain and West Germany', *Sociology*, 17: 63–78.

Child, J., Loveridge, R., Harvey, A. and Spencer, A. (1984) 'Microelectronics and the quality of employment in services', in Marstrand (ed.).

Chodorow, N. (1978) *The Reproduction of Mothering: psychoanalysis and the sociology of gender*, Berkeley, Calif.: California University Press.

Clawson, D. (1980) *Bureaucracy and the Labor Process*, New York: Monthly Review Press.

Claydon, T. (1989) 'Union derecognition in Britain in the 1980's', *British Journal of Industrial Relations*, 27: 214–23.

Clegg, H. A. (1975) 'Pluralism in industrial relations', *British Journal of Industrial Relations*, 13: 309–16.

Clegg, S. (1990) *Modern Organisations: organisation studies in the postmodern world*, London: Sage.

Coates, R. V. and Pellegrin, R. J. (1962) 'Executives and supervisors', in Stoodley, B. H. (ed.) *Society and Self*, New York: Free Press.

Cockburn, C. and Ormrod, S. (1993) *Gender and Technology in the Making*, London: Sage.

Cohen, M. D., March, J. G. and Olsen, J. P. (1972) 'A garbage can model of organisational choice', *Administrative Science Quarterly*, 17(1): 1–25.

Cohen, S. S. and Zysman, J. (1987) *Manufacturing Matters: the myth of the post industrial economy*, New York: Basic Books.

Collin, A. (1986) 'Career development: the significance of subjective career', *Personnel Review*, 15(2): 22–8.

Collinson, D. L. (1992) *Managing the Shopfloor*, Berlin: de Gruyter.

Collinson, D. L. (1994) 'Strategies of resistance', in Jermier, Knights and Nord (eds).

Collinson, D., Knights. D. and Collinson, M. (1990) *Managing to Discriminate*, London: Routledge.

Cotgrove, S., Dunham, J. and Vamplew, C. (1971) *The Nylon Spinners*, London: Allen & Unwin.

Craig, C., Rubery, J., Tarling, R. and Wilkinson, F. (1982) *Labour Market Structure, Industrial Organisation and Low Pay*, Cambridge: Cambridge University Press.

Crompton, R. (1976) 'Approaches to the study of white collar unionism', *Sociology*, 10.

Crompton, R. (1990) 'Professions in the current context', *Work, Employment and Society*, Additional Special Issue: 'The 1980's: a decade of change?'.

Crompton, R. (1993) *Class and Stratification: an introduction to current debates*, Cambridge: Polity.

Crompton, R. and Jones, G. (1984) *White-Collar Proletariat: deskilling and gender in clerical work*, London: Macmillan.

Crompton, R. and Sanderson, K. (1990) *Gendered Jobs and Social Change*, London: Unwin Hyman.

Crompton, R., Gallie, D. and Purcell, K. (eds) (1996) *Corporate Restructuring and Labour Markets*, London: Routledge.

Crook, S., Pakulski, J. and Waters, M. (1992) *Postmodernisation: change in advanced society*, London: Sage.

Crouch, C. (1982) *Trade Unions: The Logic of Collective Action*, Glasgow: Fontana.

Crouch, C. (1993) *Industrial Relations and the European State Traditions*, Oxford: Oxford University Press.

Crouzet, F. (1985) *The First Industrialists: the problem of origins*, Cambridge: Cambridge University Press.

Crozier, M. (1964) *The Bureaucratic Phenomenon*, London: Tavistock.

Curran, J. and Burrows, R. (1986) 'The Sociology of Petit Capitalism: a trend report', *Sociology*, 20(2): 265–79.

Curran, J. and Burrows, R. (1988) *Enterprise in Britain: a national profile of small business owners and the self-employed*, London: Small Business Research Trust.

Curran, M. M. (1988) 'Gender and recruitment: people and places in the labour market', *Work, Employment and Society*, 2(3): 335–51.

Cyert, R. M. and March, J. G. (1963) *A Behavioural Theory of the Firm*, Englewood Cliffs, NJ: Prentice-Hall.

Dalton, M. (1951) 'Informal factors in career achievement', *American Journal of Sociology*, 56.

Dalton, M. (1959) *Men Who Manage*, New York: Wiley.

Daniel, W. W. (1973) 'Understanding employee behaviour in its context', in Child (ed.).

Darlington, R. (1994) *The Dynamics of Workplace Unionism: shop stewards' organisation in three Merseyside plants*, London: Mansell.

Davis, F. (1959) 'The cabdriver and his fare', *American Journal of Sociology*, 65.

Davis, K. and Moore, W. E. (1945) 'Some principles of stratification', *American Sociological Review*, 10.

Davis, L. E. (1966) 'The design of jobs', *Industrial Relations*, 6: 21–45.

Davis, L. E. and Taylor, J. (1979) *The Design of Jobs* (2nd edn), Santa Monica, California: Goodyear.

Dawes, L. (1993) *Long-term Unemployment and Labour Market Flexibility*, Leicester: University of Leicester Centre for Labour Market Studies.

Dawson, P. (1994) *Organisational Change: a processual approach*, London: Chapman.

Dawson, P. and Webb, J. (1989) 'New production arrangements: the totally flexible cage?', *Work, Employment and Society*, 3(2): 221–38.

Deal, T. E. and Kennedy, A. A. (1982) *Corporate Cultures: the rites and rituals of corporate life*, Reading, Mass.: Addison-Wesley.

Delphy, C. and Leonard, D. (1992) *Family Exploitation: a new analysis of marriage in contemporary western societies*, Cambridge: Polity.

Devine, F. (1992a) 'Gender segregation in the engineering and science professions: a case of continuity and change', *Work, Economy and Society*, 6(4): 557–75.

Devine, F. (1992b) *Affluent Workers Revisited: privatism and the working class*, Edinburgh: Edinburgh University Press.

Dex, S. (1988) *Women's Attitudes towards Work*, London: Macmillan.

Dimaggio, P. (1988) 'Interest and agency in institutional theory', in Zucker (ed.).

Ditton, J. (1974) 'The fiddling salesman', *New Society*, 28 November.

Ditton, J. (1977) *Part-time Crime*, London: Macmillan.

Doeringer, P. B. and Piore, M. J. (1971) *Internal Labor Markets and Manpower Analysis*, Lexington, Mass.: D. C. Heath.

Dopson, S. and Stewart, R. (1990) 'What is happening to middle management', *British Journal of Management*, 1(1): 3–16.

Draper, P. (1975) '!Kung Women: contrasts in sexual egalitarianism in foraging and sedentary contexts', in Reiter, R. R. (ed.) *Towards an Anthropology of Women*, New York: Monthly Review Press.

Drucker, P. (1992) *Managing for the Future: the 1990s and beyond*, Hemel Hempstead: Butterworth Heinemann.

du Gay, P. (1994) 'Colossal immodesties and hopeful monsters', *Organisation*, 1(2): 125–48.

Dubin, R. (1956) 'Industrial workers' worlds: a study of the central life interests of industrial workers', *Social Problems*, 3: 1312.

Dubin, R., Champoux, J. E. and Porter, L. W. (1975) 'Central life interests and organisational commitment of blue-collar and clerical workers', *Administrative Science Quarterly*, 20: 411–21.

Dunkerley, D. (1975) *The Foreman*, London: Routledge & Kegan Paul.

Dunlop, J. T. (1958) *Industrial Relations Systems*, New York: Holt.

Dunn, S. and Gennard, J. (1984) *The Closed Shop in British Industry*, London: Macmillan.

Durkheim, E. (1984) *The Division of Labour in Society*, transl. W. D. Halls, London: Macmillan.

Edgell, S. (1980) *Middle Class Couples*, London: Allen & Unwin.

Edwards, P. (1986) *Conflict at Work*, Oxford: Blackwell.

Edwards, P. K. and Scullion, H. (1982) *The Social Organisation of Industrial Conflict*, Oxford: Blackwell.

Edwards, P. K. and Whitson, C. (1989) 'Industrial discipline, the control of attendance and the subordination of labour', *Work, Employment and Society*, 3: 1–28.

Edwards, R. (1979) *Contested Terrain*, London: Heinemann.

Eisenstadt, S. N. (1973) *Tradition, Change and Modernity*, New York: Wiley.

Eldridge, J. E. T. (1971a) *Sociology and Industrial Life*, London: Michael Joseph.

Eldridge, J. E. T. (1971b) 'Weber's approach to the study of industrial workers', in Sahay (ed.).

Eldridge, J. E. T. (1975) 'Industrial relations and industrial capitalism', in Esland *et al.* (eds).

Eldridge, J., Cressey, P. and MacInnes, J. (1991) *Industrial Sociology and Economic Crisis*, Hemel Hempstead: Harvester Wheatsheaf.

Elliot, P. (1972) *The Sociology of the Professions*, London: Macmillan.

Elliot, P. (1973) 'Professional ideology and social situation', *Sociological Review*, 21.

Esland, G., Salaman, G. and Speakman, M. (eds) (1975) *People and Work*, Edinburgh: Holmes McDougall.

Evans, P. and Bartolemé, F. (1980) *Must Success Cost So Much?* London: Grant McIntyre.

Fayol, H. (1949, orig. 1916) *General and Industrial Management* (transl. C. Stores) London: Pitman.

Feldberg, R. L. and Glenn, E. N. (1982) 'Male and female: job versus gender models in the sociology of work', in Kahn-Hut *et al.* (eds).

Ferner, A. and Hyman, R. (eds) (1992) *Industrial Relations in the New Europe*, Oxford: Blackwell.

Filby, M. P. (1987) 'The Newmarket racing lad: tradition and change in a marginal occupation', *Work, Employment and Society*, 1(2): 205–24.

Filby, M. P. (1992) '"The figures, the personality and the bums": service work and sexuality', *Work, Employment and Society*, 6(1): 23–42.

Finch, J. (1983) *Married to the Job: wives' incorporation into men's work*, London: Allen & Unwin.

Finch, J. and Mason, J. (1993) *Negotiating Family Responsibilities*, London: Routledge.

Fineman, S. (ed.) (1987) *Unemployment: personal and social consequences*, London: Tavistock.

Fineman, S. (ed.) (1993a) *Emotion in Organisations*, London: Sage.

Fineman, S. (1993b) 'Organisations as emotional areas', in Fineman (ed.).

Fineman, S. (1994) 'Organizing and emotion: towards a social construction', in Hassard and Parker (eds).

Fletcher, R. (1971) *The Making of Sociology, Vol. 1*, London: Michael Joseph.

Fosh, P. (1981) *The Active Trade Unionist*, Cambridge: Cambridge University Press.

Fosh, P. and Heery, E. (eds) (1990) *Trade Unions and their members: studies in union democracy and organisation*, London: Macmillan.

Foster, J. (1974) *Class Struggle and the Industrial Revolution*, London: Weidenfeld & Nicolson.

Foucault, M. (1980) *Power/Knowledge: selected interviews and other writings*, Brighton: Harvester.

Fox, A. (1966) *Industrial Sociology and Industrial Relations*, London: HMSO.

Fox, A. (1973) 'Industrial Relations: a social critique of pluralist ideology', in Child (ed.).

Fox, A. (1974) *Beyond Contract: work, power and trust relations*, London: Faber.

Fox, A. (1979) 'A note on industrial relations pluralism', *Sociology*, 13(1).

Fox, A. (1985) *History and Heritage: the social origins of the British industrial relations system*, London: Allen & Unwin.

Frankel, B. (1987) *The Post-Industrial Utopians*, Oxford: Polity.

Freidson, E. (1973) 'Professionalisation and the organisation of middle-class labour in post-industrial society', *Sociological Review Monograph*, 20.

Freidson, E. (1994)) *Professionalism Reborn: theory, prophecy and policy*, Cambridge: Polity.

Friedman, A. L. (1977) *Industry and Labour*, London: Macmillan.

Friedmann, E. A. and Havighurst, R. J. (1954) *The Meaning of Work and Retirement*, Chicago: University of Chicago Press.

Frobel, F., Heinrichs, J. and Kreye, O. (1980) *The New International Division of Labour*, Cambridge: Cambridge University Press.

Fukuyama, F. (1992) *The End of History and The Last Man*, London: Hamilton.

Gabriel, Y. (1988) *Working Lives in Catering*, London: Routledge.

Galbraith, J. K. (1972) *The New Industrial State*, Harmondsworth: Penguin.

Gallie, D. (1978) *In Search of the New Working Class*, Cambridge: Cambridge University Press.

Gallie, D. (1984) *Social Inequality and Class Radicalism in Britain and France*, Cambridge: Cambridge University Press.

Gallie, D. (1985) 'Directions for the future', in Roberts *et al.* (eds).

Gallie, D. (ed.) (1988) *Employment in Britain*, Oxford: Blackwell.

Gallie, D. (1996) 'Changing patterns of skill and responsibility at work', in Crompton, Gallie and Purcell (eds).

Gallie, D. and Marsh, C. (1994) 'The experience of unemployment', in Gallie, Marsh and Vogler (eds).

Gallie, D. and Vogler, C. (1994) 'Unemployment and attitudes to work', in Gallie, Marsh and Vogler (eds).

Gallie, D., Marsh, C. and Vogler, C. (eds) (1994) *Social Change and the Experience of Unemployment*, Oxford: Oxford University Press.

Garrahan, P. and Stewart, P. (1992) *The Nissan Enigma*, London: Cassell.

Geer, B. *et al.* (1968) 'Learning the ropes', in Deutscher, J. and Thompson, J. (eds) *Among the People*, New York: Basic Books.

Gergen, K. J. (1992) 'Organisation theory in a postmodern era', in Reed, M. and Hughes, M. (eds) *Rethinking Organisation*, London: Sage.

Gershuny, J. (1978) *After Industrial Society*, London: Macmillan.

Gershuny, J. (1983) *Social Innovation and the Division of Labour*, Oxford: Oxford University Press.

Gershuny, J. (1992) 'Change in the domestic division of labour in the UK, 1975–87', in Abercrombie and Warde (ed.): 70–94.

Gershuny, J. (1994) 'The psychological consequences of unemployment: an assessment of the Jahoda thesis', in Gallie, Marsh and Vogler (eds).

Gerstl, J. E. and Hutton, S. P. (1966) *Engineers: the anatomy of a profession*, London: Tavistock.

Giddens, A. (1971) *Capitalism and Modern Social Theory*, Cambridge: Cambridge University Press.

Giddens, A. (1973) *The Class Structure of the Advanced Societies*, London: Hutchinson.

Giddens, A. (1982) *Sociology: a brief but critical introduction*, London: Macmillan.

Giddens, A. (1984) *The Constitution of Society: outline of the theory of structuration*, Cambridge: Polity.

Giddens, A. (1991) *Modernity and Self-identity: self and society in the modern age*, Cambridge: Polity Press.

Giddens, A. and Mackenzie, G. (eds) (1982) *Social Class and the Division of Labour*, Cambridge: Cambridge University Press.

Gilbert, N., Burrows, R. and Pollert, A. (eds) (1992) *Fordism and Flexibility: divisions and change*, London: Macmillan.

Gill, C. (1985) *Work, Unemployment and New Technology*, Oxford: Polity Press.

Gillespie, R. (1991) *Manufacturing knowledge: a history of the Hawthorne experiments*, Cambridge: Cambridge Universtity Press.

Ginzberg, E. J., Sinzberg, S. W., Axelrad, S. and Herma, J. L. (1951) *Occupational Choice*, New York: Columbia University Press.

Glaser, B. G. and Strauss, A. L. (1967) *The Discovery of Grounded Theory*, New York: Aldine.

Goffee, R. and Scase, R. (1985) *The Experience of Female Entrepreneurs*, London: Allen & Unwin.

Goffman, E. (1968) *Asylums*, Harmondsworth: Penguin.

Goldner, F. H. (1970) 'The division of labor: process and power', in Zald (ed.).

Goldthorpe, J. (1971) 'Theories of industrial society', *European Journal of Sociology*, 12.

Goldthorpe, J. H. (1974) 'Industrial relations in Great Britain: a critique of reformism', *Politics and Society*, 4: 419–52.

Goldthorpe, J. H. (1982) 'On the service class, its formation and future', in Giddens and Mackenzie (eds).

Goldthorpe, J. H. (1985) 'The end of convergence: corporatist and dualist tendencies in modern western societies', in Roberts, Finnegan and Gallie (eds).

Goldthorpe, J. H., Llewellyn, C. and Payne, C. (1980) *Social Mobility and Class Structure in Modern Britain*, Oxford: Clarendon Press.

Goldthorpe, J. H., Lockwood, D., Bechhofer, F. and Platt, J. (1968) *The Affluent Worker: industrial attitudes and behaviour*, Cambridge: Cambridge University Press.

Goode, W. J. (1957) 'Community within a community: the professions', *American Sociological Review*, 22.

Goodman, J. F. B. and Whittington, T. G. (1973) *Shop Stewards*, London: Pan.

Goodman, P. S. and Pennings, J. M. *et al.*(eds) (1977) *New Perspectives on Organisational Effectiveness*, San Francisco: Jossey Bass.

Gordon, D., Edwards, R. and Reich, M. (1982) *Segmented Work, Divided Workers*, Cambridge: Cambridge University Press.

Gorz, A. (1985) *Paths to Paradise: on liberation from work*, London: Pluto.

Gouldner, A. W. (1957) 'Cosmopolitans and locals', *Administrative Science Quarterly*, 2.

Gouldner, A. W. (1964) *Patterns of Industrial Bureaucracy*, New York: Free Press.

Gouldner, A. W. (1971) *The Coming Crisis of Western Sociology*, London: Heinemann.

Gregson, N. and Lowe, M. (1994a) *Servicing the Middle Classes: waged domestic labour in Britain in the 1980s and 1990s*, London: Routledge.

Gregson, N. and Lowe, M. (1994b) 'Waged domestic labour and the renegotiation of the domestic division of labour within dual career households', *Sociology*, 28(1): 55–78.

Grey, C. (1994) 'Career as a project of the self and labour process discipline', *Sociology*, 28(2): 479–97.

Grieco, M. (1987) *Keeping it in the Family: Social Networks and Employment Chance*, London: Tavistock.

Grint, K. (1991) *Work: an introduction*, Cambridge: Polity.

Guest, D. (1991) 'Personnel management: the end of an orthodoxy', *British Journal of Industrial Relations*, 29(2): 149–76

Guest, R. H. (1962) *Organisational Change*, Homewood, Ill.: Dorsey Press.

Gulick, L. and Urwick, L. (1937) *Papers on the Science of Administration*, New York: Columbia University Press.

Habermas, J. (1987) *Lectures on the Philosophical Discourse of Modernity*, Cambridge, Mass.: MIT Press.

Hakim, C. (1979) *Occupational Segregation – Research Paper 9*, Department of Employment, London: HMSO.

Hakim, C. (1988) 'Self-employment in Britain: recent trends and current issues', *Work, Employment and Society*, 2(4): 421–50.

Hakim, C. (1990) 'Core and periphery in employers' workplace strategies', *Work, Employment and Society*, 4(2): 157–88.

Hakim, C. (1993) 'The myth of rising female employment', *Work, Employment and Society*, 7(1): 97–120.

Hall, C. (1979) 'The early formation of Victorian domestic ideology', in Burman (ed.).

Halmos, P. (1970) *The Personal Service Society*, London: Constable.

Hamilton, R. (1978) *The Liberation of Women*, London: Allen & Unwin.

Hammersley, M. (1992) *What's Wrong with Ethnography?*, London: Routledge.

Harding, P. and Jenkins, R. (1989) *The Myth of the Hidden Economy: towards a new understanding of informal economic activity*, Milton Keynes: Open University Press.

Harris, R. (1987) *Power and Powerlessness in Industry*, London: Tavistock.

Hassard, J. and Parker, M. (eds) (1993) *Postmodernism and Organisations*, London: Sage.

Hassard, J. and Parker, M. (eds) (1994) *Towards a New Theory of Organisations*, London: Routledge.

Hatt, P. K. (1950) 'Occupations and social stratification', *American Journal of Sociology*, 55.

Hayter, T. and Harvey, D. (1993) *The Factory and the City: the story of the Cowley automobile workers in Oxford*, Poole: Mansell.

Hearn, J. and Parkin, W. (1987) '"Sex" at "Work": the power and paradox of organisation sexuality', Brighton: Wheatsheaf.

Heery, E. and Kelly, J. (1994) 'Professional, participative and managerial unionism: an interpretation of change in trade unions', *Work, Employment and Society*, 8(1): 1–22.

Henderson, J. (1989) *The Globalisation of High Technology Production*, London: Routledge.

Hendry, C. and Pettigrew, A. (1990) 'Human resource management: an agenda for the 1990's', *International Journal of Human Resource Management*, 1(1).

Henry, S. (1978) *The Hidden Economy*, London: Martin Robertson.

Herzberg, F. (1966) *Work and the Nature of Man*, Cleveland, Ohio: World Publishing Company.

Hickson, D. J. (1990) 'Politics permeate', in Wilson and Rosenfeld.

Hickson, D. J., Hinings, C. R., Lee, C. A., Schneck, R. E. and Pennings, J. M. (1971) 'A strategic contingencies theory of intra-organisational power', *Administrative Science Quarterly*, 16: 216–29.

Hill, C. (1974) *Change and Continuity in Seventeenth Century England*, London: Weidenfeld and Nicolson.

Hill, L. A. (1992) *Becoming a Manager: mastery of a new identity*, Boston, Mass.: Harvard Business School.

Hill, S. (1976) *The Dockers*, London: Heinemann.

Hill, S. (1988) *The Tragedy of Technology*, London: Pluto.

Hill, S. (1991) 'How do you manage a flexible firm? The total quality model', *Work, Employment and Society*, 5(3): 397–415.

Hinton, J. (1973) *The First Shop Stewards' Movement*, London: Allen & Unwin.

Hirst, P. and Zeitlin, J. (1991) 'Flexible specialisation versus Post-Fordism: theory, evidence and policy implications', *Economy and Society*, 20(1): 1–55.

Hobsbawm, E. J. (1969) *Industry and Empire*, Harmondsworth: Penguin.

Hochschild, A. R. (1985) *The Managed Heart: the commercialisation of human feeling*, Berkeley, Calif.: University of California Press.

Hollowell, P. G. (1968) *The Lorry Driver*, London: Routledge & Kegan Paul.

Holton, R. J. (1985) *The Transition from Feudalism to Capitalism*, London: Macmillan.

Hopper, E. and Pearce, A. (1973) 'Relative deprivation, occupational status and occupational "situs"', in Warner (ed.).

Huczynski, A. (1993) *Management Gurus: what makes them and how to become one*, London: Routledge.

Huczynski, A. and Buchanan, D. (1991) *Organisational Behaviour: an introductory text*, Hemel Hempstead: Prentice-Hall.

Hughes, E. C. (1937) 'Institutional office and the person', *American Journal of Sociology*, 43: 404–13.

Hughes, E. C. (1958) *Men and their Work*, New York: Free Press.

Hunter, L. and MacInnes, J. (1992) 'Employers and labour flexibility: the evidence from case studies', *Employment Gazette*, June, 307–15.

Huws, U. (1984) 'New technology homeworkers', *Employment Gazette*, 92(1): 13–17.

Hyman, R. (1978) 'Pluralism, procedural consensus and collective bargaining', *British Journal of Industrial Relations*, 13: 16–40.

Hyman, R. (1987) 'Strategy or structure: capital, labour and control', *Work, Employment and Society*, 1(1): 25–55.

Hyman, R. (1989) *The Political Economy of Industrial Relations*, London: Macmillan.

Hyman, R. (1991) 'Plus ça change? The theory of production and the production of theory', in Pollert (ed.).

Hyman, R. and Ferner, A. (eds) (1994) *New Frontiers in European Industrial Relations*, Oxford: Blackwell.

ILO (1995) *World Employment 1995*, Geneva: International Labour Organisation.

Israel, H. (1966) 'Some religious factors in the emergence of industrial society in England', *American Sociological Review*, 31.

Jackall, R. (1988) *Moral Mazes: the world of corporate managers*, New York: Oxford University Press.

Jahoda, M. (1982) *Employment and Unemployment: a social psychological analysis*, Cambridge: Cambridge University Press.

James, L. (1973) 'On the game', *New Society*, 24 May.

Jenkins, R. (1986) *Racism and Recruitment: managers, organisations and equality in the labour market*, Cambridge: Cambridge University Press.

Jermier, J., Knights, D. and Nord, W. R. (eds) (1994) *Resistance and Power in Organisations*, London: Routledge.

Johnson, T. J. (1977) 'The professions in the class structure', in Scase, R. (ed.) *Industrial Society*, London: Allen & Unwin.

Jones, B. (1982) 'Destruction or redistribution of engineering skills?', in Wood.

Joyce, P. (1980) *Work, Society and Politics: the culture of the factory in late Victorian England*, Brighton: Harvester Press.

Joyce, P. (ed.) (1987) *The Historical Meanings of Work*, Cambridge: Cambridge University Press.

Kahn-Hut, R., Daniels, A. K. and Colvard, R. (eds) (1982) *Women and Work: problems and perspectives*, New York: Oxford University Press.

Kanter, R. M. (1982) 'The impact of hierarchical structures on the work behaviour of women', in Kahn-Hut *et al.* (eds).

Keat, R. and Abercrombie, N. (eds) (1991) *Enterprise Culture*, London: Routledge.

Keenoy, T. (1991) 'The roots of metaphor in the old and new industrial relations', *British Journal of Industrial Relations*, 29(2): 313–27.

Kelly, J. E. (1982) *Scientific Management, Job Redesign and Work Performance*, London: Academic Press.

Kelly, J. and Heery, E. (1994) *Working for the Union: British trade union officers*, Cambridge: Cambridge University Press.

Kenney, M. and Florida, R. (1993) *Beyond Mass Production: the Japanese system and its transfer to the US*, New York: Oxford Univeristy Press.

Kerfoot, D. and Knights, D. (1994) 'Empowering the "quality worker": the seduction and contradiction of the total quality mangement phenomenon', in Wilkinson and Willmott (eds).

Kerr, C., Dunlop, J. T., Harbison, F. and Myers, C. A. (1973) *Industrialism and Industrial Man*, Harmondsworth: Penguin.

Kerr, C. and Rostow, J. M. (eds) (1979) *Work in America: the decade ahead*, New York: Van Nostrand.

Kerr, C. and Siegal, A. J. (1954) 'The inter-industry propensity to strike', in Kornhauser *et al.* (eds) *Industrial Conflict*, New York: McGraw-Hill.

Kerr, C. (1983) *The Future of Industrial Societies: convergence or continuing diversity?*, Cambridge, Mass.: Harvard University Press.

Klein, L. (1976) *A Social Scientist in Industry*, London: Gower.

Klein, L. and Eason, K. (1991) *Putting Social Science to Work*, Cambridge: Cambridge University Press.

Knights, D. and Morgan, G. (1990) 'The concept of strategy in sociology: a note of dissent', *Sociology*, 24: 475–83.

Knights, D. and Willmott, H. (1985) 'Power and identity in theory and practice', *Sociological Review*, 33(1): 22–46.

Knights, D. and Willmott, H. (eds) (1986) *Managing the Labour Process*, Aldershot: Gower.

Knights, D. and Willmott, H. (eds) (1989a) *Labour Process Theory*, London: Macmillan.

Knights, D. and Willmott, H. (1989b) 'Power and subjectivity at work: from degradation to subjugation at work', *Sociology*, 23(4): 535–58.

Knights, D., Collinson, D. and Willmott, H. (eds) (1984) *Job Redesign: the organisation and control of work*, Aldershot: Gower.

Kohn, M. (1969) *Class and Conformity*, Homewood, Ill.: Dorsey Press.

Kohn, M. (1971) 'Bureaucratic man: a portrait and an interpretation', *American Sociological Review*, 36.

Kotter, J. P. (1982) *The General Manager*, New York: Free Press.

Kuhn, J. W. (1961) *Bargaining in Grievance Settlement*, New York: Columbia University Press.

Kumar, K. (1978) *Prophecy and Progress*, Harmondsworth: Penguin.

Kunda, G. (1992) *Engineering Culture: control and commitment in a high-tech corporation*, Philadelphia, Pa.: Temple University Press.

Land, H. (1981) *Parity Begins at Home*, London: EOC/SSRC.

Landsberger, H. A. (1958) *Hawthorne Revisited*, Ithaca, NY: Columbia University Press.

Landsberger, H. A. (1961) 'The horizontal dimension in bureaucracy', *Administrative Science Quarterly*, 6.

Lane, C. (1985) 'White-collar workers in the labour process: the case of the Federal Republic of Germany', *Sociological Review*, 33(2): 298–326.

LaNuez, D. and Jermier, J. (1994) 'Sabotage by managers and technocrats', in Jermier, Knights and Nord (eds).

Larson, M. S. (1977) *The Rise of Professionalism: a sociological analysis*, Berkeley, Calif.: University of California Press.

Larson, M. S. (1991) 'In the matter of experts and professionals, or how impossible it is to leave nothing unsaid', in Burrage and Torstendahl (eds).

Lash, S. (1984) *Militant Workers: class and radicalism in France and America*, Aldershot: Gower.

Lash, S. and Urry, J. (1987) *The End of Organised Capitalism*, Cambridge: Polity.

Latour, B. (1987) *Science in Action*, Milton Keynes: Open University Press.

Latour, B. (1993) *We Have Never Been Modern*, Brighton: Harvester Wheatsheaf.

Lawrence, P. R. and Lorsch, J. W. (1967) *Organisation and Environment*, Cambridge, Mass.: Harvard University Press.

Layder, D. (1994) *Understanding Social Theory*, London: Sage.

Layder, D., Ashton, D. and Sung, J. (1991) 'The empirical correlates of action and structure: the transition from school to work', *Sociology*, 25(3): 447–64.

Lazonick, W. (1991) *Business Organisation and the Myth of the Market Economy*, Cambridge: Cambridge University Press.

Lee, G. and Loveridge, R. (1987) *The Manufacture of Disadvantage*, Milton Keynes: Open University Press.

Lewis, J. (1984) *Women in England, 1970–1950: sexual divisions and social change*, Brighton: Wheatsheaf.

Likert, R. (1967) *The Human Organisation*, New York: McGraw-Hill.

Linstead, S. (1985) 'Jokers wild: the importance of humour in the maintenance of organisational culture', *Sociological Review*, 33(4): 741–67.

Lipietz, A. (1987) *Miracles and Mirages: the crisis in global Fordism*, London: Verso.

Lipset, S. M. (1976) 'Social structure and social change', in Blau (ed.).

Lipset, S. M., Trow, M. and Coleman, J. (1956) *Union Democracy*, Chicago: Free Press.

Littler, C. (1982) *The Development of the Labour Process in Capitalist Societies*, London: Heinemann.

Littler, C. R. and Salaman, G. (1982) 'Bravermania and beyond: recent theories of the labour process', *Sociology*, 16(2).

Littler, C. R. and Salaman, G. (1984) *Class at Work*, London: Batsford.

Lockwood, D. (1989) *The Blackcoated Worker: a study in class consciousness* (2nd edn), Oxford: Oxford University Press.

Lorber, J. (1985) *Women Physicians: careers, status and power*, London: Tavistock.

Lupton, T. (1963) *On the Shopfloor*, Oxford: Pergamon.

Lyotard, J. F. (1986) *The Postmodern Condition: a report on knowledge*, Manchester: Manchester University Press.

McDermott, J. (1991) *Corporate Society: class, property and contemporary capitalism*, Boulder, Colo.: Westview.

McGregor, D. C. (1960) *The Human Side of Enterprise*, New York: McGraw-Hill.

MacInnes, J. (1987) *Thatcherism at Work: Industrial Realtions and Economic Change*, Milton Keynes: Open University Press.

Mackenzie, G. (1975) 'World images and the world of work', in Esland *et al.* (eds).

McLoughlin, I. and Clark, J. (1994) *Technological Change at Work* (2nd edn), Milton Keynes: Open University Press.

McLoughlin, I. and Gourlay, S. (1994) *Enterprise without Unions*, Milton Keynes: Open University Press.

McNally, F. (1979) *Women for Hire: a study of the female office worker*, London: Macmillan.

McNeil, K. (1978) 'Understanding organisational power', *Administrative Science Quarterly*, 23.

Madge, C. (1963) *The Origins of Scientific Sociology*, London: Tavistock.

Mair, A. (1994) *Honda's Local Global Corporation*, London: Macmillan.

Mallet, S. (1975) *The New Working Class*, Nottingham: Spokesman Books.

Mann, M. (1973) *Workers on the Move*, Cambridge: Cambridge University Press.

Manning, P. K. (1977) *Police Work: the social organisation of policing*, Cambridge, Mass.: MIT Press.

Marceau, J. (1989) *A Family Business? The making of an international business elite*, Cambridge: Cambridge University Press.

March, J. G. and Olsen, J. P. (1976) *Ambiguity and Choice in Organisations*, Oslo: Universitetsforlagtt.

Marchington, M. (1992) 'Managing labour relations in a competitive environment', in Sturdy, Knights and Willmott (eds).

Marglin, S. (1980) 'The origins and function of hierarchy in capitalist production', in Nichols (ed.).

Mars, G. (1974) 'Dock pilferage', in Rock, P. and McIntosh, M. (eds) *Deviance and Control*, London: Tavistock.

Mars, G. (1982) *Cheats at Work*, London: Allen & Unwin.

Mars, G. and Nicod, M. (1984) *The World of Waiters*, London: Allen & Unwin.

Marsh, D. (1992) *The New Politics of British Trade Unionism: union power and the Thatcher legacy*, London: Macmillan.

Marshall, G., Newby, H., Rose, D. and Vogler, C. (1988) *Social Class in Modern Britain*, London: Hutchinson.

Marstrand, P. (ed.) (1984) *New Technology and the Future of Work Skills*, London: Pinter.

Martin, J. and Roberts, C. (1984) *Women and Employment*, London: HMSO.

Martin, R. M. (1989) *Trade Unionism: purposes and forms*, Oxford: Oxford University Press.

Martin, R. M. (1992) *Bargaining Power*, Oxford: Clarendon Press.

Maslow, A. (1943) 'A theory of human motivation', *Psychological Development*, 50: 370–96.

Maslow, A. (1954) *Motivation and Personality*, New York: Harper & Row.

Massey, D. S. and Denton, N. A. (1993) *American Apartheid: segregation and the making of the underclass*, Cambridge, Mass.: Harvard University Press.

Mayo, E. (1933) *The Human Problems of an Industrial Civilisation*, New York: Macmillan.

Mayo, E. (1949) *The Social Problems of an Industrial Civilisation*, London: Routledge & Kegan Paul.

Mead, G. H. (1962) *Mind, Self and Society*, Chicago: University of Chicago Press.

Mead, M. (1962) *Male and Female*, Harmondsworth: Penguin.

Meissner, M. (1971) 'The long arm of the job', *Industrial Relations*, 2.

Meissner, M. (1976) 'The language of work', in Dubin, R. (ed.) *The Handbook of Work, Organisation and Society*, Chicago: Rand-McNally.

Merton, R. K. (1957) 'Bureaucratic structure and personality', in *Social Theory and Social Structure*, New York: Free Press.

Meyer, J and Rowan, B. (1977) 'Institutionalised organisations: formal structure and myth and ceremony', *American Journal of Sociology*, 83: 340–63.

Michels, R. (1949) *Political Parties*, Chicago, Ill.: Free Press.

Michie, J. and Grieve Smith, J. (1995) *Managing the Global Economy*, Oxford: Oxford University Press.

Miles, I. (1984) 'Work, well-being and unemployment', in Marstrand (ed.).

Miles, R. H. (1980) *Macro Organisational Behaviour*, Santa Monica, Calif.: Goodyear.

Miller, D. and Swanson, G. (1958) *The Changing American Parent*, New York: Wiley.

Millerson, G. (1964) *The Qualifying Associations*, London: Routledge & Kegan Paul.

Mills, C. W. (1953) *White Collar*, New York: Oxford University Press.

Mills, C. W. (1970) *The Sociological Imagination*, Harmondsworth: Penguin.

Millward, N., Stevens, M., Smart, D. and Hawes, W. R. (1992) *Workplace Industrial Relations in Transition*, Aldershot: Dartmouth.

Mintzberg, H. (1973) *The Nature of Managerial Work*, New York: Harper & Row.

Mintzberg, H. (1994) *The Rise and Fall of Strategic Planning*, Hemel Hempstead: Prentice-Hall.

Mooney, J. D. and Riley, A. C. (1931) *Onward Industry*, New York: Harper.

Moore, R. (1975) 'Religion as a source of variation in working class images of society', in Bulmer, M. (ed.) *Working Class Images of Society*, London: Routledge & Kegan Paul.

Moore, W. (1965) *The Impact of Industry*, Englewood Cliffs, NJ: Prentice-Hall.

Morgan, G. (1990) *Organisations in Society*, London: Macmillan.

Morgan, G. and Knights, D. (1991) 'Gendered jobs: corporate strategy, managerial control and the dynamics of job segregation', *Work, Employment and Society*, 5(2): 181–97.

Morris, L. (1988) 'Employment, the household and social networks', in Gallie (ed.): 376–405.

Morris, R. T. and Murphy, R. J. (1959) 'The situs dimension in occupational sociology', *American Sociological Review*, 24.

Morris, T. and Morris, P. (1973) 'The prison officer', in Weir (ed.).

Morse, N. C. and Weiss, R. S. (1955) 'The function and meaning of work and the job', *American Sociological Review*, 20.

Moses, J. A. (1990) *Trade Union Theory from Marx to Walesa*, New York: Berg.

Mott, J. (1973) 'Miners, weavers and pigeon racing', in Smith *et al.* (eds).

MOW International Research Team (1987) *The Meaning of Work*, London: Academic Press.

Mulkay, M. (1988) *On Humour: style and technique in comic discourse*, Cambridge: Polity.

Musgrave, P. W. (1967) 'Towards a sociological theory of occupational choice', *Sociological Review*, 15.

Myrdal, A. and Klein, V. (1968) *Women's Two Roles*, London: Routledge & Kegan Paul.

Newby, H., Vogler, C., Rose, D. and Marshall, G. (1985) 'From class structure to class action: British working-class politics in the 1980's', in Roberts *et al.* (eds).

Nichols, T. (1969) *Ownership, Control and Ideology*, London: Allen & Unwin.

Nichols, T. (1975) 'The sociology of accidents and the social production of industrial accidents', in Esland *et al.* (eds).

Nichols, T. (ed.) (1980) *Capital and Labour*, Glasgow: Fontana.

Nichols, T. and Beynon, H. (1977) *Living with Capitalism*, London: Routledge & Kegan Paul.

Niethammer, L. (1993) *Posthistoire: has history come to an end?*, London: Verso.

Niland, J. R., Lansbury, R. D. and Verevis, C. (eds) (1994) *The Future of Industrial Relations*, London: Sage.

Nisbet, R. (1970) *The Sociological Tradition*, London: Heinemann.

Nisbet, R. (1979) *Social Change and History*, Oxford: Oxford University Press.

Noble, D. F. (1984) *Forces of Production: a social history of industrial automation*, New York: Alfred A. Knopf.

Oakley, A. (1974) *Housewife*, London: Allen Lane.

Oakley, A. (1981) *Subject Women*, London: Martin Robertson.

O'Connell Davidson, J. (1994) 'Resistance in a privatised utility', in Jermier, Knights and Nord (eds).

O'Connell Davidson, J. (1995) 'The anatomy of "free choice" prostitution', *Gender, Work and Organisation*, 2(1): 1–10.

Offe, C. (1976) *Industry and Inequality*, London: Edward Arnold.

Oliver, N. and Wilkinson, B. (1988) *The Japanisation of British Industry?*, 2nd edn, Oxford: Blackwell.

Oppenheimer, M. (1973) 'The proletarianisation of the professional', *Sociological Review Monograph*, 20.

Orzack, L. (1959) 'Work as a central life interest of professionals', *Social Problems*, 6.

Pahl, J. M. and Pahl, R. E. (1972) *Managers and their Wives*, Harmondsworth: Penguin.

Pahl, R. E. (1984) *Divisions of Labour*, Oxford: Blackwell.

Pahl, R. (ed.) (1988) *On Work: historical, comparative and theoretical approaches*, Oxford: Blackwell.

Pahl, R. E. and Winkler, J. T. (1974) 'The economic élite', in Stanworth, P. and Giddens, A. (eds) *Elites and Power in British Society*, Cambridge: Cambridge University Press.

Parker, S. (1982) *Work and Retirement*, London: Allen & Unwin.

Parker, S. (1983) *Leisure and Work*, London: Allen & Unwin.

Parkin, F. (1972) *Class, Inequality and Political Order*, London: Paladin.

Parkin, F. (ed.) (1974) *The Social Analysis of Class Structure*, London: Tavistock.

Parry, N. and Parry, J. (1977) 'Social closure and collective mobility', in Scase, R. (ed.) *Industrial Society*, London: Allen & Unwin.

Penn, R. (1985) *Skilled Workers in the Class Structure*, Cambridge: Cambridge University Press.

Penn, R. (1990) *Class, Power and Technology: skilled workers in Britain and America*, Oxford: Polity.

Perkin, H. (1989) *The Rise of Professional Society*, London: Routledge.

Perrow, C. (1970a) 'Departmental Power', in Zald (ed.).

Perrow, C. (1970b) *Organisational Analysis*, London: Tavistock.

Perrow, C. (1977) 'Three types of effectiveness studies', in Goodman, Pennings *et al.* (eds).

Perrow, C. (1986) *Complex Organisations: a critical essay*, New York: Random House.

Peters, T. J. and Waterman, R. H. Jnr (1982) *In Search of Excellence*, New York: Harper & Row.

Pettigrew, A. (1973) *The Politics of Organisational Decision Making*, London: Tavistock.

Pfeffer, J. and Salancik, G. R. (1978) *The External Control of Organisations: a resource dependence approach*, New York: Harper & Row.

Phizacklea, A. (1990) *Unpacking the Fashion Industry: gender, racism and class in production*, London: Routledge.

Pickford, L. J. (1985) 'The superstructure of myths supporting the subordination of women', in Stead (ed.).

Piore, M. J. (1979) *Birds of Passage: migrant labour and industrial societies*, Cambridge: Cambridge University Press.

Piore, M. J. (1980) 'Economic fluctuation, job security and labor-markets duality in Italy, France and the U.S.', *Politics and Society*, 9(4).

Piore, M. J. (1986) 'The decline of mass production and challenge to union survival', *Industrial Relations Journal*, 17(3): 207–13.

Piore, M. and Sabel, C. F. (1984) *The Second Industrial Divide: possibilities of prosperity*, New York: Basic Books.

Poggi, G. (1983) *Calvinism and the Capitalist Spirit*, London: Macmillan.

Pollert, A. (1981) *Girls, Wives, Factory Lives*, London: Macmillan.

Pollert, A. (ed.) (1991) *Farewell to Flexibility*, Oxford: Blackwell.

Pondy, L. R., Frost, P. J., Morgan, G. and Dandridge, T. C. (eds) (1983) *Organisational Symbolism*, Greenwich, Conn.: JAI.

Poole, M. (1986) *Industrial Relations: origins and patterns of national diversity*, London: Routledge.

Poole, M., Mansfield, R., Blyton, P. and Frost, P. (1981) *Managers in Focus*, Farnborough, Hants: Gower.

Popper, K. (1957) *The Poverty of Historicism*, London: Routledge & Kegan Paul.

Poulantzas, N. (1975) *Classes in Contemporary Capitalism*, London: New Left Books.

Pringle, R. (1989) *Secretaries Talk: sexuality, power and work*, London: Verso.

Proctor, S. J., Rowlinson, M., McArdle, L., Hassard, J. and Forrester, P. (1994) 'Flexibility, politics and strategy: in defence of the model of the flexible firm', *Work, Employment and Society*, 8(2): 221–42.

Pugh, D. S. and Hickson, C. D. (1976) *Organisational Structure: extensions and replications*, Farnborough, Hants: Saxon House.

Pugh, D. S. and Hinings, C. R. (eds) (1976) *Organisation Structure: extensions and replications, the Aston Studies II*, Farnborough, Hants: Gower.

Pugh, D. S. and Payne, R. L. (1977) *Organisational Behaviour in its Context: the Aston programme III*, London: Saxon House.

Purcell, J. and Sisson, K. (1983) 'Strategies and practices in the management of industrial relations', in Bain, G. S. (ed.) *Industrial Relations in Britain*, Oxford: Blackwell.

Purcell, K. (1978) 'Working women, women's work and the occupational sociology of being a woman', *Women's Studies International Quarterly*, 1: 153–63.

Purcell, K. (1982) 'Female manual workers: fatalism and the reinforcement of inequality', in Robbins, D. (ed.) *Rethinking Inequality*, Aldershot: Gower.

Quinney, E. R. (1963) 'Occupational structure and criminal behaviour', *Social Problems*, 11.

Radcliffe-Brown, A. R. (1965) *Structure and Function in Primitive Society*, New York: Free Press.

Ram, M. (1993) *Managing to Survive: working lives in small firms*, Oxford: Blackwell.

Rapoport, R. and Rapoport, R. (1976) *Dual Career Families Re-examined*, London: Martin Robertson.

Ray, L. J. and Reed, M. (eds) (1994) *Organizing Modernity: new Weberian perspectives on work*, London: Routledge.

Reed, M. (1992) *The Sociology of Organisations: themes, perspectives and prospects*, Hemel Hempstead: Harvester Wheatsheaf.

Regini, M. (ed.) (1992) *The Future of Labour Movements*, London: Sage.

Rice, A. K. (1958) *Productivity and Social Organisation*, London: Tavistock.

Richman, J. (1969) 'Busmen v. the public', *New Society*, 14 August.

Richman, J. (1983) *Traffic Wardens: an ethnography of street administration*, Manchester: Manchester University Press.

Ritchie, J. (1991) 'Enterprise cultures: a frame analysis', in Burrows (ed.).

Ritzer, G. (1972) *Man and his Work*, New York: Appleton-Century-Crofts.

Ritzer, G. (1993) *The McDonaldization of Society*, Thousand Oaks, Calif.: Pine Forge.

Roberts, B., Finnegan, R. and Gallie, D. (eds) (1985) *New Approaches to Economic Life – economic restructuring: unemployment and the social division of labour*, Manchester: Manchester University Press.

Roberts, K. (1975) 'The developmental theory of occupational choice', in Esland *et al.*

Roberts, K., Cook, F. G., Clark, S. C. and Semeonoff, E. (1977) *The Fragmentary Class Structure*, London: Heinemann.

Robertson, R. (1993) *Globalisation: social theory and global culture*, London: Sage.

Roethlisberger, F. J. (1945) 'The foreman: master and victim of double talk', *Harvard Business Review*, 23.

Roethlisberger, F. J. and Dickson, W. J. (1939) *Management and the Worker*, Cambridge, Mass.: Harvard University Press.

Rojek, C. (ed.) (1989) *Leisure for Leisure*, London: Macmillan.

Roper, M. (1994) *Masculinity and the British Organisation Man since 1945*, Oxford: Oxford University Press.

Rose, M. (1985) *Re-Working the Work Ethic*, London: Batsford.

Rose, M. (1988a) 'Attachment to work and social values', in Gallie (ed.).

Rose, M. (1988b) *Industrial Behaviour*, London: Allen Lane.

Rose, M. (1994) 'Level of strategy amd regimes of control', in Rubery and Wilkinson (eds).

Rose, M. and Jones, B. (1984) 'Managerial strategy and trade union response in plant level reorganisation of work', in Knights *et al.* (eds).

Rosenberg, M. (1957) *Occupations and Values*, Chicago, Ill.: Free Press.

Rosenbrock, H. (1982) 'Technology and policy options', in Bjorn-Anderson *et al.* (eds).

Rowthorn, R. E. and Wells, J. N. (1987) *Deindustrialisation and Foreign Trade*, Cambridge: Cambridge University Press.

Roy, D. (1952) 'Quota restriction and goldbricking in a machine shop', *American Journal of Sociology*, 57.

Roy, D. (1953) 'Work satisfaction and the reward in quota achievement', *American Sociological Review*, 18.

Roy, D. (1954) 'Efficiency and "the Fix"', *American Journal of Sociology*, 60.

Rubenstein, D. (1978) 'Love and Work', *Sociological Review*, 26.

Rubery, J. (1978) 'Structured labour markets, worker organisation and low pay', *Cambridge Journal of Economics*, 2: 17–36.

Rubery, J. and Wilkinson, F. (eds) (1994) *Employer Strategy and the Labour Market*, Oxford: Oxford University Press.

Rubery, J., Tarling, R. and Wilkinson, F. (1987) 'Flexibility, marketing and the organisation of production', *Labour and Society*, 12: 131–51.

Sahay, A. (ed.) (1971) *Max Weber and Modern Sociology*, London: Routledge & Kegan Paul.

Salaman, G. (1974) *Community and Occupation*, Cambridge: Cambridge University Press.

Salaman, G. (1981) *Class and the Corporation*, Glasgow: Fontana.

Salaman, G. (ed.) (1992) *Human Resource Strategies*, London: Sage.

Salaman, G. and Thompson, K. (eds) (1973) *People and Organisations*, London: Longman.

Salaman, G. and Thompson, K. (1978) 'Class culture and the persistence of an elite', *Sociological Review*, 26.

Salutin, M. (1971) 'Stripper Morality', *Transaction*, 8.

Saussure, F. de (1974) *Course in General Linguistics*, London: Fontana.

Savage, M., Barlow, J., Dickens, P. and Fielding, A. (1992) *Property, Bureaucracy and Culture: middle class formation in contemporary Britain*, London: Routledge.

Sayer, A. and Walker, R. (1992) *The New Social Economy*, Oxford: Blackwell.

Sayles, L. R. (1958) *The Behaviour of Industrial Work Groups*, New York: Wiley.

Scarborough, H. and Corbett, J. M. (1992) *Technology and Organisation*, London: Routledge.

Scase, R. and Goffee, R. (1982) *The Entrepreneurial Middle-Class*, London: Croom Helm.

Scase, R. and Goffee, R. (1989) *Reluctant managers: their work and lifestyles*, London: Unwin Hyman.

Schacht, R. (1970) *Alienation*, London: Allen & Unwin.

Schein, E. (1978) *Career Dynamics*, Reading, Mass.: Addison-Wesley.

Schienstock, G. (1981) 'Towards a theory of industrial relations', *British Journal of Industrial Relations*, 19(2).

Schmidt, G. (1976) 'Max Weber and modern industrial sociology', *Sociological Analysis and Theory*, 6.

Schwartzman, H. B. (1993) *Ethnography in Organisations*, Newbury Park, Calif.: Sage.

Scott, J. (1979) *Corporations, Classes and Capitalism*, London: Hutchinson.

Scott, J. and Griff, C. (1984) *Directors of Industry: the British Corporate Network, 1904–76*, Oxford: Polity Press.

Seabrooke, J. (1988) *The Leisure Society*, Oxford: Blackwell.

Selden, R. (1991) 'The Rhetoric of Enterprise', in Keat and Abercrombie (eds).

Selznick, P. (1949, 1966) *TVA and the Grassroots*, Berkeley, Calif.: University of California Press.

Selznick, P. (1957) *Leadership in Administration: a sociological interpretation*, New York: Harper and Row.

Sennett, R. and Cobb, J. (1977) *The Hidden Injuries of Class*, Cambridge: Cambridge University Press.

Sewell, G. and Wilkinson, B. (1992) '"Someone to watch over me": surveillance, discipline and just-in-time labour process', *Sociology*, 26(2): 271–89.

Shalev, M. (1992) 'The resurgence of labour quiescence', in Regini (ed.).

Sharpe, S. (1984) *Double Identity: the lives of working mothers*, Harmondsworth: Penguin.

Silverman, D. (1970) *The Theory of Organisations*, London: Heinemann.

Silverman, D. (1993) *Interpreting Qualitative Data*, London: Sage.

Silverman, D. (1994) 'On throwing away ladders: rewriting the theory of organisations', in Hassard and Parker (eds).

Silverman, D. and Jones, J. (1976) *Organisational Work*, London: Collier Macmillan.

Simon, H. A. (1957) *Models of Man*, New York: Wiley.

Sims, D., Fineman, S. and Gabriel, Y. (1993) *Organizing and Organizations*, London: Sage.

Sisson, K. (ed.) (1994) *Personnel Management*, Oxford: Blackwell.

Skipper, J. and McCaghy, C. (1970) 'Stripteasers', *Social Problems*, 17.

Small Business Research Trust (1995) *Natwest Review of Small Business Trends*, Milton Keynes: Small Business Research Trust.

Smart, B. (1992) *Modern Conditions, Postmodern Controversies*, London: Routledge.

Smith, C. (1987) *Technical Workers: class, labour and trade unionism*, London: Macmillan.

Smith, J. H. (1987) 'Elton Mayo and the hidden Hawthorne', *Work, Employment and Society*, 1(1): 107–20.

Smith, M. A., Parker, S. and Smith, C. S. (eds) (1977) *Leisure and Society in Britain*, London: Allen Lane.

Smith, P. and Morton, G. (1990) 'A change of heart: union exclusion in the provincial newspaper sector', *Work, Employment and Society*, 4(1): 105–24.

Smith, V. (1990) *Managing in the Corporate Interest: control and resistance in an American bank*, Berkeley, Calif.: University of California Press.

Sofer, C. (1970) *Men in Mid-Career*, Cambridge: Cambridge University Press.

Spradley, J. P. and Mann, B. J. (1975) *The Cocktail Waitress*, New York: Wiley.

Stanworth, J. and Stanworth, C. (1992) *Telework: the human resource implications*, London: IPM.

Starkey, K. and McKinlay, A. (1989) 'Beyond Fordism: strategic choice and labour relations in Ford UK', *Industrial Relations Journal*, 20(2): 93–100.

Stead, B. A. (ed.) (1985) *Women in Management*, 2nd edn, Englewood Cliffs, NJ: Prentice Hall.

Stewart, R. and Barsoux, J. (1994) *The Diversity of Management*, London: Macmillan.

Storey, J. (1989) *New Perspectives on Human Resource Management*, London: Routledge.

Storey, J. (1992) *Developments in the Management of Human Resources*, Oxford: Blackwell.

Storey, J. (1994a) 'The take-up of human resource management by mainstream companies: key lesson from research', in Niland, Lansbury and Verevis (eds).

Storey, J. (ed.) (1994b) *New Wave Manufacturing Strategies: organisational and human resource management dimensions*, London: Chapman.

Strauss, A., Shatzman, L., Erlich, D., Bucher, R. and Sabshim, M. (1963) 'The hospital and its negotiated order', in Friedson, E. (ed.) *The Hospital in Modern Society*, New York: Macmillan.

Sturdy, A. (1992) 'Clerical consent: "Shifting" work in the insurance office', in Sturdy *et al.* (eds).

Sturdy, A., Knights, D. and Willmott, H. (1992) *Skill and Consent: contemporary studies in the labour process*, London: Routledge.

Super, D. E. (1957) *The Psychology of Careers*, New York: Harper & Row.

Sykes, A. J. M. (1969) 'Navvies: their work attitudes', *Sociology*, 3.

Sztompka, P. (1994) *The Sociology of Social Change*, Oxford: Blackwell.

Tailby, S. and Whitson, C. (1989a) 'Industrial relations and restructuring', in Tailby and Whitson (eds).

Tailby, S. and Whitson, C. (eds) (1989b) *Manufacturing Change: industrial relations and restructuring*, Oxford: Blackwell.

Taylor, F. W. (1911a) *The Principles of Scientific Management*, New York: Harper.

Taylor, F. W. (1911b) *Shop Management*, New York: Harper.

Taylor, I. and Walton, P. (1971) 'Industrial sabotage: motives and meanings', in Cohen, S. (ed.) *Images of Deviance*, Harmondsworth: Penguin.

Taylor, R. (1982) *Workers and the New Depression*, London: Macmillan.

Terkel, S. (1977) *Working*, Harmondsworth: Penguin.

Thompson, E. P. (1967) 'Time, work discipline and industrial capitalism', *Past and Present*, 38.

Thompson, E. P. (1968) *The Making of the English Working Class*, Harmondsworth: Penguin.

Thompson, J. D. (1967) *Organisations in Action*, New York: McGraw-Hill.

Thompson, P. (1983a) *The Nature of Work*, London: Macmillan.

Thompson, P. (1983b) *Living the Fishing*, London: Routledge & Kegan Paul.

Thompson, P. (1989) *The Nature of Work: an introduction to debates on the labour process*, London: Macmillan.

Thompson, P. (1993) 'Fatal distraction: postmodernism and organisational analysis', in Hassard and Parker (eds).

Tichy, N. M., Fombrun, C. J. and Devanna, M. A. (1982) 'Strategic human resource management', *Sloan Management Review*, 23(2).

Tilgher, A. (1930) *Work: what it has meant to men through the ages*, New York: Harcourt Brace.

Tilly, L. and Scott, J. (1978) *Women, Work and Family*, New York: Holt, Rinehart & Winston.

Toffler, A. (1983) *The Third Wave*, London: Pan.

Tomaskovic-Devey, D. (1993) *Gender and Racial Inequality at Work: the sources and consequences of job segregation*, Ithaca, NY: ILR Press.

Touraine, A. (1971) *The Post-Industrial Society*, New York: Random House.

Townley, B. (1994) *Reframing Human Resource Management*, London: Sage.

Trist, E. L., Higgin, G. W., Murray, H. and Pollock, A. B. (1963) *Organisational Choice*, London: Tavistock.

Tunstall, J. (1962) *The Fishermen*, London: MacGibbon & Kee.

Turnbull, P. and Sapsford, D. (1992) 'A sea of discontent: the tides of organised and "unorganised" conflict on the docks', *Sociology*, 26(2): 291–309.

Turner, H. A., Clack, C. and Roberts, G. (1967) *Labour Relations in the Motor Industry*, London: Allen & Unwin.

Turner, R. (ed.) (1974) *Ethnomethodology*, Harmondsworth: Penguin.

Undy, R. and Martin, R. (1984) *Ballots and Trade Union Democracy*, Oxford: Blackwell.

Visser, J. (1994) 'European Trade Unions: the transition years', in Hyman and Ferner (eds).

Vokins, N. (1993) 'The Minerva matrix women entrepreneurs: their perceptions of their managerial style', in Allen and Truman (eds).

Walby, S. (1986) *Patriarchy at Work: patriarchal and capitalist relations in employment*, Oxford: Polity.

Walker, C. R. and Guest, R. H. (1952) *The Man on the Assembly Line*, Cambridge, Mass.: Harvard University Press.

Walton, R. E. (1985) 'From control to commitment in the workplace', *Harvard Business Review*, March–April: 76–84.

Walton, R. E. and Lawrence, R. R. (eds) (1985) *Human Resource Management: trends and challenges*, Boston, Mass.: Harvard Business School Press.

Ward, R. (1987) 'Resistance, accommodation and advantage: strategic development in ethnic business', in Lee and Loveridge (eds).

Warde, A. and Hetherington, K. (1993) 'A changing domestic division of labour? Issues of measurement and interpretation', *Work, Employment and Society*, 7(1): 23–45.

Warner, M. (ed.) (1973) *Sociology of the Workplace*, London: Allen & Unwin.

Warr, P. (1983) 'Unemployment and mental health', *SSRC Newsletter*, 48.

Warwick, D. and Littlejohn, G. (1992) *Coal, Capital and Culture: a sociological analysis of mining communities in West Yorkshire*, London: Routledge.

Watson, D. H. (1988) *Managers of Discontent: trade union officers and industrial relatons managers*, London: Routledge.

Watson, D. H. (1992) 'Power, conflict and control at work', in Allen, J., Brayham, P. and Lewis, P. (eds) *Political and Economic Forms of Modernity*, Cambridge: Polity.

Watson, T. J. (1976) 'The professionalisation process: a critical note', *Sociological Review*, 24: 599–608.

Watson, T. J. (1977) *The Personnel Managers: a study in the sociology of work and employment*, London: Routledge.

Watson, T. J. (1982) 'Group Ideologies and Organisational Change', *Journal of Manage-*

ment Studies, 19(3): 259–75.

Watson, T. J. (1986) *Management, Organisation and Employment Strategy*, London: Routledge & Kegan Paul.

Watson, T. J. (1994a) *In Search of Management: culture, chaos and control in managerial work*, London: Routledge.

Watson, T. J. (1994b) 'Managing, crafting and researching: words, skill and imagination in shaping management research', *British Journal of Management*, 5, Special Issue: 77–87.

Watson, T. J. (1994c) 'Towards a managerially relevant but non-managerialist organisation theory', in Hassard and Parker (eds).

Watson, T. J. (1994d) 'Management "flavours of the month": their role in managers' lives', *The International Journal of Human Resource Management*, 5(4): 889–905.

Watson, T. J. (1995a) 'Entrepreneurship and professional management: a fatal distinction', *International Small Business Journal*, 13(3): 34–46.

Watson, T. J. (1995b) 'Theorising managerial work: a pragmatic pluralist approach to interdisciplinary research', *British Journal of Management*, forthcoming.

Watson, T. J. (1995c) 'Professing postmodernism – soft postmodernist thoughts on education and management', in Watson, T. J. (ed.) *Professorial Papers*, Nottingham: The Nottingham Trent University.

Watson, T. J. (1995d) 'Rhetoric, discourse and argument in organisational sense-making: a reflexive tale', *Organisation Studies*, 16 (5).

Watson, W. (1964) 'Social mobility and social class in industrial communities', in Gluckman, M. and Devon, E. (eds) *Closed Systems and Open Minds*, Edinburgh: Oliver & Boyd.

Weber, M. (1927) *General Economic History*, New York: Free Press.

Weber, M. (1965) *The Protestant Ethic and The Spirit of Capitalism*, London: Allen & Unwin.

Weber, M. (1968) *Economy and Society*, New York: Bedminster Press.

Webster, F. and Robins, K. (1993) '"I'll be watching you": comment on Sewell and Wilkinson', *Sociology*, 27(2): 243–52.

Wedderburn, D. and Crompton, R. (1972) *Workers' Attitudes and Technology*, Cambridge: Cambridge University Press.

Weick, K. E. (1979) *The Social Psychology of Organizing*, Reading, Mass.: Addison-Wesley.

Weir, D. (ed.) (1973) *Men and Work in Modern Britain*, Glasgow: Fontana.

West, J. (ed.) (1982) *Work, Women and the Labour Market*, London: Routledge & Kegan Paul.

Westergaard, J., Noble, I. and Walker, A. (1989) *After Redundancy*, Oxford: Polity.

Wheelock, J. (1990) *Husbands at Home: the domestic economy in a post industrial society*, London: Routledge.

Whipp. R. (1992) *Patterns of Labour: work and social change in the pottery industry*, London: Routledge.

Whitehead, T. N. (1938) *The Industrial Worker*, New York: Oxford University Press.

Whitley, R. (1994) 'The internationalisation of firms and markets: its significance and institutional structuring', *Organisation* 1(1): 101–34.

Whyte, W. H. (1961) *The Organisation Man*, Harmondsworth: Penguin.

Wild, R. and Birchall, D. W. (1975) 'Job structuring and work organisation', *Journal of Occupational Psychology*, 48: 169–77.

Wilkinson, A. and Willmott, H. (1994) 'Introduction', to Wilkinson and Willmott (eds).

Wilkinson, A. and Willmott, H. (eds) (1994) *Making Quality Critical*, London: Routledge.

Wilkinson, A., Marchington, M., Goodman, J. and Ackers, P. (1992) 'Total Quality Management and employee involvement', *Human Resource Management Journal*, 2(4): 1–20.

Wilkinson, B. (1983) *The Shopfloor Politics of New Technology*, London: Heinemann.

Williams, C. C. (1988) *Examining the Nature of Domestic Labour*, Aldershot: Avebury.

Williams, K., Cutler, T., Williams, J. and Haslam, C. (1987) 'The end of mass production', *Economy and Society*, 16(3): 405–39.

Williams, R. (1965) *The Long Revolution*, Harmondsworth: Penguin.

Williams, R. (1976) *Keywords*, Glasgow: Fontana.

Williams, R. (1981) *Culture*, Glasgow: Fontana.

Willis, P. E. (1977) *Learning to Labour*, London: Saxon House.

Willman, P. (1980) 'Leadership and trade union principles: some problems of management sponsorship and independence', *Industrial Relations Journal*, 11(4).

Willman, P., Morris, T. and Aston, B. (1993) *Union Business: trade union organisation and financial reform in the Thatcher years*, Cambridge: Cambridge University Press.

Willmott, H. (1995) 'Strength is ignorance; slavery is freedom: managing culture in modern organisations', *Journal of Management Studies*, 30(4): 511–12.

Wilson, A. (1991) *Teleworking: flexibility for a few*, Brighton: Institute of Manpower Studies.

Wilson, D. C. and Rosenfeld, R. H. (1990) *Managing Organisations*, London: McGraw Hill.

Wilson, W. J. (1987) *The Truly Disadvantaged*, Chicago, Ill.: University of Chicago Press.

Winchester, D. and Clegg. H. (1993) *The Changing Systems of Industrial Relations in Great Britain*, Oxford: Blackwell.

Witz, A. (1992) *Professions and Patriarchy*, London: Routledge.

Womack, J. P., Jones, D. J. and Roos, D. (1990) *The Machine that Changed the World*, New York: Rawson.

Wood, S. (ed.) (1982) *The Degradation of Work?*, London: Hutchinson.

Wood, S. (ed.) (1989) *The Transformation of Work?*, London: Unwin Hyman.

Woodward, J. (1965) *Industrial Organisation*, Oxford: Oxford University Press.

Woolgar, S. (1988) *Science: the very idea*, London: Ellis Horwood.

Wray, D. (1949) 'Marginal men of industry: the foremen', *American Journal of Sociology*, 54.

Wright, E. O. (1985) *Classes*, London: Verso/NLB.

Young, M. and Willmott, P. (1975) *The Symmetrical Family*, Harmondsworth: Penguin.

Zald, M. (ed.) (1970) *Power in Organisations*, Vanderbilt University Press.

Zeitlin, M. (1989) *The Large Corporation and Contemporary Classes*, Oxford: Polity Press.

Zimmerman, D. H. (1973) 'The practicalities of rule use', in Salaman and Thompson (eds).

Zuboff, S. (1988) *In the Age of the Smart Machine*, Oxford: Heinemann.

Zucker, L. G. (ed.) (1988) *Institutional Patterns and Organisations*, Cambridge, Mass.: Ballinger.

■　■　■

Author index

Subject index